THE CASE FOR PATENTS

THE CASE FOR PATENTS

Daniel Spulber
Northwestern University, USA

World Scientific
NEW JERSEY • LONDON • SINGAPORE • BEIJING • SHANGHAI • HONG KONG • TAIPEI • CHENNAI • TOKYO

Published by

World Scientific Publishing Co. Pte. Ltd.
5 Toh Tuck Link, Singapore 596224
USA office: 27 Warren Street, Suite 401-402, Hackensack, NJ 07601
UK office: 57 Shelton Street, Covent Garden, London WC2H 9HE

Library of Congress Cataloging-in-Publication Data
Names: Spulber, Daniel F., author.
Title: The case for patents / Daniel Spulber, Northwestern University, USA.
Description: New Jersey : World Scientific, 2021. | Includes bibliographical references and index.
Identifiers: LCCN 2020043384 | ISBN 9789811225635 (hardcover) |
ISBN 9789811225666 (ebook)
Subjects: LCSH: Patent laws and legislation. | Patents--Economic aspects. |
Patent infringement. | Patents and government-developed inventions.
Classification: LCC K1505 .S68 2021 | DDC 346.04/86--dc23
LC record available at https://lccn.loc.gov/2020043384

British Library Cataloguing-in-Publication Data
A catalogue record for this book is available from the British Library.

For any available supplementary material, please visit
https://www.worldscientific.com/worldscibooks/10.1142/11976#t=suppl

Desk Editor: Lum Pui Yee

Typeset by Stallion Press
Email: enquiries@stallionpress.com

Endorsements

The Case for Patents provides a robust and convincing economic justification for patent rights by one of the leading scholars in the field. The book is accessible to non-economists and policy analysts, as well as economists, and deserves to be widely read. Based on wide-ranging analysis of the roles patents serve and an impressive marshaling of empirical evidence, Spulber emphasizes how patents do far more than provide an innovation incentive; most importantly, they underpin market transactions in technology. This promotes access to capital and the ability to monetize the returns to inventions for small entrepreneurial companies, and thus improves the efficiency of vertical specialization. But, this only works if there is effective patent screening (and enforceability), so that patents are informative signals to the market and are socially desirable as well. While there are social costs from patents, this book is an important reminder of the need to protect patent rights and to facilitate markets for technology.

Mark Schankerman
Professor of Economics, London School of Economics

Professor Spulber's book is a pathbreaking synthesis of economics, business strategy, and law that makes the case for a robust patent system. *The Case for Patents* is a must-read book for the academic and policy communities.

D. Daniel Sokol
Professor, University of Florida Levin College of Law

Few subjects today deserve robust economic analysis more keenly than innovation and entrepreneurship, and few issues spark more vigorous debate than the role that intellectual property rights play in increasing, or impairing, economic performance and social welfare. For those interested in understanding how the modern economy works, *The Case for Patents* is essential reading.

Stuart Graham
Scheller College of Business @ Georgia Tech and Former Chief Economist, United States Patent and Trademark Office

Contents

Introduction

In this book, I present an affirmative case for the patent system. I emphasize the importance of incentives for invention, innovation, and technology adoption. Preserving these incentives requires protecting the patent system. More than simply a defense, The Case for Patents is an argument for strengthening Intellectual Property (IP) rights.

I seek to increase awareness of the many economic contributions of the patent system. I observe that the patent system has fostered the economic growth and prosperity of the industrial world. I identify some important functions of the patent system that have not been fully understood before. I explain why patents are so effective in supporting technological change.

My main purpose is to increase understanding of what patents do. The book provides a non-technical introduction to the law and economics of patents. At the same time, the book introduces new concepts and frameworks that explain the functions and effects of IP rights. The book shows why IP rights support the efforts, investment, and creativity of inventors and innovators.

This book is for scientists, engineers, social scientists, inventors, managers, and entrepreneurs. The book also is for attorneys, judges, experts, and leaders in government agencies. My hope is that the book helps restore some balance to public policy debates by recognizing the important contributions of the patent system.

Patents play a significant role in the extensive global market for IP. Patents contribute to the intangible real assets of corporations. Patents support a wide variety of transactions including licensing, cross-licensing, transfers, joint ventures, mergers, and financing of research and development ("R&D").

The patent system protects incentives for invention, innovation, and technology adoption. Patents provide a system of IP rights for inventors and innovators. Patents allow inventors and innovators to stake out new areas for exploration. Patents are part of the system of IP rights that is essential for investments in invention and innovation. Patents increase transaction efficiencies that are fundamental to the operation of the market for technology. Patents provide incentives for advances in medicines, computers, software, communication systems, energy, transportation, and transaction methods. Patents continue to drive employment, development, and progress throughout the modern economy.

Making the case for patents is necessary because the system is in serious danger. Despite its great success, the patent system faces a host of critics. These critics seek to weaken or even abolish IP rights for inventors and innovators. These critics have dominated academic discussions and public policy forums. Major corporations that use patented inventions have engaged in extensive lobbying for regulations limiting the exercise of IP rights.

Many of the criticisms of the patent system are based on inaccurate data and faulty economic reasoning. Patent critics rely on incorrect characterizations of patents as economic monopolies causing deadweight welfare losses. Some critics of the patent system are opposed to competitive markets and private property in general, with IP rights serving as a convenient target.

The United States patent system faces a war of attrition. Advocates who oppose patents have influenced judges and legislators. Perhaps because the patent system has worked so well, it is nearly invisible and often taken for granted. Although some inventors with valuable patents make headlines, many inventors find it increasingly difficult to obtain patents. Inventors that do obtain patents encounter difficulties in defending their patents against infringers and legal challenges.

Protecting the patent system requires removing various roadblocks faced by inventors and avoiding proposals for more roadblocks. Various legal decisions and public policy efforts have weakened patent protections for inventors. The Patent Trial and Appeal Board (PTAB) at the United States Patent and Trademark Office (USPTO) "conducts trials, including *inter partes*, post-grant, and covered business method patent reviews and derivation proceedings, hears appeals from adverse examiner decisions in patent applications and reexamination proceedings, and renders decisions in interferences."[1]

The Supreme Court in *eBay* limited injunctions in patent disputes, determining that the basic principles of injunctions "apply with equal force to disputes arising under the Patent Act."[2] This reduces the ability of inventors to deter infringement and diminishes the incentives for infringers to negotiate patent license agreements. Also, a series of Supreme Court decisions constrained what types of inventions can be patented. These decisions limit the ability of inventors to obtain patents in a variety of areas including business method inventions.

Chapter 1 develops a comprehensive framework demonstrating how patents provide the foundation of the market for inventions. Patents support the establishment of the market in several key ways. First, patents provide a system of IP rights that increases transaction efficiencies and stimulates competition by offering exclusion, transferability, disclosure, certification, standardization, and divisibility. Second, patent transfers and licensing constitute what I call "the market for innovative control" that provides incentives for efficient investment in invention, innovation, and complementary assets. Third, patents as intangible real assets promote the financing of invention and innovation. The market foundation role of patents refutes the economically incorrect "rewards" view of patents. The discussion considers how economic benefits of the market for inventions should guide IP policy and antitrust policy.

Chapter 2 argues that the current system of patents and market prices provide far better incentives for invention and innovation than would a system of public contests and government ownership and distribution of technology. The question of public prizes versus market prices is important because the America COMPETES Reauthorization Act of 2010 established a framework for government contests. First, the chapter finds fundamental flaws in the deadweight welfare loss arguments for replacing market prices with public prizes. Second, the chapter shows how the market for inventions allocates inventions much more efficiently than would government diffusion. Third, the chapter demonstrates that the market for inventions, in contrast to contests, provides guidance for investment in invention, commercialization, innovation, and complementary inventions. The chapter concludes that replacing market prices with public prizes would substantially harm invention and innovation.

Chapter 3 examines limits on the subject matter of inventions that can be granted patents. Excessive limits on what types of inventions are eligible for patents tend to diminish the benefits of the patent system. Often occurring at the cutting edge of technological change, legal and regulatory limits on what can be patented can stifle invention and innovation. There has been a tightening of restrictions on patent subject matter eligibility to include some types of software, business methods, and biotechnology.

Chapter 3 considers the role of business method patents and their contribution to what I call the "Business Revolution." The "Business Revolution" includes the augmentation and replacement of human effort in business transactions by computers, communications systems, and the Internet.

A business method invention is the discovery of a commercial technique that firms can apply to address market opportunities. The initial implementation of a business method invention by firms is a Schumpeterian innovation. I advance several arguments in favor of business method patentability. Business method inventions are an important foundation for entrepreneurship and a channel for the commercialization of scientific and technological inventions. IP protections for business method inventions are essential for economic efficiency, including incentives for invention, efficient allocation of inventions, and transaction efficiencies in the market for discoveries. I conclude that the patent system should continue to provide intellectual property protections for business method inventions just as it does for other types of inventions.

Chapter 4 examines enforcement of IP rights through remedies for patent infringement. Damages for infringement are important for enforcing inventors' IP rights and inducing patent licensing agreements. There is considerable controversy regarding how to calculate damages in patent infringement cases. To help resolve this controversy, Chapter 4 introduces a contract approach to patent infringement and develops a methodology for finding reasonable royalty damages.

The proposed contract approach to infringement remedies serves to complement other approaches that are based on property and tort. This general perspective provides a more complete understanding of damages for infringement. The chapter introduces the concept of an "informed contract" as the basis for damages. The chapter argues that an "informed contract" improves estimation of damages by taking into account information revealed during the period of infringement. The chapter also introduces a "market value method" for calculating reasonable royalty damages based on patent transfer prices. The contract approach helps calculate reasonable royalty damages based on royalties in comparable patent licenses. The contract approach addresses various controversies over reasonable royalty damages.

Chapter 5 offers a general legal framework for addressing technological change. Technological change is altering the nature of contract law toward a greater focus on intangible assets. The direction of technological change toward greater connectivity, interoperability, mobile communications, the Internet of Things (IoT), artificial intelligence (AI), virtual inventions, and cooperative research and development (R&D) has profound implications.

I develop a new framework that I refer to as "Intellectual Law" to address this shift. I introduce the concept of "Intellectual Contract" (IC) to characterize an agreement for invention, innovation, and technology adoption. I also introduce the concept of "Intellectual Tort" (IT) to describe liability including but not limited to misappropriation of trade secrets and infringement of patents, trademarks, and copyrights. Intellectual Law provides a consistent framework that includes IC, IT, and IP.

Chapter 5 observes that legal protections for inventors cannot rely solely on what has proven to be a flawed combination of IT and IP. I argue that greater emphasis on IC rules would improve both IT and IP. Because an IC protects expectation interests, it is essential for creating, developing, sharing, and applying intangible assets. An IC generates gains from trade that enhance the benefits of inventors, innovators, and adopters beyond what can be achieved by IT and IP alone. I set forth some broad principles for IC law. I examine the differences between an IC and a standard contract and identify the main forms of ICs. ICs help to realize the full potential of the patent system.

Acknowledgements

The chapters draw on some of my publications, particularly the following articles.

Daniel F. Spulber, How patents provide the foundation of the market for inventions, 2015, *Journal of Competition Law and Economics*, June, 11, 2, pp. 271–316, doi:10.1093/joclec/nhv006, Oxford University Press.

Daniel F. Spulber, Public prizes versus market prices: Should contests replace patents?, 2015, *Journal of the Patent and Trademark Office Society*, 97, 4, December, pp. 690–735.

Daniel F. Spulber, Should business method inventions be patentable?, 2011, *Journal of Legal Analysis*, 3, 1, Spring, pp. 265–340. Oxford University Press.

Daniel F. Spulber, Finding reasonable royalty damages: A contract approach to patent infringement, 2019, *University of Illinois Law Review*, 2019, 2, pp. 615–700.

Daniel F. Spulber, Intellectual contract and intellectual law, 2018, *Journal of Technology Law & Policy*, Fall, 23(1), pp. 1–67.

Some of the work in these articles benefitted from comments at various seminars and conference presentations. These include the following: The Research Roundtable on Innovation Policy, Intellectual Property, and Entrepreneurship in April, 2011 at the Searle Center for Law, Regulation, and Economic Growth, Northwestern University School of Law; Inventions and U.S. Patent System Conference, Working Group on Intellectual Property, Innovation, and Prosperity, Hoover Institution, Stanford University, May 19–20, 2014, Stanford, CA; the Research Roundtable on Software and Business Method Patents, Searle Center on Law, Regulation and Economic Growth, Northwestern University School of Law, April 24–25, 2014; and the Eleventh Annual Searle Center/USPTO Conference on Innovation Economics, June 21–22, 2018, Northwestern University Pritzker School of Law.

I am particularly grateful for research support from Qualcomm and the Kellogg School of Management. I also gratefully acknowledge research support from the Ewing Marion Kauffman Foundation and Nokia. I have also received research support from the United States Patent and Trademark Office (USPTO) for academic conferences

I have received many helpful comments on the earlier published work. I particularly thank Alexei Alexandrov, Richard Epstein, Kirti Gupta, Paul Heald, Byron Holz, John Howells, Ron Katznelson, Scott Kieff, Robert Merges, Ivan Png, Mark Snyder, Danny Sokol, Robin Stitzing, and Andrew Toole.

Chapter 1

Patents and the Market for Innovative Control

1.1 Introduction

The U.S. patent system issued its first patent on July 31, 1790, which was signed by President George Washington.[1] Samuel Hopkins obtained that patent for a process of making potash, an ingredient used in fertilizer.[2] The United States has issued over 10 million patents since then.[3]

According to the United States Patent and Trademark Office (USPTO), patent 10 million was for "Coherent Ladar Using Intra-Pixel Quadrature Detection." The USPTO observes that the patent "symbolizes the breadth of American invention, with applications in such varied fields as autonomous vehicles, medical imaging devices, military defense systems, and space and undersea exploration."[4] The inventor is Joseph Marron and the patent is owned by the Raytheon Company.[5]

Patents have supported the market development of steamships, automobiles, electric power, electric appliances, aviation, aerospace, telecommunications, mobile communications, computers, the Internet, biotechnology, and nanotechnology. Despite these significant achievements, the U.S. patent system is facing a perfect storm of criticism from academics, politicians, judges, journalists, and industry groups, with calls for abolishing or heavily regulating patents. In this chapter, I suggest that the anti-patent storm in part reflects a basic misunderstanding of the purpose of the patent system. A better understanding of the contributions of patents may help calm the anti-patent storm and avoid disrupting the highly successful U.S. system of invention and innovation.

The U.S. Constitution offers valuable guidance, granting Congress the power "[t]o promote the Progress of Science and useful Arts, by securing for limited Times to Authors and Inventors the exclusive Right to their respective Writings and Discoveries."[6] Patents serve this purpose because they provide the foundation of the market for inventions.

I develop a comprehensive economic framework for the study of patents that extends work I have done on market microstructure, the theory of the firm, invention, and innovation.[7] Applying this framework, I demonstrate that patents support the market for inventions in several important ways: (1) by increasing transaction efficiencies and stimulating competition, (2) by establishing what I term "the market for innovative control" that provides incentives for efficient investment, and (3) by promoting the financing of invention and innovation.[8] I show that the market foundation role of patents has important implications for antitrust and public policy toward intellectual property (IP).

Yet, for many academics, the patent system is a "failure,"[9] in a "crisis,"[10] and a "major wound" that should be abolished.[11] The press tends to agree: "Abusive and frivolous lawsuits brought by holders of patents are costing the American economy billions of dollars."[12] Antitrust policymakers seeking "a proper balance between exclusivity and competition" argue that "[i]nvalid or overbroad patents disrupt that balance by discouraging follow-on innovation, preventing competition, and raising prices through unnecessary licensing and litigation."[13] The Supreme Court in a series of opinions has ruled claims for a wide range of subject matters as patent-ineligible.[14] Commentators have noted the "hostility to patents" by the Executive Branch.[15] Congress is in the midst of extensive bipartisan patent reform efforts.[16] According to industry lobbyists, such as the Electronic Frontier Foundation, "[w]e happen to be at a special point in time when every branch of government is itching for patent reform."[17]

I demonstrate that, contrary to these assertions, patents create economic benefits, because the market for inventions generates efficient incentives for invention and innovation. This is important because the market for inventions is vast. The market for inventions includes disembodied inventions in the form of licensing, cross-licensing, assignments, and contractual research and development (R&D). The market for inventions also includes technologies embodied in goods and services, production processes, transaction techniques, and firms themselves.[18] The market for inventions further includes financing of invention and innovation through entrepreneurial and corporate finance.

First, I show that key features of the patent system — exclusion, transferability, disclosure, certification, standardization, and divisibility — increase *transaction efficiencies and stimulate competition* in the market for inventions. These properties of patents reduce transaction costs associated with transferring, licensing, cross-licensing, combining, implementing, and developing inventions. Patents give owners rights to exclude others from making, using, or selling their inventions.[19] Patents help convert inventions into transferable assets, so that inventors and adopters can transact more efficiently in the market for inventions. Patents promote disclosure of inventions, which reduces costs of search and bargaining in the market for inventions. Patents provide certification of technologies, which decreases information asymmetry in the market for inventions. Patents provide standardization in IP, which reduces the costs of contracting in the market for inventions. Finally, patents allow greater divisibility of technology, which promotes modularity and increases gains from trade in the market for inventions. Patents thus generate economic benefits that are based on more efficient transactions and greater competition in the market for inventions.

Second, I introduce the concept of *the market for innovative control.* Patent owners not only obtain residual returns from their inventions but also have residual rights to choose how their inventions are made, used, and sold.[20] The market for innovative control helps determine the value of inventions, selects the best inventions, and allocates inventions to the highest-value users. The market for inventions is a market for innovative control because patent owners have rights to develop inventions, apply inventions to produce innovations, and invest in complementary assets. The market for inventions provides incentives for the efficient organization of firms and industries in terms of the extent of vertical integration of R&D and manufacturing.

Third, I emphasize that patents facilitate the *financial separation* of inventions from their inventors, helping inventors obtain financing.[21] By serving as *intangible real assets*, patents are useful for contracts that finance invention, as indicated by the use of licensing or transfer options for companies funding university research. Entrepreneurs report that patents can be important in securing financing for startups and establishment of firms.[22] Patents also are important for corporate finance and appear as intangible real assets in the balance sheets of corporations. Patents affect the value of corporations in two main ways.[23] Patents that are "assets in place" affect the firm's earnings either through licensing royalties or through own-use of the technology as a productive input. Patents that offer "growth opportunities" affect the firm's expected value because they indicate the potential to invest in innovation based on the firm's IP or to invest in invention of related technology. Financial contracts and the capital structure of firms help provide incentives for invention and innovation.

Patents are *forward-looking* — they perform most of their economic functions in the market for inventions after they are granted. The market foundation role of patents stands in stark contrast to the common view that patents provide "rewards" for inventors. The "rewards" view tends to be *backward-looking*; according to this view, patents complete most of their economic functions at the time they are granted. The "rewards" view of patents is highly misleading for public policy because it does not accurately describe public and private institutions. Contrary to the "rewards" view, markets, not government agencies, determine what rewards inventors and innovators receive and market participants provide those rewards. The "rewards" view considers patents as sources of residual returns for IP owners rather without considering that ownership provides the basis for innovative control. Based on the "rewards" view, some researchers recommend weakening patents through antitrust, limits on litigation, compulsory licensing, government ownership, price controls, taxes, and subsidies.[24] These regulatory approaches would stifle or eliminate the economic benefits that result from the market for inventions.

The market foundation role of patents offers insights into public policy toward IP. With patent protections for IP, the market for inventions determines the market value of inventions and the returns to invention, innovation, and complementary inventions. IP policy should maintain the property rights system because of its benefits for competition and transaction efficiencies. This implies maintaining the key features of the patent system: exclusion, transferability, disclosure, certification, standardization, and divisibility. In addition, to support the market for innovative control and the financing of invention and innovation, patents should have sufficient scope to provide IP protections for development of inventions and innovations. Weakening patent rights would reduce transaction efficiencies and competition, distort incentives and guidance in the market for innovative control, and reduce incentives to finance invention, commercialization, and innovation. Public policymakers should not attempt to determine rewards for inventors, because governments lack the vast amounts of information dispersed in the market place, as Friedrich Hayek understood.[25]

The market foundation role of patents implies that antitrust policy should support rather than weaken IP protections. When there is a market for inventions, *competitive pressures*, both among inventors and among producers who apply inventions, increase incentives to invent and to innovate.[26] On the supply side of the market for inventions, competitive pressures increase incentives to invent and decrease royalties for inventions. On the demand side of the market for inventions, competition drives adopters' incentives to purchase or license discoveries, introduce economic innovations based on those discoveries, and invest in complementary activities. Weakening of patents reduces incentives to participate in the market for inventions, leading inventors to protect their IP through other means such as trade secrets, R&D alliances, and vertical integration. In the absence of a market for inventions, competitive pressures tend to reduce incentives to invent and to innovate.

There are a number of important works that are related to the market foundation role of patents discussed here. Judge Giles Rich, in a series of writings, emphasizes the importance of patents for innovation. Giles Rich observes, "A time-limited exclusive right to subject matter which was neither known, nor obvious from what was known, *takes nothing from the public which it had before*. As a necessary corollary, the disclosure in a valid patent gives to the public knowledge it did not possess, actually or potentially, and thereby makes for progress."[27] Harold Demsetz points out that the problem of indivisibility of information is best handled by "a private property system that reduces the cost of contracting and raises the cost of free-loading while, at the same time, it provides incentives and guidance for investment in producing information."[28] Robert Merges emphasizes that patents and other IP play an important role in promoting transaction efficiencies by providing protections for the disclosure of information in contract formation and by adding flexibility in contractual enforcement.[29]

An important contribution by Edmund Kitch argues that the function of patents is to help attract resources to innovative "prospects."[30] Kitch contrasts his "prospects" view of the patent system with the "rewards" view. Patents are "prospects," because a patent generally discloses an invention *before* it is fully developed and covers *potential* innovations based on that invention. He correctly points out that patents allow owners to coordinate the search for technological and market improvements, invest in innovation based on the invention, invest in distribution and marketing of the invention, contract more readily with providers of complementary information, resources, and financing, avoid duplicating investment of other patent holders, and exercise control over the technology. This chapter extends Kitch's insightful analysis and offers an economic framework for understanding the role of patents in the market for inventions.[31]

F. Scott Kieff's valuable discussion of patents finds that "the treatment of patents as property rights is necessary to facilitate investment in the complex, costly, and risky commercialization activities required to turn nascent inventions into new goods and services.[32] Furthermore, property treatment is equally necessary to help society decide which inventive activities are worth protecting in the first instance."[33] Kieff critiques the "rewards" view of patents, pointing out that reward systems do not account for innovative activities after inventions have been made.[34] He highlights both coordination and investment in commercialization: "The patent right to exclude competitors who have not shared in bearing these initial costs provides incentives for the holder of the invention and the other players in this market to come together and incur all costs necessary to facilitate commercialization of the patented invention."[35] The analysis of the market for inventions presented here encompasses the coordination and commercialization aspects of patents discussed by Kieff.

Richard Epstein emphasizes that exclusivity "seeks to maximize the gains from both the creation and dissemination of protected information."[36] Epstein demonstrates the fundamental connections between tangible and intangible property. The limited term of exclusion for patents allows the application of rules concerning exclusion, use and disposition in real property, which is also subject to limitations such as antitrust law and the law of private and public necessity. Epstein explains that the evolution of property rights in inventions (and writings) is "a conscious extension of the classical liberal conception of property that is associated with such writers as John Locke, William Blackstone, and Adam Smith."[37]

Henry Smith emphasizes the modularity of IP: "The traditional view of markets has a strongly modular flavor, and one role of modular property is to support markets."[38] Smith notes that a modular system involves greater interaction within modules than across modules. IP rights allow the establishment of boundaries by exclusion of others, which allows asset partitioning, greater interaction within modules, usage of local information, and grouping of complementary activities. IP rights also allow interaction and exchange of information across modular boundaries. Smith also emphasizes the reduction of transaction costs by exclusivity in property.[39]

This chapter is organized as follows. Section 1.2 examines how patents improve transaction efficiencies and competition in the market for inventions. Section 1.3 considers how the market for inventions is a market for innovative control that provides incentives for invention and innovation, promotes selection of the best inventions, allocates inventions efficiently, maximizes gains from trade, and encourages investment in complementary assets. Section 1.4 considers how patents are useful for financing invention and innovation. Sections 1.5 and 1.6 discuss implications for IP policy and antitrust policy. Section 1.7 concludes the discussion.

1.2 Transaction Efficiencies and Competition in the Market for Inventions

Patents increase the efficiency of transactions and intensify competition in the market for inventions. This is because the patent system offers a sophisticated property rights framework that combines exclusion with other mechanisms that facilitate exchange. Patents are forward-looking, because property rights support market transactions that take place after the patent is granted. The discussion in this section identifies some key elements of the patent system that are fundamental for market exchange.

1.2.1. *Exclusion*

The United States Patent and Trademark Office (USPTO) defines a *patent* as "an intellectual property right granted by the Government of the United States of America to an inventor 'to exclude others from making, using, offering for sale, or selling the invention throughout the United States or importing the invention into the United States' for a limited time in exchange for public disclosure of the invention when the patent is granted."[40] Although the present discussion applies to IP generally, my focus is on *utility patents* that "may be granted to anyone who invents or discovers any new and useful process, machine, article of manufacture, or composition of matter, or any new and useful improvement thereof."[41] Inventions include commercial, scientific, and technological discoveries.

The right to exclude provides property rights needed to establish a market for inventions. Patents are forward-looking because patent-related transactions, such as licensing and assignments, generally take place after the patent is granted. Patents protect investment-backed expectations; inventors usually invest in developing and commercializing their inventions after the patent is granted. Patent owners invest in innovation and complementary assets after patents are granted. An inventor's returns, if any are ever obtained, are based on the inventor's commercialization efforts and the market value of the invention.

Patents also are forward-looking because the market value of inventions is often determined after the patent is granted. Exclusivity gives inventors the opportunity to obtain the market value of their patents. The value of the inventor's asset is determined after the fact and depends on the demand for the invention and the supply of competing technologies. The price of inventions can be explicit for disembodied inventions. The prices of inventions can be implicit for inventions embodied in products, production processes, transaction methods, and firms. The prices of inventions change continually in response to variations in demand for inventions and the supply of alternative technologies.

Patents are forward-looking because, after the patent is granted, the patent owner invests in enforcement by defending challenges of validity, monitoring infringement, and seeking injunctions and damages for infringement. According to the USPTO, "it is up to the patent holder to enforce his or her own rights if the USPTO does grant a patent."[42] The patent system provides a legal framework for determining infringement and damages. Legal battles over infringement are a natural aspect of the patent system and do not in themselves indicate problems with patents.

Indeed, the legal costs of the patent system are part of the costs of operating a system of property rights. The number of patent lawsuits constitutes a tiny fraction of the number of active patents. Patent lawsuits are less than two tenths of one percent of patents in force each year from 1920 to 2010.[43] Patents are only about one percent or less of all civil law suits in U.S. District Courts for almost every year since the Second World War.[44] Some studies of the patent system exaggerate litigation costs by incorrectly counting licensing, settlements, and judgments as social costs rather than economic transfers.[45]

Many studies that are critical of the patent system tend to emphasize litigation costs without comparing these costs to the economic benefits of the patent system.[46] The legal costs of the patent system are relatively low in comparison to the value of IP. For example, Kevin A. Hassett and Robert J. Shapiro estimate that the value of the intellectual capital in the U.S. economy in 2011 was between \$8.1 trillion and \$9.2 trillion.[47]

Patents generate economic benefits because appropriability of the returns to invention and innovation is critical to the development of the market for inventions. In university licensing, Gaétan de Rassenfosse, Alfons Palangkarya, and Elizabeth Webster find empirical support for the appropriability effect by showing that negotiations involving a granted patent instead of a pending patent are more likely to be successful in fields with more effective IP protections such as biotech, chemicals, medical equipment, and pharmaceuticals.[48] Lee Branstetter, Ray Fisman, and C. Fritz Foley demonstrate empirically that strengthening patent rights increases technology transfers among U.S. multinationals.[49]

Paul Heald observes that exclusivity reduces the costs of transferring IP by providing asset partitioning that protects both sellers and buyers of patents from expropriation of the idea by the other party. Not only does a patent protect sellers from potential buyers who would steal the idea but it also protects buyers from sellers who would use the idea or transfer it to others after the sale takes place. Heald notes that exclusivity in patents is comparable to asset partitioning provided by the corporate form of organization.[50]

Economic historians have documented extensively the importance of the patent system in the establishment of the market for inventions.[51] B. Zorina Khan's study of the U.S. patent system from 1790 to 1920 finds that "[s]ecure property rights in patented inventions helped to create tradeable assets."[52] During this period, the U.S. patent system "stood out as conduit for creativity and achievement among otherwise disadvantaged groups" and "comprised a key institution in the progress of technology."[53] Khan examines the international market for inventions from 1790 to 1930 and shows that international trade in patented inventions responded to incentives from IP protections.[54] She finds that greater protections for IP rights encouraged the formation of a global market for inventions.[55]

An indication of the benefits of IP protection is that companies conducting in-house R&D choose to obtain patents for their inventions. For example, the ten leading patent holders in the US in 2013 were corporations conducting in-house R&D: IBM (6,809), Samsung (4,675), Canon (3,825), Sony (3,098), Microsoft (2,660), Panasonic (2,601), Toshiba (2,416), Hon Hai (2,279), Qualcomm (2,103), and LG Electronics (1,947).[56] Extensive and growing patenting by universities and public research organizations also provides evidence of the benefits offered by the patent system.[57]

The growing volume of patent applications provides some evidence that the patent system is an effective institution. Because applying for patents is costly, this provides some indication of inventors' demand for patent protection. The USPTO receives over 600,000 applications per year.[58] However, increases in the number of patents or the number of citations need not increase innovation and productivity, a phenomenon known as the "patent puzzle." Michele Boldrin and David Levine conclude based on a literature survey that "strengthening the patent regime increases patenting!"[59] However, evaluating the market value of patents for both disembodied and embodied inventions provides a better indication of the connection between patents and innovation.

1.2.2. *Transferability*

Transferability of patent usage and ownership contributes significantly to the establishment and operation of the market for inventions. Because they are transaction institutions, markets require legal transferability of products. John R. Commons states, "Transactions are the means, under operation of law and custom, of acquiring and alienating legal control of commodities, or legal control of the labor and management that will produce and deliver or exchange the commodities and services, forward to the ultimate consumers."[60] Technology transfers that occur through infringement, imitation, and spillovers are not market transactions. Patent owners often license patents after infringement occurs, which can convert such technology transfers into market transactions. Kieff emphasizes the importance of patents as property rights for commercialization and identifies problems with liability rules.[61]

Transactions involving disembodied technology include selling patents, licensing patents, and cross-licensing patents. Patent owners may bundle knowledge transfers with patent licensing or transfers, particularly when patent owners are inventors who have tacit knowledge. The returns to selling the bundle cover the market value of the IP and the inventor's costs of codifying and communicating tacit knowledge.[62] The market for disembodied inventions includes transfers of knowledge, discoveries, ideas, and technologies that are protected by IP other than patents, including trademarks, copyright, and trade secrets. The market for inventions also includes contractual R&D and R&D consortia.[63] R&D outsourcing contracts and R&D partnership contracts specify ownership of the inventions created by the project. Employment contracts specify who owns inventions created by employees. Contracts for education and training specify ownership of information contained in courses and instruction materials.

The market for inventions also includes goods and services that embody inventions, products manufactured using inventions, and transaction techniques that apply business method inventions. Patents often provide IP protections for inventions embodied in products, production processes, and transaction techniques. The market for inventions includes mergers and acquisitions (M&A) involving companies that own or embody inventions. M&A involves the purchase of a firm's assets, including their patent portfolios.

Markets are transaction institutions that are created and managed by individuals and firms.[64] Markets are endogenous to the economy and involve formal and informal rules of exchange that can be characterized as "market microstructure."[65] Firms that create markets choose profit-maximizing market designs. Firms generate and operate a wide variety of physical and virtual market places, such as stores, websites, intermediaries, and auctions. The market for inventions involves these types of institutions, as do markets for other types of goods and services and financial assets.

The market for inventions includes direct exchange between inventors and adopters of technology and intermediated exchange through a wide variety of market makers, dealers, brokers, insurers, and other specialists. Firms create and operate markets through intermediation, price adjustment, marketing, sales, communication, and other coordination mechanisms.[66] Because markets are endogenous, their institutional features depend on the decisions of market-making firms, the characteristics of buyers and sellers that participate in the market, and the types of goods and services that are exchanged. Market institutions can be efficient for the task at hand without necessarily resembling financial commodity markets. Firms create and operate transaction institutions in the market for inventions.

1.2.3. *Disclosure*

Disclosure is often portrayed as a quid pro quo — the patentee provides disclosure of the invention in return for the patent grant. However, disclosure has value to inventors and adopters as a foundation for market transactions. Disclosure provides a description of the invention, the list of claims, and other information in the patent that is useful for transactions. It is not necessary for buyers and sellers to spell out all this information every time a transaction occurs. This reduces the costs of licensing and technology transfer contracts. Patents provide transaction efficiencies in a manner that is similar to other forms of ownership registration including securities, real estate, and motor vehicles.[67]

Disclosure reduces potential adopters' costs of determining which technologies are available for licensing or transfer and what types of prior work has been done. This can reduce the costs of innovation for potential adopters. Disclosure also reduces the costs to other inventors who can learn about prior art and avoid duplicating past research. Inventors can also benefit by extending and improving existing inventions. Disclosure is also useful for potential adopters, allowing them to reduce their risk of infringement.

Disclosure also increases transaction efficiencies by reducing search costs in the market for inventions. The USPTO provides a centralized searchable database for patents. Potential adopters can reduce their costs of obtaining technology by finding out which patented technologies are available. Inventors also benefit from lower search costs, because disclosure reduces their costs of publicizing their inventions to potential adopters. For university inventions, Daniel Elfenbein finds that "although a majority of technologies are licensed prior to the receipt of a patent, a patent more than doubles the likelihood of finding a license partner."[68]

Disclosure to the USPTO also mitigates adverse selection in bargaining between inventors and adopters. Adverse selection in bargaining can result in the failure of a buyer and a seller to come to an agreement, even though the transaction would offer gains from trade. When the quality of the seller's good is observable to the buyer but not to the seller, the seller's offer may not be sufficient to compensate the buyer. Disclosure increases the information about inventions available to potential adopters, thus reducing asymmetry of information in negotiations between inventors and adopters.

Kieff argues that inventors have incentives to disclose their inventions accurately to the USPTO, so as to increase the likelihood that their patent will be valid if challenged in court.[69] He points out that disclosure reduces social costs by providing information about property rights, so that registration in itself generates transaction efficiencies.[70] Kieff emphasizes that the patent system promotes commercialization through incentives for accurate disclosure.[71] Deepak Hegde and Hong Luo find that information disclosure through patent publications generates transaction efficiencies in the market for inventions and accelerates commercialization of inventions.[72]

1.2.4. *Certification*

The USPTO performs a variety of certification tasks that reduce transactions costs in the market for inventions. These tasks include patent review, which determines whether the patent satisfies various criteria that determines whether the invention is useful, novel, and non-obvious. The USPTO provides a recognized method of screening and certification that allows market participants to avoid duplicating these costs. The certification role offered by the USPTO and the courts provides generic information that supplements the important certification contributions of specialized market intermediaries.

The USPTO's patent review alleviates adverse selection in the market for inventions by certifying the disclosure of information about the invention. Certification provides potential adopters with more information about inventions than might otherwise be disclosed in transactions involving trade secrets. This reduces the effects of adverse selection, also known as the "lemons" problem, in which bad products drive out good ones. Better information reduces the likelihood that suppliers of higher-quality inventions will exit the market and suppliers of lower-quality inventions will stay in the market, possibly leading to the collapse of the market entirely. Economic analysis shows that adverse selection problems can be alleviated by intermediaries that invest in certifying the quality of goods.[73]

The certification system is accompanied by *ex post* review in the courts that determines not only the validity of patents but also implicitly provides a check on the patent system itself. The certification system is also subject to *ex post* review in the market for inventions itself. Market transactions provide indications of the performance of the certification system. Simply having a patent does not guarantee that the patent has market value — indeed, many patents do not have market value. The fact that many patents have value provides an indication of the services provided by the USPTO certification system.

Thus, licensing of patented inventions, patent transfers, and the production of goods and services that embody patented inventions provide evidence of the market value of the USPTO certification system. This serves to refute the assertions of some critics that the patent system creates "bad patents." A number of critics suggest that the USPTO's examination processes have generated patents that are invalid in terms of usefulness, novelty, and non-obviousness.[74] Ron Katznelson demonstrates that various studies purporting USPTO standards to be inferior to agencies abroad are based on incorrect statistical analysis.[75,76] Katznelson observes that "even accurate patent grant rate comparisons among national patent offices are of little probative value and should not be used as indicators of examination rigor or patentability standards."[77]

Some critics of the patent system argue that particular types of inventions generate "bad patents." For example, Robert Merges objects to patenting software and business method inventions, because such technologies were formerly "impossible" to patent.[78] As I argue elsewhere, business method inventions reflect commercial discoveries and should not be treated differently from traditionally-defined scientific and technological discoveries.[79] Critics of these types of inventions reflect familiar biases against entrepreneurs and market transactions. There is evidence that software and business method patents are, if anything, higher in quality than other types of inventions.[80]

Certification also reduces transaction costs by determining the identity of the initial patent owner. The US patent system traditionally granted a patent to the inventor that was the first to invent, which required an initial determination of the identity of the first inventor. Under the America Invents Act, the patent is granted to the first to file.[81] Although there are costs and benefits associated with either system, there are benefits to determination of the initial assignment. This reduces the costs of search in the market place by specifying the assignment of property rights.

1.2.5. *Standardization*

Standardization is an important feature of the patent system that has not received sufficient attention. Although each invention is different, patents have consistent features. Patents are standardized documents with an application number, a bar code, an application date, a date of the grant, names of inventors, names of assignees, a title, an abstract, citations to prior patents, and formal specification of claims. Patents are standardized in terms of duration, which is generally 20 years from the time the application is filed. The patent application procedure and examination process are standardized.[82] There is a complex set of rules that apply to all patent applications and patent grants.[83] In addition to these rules, there are standardized legal procedures for patent owners seeking injunctions and damages for infringement.

The patent system provides a set of rules governing licensing and transfer of ownership.[84] According to the USPTO, an assignment must include "all of the bundle of rights that are inherent in the right, title and interest in the patent or patent application."[85] A patent licensing agreement "transfers a bundle of rights which is less than the entire ownership interest, e.g., rights that may be limited as to time, geographical area, or field of use."[86] The USPTO maintains public records on assignments.

In general, standardization can improve the efficiency of markets. Standardization allows buyers and sellers to focus their attention on the idiosyncratic features of the transaction at hand. Standardization allows for economies of scale in transactions. Also, standardization allows buyers and sellers to make comparisons with other transactions, thus facilitating competition. Standard definitions of patent attributes lower the costs of communication and negotiation.

The patent system offers a standard vocabulary that is common usage in market transactions. Patent numbering and public records of patents and applications offer a highly convenient system for asserting IP; it is sufficient for a company to state the patent number or application number on a product or its packaging. Under the America Invents Act, companies have the option of virtual marking by listing a website with patent information. This lowers transaction costs by separating patent marking from product manufacturing and distribution.[87]

In the market for inventions, standardization in patents simplifies licensing contracts, technology transfer agreements, and other transactions. The patent document is part of the agreement, and the technology does not have to be fully described each time a transaction occurs. Prices and other contract terms adjust to reflect the unique features of the technology itself and the purposes of the agreement between the buyer and seller. Standardization offered by patents facilitates financial transactions, including the financing of invention and innovation, entrepreneurial finance, and corporate finance.

Standardization in patents reduces transaction costs associated with the development and adoption of technology standards. Patents provide a means for IP owners to convey information to standards organizations. Companies with patents that read on a standard can readily declare patents "essential" to a standard by communicating the patent numbers to the organizations. Companies that develop new technologies related to existing standards can obtain patents for those standards and report those to standards organizations. Companies seeking to adopt technology standards can determine what IP may be relevant to the standard by observing what patents are declared "essential." Patents serve as standard building blocks for technology standards.

Conversely, technology standards are useful to patent examiners in determining the novelty of inventions. Willingmyre observes, "Standards, publicly available draft standards, and publicly available discussions during standards setting can be a rich source of information about 'prior art.'"[88] Willingmyre points out that the "public pair" database at the USPTO contains useful references to technology standards and standard setting meetings.[89]

1.2.6. *Divisibility*

Patents are useful for the divisibility of technology into discrete units. Although there is considerable debate over whether patents should be broader or narrower, patents serve to define boundaries between inventions. This has important benefits for transactions in the market for inventions. Modularity of technologies enhances competition by allowing component-level rivalries without the need to recreate entire systems.

Patents necessarily impose boundaries on inventions as spelled out in patent claims and the specifics of the technological descriptions. There are numerous transaction advantages of the resulting divisibility. The most important benefit of discreteness is that buyers and sellers can enter more easily into transactions that only involve a specific technology. The technology can meet the particular purposes of the adopter without having to purchase a host of costly technologies that they might not need.

Patents as discrete inventions are the building blocks for collections of inventions. Patents can be combined to form a patent portfolio. Firms can assemble a portfolio of patents with different technologies to meet their production needs. Buyers can license or purchase patents from different patent owners. Patent bundling offers transaction efficiencies by providing convenience to buyers and sellers. Because they represent discrete inventions, the particular needs of buyers and sellers can be satisfied by choosing the best combination of patents.

By offering divisibility, patents promote efficiency in the organization of firms and industries. A firm need not conduct R&D on all the technologies necessary to produce a product or service. Instead, firms can specialize in a particular type of R&D. Then, buyers can assemble the technologies they need through the market for inventions. In this way, patents help foster *modularity* of technologies, which allows the separation and combination of different parts of a technology platform.

Modularity of technologies generates efficiencies from specialization and division of labor. Different companies can focus on invention, innovation, and manufacturing. Also, companies can focus on different types of R&D. For example, in the computer industry, different firms can focus on R&D in software, microprocessors, memory, and screens. This type of specialization improves inventors' knowledge and experience in comparison with what would occur if firms needed to be proficient in all technologies used to produce a particular product.

1.3 The Market for Innovative Control

Because patents provide protections for developing inventions and creating innovations, the market for innovative control generates efficient investment decisions. The residual returns from licensing, selling, or using patented inventions are only part of patent ownership. Patent owners exercise *residual rights of control*, because they can exclude others from making, using, or selling the invention.[90] These rights are transferable so that the market for innovative control provides incentives for efficient investments in invention, innovation, and complementary assets. The concept of the market for innovative control is useful because it helps explain patent transfers and what types of firms acquire patents.

1.3.1. *The Market for Innovative Control and Incentives for Investment*

How well patent owners manage innovation affects the market value of patents. The market for innovative control thus provides incentives for patent owners to develop and commercialize inventions and create innovations that are desirable for consumers and producers. After patents are awarded, patent owners can improve the technology, commercialize the invention, and generate innovations based on the invention, as Kitch observed.[91]

Patents provide incentives for efficient invention and innovation because ownership is transferable. Competition among potential adopters helps the market for innovative control allocate patented inventions to the highest-value users. Patent owners have incentives to transfer their IP when others can increase its market value.

The market for innovative control provides valuable guidance for investment in invention and innovation. The market for innovative control determines the returns to invention, commercialization, and innovation. What matters are innovations — that is, the *outputs* of development, commercialization, and application of inventions — rather than the level of inventive and innovative efforts — that is, the *inputs* of R&D and the innovative process. Simply subsidizing invention or rewarding inventive efforts could produce more efforts, but not necessarily better inventions and innovations. Government subsidies or rewards for invention in the absence of IP protections would not provide incentives for development, commercialization, or application of inventions, which are essential for diffusion of technology and innovation.

The interaction of demand and supply in the market for innovative control determines the market value of inventions. Inventors compete to supply producers with inventions, and producers compete to obtain inventions or develop their own inventions.[92] The market value of an invention reflects competition from both substitute and complementary inventions on the supply side of the market for inventions. The market value of inventions depends on the stock of inventions and anticipation of future discoveries that may enhance the demand for particular inventions or render those inventions obsolete. The market value of an invention also reflects the returns to applying inventions obtained by adopters on the demand side of the market for inventions.

A patented invention is an intangible real asset with potentially valuable control rights. The market value of patents is subject to random shocks due to randomness in the outcomes of the development process, in the costs of the development process, and in market valuations of the outcomes of innovation. The market value of the asset can also depend on the extent of the claims in the patent.[93] The patent owner can invest in development and commercialization, so that the probability distribution of the market value of the patent depends on the level of investment. The patent owner can choose among various investment projects with random outcomes, so that the probability distribution of the value of the patent also depends on the choice of projects.

The market for innovative control provides guidance to inventors regarding investment in R&D and the choice of R&D projects. Because market values of individual inventions differ, the returns to producing inventions through R&D depend on how the resulting inventions will be valued in the market. The expected returns to different directions in R&D will depend on scientific and technical opportunities and the potential market value of successful outcomes. Efficient levels of investment in R&D will be targeted to particular areas on the basis of expected returns to different types of inventions.

The market for innovative control also provides guidance on how much to invest in commercialization and how to commercialize particular inventions. Commercialization of inventions requires investment in communication, marketing, and sales efforts. Patent owners also need to identify potential adopters who might license or purchase their inventions. Patent owners need to choose among different methods of commercialization including transfers, licensing, cross-licensing, services, and contract R&D. In addition, patent owners must monitor potential infringement and if necessary invest in the legal costs of obtaining damages and injunctions. The market for inventions contains many types of transactions including embodied inventions. This implies that limited licensing does not indicate market failure, contrary to some studies.[94]

Patents are important for commercializing inventions through licensing. Using data from the Securities Data Corporation (SDC), Bharat Anand and Tarun Khanna find significant licensing activity in the chemicals, computers, and electronics industries.[95] Ashish Arora, Marco Ceccagnoli, and Wesley Cohen apply extensive survey data on research labs in the U.S. manufacturing sector and show that patent protection of IP supports the market for technology licensing and the provision of specialized technology services.[96] The market for inventions includes not only domestic markets but also international transactions related to IP; royalty and licensing fees in international transactions grew faster than global GDP, reaching $2.8 billion in 1970, $27 billion in 1990, and $180 billion in 2009.[97]

1.3.2. *Explaining Patent Licensing and Transfers*

The concept of the market for innovative control helps to explain why there are patent transfers. Firms have incentives to acquire patents as a means of adding value to the patent. Firms add to the market value of patents when they can improve on the invention, commercialize the invention more effectively, or better develop innovations based on the patent. Firms also have incentives to acquire patents when they can realize economies of scale and scope in the management of IP. Firms also have additional incentives to acquire patents when they can offer greater capabilities in the management of IP than existing owners. Producers acquire patents that they can apply in developing innovations in products, production processes, or transaction methods.

The concept of the market for innovative control is also helpful in understanding the many types of firms that buy or sell patents. Different types of firms are needed for different types of technologies and for different tasks involved in invention, commercialization, and innovation. Christopher A. Cotropia, Jay P. Kesan, and David L. Schwartz point out that many types of companies engage in patent transactions, including universities, individual inventors, mass patent aggregators, failed startups and operating companies, patent holding companies, operating companies, IP holding companies owned by operating companies, and technology development companies.[98]

Different business models are an important aspect of the market for innovative control. Because the market for innovative control helps to allocate patents to the highest-value users, the types of firms that acquire patents will be those that provide the greatest market value. In a well-functioning market for innovative control, the business model of the acquiring firm acquiring IP will be the best suited to efficient management of that IP, all other things being equal. Restricting IP rights on the basis of the business model of the firm that owns the patent would create inefficiencies in the market for innovative control.

The market for innovative control also allows the entry of specialized intermediaries who can invest in commercialization, innovation, and complementary assets.[99] The allocation of patents in the market for innovative control implies that there should not be regulatory restrictions on patent transactions and ownership that are based on the characteristics of companies acquiring patents. Various commentators critically refer to some types of firms that acquire patents as "patent trolls," "patent monetizing entities" (PMEs), "non-practicing entities" (NPEs), or "patent assertion entities" (PAEs). Some types of firms that acquire patents have a particular expertise as market intermediaries.[100] Market intermediaries perform many types of activities that reduce various types of transaction costs, including search costs, bargaining costs, moral hazard, adverse selection, and contracting costs.[101] Intermediaries in the market for innovative control reduce transaction costs by evaluating patent quality, handling licensing transactions, or marketing and reselling patents. Intermediaries in the market for innovative control can act as market makers, bringing buyers and sellers together, clearing markets and adjusting prices.[102] Andrei Hagiu and David Yoffie identify different types of patent intermediaries.[103]

The market for innovative control also promotes efficiencies in the organization of firms and industries. Weaker IP protections increase transaction costs for inventors and innovators. Inventors and innovators will have incentives to replace patent protections with other mechanisms including trade secrets, contracts, and vertical integration.[104] With stronger IP protections, inventors and innovators can make decisions about transactions, outsourcing, and vertical integration based on other business considerations. The market for innovative control generates differences in patent transfers across industries depending on technologies. Carlos Serrano shows that there are surplus enhancing patent transfers and finds that higher rates of transfers occur in information and communications technology (ICT) and the pharmaceutical and medical industries.[105] In some industries, consortia form to exercise innovative control. For example, in 2011, Nortel Networks sold about 6000 patents and patent applications for $4.5 billion to a consortium of companies that included Apple, EMC, Ericsson, Microsoft, RIM, and Sony.[106]

As with securities markets, the market for innovative control allows separation of ownership and control. The patent owner can obtain returns from the patented invention while delegating control over innovation to licensees who employ the technology. The patent owner does not need to undertake all the transactions needed to apply the invention, but instead can rely on others to manage the IP. Delegation of control to licensees also provides benefits from specialization and division of labor. The patent owner can obtain returns from licensing, and the licensees can apply their expertise to developing, commercializing and applying the invention.

The market for innovative control promotes gains from trade in inventions. Because patents offer divisibility, as well as exclusivity and transferability, companies can engage in specialized R&D and exchange technologies in the market for innovative control. This allows a division of labor in invention, commercialization, innovation, and manufacturing. Specialization allows companies to take advantage of economies of scale and scope and to build capabilities and expertise. Market exchange of patented inventions generates gains from trade by selection of the best inventions and matching inventions with specialized firms.[107] The market for innovative control also interacts with the market for corporate control. M&A, including hostile takeovers, provides a mechanism for acquiring patented inventions and improving the management of IP. There is some evidence that complementarities in innovation capabilities help explain M&A.[108]

1.3.3. *Investment in Complementary Assets*

The market for innovative control also provides incentives to invest efficiently in *complementary assets*. Assets that are complementary to inventions include human resources, absorption of inventions, IP, product design, capital equipment, marketing, sales, procurement, and establishment of new firms. Patent protections allow companies to make investments in those complementary assets that are specific to particular inventions rather than in generic complementary assets. Invention-specific investment can generate greater economic returns than generic investment.[109]

The following example illustrates how patents help the market for innovative control guide investment in complementary assets. Inventors at Amazon Technologies obtained patent number 8,615,473 B2 for a "[m]ethod and system for anticipatory package shipping":

> According to one embodiment, a method may include packaging one or more items as a package for eventual shipment to a delivery address, selecting a destination geographical area to which to ship the package, shipping the package to the destination geographical area without completely specifying the delivery address at time of shipment, and while the package is in transit, completely specifying the delivery address for the package.[110]

The basic invention is the discovery that the delivery address can be specified after shipping has begun. This type of invention is valuable for a major e-commerce company such as Amazon.com because it can improve the speed and efficiency of shipping. Amazon's services depend on the quality of shipping, which also constitutes a significant part of the company's costs.

The Amazon patent specifies not only the basic invention but also looks ahead to innovations that will be introduced to the market based on that invention. Among the 24 claims, the patent contemplates different embodiments of the invention, including multiple computer systems that will communicate with each other, with one computer system initiating the shipment and the second computer system determining the destination and communicating with this first computer system.

Implementing a complex shipment system as envisioned in Amazon's patent will require investment in complementary assets, including computer software and hardware and machinery in the company's warehouses.

To get some idea of the extent of this investment, consider that Amazon has spent over $5 billion on its facilities in five years, operates 40 fulfillment centers, and has plans to build more. Amazon's fulfillment center in Phoenix, Arizona, covers an area greater than 28 football fields.[111]

Amazon's patent allows it to exclude others from making, using, or selling its business method invention. Amazon's incentives to develop better shipping techniques are based on the market returns to improved shipping services and the lower costs of more efficient shipping technologies. Amazon has incentives to offer products and services based on its basic invention because of the market returns to developing and implementing its invention. Amazon has incentives to invest in complementary assets such as computers, fulfillment centers, and specialized equipment to realize the full returns to its invention and related innovations. As illustrated by Amazon's shipping method patent, patents protect market incentives for invention, commercialization, and innovation. The market for innovative control provides guidance for what types of inventions to pursue and the direction of subsequent investments in development, innovation, and complementary assets.

1.4 Financing Invention and Innovation

Patents facilitate financing of invention and innovation in two critical ways. First, patented inventions serve as intangible real assets that allow a separation of the invention from the inventor, which is necessary for obtaining financing. In turn, financing helps inventors achieve financial separation between their innovative decisions and their personal consumption and saving decisions. Second, patents reduce the transaction costs of financing for entrepreneurial entrants and established companies, thus generating greater invention and innovation.

1.4.1. *Patents and Financial Separation*

Separation of the invention from the inventor is critical for financing of invention and innovation. Inventors create inventions by applying effort, knowledge, ingenuity, capabilities, insights, and scientific observations.

If R&D is successful, the discovery may be valuable in commercial applications or as an input to further R&D. The discovery is the knowledge of the inventor, whether explicit or tacit, so it can be difficult to separate the discovery from the inventor.

The patented invention is an intangible real asset that embodies the inventor's discovery as well as subsequent development of the invention. The separation of the invention from the inventor is analogous to the creation of a firm by an entrepreneur. Stewart Myers observes, "The company starts up with human capital. As and if it succeeds, an intangible real asset is created: the technology is embodied in product design; the production process used, and in the product's reputation with customers."[112] Myers points out that "[t]his real asset separates from the people who created it and can in due course be appropriated by financial investors. The venture could not raise outside money otherwise."[113] The patented invention is a real asset that separates from the inventor who creates it.

By separating inventions from inventors, patents facilitate the financing of R&D for independent inventors, specialized firms, and corporations. Stuart Graham, Robert Merges, Pam Samuelson, and Ted Sichelman find that startups patent to obtain financing as well as to seek a competitive advantage and deter infringement.[114] Pere Arqué-Castells shows that investment by venture capitalists (VCs) funds the development of inventions and increases patenting by startups.[115] Studies using aggregate industry data show that VC funding tends to increase patenting.[116]

By separating inventions from inventors, patents also facilitate the financing of commercialization and innovation. Commercialization is costly because inventors must invest in communicating the discovery to others by codifying it in the form of technical reports, diagrams, blueprints, computer code, statistical analyses, and mathematical formulas. The inventor incurs costs of developing the invention in the form of models, prototypes, equipment, materials, chemical compounds, and biological matter. Financing also allows inventors to innovate by investing in the development of new products, new manufacturing technologies, or new transaction methods. Invention, commercialization, and innovation may be inefficient if inventors do not have sufficient funds to invest in these activities. The inventor may not be able to carry out R&D projects in an efficient way or may not be able to undertake R&D at all. The inventor may not be able to effectively commercialize an invention. Also, the inventor may not be able to develop innovations based on the invention due to limited resources.

Because patents facilitate financing, they allow for another type of separation, that is, financial separation between inventors' innovative decisions and inventors' personal consumption and saving decisions. When inventors have sufficient resources for invention, commercialization, or innovation, the conditions of the Fisher Separation Theory apply.[117] Investment projects can be managed efficiently to maximize net present value. In a two-period setting, for example, the optimal investment equates the expected marginal return to investment to the per-unit cost of investment. The optimal investment level is independent of the preferences or endowment of the inventor.

When inventors do not have sufficient resources for invention, commercialization, or innovation, the conditions of the Fisher Separation Theory no longer apply. The inventor cannot achieve the optimal investment level. The inventor's investment decisions are financially intertwined with the inventor's personal consumption and saving decisions.[118] Suppose that the inventor is financially constrained and does not have sufficient funds to efficiently invest in innovation. Also, suppose that the inventor cannot obtain financing to develop and commercialize the invention. The innovator will be forced to underinvest in innovation, and, if a minimum level of investment is needed, the innovator may be unable to develop the innovation at all. An inventor who cannot transfer the invention to others and is financially and liquidity constrained faces interconnected consumption and investment decisions. The inventor's investment in innovation will reflect his marginal utility of consumption, subjective discount rate, and initial endowment.

The market for innovative control addresses problems resulting from the inventor's liquidity or financing constraints. These problems are readily solved if the inventor can transfer the invention to buyers that do not face such constraints. Buyers that are not subject to these constraints will be willing to pay up to the maximum value of the innovative project. Buyers can develop the innovation efficiently either through investment of their own funds or by obtaining financing for the costs of innovation.

Patents thus generate gains from trade by facilitating the financial separation of inventors' innovative decisions and personal consumption and saving decisions. Inventors who face liquidity and financing constraints will be made strictly better off by transferring the invention to others than by developing innovations themselves. Innovators who acquire inventions benefit by investing efficiently in developing and commercializing inventions.

1.4.2. *Patents and the Financing of Innovation*

Patents also can reduce the transaction costs of financing invention and innovation. Independent inventors and specialized firms can obtain financing for the invention by offering to license or transfer the patent to a company that provides financing. Companies that fund research can obtain an option to license or purchase the inventions after they are patented. If the inventor or specialized firm has already obtained a patent, the patent can serve as collateral for financing to develop the invention and to innovate based on the invention. Nathan Myhrvold recommends the creation of patent-backed securities and suggests that "the business of invention would function better if it were separated from manufacturing and developed on its own by a strong capital market that funded and monetized inventions."[119]

Patents are intangible real assets that contribute to the market value of the firm. The patent provides IP protections for an investment project with uncertain market value V. Suppose that the firm's assets consist of a patent with expected market value EV. Corporations obtain financing based on their patents. In the balance sheet of a firm financed by debt and equity, the market value of debt and equity equals the expected market value of the firm's intangible real asset, EV.[120]

Patented inventions can represent what Myers refers to as "assets in place."[121] Patents that are "assets in place" contribute to the market value of the corporation. The market value of patent ownership reflects the value of own-use of technology, the benefits of cross-licensing, and earnings from licensing. Studies show that patent ownership by corporations contributes significantly to their market value.[122] For example, IBM earns about $1 billion annually from licensing revenues.[123] Carol Robbins estimates that in 2002, US corporations reported about $67 billion in earnings from IP protected by patents and trade secrets.[124] David Abrams,

Ufuk Akcigit, and Jillian Popadak study the effect of patent ownership on the value of companies based on licensing revenues of specialized patent intermediaries.[125]

Patented inventions also can represent assets that Myers refers to as "growth opportunities."[126] This is because the company can develop the invention, innovate based on the invention, and invest in complementary assets. Also, the company can develop new technologies that extend their patented inventions. Myers points out that assets that are "growth opportunities" can function as call options because they involve investment decisions under uncertainty.[127] In this way, patented inventions that are growth opportunities can function as call options.

The capital structure of the firm can affect incentives for investment in invention and innovation. Myers shows that equity financing is best for inducing firms to maximize expected value of projects.[128] This is because debt financing could cause the firm to avoid some projects that have positive expected value. Equity financing provides incentives for efficiency in the choice of R&D projects as well.

Debt financing is useful as an incentive mechanism for inducing effort. Michael Jensen and William Meckling argue that with moral hazard, debt financing gives managers incentives for more efficient performance in comparison to equity financing.[129] Joaquín Poblete and Daniel Spulber show that generally the optimal contract with moral hazard and limited liability takes the form of debt.[130] This is because debt-style contracts serve to concentrate payments to the agent in the best states, which induces efficient levels of effort. Poblete and Spulber extend this analysis to R&D and show that debt-style contracts are the optimal contract for inducing R&D effort.[131]

Investment in R&D by companies provides evidence that the exclusivity provided by patents protects investment-backed expectations. Carol Corrado, Charles Hulten, and Daniel Sichel consider average annual capital spending from 2000 to 2003 and estimate that companies invested approximately $640 billion in R&D and development of computer software.[132] Investment in IP contributes significantly to the market value of companies. Hassett and Shapiro find that ten of the twenty four industries they study hold intellectual capital equal to one-half or more of their total market value and accounts for a significant share of market value in practically every industry.[133]

The role of patents as intangible real assets further shows that patents are not "rewards" for inventors. Inventors are no more rewarded by patents than companies are rewarded by registering securities. Indeed, patented inventions are intangible real assets that are analogous to *financial assets* in various ways. Inventors seeking patents must make filings and disclosures to the USPTO including a description of the invention and information showing that the invention is useful, novel, and non-obvious. Firms selling securities must register those securities with the Securities and Exchange Commission (SEC) and make various disclosures including a description of the security, an explanation of the company's properties and business, information about the company's management, and certified financial statements.[134] Just as each patent is different, so each corporate security is different — Procter & Gamble stock is not the same as ExxonMobil stock.

1.5 Public Policy toward IP

The present analysis of the market for inventions has implications for public policy toward IP. The design of IP policy should consider the patent system overall, which includes the market for inventions and other private institutions, such as industry consortia and standard-setting organizations (SSOs). The patent system also includes public institutions, which in the U.S. involve all three branches of government. The Congress establishes the rules of the system through legislation such as the 2011 America Invents Act (AIA). The executive branch reviews patent applications and grants patents through the USPTO, which is an agency of the Department of Commerce. Finally, the judiciary adjudicates legal cases involving patent grants and patent infringement. Patent law encompasses a rich set of legal precedents including many Supreme Court decisions.

1.5.1. *The Market Foundation View vs. the "Rewards" View of Patents*

The market foundation role of patents refutes the notion that patents are government-provided "rewards" for inventors. The "rewards" view is a mischaracterization of the purpose and institutions of the patent system.

The market foundation role of patents and the "rewards" view suggest substantially different public policies toward IP.

At first glance, it is easy to see why many believe that patents are "rewards" for inventors. The USPTO states, "A patent is an intellectual property right granted by the Government of the United States of America."[135] Because some patented inventions are quite valuable in the market place, one might well be tempted to conclude that the U.S. government has given a valuable property right to the patentee. Yet the meaning of the word "grant" in this context is not an award, gift, donation, or subsidy. Rather the word "grant" indicates that the government recognizes the inventor's right to exclude others from making, using, or selling the invention.

The government does not transfer a valuable asset to inventors, but instead recognizes the ownership of the asset by the inventor. The inventor's efforts, not the government patent grant, generate the invention. The patent grant is based on the features of the invention, the details of the application, and is contingent on whether the invention is useful, novel, and non-obvious. The patent certifies that the inventor meets criteria such as the first to invent, or now, the first to file.

The "rewards" view of patents is inconsistent with the institutions of the patent system. The returns received by the patent owner are provided by market participants, not by the government. The patent grant does not involve any asset or monetary transfers from the government to the patentee. The patent grant does not specify the market value of the patented invention, which is determined by the features of the invention and by demand and supply in the market for inventions. In addition, the patent owner's returns are generated by investment in developing, commercializing, and applying the invention. Many of these investments are made after the patent is granted.

The "rewards" view suggests that anticipation of obtaining patents provides incentives for invention. Inventors would not devote effort and make investments in R&D unless they expected to obtain economic returns. However, patent owners only receive the market value of the patented invention net of the costs of invention and commercialization. Inventors bear the risks associated with invention and commercialization. The inventor's R&D project may not succeed and the invention may not meet the criteria for patentability. The patenting process itself is costly and many applicants do not receive patents. Even if the inventor receives a patent, most patents have little if any market value. The patent grant does not provide incentives; rather, it provides the basis for further developing the invention, commercializing the technology, and introducing innovations to the market.

The patent grant is not designed to provide a reward for any particular type of invention, as if it were a "prize" for winning a contest, a government subsidy, or an employer bonus.[136] The patent grant is not a financial reward designed to induce some type of inventive behavior or level of effort. Also, the grant of a patent by the USPTO is not based on the costs of R&D or the efforts of the inventor in making the discovery.[137] The patent grant does not reward the inventor for disclosing the invention. As already noted, disclosure provides benefits to both patentees and potential adopters by reducing transaction costs in the market for inventions. Disclosure identifies the features of the invention and helps to guard against infringement.

1.5.2. *The Scope of Patents*

An important implication of the market foundation role of patents is that patent claims should be viewed prospectively. This confirms and extends Kitch's argument that patents should have sufficient scope to encourage further invention and innovation and to foster coordination.[138] Patents not only recognize creative work but they also provide IP protections for future creative work. The patent's claims extend beyond the completed work because inventors and patent owners plan to develop the invention and to invest in innovation. Patents do much of their work after they have been granted. As already noted, the terms of transactions in the market for inventions provide guidance on how to develop the invention, what innovations will apply the invention, what types of complementary assets should be obtained, and financial investments in invention and innovation.

Patents must be sufficiently broad as to provide guidance to inventors, innovators, and investors through the market for innovative control. This policy recommendation contrasts with the "rewards" view of patents, which suggests that patent scope should be narrow to limit the returns to inventors receiving the patent and to open the way for other patents to give additional rewards to future inventors. For example, Robert Merges and Richard Nelson argue that the scope of patents should be constrained, because "[i]n many industries the efficiency gains from the pioneer's ability to coordinate are likely to be outweighed by the loss of competition for improvements to the basic invention."[139] Merges and Nelson are concerned that broad patent scope will discourage "subsequent inventions that not only substitute for the initial invention, but also improve on it in some way."[140]

The market foundation role of patents supports broader patent scope because patents are forward-looking. Patents increase transaction efficiencies in the market for invention, provide innovative control, and facilitate financing of invention and innovation. These functions encourage competition — property rights increase entry into the market for inventions. Greater financing of invention and innovation increases entrepreneurial entry and competition in the market. Patents can cover development, commercialization, and innovation without ruling out improvements offered by others. Also, the patent examination process and the courts limit the scope of patent claims. Patent owners have incentives to limit the scope of their claims to increase the likelihood that the USPTO will grant the patent. Patent owners also have incentives to limit the scope of claims to reduce the risk that patents will be challenged and found invalid in the courts.

1.5.3. *Incremental Inventions, "Patent Hold-Up," and "Patent Thickets"*

Another common critique of patents that is based largely on the "rewards" view is that IP rights block incremental inventions.[141] This concern is applied to both individual patents and to sets of complementary patents, referred to as patent hold-ups, patent thickets, patent logjams, or the anticommons. Little if any evidence is advanced for these policy concerns.

However, the history of patents demonstrates that the patent system has accommodated a continual stream of both major inventions and incremental inventions. As Adam Mossoff observes, "From the sewing machine to automobiles to airplanes to radios, incremental innovation is omnipresent in the historical evolution of science and technology."[142] George Selgin and John Turner explain how James Watt's steam engine patent did not prevent subsequent innovations, but "may actually have hastened the development of the high-pressure steam engine by inspiring Richard Trevithick to revive a supposedly obsolete technology so as to invent around them."[143]

The many contributions of patents to the development of inventions and the introduction of innovations are well documented. Ron Katznelson and John Howells find that "court decisions upholding Edison's patent generated a surge of patent filings in the incandescent lamp classes."[144] In the early aircraft industry, Katznelson and Howells find "plentiful evidence of robust US aircraft developments in 1912–1916, the period of the alleged patent hold-up."[145] In the early radio industry, Howells and Katznelson demonstrate that the diode patent was followed by extensive and vigorous development of the later triode technology.[146]

Mark Lemley defines broad categories of technologies as individual inventions and concludes that there were many simultaneous inventors:

> Any elementary school student can recite a number of canonical American invention stories. Thomas Edison invented the lightbulb from his famous home laboratory in Menlo Park, New Jersey. Alexander Graham Bell invented the telephone, again from his home invention laboratory, and famously used the phone to call his assistant, saying "Come here, Watson, I need you." Orville and Wilbur Wright invented the airplane from their bicycle shop, taking it to Kitty Hawk, North Carolina to put it in the air. The list of lone genius inventors goes on and on: Samuel Morse and his telegraph, Eli Whitney and his cotton gin, Robert Fulton and his steamboat, Philo Farnsworth and the television, and so on.[147]

Lemley suggests that incentives for invention, commercialization, or disclosure are not good descriptions of the patent system.[148] Instead, based on simultaneous invention, Lemley argues that racing is the best description of the patent system.[149]

Howells and Katznelson observe that the problem with Lemley's analysis stems from his overly broad description of inventions.[150] In practice, there were many inventors of what Lemley refers to as "the lightbulb," because such technologies typically consist of many inventions. However, the patent system grants patents to inventors for specific inventions not broad technological categories. Howells and Katznelson demonstrate that Lemley's evidence for simultaneous invention is historically inaccurate.[151] Howells and Katznelson conclude, "But the *direct* purpose of the patent system that Lemley ignores, and from which the other incentives naturally flow, is to encourage *investment* in new inventions *once they have been made and disclosed.*"[152]

A related criticism of patents on the basis of the "rewards" view is that IP rights are unnecessary because incremental inventions would occur anyway. According to this view, rewards from patent ownership must be "excessive" because inventors have sufficient incentives to develop inventions with weaker IP rights. Indeed, Lemley suggests that inventors develop distinct inventions "because of an accident or error in the experiment rather than a conscious effort to invent."[153] Who needs patents if inventors are just stumbling over inventions? Carl Shapiro suggests that when public knowledge advances rapidly, incremental improvements are "in the air."[154] Shapiro further argues that independent invention is more likely for inventions that are "easily achieved."[155]

The market foundation role of patents emphasizes that patents provide transaction efficiencies, innovative control, and financing. These economic benefits are present regardless of whether or not the initial invention was "in the air" or "easily achieved." In practice, it is difficult if not impossible to distinguish between inventions that are easy or hard to obtain. Inventions often involve a complex mixture of inspiration and hard work. It is also not feasible to distinguish between inventions that are breakthroughs or "in the air" for the purpose of regulating royalties.

Criticisms of the patent system based on the "rewards" view suggest that patents are granted for inventions that fail the tests of being useful, novel, and non-obvious.[156] These issues have to do with the functioning of the patent examination process and can be addressed through improvements in management and organizational design. However, such administrative issues differ from the question of whether patents support exchange in the market for inventions.

Some complaints about the patent examination process are the product of hindsight. Many inventions that were once useful, novel, and non-obvious no longer are, as technological change reveals alternatives and makes past inventions not only obsolete but quaint by comparison. Rapid technological change can speed up change in subjective perceptions of past inventions.

Another common criticism of patents based on the "rewards" view is that patents restrict innovation by discouraging the use of patented inventions. According to this argument, patent owners can "hold up" infringers by threatening injunctions and damage remedies for infringement.[157] Infringers are said to be unaware of the patents and surprised by legal claims. The "hold-up" argument further assumes that infringers are locked in to the technology because of high costs of designing around the patented technology and the costs of switching to a new technology. The "hold-up" argument concludes that patent owners will take advantage of these costs to increase royalty demands in license negotiations.

The theoretical "hold-up" argument tends to ignore incentives for coordination through the market for inventions.[158] Patent owners and producers have incentives to contract before any infringement occurs and before producers make complementary investments. Evidence for this comes from extensive investment and industry growth that occurs after licensing and cross-licensing of inventions.

Even after infringement is discovered, patent owners and producers have incentives to negotiate licensing agreements. Patent owners do not have incentives to seek excessive royalties because they benefit from producers' marketing and sales efforts that increase usage of the patented invention. Patent owners also benefit from producers' making investments in new products, production processes, and transaction techniques that apply the inventions. Patent owners would not wish to discourage investments in innovation and complementary assets. Also, in practice, producers can develop alternative technologies, license substitute technologies, or pursue alternative activities that do not require the infringed technology. These activities are affected by royalties; excessive royalties would discourage use of the patented invention and encourage the search for alternatives. Market forces including competition from past, present, and future inventions constrain royalties.

1.5.4. *Public Goods and the Market for Inventions*

Critics of the patent system often point out that inventions are "public goods." Consumption of inventions is "non-rivalrous" in the sense that multiple firms can apply the same invention. Unlike eating a cake, which must be divided among consumers, many firms can use the same invention without depleting the original resource. For example, Joseph Stiglitz states, "I want to emphasize that efficiency *in use* means knowledge should be freely available. The problem is that intellectual property rights circumscribe the use of knowledge and thus, almost necessarily, cause inefficiency."[159] Again applying the "rewards" view, Stiglitz observes, "The patent system can only be justified, given all its costs, in terms of dynamic efficiency: the benefits that result from an enhanced pace of innovation."[160]

The non-rivalrous or public good nature of inventions by no means implies that technology cannot be allocated efficiently by a system of property rights. Access to patented technology can readily be sold and distributed to multiple users through licensing, cross-licensing, subscriptions, and other types of contracts. There are many types of markets for goods and services that are non-rivalrous but excludable. Markets have long existed for printed matter such as books, newspapers, magazines, and journals, and other types of analog and digital media. Markets also allocate access to shows and movie presentations. All types of video and audio programming are sold and distributed through cable television or streaming over the Internet. Access to other types of content, including news, technical information, education, e-books, games, movies, music, and applications programs (apps), is sold and distributed over the Internet.

The non-rivalrous or public good nature of inventions also does not imply that such goods should be freely available. There are marketing, distribution, sales, and other types of transaction costs for information goods such as inventions. There are also costs of communication and codification of technological information, particularly when the inventor has tacit knowledge that is difficult to transmit to potential adopters.

Even if distribution and transaction costs are zero, inventions should not be freely available because patent owners incur costs of developing the invention, creating innovations, and investing in complementary assets. The best way to recover these costs is through a price system. Simply labeling technology as a public good does not imply that inventors should rely on government subsidies obtained from general taxation. Also, labeling technology as a public good does not imply that firms employing the technology should receive it at no cost. Efficiency is achieved by the "user pays principle." Firms have incentives to make efficient technology adoption decisions and efficient R&D investments when they pay for technology. If there are efficiencies from lower per-unit royalties, access to technology can be sold using a combination of lump-sum and per-unit royalties.

Some critics of the patent system apply inappropriate benchmarks to the market for inventions. These benchmarks are based on the theoretical market model in neoclassical economics, which assumes "rivalrous" consumption. According to Troy and Werle, for example,

> [f]undamental and strategic uncertainty related to patent trading — a specific decontextualized institutional form of knowledge property — has prevented functioning markets for patents from emerging. Apparently, patent transactions are not made in perfect, anonymous neoclassical markets. Also, if we define markets less rigidly as institutional fields constituted by sellers and buyers, intermediaries and regulators, sharing rules, standards, and norms which govern transactions, we can hardly speak of a market for patents.[161]

This argument is based on the unrealistic definition of markets as centralized auctions, such as organized financial exchanges. The authors also rule out transactions involving intermediaries, regulators, standards, and norms. This definition not only eliminates financial exchanges but also most markets, because practically any market has a microstructure with these features.[162] Criteria that define almost all markets out of existence should certainly not be applied to patents and are misleading for public policy.

Markets rarely conform to the neoclassical economics paradigm of homogenous goods, anonymous trading through an exogenous auctioneer, price-taking behavior, or rivalrous consumption. This combination of features is absent from practically all markets, and certainly should not be a normative standard applied to the market for inventions. Many markets involve highly differentiated products. For example, all properties in commercial and residential real estate differ in terms of combinations of location and building features. Even securities markets have submarkets for the stocks of individual companies. For example, the New York Stock Exchange has specialists that make the market for the stock of individual firms. Many markets involve an absence of anonymity such as labor markets or markets for outsourcing contracts. Many markets involve price setting by sellers or price negotiation between buyers and sellers.

1.6 Antitrust Policy toward Patents

The present analysis of the market for inventions has implications for antitrust policy. Protection of IP and antitrust policy are complements, because protecting IP promotes competition in the market for inventions and in markets for goods and services that embody or are manufactured with patented inventions. Conversely, antitrust policy that favors competition in the market for inventions and in product markets will increase incentives to innovate. This implies that both patent policy and antitrust policy should favor stronger IP rights. Patent policy and antitrust policy should avoid making exceptions to protections of IP rights. Policymakers should thus avoid restrictions of IP rights for arbitrarily selected cutting-edge technologies such as software, business methods, or biotechnology.

1.6.1. *Patents and Competition*

The many varieties of competition in the market for inventions and related markets refute the common misconception that patents give their owners an economic monopoly. For example, Kenneth Arrow's classic analysis states "[w]ith suitable legal measures, information may become an appropriable commodity. Then the monopoly power can indeed be exerted."[163] Boldrin and Levine argue that patents provide "a monopoly as a reward for innovation" and that there is "little doubt that granting a monopoly for any reason has the equally ill consequences we associate with monopoly power."[164] The patent as monopoly argument has been refuted by John Stuart Mill, Judge Giles Rich, Edmund Kitch, Daniel Spulber, and others.[165]

Advocates of the "rewards" view of patents typically conclude that patents are "excessive" because rewards exceed the inventor's contribution to social welfare. For example, Stiglitz states, "The fundamental problem is that under the patent system the rewards do not correspond to the marginal social returns."[166] Similarly, Shapiro argues that "The core problem with the current U.S. patent system explored here is that . . . the patent system predictably provides excessive rewards to patent holders. The term 'excessive rewards' is defined here to mean rewards that exceed the patentee's actual contribution to economic welfare."[167]

There is no empirical evidence for the assertion that patent owners systematically earn "excessive" rewards. In any case, there is no intrinsic value of an invention that departs from its market value. Economic analysis has long identified the value of goods and services as being given by market prices. Competition in the market for inventions strongly suggests that patent owners earn market rewards. A patent does not confer an economic monopoly because access to the market for inventions, markets for products, or financial markets remains unimpeded.

The standard Nordhaus argument is incorrect because it *assumes* that a patent confers an economic monopoly on their owners.[168] This now standard assumption in the economics and law literature is inconsistent with reality. Competition in the market for inventions and in the product market that applies inventions means that a patent owner does not receive monopoly rents. This invalidates the standard analysis of patent policy that is based on the economic monopoly assumption.

The standard Nordhaus-style conclusion is that the duration of a patent should be just sufficient for a period of monopoly rents to cover the costs of invention. Even within this overly simplistic framework, it should be noted that more intense competition would dissipate economic rents and therefore would extend the optimal duration of a patent. The duration of a patent is not simply adding up monopoly rewards such that they exactly equal the cost of an invention.

The Nordhaus-style analysis is incorrect for more fundamental reasons. The inventor's incentives depend on anticipation of the market value of the invention. Patents serve to promote competition among inventors. Greater patent duration increases incentives to enter the market, all other things being equal, which increases competition among inventors. By reducing transaction costs in the market for inventions, patents reduce the costs of entry and operation in that market, also increasing incentives to enter the market and increasing competition among inventors.

Competition in the market for inventions *limits* inventors' rewards. Entry of inventors and competition in the market for inventions improves the quality of the best inventions. Entry of inventors also increases competition among inventors, which dissipates economic returns to inventors. This suggests that policymakers may wish to strengthen patent protections and increase their duration to increase competition in the market for inventions. A Nordhaus-style analysis will miss the beneficial effects of inventor entry because it assumes that all patents are economic monopolies.

A patent faces competition from past, present, and future inventions. For example, the USPTO issued 276,788 patents in 2012. Patents filed on or after June 8, 1995 have a term of 20 years from the time of filing, so the stock exceeds two million patents. Table 1.1 shows the number of patents issued in the US from 1963 to 2012.

Table 1.1: U.S. Patent statistics chart calendar years 1963 to 2012.

Year of application or grant	Utility patent grants, all origin total	Design patent grants	Plant patent grants	Reissue patent grants	Total patent grants
2012	253,155	21,951	860	822	276,788
2011	224,505	21,356	823	1,029	247,713
2010	219,614	22,799	981	947	244,341
2009	167,349	23,116	1,009	453	191,927
2008	157,772	25,565	1,240	647	185,224
2007	157,282	24,062	1,047	508	182,899
2006	173,772	20,965	1,149	519	196,405
2005	143,806	12,951	716	245	157,718
2004	164,290	15,695	1,016	298	181,299
2003	169,023	16,574	994	421	187,012
2002	167,331	15,451	1,133	460	184,375
2001	166,035	16,871	584	480	183,970

(Continued)

Table 1.1: (*Continued*)

Year of application or grant	Utility patent grants, all origin total	Design patent grants	Plant patent grants	Reissue patent grants	Total patent grants
2000	157,494	17,413	548	524	175,979
1999	153,485	14,732	420	448	169,085
1998	147,517	14,766	561	298	163,142
1997	111,984	11,414	394	277	124,069
1996	109,645	11,410	362	279	121,696
1995	101,419	11,712	387	316	113,834
1994	101,676	11,095	499	317	113,587
1993	98,342	10,630	442	332	109,746
1992	97,444	9,269	321	360	107,394
1991	96,511	9,569	353	263	106,696
1990	90,365	8,024	318	370	99,077
1989	95,537	6,092	587	317	102,533
1988	77,924	5,679	425	244	84,272
1987	82,952	5,959	229	245	89,385
1986	70,860	5,518	224	260	76,862
1985	71,661	5,066	242	276	77,245
1984	67,200	4,938	212	300	72,650
1983	56,860	4,563	197	362	61,982
1982	57,888	4,944	173	271	63,276
1981	65,771	4,745	183	365	71,064
1980	61,819	3,949	117	285	66,170
1979	48,854	3,119	131	309	52,413
1978	66,102	3,862	186	364	70,514
1977	65,269	3,929	173	410	69,781
1976	70,226	4,564	176	422	75,388
1975	72,000	4,282	150	378	76,810
1974	76,278	4,304	261	435	81,278
1973	74,143	4,033	132	314	78,622
1972	74,810	2,901	199	275	78,185
1971	78,317	3,156	71	246	81,790

Table 1.1: (*Continued*)

Year of application or grant	Utility patent grants, all origin total	Design patent grants	Plant patent grants	Reissue patent grants	Total patent grants
1970	64,429	3,214	52	269	67,964
1969	67,559	3,335	103	233	71,230
1968	59,104	3,352	72	186	62,714
1967	65,652	3,165	85	196	69,098
1966	68,405	3,188	114	179	71,886
1965	62,857	3,424	120	246	66,647
1964	47,375	2,686	128	200	50,389
1963	45,679	2,965	129	198	48,971

Source: *Calendar Year Patent Statistics (January 1 to December 31)*, United States Patent and Trademark Office, http://www.uspto.gov/web/offices/ac/ido/oeip/taf/reports.htm.

A patented invention also faces *potential* competition from future inventions. Thus, a patent does not create a barrier to entry into the market for inventions because any other patented invention can enter the market for inventions. Any invention that is novel and thus does not infringe on patented inventions can enter the market for inventions.

A patented invention faces additional competition from inventions that are not protected by IP rights, including inventions that were patented but whose term has expired. For example, patented pharmaceuticals face competition from generics. A patented invention faces competition both within and across the patent categories established by the USPTO. This is because the patent categories have to do with the properties of the inventions, which need not correspond to adopters' uses for inventions. For example, a computer software invention, such as an email program, can compete with a computer hardware invention, such as a fax machine.

The patent system, by creating transferable assets from inventions, translates market competition into incentives for invention, commercialization, and innovation. When there is a market for inventions, competition among inventors increases incentives for invention and innovation.[169] Additionally, when there is a market for inventions, competition among adopters increases incentives for invention and innovation. Without such protections, companies resort to secrecy and vertical integration, which can cause competitive pressures to reduce incentives to invent and to innovate.[170]

1.6.2. *Antitrust Policy and the Market for Inventions*

Antitrust policy toward patents should consider their role as the foundation of the market for inventions. This immediately eliminates the false conflict between patents as monopoly rewards for inventors and antitrust as rent control. The antitrust policy objectives of promoting competition and consumer welfare complement the market foundation role of patents.

Further, a patent does not create barriers to entry in product markets. Any product that uses other patented inventions or that uses any technology that does not infringe on the patented invention can enter the product market. Thus, producers that offer products applying a patented invention face competition in the product market. Competition in the product market from firms using other technologies limits the economic returns to a particular invention.

A patented invention faces competition both from inventions that are substitutes and from inventions that are complements. The economic definition of substitute (complementary) products refers to those products whose demand increases (decreases) with an increase in the price of the other products. Products are economic substitutes if some buyers are willing to switch some of their consumption from one good to another in response to changes in the relative prices. The concept of economic substitutes only requires products to be comparable rather than identical, which is referred to as perfect substitutes. Products are economic complements if some buyers derive benefits from joint consumption. Buyers can derive benefits from consuming a selection of complementary products, so that joint consumption of all complementary products is not necessary, in contrast to perfect complements.

Entry of and competition from substitutes in the market for inventions limit or eliminate the market power of inventions. When inventions are vertically differentiated — that is, buyers can rank inventions consistently on the basis of quality — buyers' willingness to pay for a particular invention is limited by the incremental contribution of that invention to their profits. Inventions other than the best invention are not adopted and inventors need not recover their costs of invention. Buyers will tend to apply the best invention, and royalties are less than or equal to the incremental benefits of the best invention as compared to the best alternative. This outcome corresponds to dominant designs or to technology standards based on the best technology. The best technology is subject to change as new inventions continue to enter the market.

When inventions are horizontally differentiated, multiple technologies may be adopted in the market for inventions. Edward Chamberlin's model of monopolistic competition is useful for characterizing competition in a particular segment of the market for inventions. This model features price setting by suppliers and competitive entry.[171] Although suppliers have pricing power, entry dissipates rents. With up-front fixed-fee royalties, the equilibrium royalty will equal the cost of invention divided by the number of licenses offered by every inventor plus licensing costs. A similar argument can be made when inventors charge a royalty based on the units of output sold by adopters.[172] Even if inventors have pricing power, entry of substitute inventions drives inventors' economic profits toward zero.

Even in the absence of substitutes, inventions compete for economic rents with complementary inventions. The entry of additional complementary inventions tends to diminish the returns to each invention when adopters of the inventions have a given total benefit. This is the case even when complementary inventions are necessary for adopters to produce final products. When complementary inventions are not necessary, competition among inventions constrains the returns to a particular invention based on its incremental contributions to the final products. The presence of substitutes for individual complementary inventions and substitutes for entire technology platforms provide competitive pressures that limit royalties.[173]

1.7 Conclusion

The economic benefits of patents derive from their major contributions to the formation of the market for inventions. The U.S. patent system offers many important features that contribute to transaction efficiencies and increase competition. The patent system provides IP protections that support the market for innovative control. The patent system facilitates financing of invention and innovation. The market foundation role of the U.S. patent system has a proven record of performance, having fostered significant technological change and economic growth.

The market foundation role of patents presents a complex but realistic analysis of invention and innovation. The "rewards" view of patents does not take full account of either public or private institutions that form the patent system. Critics of the patent system often highlight the legal costs of the patent enforcement. The legal costs of the patent system should not be viewed as a reward to inventors, but instead can be better understood as a cost of deterring infringement. Such costs cannot be taken in isolation; they must be weighed against the benefits generated by the market for inventions.

The analysis in this chapter suggests that public policy toward IP should be based on long experience with markets for all types of goods, services, and financial assets. The economic understanding of how market mechanisms contribute to allocative and dynamic efficiency extends readily to invention and innovation. The market for inventions, whether in the form of disembodied technology or discoveries embodied in products, services, or production processes, offers efficiencies that are closely related to how markets perform in other areas of the economy. Private ordering offers a variety of institutions such as licensing, cross-licensing, transfers, and contractual R&D for addressing the specific features of invention and innovation.

Antitrust policy toward IP should be based on the tradition of promoting competition and economic efficiency in other types of markets. The market foundation role of patents shows that stronger IP rights increase competition, innovation, and consumer welfare. Antitrust policy most effectively promotes innovation, competition, and transaction efficiency when it recognizes the market foundation role of patents.

Chapter 2

Patents versus Prizes

2.1 Introduction

The patent system supports the market for inventions, as explained in the previous chapter. The market for inventions establishes prices for technology transfers, allocates technologies, and guides investment in R&D. The market for inventions is a market for innovative control. It generates both allocative and dynamic economic efficiency. The patent system and the market for inventions promote social welfare and economic growth

Calls to replace the patent system with public contests are misguided. With public contests, government agencies would design games, choose prizes, select winning inventions, take ownership of technologies, and allocate technologies to producers. Reliance on such public contests would significantly decrease incentives for invention and innovation. Replacing the patent system with public contests would damage the market for inventions and harm economic efficiency.

The America COMPETES Reauthorization Act of 2010 (the Act) establishes a legal framework for replacing some types of patents with prizes and government control of technology.[1] The Act specifies the elements of prize contests: "the subject of the competition;" "the rules for being eligible to participate in the competition;" "the process for participants to register for the competition;" "the amount of the prize;" and "the basis on which a winner will be selected."[2] The Act also allows the government to license intellectual property (IP) from inventors: "The Federal Government may negotiate a license for the use of intellectual property developed by a participant for a competition."[3] The Act specifies that transfers of technology and licensing of IP to the government are voluntary.[4] However, the government can apply various mechanisms to induce participation in contests, such as antitrust, regulation, subsidies, or procurement. The Act empowers the heads of all federal agencies in the Executive branch to create prize competitions.[5] The Act authorizes the use of both tax revenues and private funds to pay cash prizes.[6]

Some provisions of the Act have been put into practice: "The Administration will continue to focus on using prizes to encourage new ways to speed commercialization."[7] For example, the U.S. government is applying prizes such as "Challenge Grants" competitions to promote commercialization of new technologies.[8] In addition, prizes are part of various public–private partnerships, including partnerships with universities.[9] According to the Department of Commerce, "To support these communities [of innovators], the Administration has partnered with organizations to inspire participation in innovative activities through the use of challenges and prizes."[10]

In this chapter, I explain why arguments for replacing market prices with public prizes are incorrect. First, I show that the standard deadweight welfare loss argument is a fallacy because it assumes government prizes create no economic distortions — a classic case of a "free lunch." Yet, the government must collect taxes to pay for the prizes and such taxes create substantial deadweight welfare losses.[11] The bureaucratic and compliance costs of the taxation system are substantial as well. The standard argument for public prizes assumes that the government would incur no costs of administering the prize system or managing subsequent technology diffusion and commercialization — another free lunch. Yet, the administrative costs of operating a government prize system and commercializing technologies are significant.

The standard argument for public prizes further assumes that market prices create monopoly deadweight welfare losses. This assumption is inaccurate because extensive competition in the markets for inventions and products reduces prices and mitigates deadweight welfare loss. Also, market competition promotes efficiency because firms have incentives to reduce the transaction costs of commercialization and innovation. I conclude that the deadweight welfare losses resulting from a government prize system are likely to substantially exceed any such losses from competitive markets — replacing prices with prizes would lower social welfare.

Second, I emphasize that government prizes, in contrast to the market for inventions, cannot achieve an efficient allocation of technology. A public prize system with government diffusion of technology can do little to promote efficient commercialization and innovation. Public prizes require planners to choose the best technology in advance, and government diffusion of technology eliminates many of the benefits of competition. Government contests and the selection of winners reflect the specific priorities of public policymakers rather than economic benefits of invention and innovation. In contrast, prices in the market for inventions are generated by competition and coordination that selects the best inventions and innovations. Patents, along with copyrights, trademarks, trade secrets, and other IP, support invention, commercialization, and innovation by providing the foundation of the market for inventions.[12] Competitive pressures among inventors and among producers increase incentives to invent.[13] Inventions and innovations are not exogenous forces but instead are the results of economic decisions and transactions among many participants in the market for inventions. As Friedrich Hayek points out, competition is a discovery procedure because it helps inventors and producers discover the best inventions and innovations.[14]

Third, I explain that government prizes cannot achieve dynamic economic efficiency because they do not provide guidance for investment in commercialization and innovation. Public ownership and distribution of the winning technology at a zero price does not provide incentives for innovation. In contrast, investment in developing patented inventions occurs both before and after the patent is granted because a patent often covers the initial invention, development of the invention, and innovative applications, as Edmund Kitch recognized.[15] Prices in the market for inventions *guide economic decisions* of inventors, innovators, producers, investors, and consumers. Market prices for inventions convey signals about seller cost and buyer willingness to pay. Market prices for inventions thus promote innovation and competition and increase both static and dynamic efficiencies. Prices are *state-contingent* because they reflect technological change and the features of complementary and substitute inventions. Market forces change prices without the transaction costs of establishing contingent contracts. Prices for inventions therefore guide decision-making under uncertainty. The market for inventions is a market for innovative control because ownership of patented inventions not only generates residual returns but allows owners to exercise residual control over the development and application of inventions.[16]

I do not argue against either public or private prizes generally — I only address the question of whether prizes should replace prices.[17] Both public and private prizes can provide incentives and information that are complements to — but not close substitutes for — the market for inventions. Gary Becker, winner of the Nobel Prize in Economic Sciences, observes that prizes may be useful because of the limited patentability of basic discoveries: "To offset the effect of this exclusion from patent protection on the incentive to discover, individuals and governments have created prizes and awards, like the Fields Medal and Nobel Prizes, for mathematical and scientific discoveries."[18] Public and private prizes can achieve various complementary objectives against the backdrop of IP rights, as long as policymakers do not seek to replace IP rights and the market for inventions.[19] Petra Moser and Tom Nicholas find historical evidence that prizes provide publicity that encourages patenting and innovation.[20] Fiona S. Murray *et al.* find that Grand Innovation Prizes are not substitutes for patents but instead serve such goals as awareness, education, and demonstrating the viability of alternatives.[21] Prizes can serve as an inducement to innovation when winners can patent their inventions and indeed find that winning a prize increases patenting.[22] Glen Weyl and Jean Tirole provide a general model of market incentives in which public subsidies supplement market prices.[23]

The chapter is organized as follows. Section 2.2 shows why the deadweight welfare loss argument for replacing market prices with public prizes is fundamentally flawed. Section 2.3 shows why market prices promote greater allocative efficiency than public prizes. Section 2.4 discusses how market prices promote greater dynamic efficiency than public prizes because they help to guide individual technological decisions and serve as condensed indicators of technological change.

2.2 The Flawed Deadweight Welfare Loss Argument

Prize advocates writing in the economics and law literatures generally make a set of inconsistent assumptions about market prices and central planning. First, prize advocates either understate or ignore the deadweight welfare losses from taxes that would be needed to finance prizes and the administrative costs of a prize system. Prize advocates then assume incorrectly that IP creates economic monopolies, so that any patent owner prices at a monopoly price, which allegedly creates monopoly deadweight welfare losses. The monopoly welfare loss assumption ignores contractual alternatives to running royalties per unit of output. The monopoly argument generally mischaracterizes restrictions on access to inventions as an economic monopoly. The characterization of patents as sources of monopoly ignores competition among inventors and among producers.

2.2.1. *Deadweight Welfare Losses and Inconsistent Assumptions*

Many academics advocate replacing market prices with a system of government prizes. Benjamin Roin points out that "the past two decades have seen a virtual explosion of scholarship on prize systems."[24] Evaluating this literature, Roin states "The consensus view is that if the government can set prizes that offer equivalent incentives for innovation as intellectual property, it should grant prizes instead of intellectual property because the public would receive the same benefits of innovation without the deadweight loss from higher consumer prices."[25] The law literature advocating replacing patents with prizes is extensive and advances a variety of arguments, including equitable allocation of resources.[26]

The economics literature advocating prizes over prices is also extensive.[27] An early advocate of prizes, Michael Polanvyi states: "In order that inventions may be used freely by all, we must relieve inventors of the necessity of earning their rewards commercially and must grant them instead the right to be rewarded from the Public purse."[28] Two winners of the Nobel Prize in Economic Sciences argue for government prizes replacing market prices.[29] According to Kenneth Arrow,

> "In an ideal socialist economy, the reward for invention would be completely separated from any charge to the users of the information. In a free enterprise economy, inventive activity is supported by using the invention to create property rights; precisely to the extent that it is successful, there is an underutilization of the information. The property rights may be in the information itself, through patents and similar legal devices, or in the intangible assets of the firm if the information is retained by the firm and used only to increase its profits."[30]

Joseph Stiglitz argues that "Patents are not the only way of stimulating innovation. . . . The alternative of awarding prizes would be more efficient and more equitable."[31] For Stiglitz, "The innovation incentives are strong in the patent system, but they are distorted, whereas the prize system can provide equivalently strong incentives that are less distorted."[32]

The standard argument for government prizes replacing market prices is simple enough.[33] Prize advocates maintain that because inventions are public goods, they should be priced at $0, so that any positive price is inefficient. The market price of an invention equals say $1.00, which is necessarily greater than the marginal cost of $0. Patents create economic monopolies the argument goes, so that market prices necessarily create a monopoly deadweight welfare loss.

To correct this problem, it is argued, the government should hold a contest, pay the winning inventor a prize of $1.00 or less, take possession of the invention, and make it available to producers at a cost of $0 — problem solved! Or is this simple solution just too good to be true?

To evaluate the economic effects of a public prize system and the patent system, it is necessary to make a consistent comparison of their costs and benefits.[34] Many economic models showing that public contests should replace patents make inconsistent and unrealistic assumptions about both taxes and market prices. Some of these analyses assume that government taxes used to finance a prize system do not create any economic distortions so that prizes involve zero deadweight welfare losses. Prize advocates further assume that prices in markets for inventions create the maximum possible economic distortions so that they generate monopoly deadweight welfare losses. The combination of these extreme assumptions inevitably generates the theoretical conclusion that public prizes are better than market prices.

A related inconsistency in many economic models of prizes is the assumption that governments can finance prizes with lump-sum taxes but IP owners cannot license patents using lump-sum royalties. In practice, patent licensing contracts involve fixed fees, cross-licensing, and other contractual arrangements that mitigate the potential effects of per-unit royalties. Lump-sum payments for patent licensing reduce welfare losses from increases in per-unit prices. In addition, patents need not be licensed because many patent owners use their own inventions. Patents provide protection for own-use of IP and for transfers of IP to other users. Own use of patented technology does not involve deadweight welfare losses from patent licensing royalties.

For example, Chari *et al.* assume that there is no deadweight welfare loss associated with taxation to pay for prizes: "Since a prize is a lump sum transfer financed by lump sum taxes on consumers, it does not affect the social surplus."[35] At the same time, Chari *et al.* assume that patent ownership causes a monopoly deadweight welfare loss.[36] This difference in assumptions generates a theoretical advantage of public prizes over market prices. In their setting, market prices may still be preferable to public prizes, but only because patent owners have private information not available to government planners.[37]

Steven Shavell and Tanguy van Ypersele assume that patent owners make monopoly profits and the patent system generates monopoly deadweight welfare losses.[38] However, their model does not explicitly account for deadweight welfare losses from taxation to finance prizes. Shavell and van Ypersele concede that "Reward systems have to be financed, and we presume through income taxation, but that involves a labor supply-related distortionary cost, something that was not considered in our model. Hence, the potential case for reward is less strong than is suggested by our analysis."[39]

Michael Kremer recommends that the government purchase inventions and make them freely available to producers. Kremer assumes that inventors are monopolists and that because of deadweight welfare losses, "competitive markets do not provide appropriate incentives for the production of ideas."[40] Kremer further assumes that government taxes to finance purchases of inventions are chosen optimally by a welfare-maximizing central planner.[41] In practice, taxes differ from optimal taxes, but even optimal taxes can generate deadweight welfare losses.[42]

Some studies suggest that government prizes are preferable to market prices for inventions because income taxes are broadly based and presumably less distortionary than taxes that are concentrated in a single market.[43] However, income taxes are distortionary for labor markets, and these distortions are increased by the complexity of tax deductions and the graduated income tax. Michael Abramowicz recognizes that general taxes used to fund prizes would be distortionary and instead recommends concentrating the taxes on users.[44] Yet, such taxes are generally equivalent to per-unit prices paid by users. Hemel and Ouellette observe that "the marginal distortion due to additional revenue-raising for credits, grants, and prizes could conceivably exceed the marginal distortion due to stronger patent rights."[45]

2.2.2. *Deadweight Welfare Losses from Taxation*

In practice, taxes generate deadweight welfare losses whether applied to goods and services or labor income. Cecil E. Bohanon, John B. Horowitz, and James E. McClure point out that in the field of public economics "Textbooks say too little, too late, about the excess burdens of taxation."[46] They argue that "When textbook authors don't explicitly discuss these costs when discussing the optimal provision of a public good, it leads students to forget that taxes are distortionary and ignore these welfare costs when doing their analyses."[47] The same may well be said about the economics and law literature that advocates public prizes and often fails to mention the costs of taxation.

The deadweight welfare losses of taxation must be estimated because they take the form of economic distortions and compliance costs. Bohanon *et al.* survey nine studies of the economic costs of raising a dollar from a labor income tax and find the average to be between $1.43 and $1.50.[48] In addition, Joel Slemrod and Jon Bakija find that there is a $0.10 compliance cost per dollar of revenue raised.[49] Using the average of economic studies of taxation, this means that the deadweight welfare losses from taxation equal $0.53 to $0.60 for every dollar of revenue.

Martin Feldstein estimates "that the deadweight loss per dollar of revenue of using a labor income tax rather than a lump-sum tax is more than twelve times as large as Harberger's classic estimate. If the existing Social Security tax and benefit structure is taken into account, the deadweight loss per dollar of personal income tax revenue is even greater."[50] Feldstein observes "The analysis implies that a marginal increase in tax revenue achieved by a proportional rise in all personal income tax rates involves a deadweight loss of two dollars per incremental dollar of revenue."[51]

Feldstein's estimate is useful because it takes into account the effect of various institutions on labor income. Applying Feldstein's estimate of the costs of taxation implies that a prize of $1.00 would generate economic costs of $3.00, which includes the $1.00 cost of the prize and another $2.00 of deadweight welfare loss. Advocates of prizes who assume that taxes do not involve a distortion evaluate market prices based only on the direct cost of the prize of $1.00. All other things equal, the proper standard of comparison for a public prize system would be whether or not market prices generated deadweight welfare losses greater than or less than $2.00 per dollar.

The costs of a public prize system that replaces patents would be prohibitive. The private returns to IP in the economy exceed hundreds of billions of dollars. The high cost of rewarding inventors and innovators would be a prohibitive amount in comparison to the existing budget of the US federal government. Monetary prizes for inventors would be financed from increases in general taxation, which would face considerable resistance by taxpayers. There would also be administrative costs of additional tax collection to finance hundreds of billions of dollars in tax increases. In addition, such high taxes would generate considerable deadweight welfare losses. This suggests that the government would be able to offer only a few prizes.

An example gives some idea of the potential costs of public prizes. Love and Hubbard propose a fixed prize fund that would be divided equally among innovators who would be compelled to surrender their IP rights.[52] Then-Congressman Bernard Sanders of Vermont, a self-described "democratic socialist," introduced a bill based on their proposal: The Medical Innovation Prize Fund Act, H.R. 417, 109th Congress, 2005. The prize system would be mandatory, difficult to enforce, and subject to political pressures and industry rent-seeking.[53]

In the proposed legislation, The Medical Innovation Prize Fund would total 0.5% of GDP. Using an estimated GDP of $17,710.7, the prize fund would have equaled approximately $88.5 billion. This large amount would cover prizes only for the relatively narrow area of medical innovation. As a standard of comparison, consider that federal funding of R&D equaled about $126 billion, about 30% of total R&D.[54] In contrast, business provided $294 billion, about 69% of total R&D.[55]

Some arguments for public funding of invention are based on income redistribution. Fisher and Syed, for example, advocate the use of progressive taxation to finance transfers to developing countries based on "social justice" arguments.[56] Arguments for prizes and subsidies based on social justice are different from the notion that prizes are a more efficient economic institution than markets for inventions. The tax system itself already involves some income redistribution through progressive taxation, tax deductions, and tax credits. Using the tax system to fund prizes increases the effects of the tax system on relative incomes.

2.2.3. *Deadweight Welfare Losses and Market Prices*

The assumptions that patent holders have an economic monopoly and charge a monopoly per-unit royalty, however unrealistic, are standard in economic studies of patents. Arrow introduces the notion that a monopolistic inventor obtains royalties that generate deadweight welfare losses.[57] William Nordhaus assumes that a patent confers an economic monopoly that generates monopoly deadweight welfare losses.[58] After the patent expires, the cost of the technology falls to zero, thereby eliminating deadweight welfare losses from the patent. Nordhaus concludes that the optimal patent duration is the shortest period of time such that the returns to an inventor exactly equal the cost of invention.

The standard assumption that prices for inventions generate monopoly deadweight welfare losses is unrealistic because ownership of IP does not in itself generate economic monopolies. There is extensive competition in the market for inventions, involving rivalries from substitute and complementary technologies. There are over 2 million active patents in the US, with more than a quarter million new patents granted every year. Many of these patents have little or no market value.

Patent owners face competition from past inventions and entry of new inventions. There is also competition in innovations that use patented inventions and other technologies in developing new products, production processes, and transaction methods.[59] These competitive forces substantially diminish the returns to patent owners. In addition, the economic returns to invention and innovation provide incentives for entry of new inventions and innovations. This leads to technological change that erodes the returns to past inventions. These market forces further constrain the returns to inventors and innovators thus limiting deadweight welfare losses over time.

The market for inventions is vast and growing.[60] It includes patent transfers, licensing, cross-licensing, and own-use of patents. Organized exchanges of patents and intermediation are growing as well.[61] Competitive pressures not only reduce the costs of IP but also tend to reduce the costs of diffusion and commercialization. Public contests are limited in scope by administrative costs, tax revenue constraints, and deadweight welfare losses from taxation.

2.2.4. *What is the Marginal Cost of an Invention?: Transaction Costs versus Administrative Costs*

Prize advocates further assume that the government would expend no resources in managing contests, selecting winners, and allocating inventions, thus assuming that there are zero administrative costs of prize systems. Prize advocates further ignore the private resource costs of developing inventions, commercializing IP, and creating innovations, which is implicit in the standard assumption that the optimal price of inventions should be zero. The deadweight welfare loss argument for public prizes is flawed because it incorrectly assumes that government prizes would eliminate monopoly deadweight welfare losses resulting from market prices.

The policy of replacing private ownership with public ownership is an attempt to achieve a "marginal cost price" for technology. Prize advocates argue that the "marginal cost price" of technology is zero so that technology is a pure public good. Both the costs of developing the technology and the cost of diffusing the technology are assumed to equal zero. Despite these standard assumptions, technology generally does not fit the textbook definition of a pure public good. Inventions may be non-rivalrous because they can be used by multiple producers. However, commercialization and innovation are not free; there are positive marginal costs of developing inventions, diffusing technology, and applying inventions. There are many types of transaction costs in markets for technology. This implies that technology shares many aspects of standard private goods. The "marginal cost price" of technology is not equal to zero.

Under proposed prize systems, government agencies would be "common carriers" in charge of obtaining and diffusing technology. Government agencies would not be in charge of producing technology, which they would outsource to participants in government prize contests. Government agencies would not apply technology but would instead provide the technology to producers. However, government agencies would be public utilities charged with procuring and allocating technology.

Prize advocates generally assume that the government prize system would operate without costs. However, in addition to the economic distortions resulting from taxes, a system of government prizes would incur both transaction costs and administrative costs.[62] The government would expend considerable resources designing and managing contests, selecting winners, and diffusing inventions to producers.

The administrative costs of a prize system would be many times the administrative costs of the current patent system. The costs of administering the US Patent and Trademark Office (USPTO) are approximately $3.5 billion per year.[63] There are over a quarter of a million patents granted per year for highly diverse inventions.[64] The USPTO covers a very wide range of scientific and technological subjects. No government agency could replace the entire patent system with contests and awards in every area of science and technology covered by the patent system without incurring astronomical administrative costs. Because of the complexities and broad range of the market for inventions, prizes could only replace a few market prices. The administrative costs of operating a public prize system suggest that the government would only offer a handful of prizes.

One indication of administrative costs of a public prize system is that private contests offer relatively few awards in only a small number of topic areas.[65] For example, the X Prize imposes very restrictive criteria: "Pushes the boundaries of human potential by focusing on problems currently believed to be unsolvable, or that have no clear path toward a solution."[66] An X Prize "Targets a range of market failures: (1) no capital is being spent, (2) capital is being spent, but without the desired result, (3) no capital is being spent because nobody knows it's a problem, (4) the problem is known, but no one can imagine that it's not already being addressed, (5) No one is addressing because a solution is thought to be impossible."[67]

Even with a limited number of government contests, the administrative costs would be significant. Government officials would need to determine what types of inventions should receive "prizes" *before discoveries are made*. This would require government officials to have foresight exceeding the combination of all scientists, engineers, and other researchers. Government officials also would need to determine what types of inventions were needed by consumers and firms. As Hayek emphasizes, this would depend on the impossible requirement that government officials' knowledge of the needs of individuals would equal individuals' own knowledge of their needs. Hayek observes that "competition . . . means decentralized planning by many separate persons."[68] Government officials would also need to know how much to reward inventors, again requiring knowledge of inventions before the fact, knowledge of inventors' costs and scientific opportunities, and knowledge of private benefits from inventions. Government officials would need to understand how to describe and disseminate technologies to potential users.

Advocates of government prizes replacing market prices also assume that the marginal cost of commercializing and distributing inventions are zero. Inventions are characterized as public goods that should have a zero price. For prize advocates, positive prices for inventions are thus evidence of market failure. The government remedies this market failure by distributing technologies at a zero price. Of course, a zero price should not be confused with zero costs. Government efforts at diffusion and commercialization would be costly and thus a zero price would involve a subsidy to producers equal to the costs of diffusion in addition to the costs of obtaining the technology itself. Also, notice that government diffusion may be inefficient compared to the private sector, both in terms of administrative costs and the effectiveness of public diffusion.

Because the efficient price of an invention can be positive, observation of positive prices in the market for inventions does not indicate economic inefficiency. It is necessary to ration access to inventions because of the resource costs of providing inventions to potential adopters. This means that market prices for inventions are positive because they necessarily include the marginal costs of providing inventions.

The benefits of patents and other protections for IP rights include reducing transaction costs.[69] Patents provide a variety of mechanisms that reduce the costs of licensing or transferring IP.[70] Because patents are a means of protecting IP, they offer an alternative that can lower transaction costs in comparison to trade secrets and other means of protecting IP. Patents allow market transactions in technology that can increase economic efficiency when transaction costs are less than the governance costs of firms that vertically integrate R&D and production.

Markets for all types of goods and services are subject to such standard transaction costs as search, communication, negotiation, contracting, moral hazard, and adverse selection.[71] Markets for inventions are subject to these transaction costs and others as well.[72] Patent owners who commercialize their inventions expend resources searching for potential licensees and negotiating licensing agreements. Inventors also expend resources in developing and demonstrating their inventions. Inventors may need to invest in codifying and transmitting tacit knowledge that is essential for producers to apply their inventions.[73] IP owners also devote effort to developing industry standards by participating in standards organizations and industry consortia, which further promotes the diffusion and application of new technologies.[74]

Marketing and sales activities are important because they serve to diffuse inventions and innovations in the economy. Marketing and sales of inventions communicate information to potential buyers and coordinate adoption decisions. The scientific and technological complexities of many inventions suggest that inventions might not diffuse without marketing and sales efforts. Inventions are by their very nature novel and unknown to potential adopters, which can require additional services that are bundled with technology transfers. Constraining prices for inventions would result in reduction of marketing and sales activities, which could then reduce diffusion of those technologies, thus generating welfare losses.

The argument for positive prices for inventions is closely related to the arguments for resale price maintenance.[75] Resale price maintenance by manufacturers may be needed to make sure that retailers that provide customer services are not undercut by retailers that do not provide customer services. In some markets, customer services may be needed to maintain customer demand for products, particularly for new products or technically complex products whose features are not well understood by customers. The Supreme Court in *Leegin* made resale price maintenance subject to the "rule of reason."[76] Inventions are clearly new products and often are technologically complex, requiring services for potential adopters.

Even if usage of inventions is non-rivalrous, the application of inventions to create economic innovations is rivalrous. Users of inventions dissipate economic rents to innovation when they compete in product markets. Innovation is a costly activity, so that users of inventions invest costly resources in applying inventions in new products, production processes, and transaction methods. Price rationing and allocation of inventions is useful in providing incentives for the development of inventions, investment in innovation, and investment in complementary assets. F. Scott Kieff emphasizes that common ownership of technology leads to the "tragedy of the commons," overuse that dissipates the value of the inventions just as overuse dissipates other types of resources.[77]

2.2.5. *Lump-Sum versus Per-Unit Running Royalties*

The literature on public prizes generates an advantage for prizes over prices because it treats taxes and market prices inconsistently. Prize advocates typically assume that taxes involve no deadweight welfare losses because they are lump-sum transfers. They further assume that market prices involve deadweight welfare losses because they are per-unit royalties. The comparison between prices and prizes changes if we treat the two alternatives consistently.

If both patent owners and government agencies can use lump-sum transfers, there is no theoretical advantage of prizes over prices in terms of allocative efficiency, and thus no argument for prizes replacing prices. Patent licensing often features two-part tariffs with an up-front lump-sum royalty and a royalty per unit of output produced using the invention. Royalties can be based on the number of units sold (the apportionment rule) or ad valorem royalty rates applied to revenues from sales (the entire market value rule). Alternative pricing methods mitigate potential distortions from per-unit prices.

If patent owners and government agencies rely on per-unit royalties or per-unit taxes, respectively, there is also no theoretical advantage of prizes over prices. Suppose for example that the government finances the prize by taxing the good that depends on the patented invention, where the tax per unit of output equals g. Suppose that with patents, inventors receive a royalty per unit of output r. Consider a process invention where producers using the patented invention have a unit cost c. Then, with prizes financed by taxes, consumers pay the sum of the tax g and a competitive price that equals the producer's cost c. With patents, the competitive market price equals the sum of the royalty r plus the producers' unit cost c. If the tax rate that would provide a prize is equivalent to market returns, the per-unit tax would need to equal the per-unit royalty, $g = r$. Consumers would pay the same amount per unit, $g + c = r + c$. Either approach would generate the same welfare loss as measured by Arnold Harberger's welfare triangle.[78] Prizes would have no *a priori* advantage over prices.

The argument that government prizes eliminate the deadweight welfare losses from market prices is thus an artifact of asymmetric assumptions. These assumptions are not only inconsistent but inaccurate. Government taxes involve all kinds of mechanisms that are highly distortionary, as has already been emphasized. The cost of funding government prizes would be significant and would require extensive tax increases. This would create substantial deadweight welfare losses from tax distortions. In addition, the administrative costs of allocating inventions under a public prize system would likely be far greater than the transaction costs of the market for inventions, further increasing deadweight welfare losses from taxation to fund administrative costs.

Conversely, prices for inventions include licensing through combinations of per-unit royalties and lump-sum royalties. Also, many inventions are owned by the companies that produce them and firms have incentives for efficient internal pricing. In addition, many patented inventions are assigned to producers through the market for inventions, so that the prices of inventions would not involve distortionary prices per unit of output. Competition in the market for inventions reduces all types of prices including licensing royalties, transfer prices, and the returns to own-use of inventions by vertically-integrated producers. This implies that prices in the market for inventions do not generate monopoly deadweight welfare losses, contrary to the assumptions of prize advocates. In practice, the deadweight welfare losses from a public prize system would far exceed any deadweight welfare losses from market prices for inventions.

2.3 Allocative Efficiency in Technology: Prizes versus Prices

The proposed government prize system would replace the market for inventions with central planning of innovation. Yet, prize advocates do not address the question of allocative efficiency directly, only making the deadweight welfare loss comparison discussed in the previous section. An economically meaningful comparison of prices and prizes requires a consistent evaluation of allocative efficiency under these two alternatives. In this section, I explain that central planning of innovation will not lead to allocative efficiency. Governments are not capable of efficiently allocating goods and services, let alone technology. I further observe that markets have a proven track record of efficiently allocating inventions and stimulating innovation based on those inventions.

2.3.1. *Patents and Markets for Technology*

The government prize system is intended to replace market allocation of inventions with public allocation. Government agencies would design contests to induce favored types of inventions and then those agencies would choose winning technologies. Having chosen particular technologies, government agencies would take possession of the IP and allocate those technologies to producers. Free distribution of technology should not be confused with an economically efficient allocation.

The public prize system itself would not be intended to provide a public good or to subsidize the provision of a public good. Governments already offer significant subsidies for R&D through grants, procurement, tax credits, and other types of subsidies, so the prize system is not meant as a subsidy to invention.

A prize system would result in an inefficient allocation of technology. Hayek points out that the price system provides coordination because it takes advantage of dispersed information.[79] Central planners cannot hope to make efficient economic decisions because they lack the staggering amount of subjective knowledge that is dispersed among individuals. In contrast, decentralized coordination by the price system offers other advantages over central planning. The allocative efficiency of markets is much greater than central planning for goods and services. The complexities of technology and specialized knowledge required by inventors and producers only serve to increase the informational advantages of markets over central planning. A government-operated market for inventions would generate even more allocative inefficiencies than government allocation of more standard goods and services.

There already is a government system for transferring technology in government labs to the private sector.[80] This system would need to be expanded to accommodate technology generated by prize competitions. Such an expansion would require additional administrative costs, which would require additional tax revenues and generate further economic distortions. Another concern with such large-scale administrative systems for government prizes and public technology transfers is that they are costly to dismantle, often taking on a life of their own. The effects on markets for inventions could be very difficult to reverse, causing long-term damage to markets for invention.[81]

Prize systems generally involve either public ownership or common ownership of inventions. With public ownership, the government would presumably make the inventions available to producers without cost, so that the outcome would be the same as with common ownership. With public ownership of inventions, government officials would need to invest in commercializing inventions or developing innovations that apply the prize-winning inventions. This would involve public expenditures for the costs of commercialization and innovation, effectively putting public agencies in the innovation business. Involving public agencies in commercialization and innovation would require public agencies to develop business expertise that is already available in the private sector.

Public commercialization and innovation would generate insurmountable problems of economic planning. Exercising command and control over economic activity has led to significant problems in socialist economies. The collapse of socialist economies such as the Soviet Union provides sufficient evidence that even the operation of traditional technologies by governments is not feasible. The diffusion of new technologies and management of innovation generally are far beyond the scope of government administration.

Governments are not very good at commercializing and diffusing inventions. The failure of government diffusion of technology is illustrated by the major benefits that resulted from the Bayh–Dole Act. The effects of the Bayh–Dole Act demonstrate how markets diffuse innovations and governments do not. The US government provides research grants to universities, non-profit organizations, and small businesses. However, the incentives for invention provided by such grants are accompanied by markets for invention, which provide additional incentives for commercialization and innovation. This was recognized by the Bayh–Dole Act, which permits organizations that receive federal government funding to own inventions rather than transferring ownership to the government.[82]

Prior to the Bayh–Dole Act, government ownership of inventions resulted in minimal commercialization or diffusion of innovations. About 5% of the 28,000 patents owned by the government were commercialized. Private ownership, in contrast, generated significant commercializing of inventions through patent licensing by universities.[83] In the first 25 years following the Act, university patent licensing generated 4,350 new products and 6,000 new firms.[84] The Bayh–Dole Act resulted in high levels of entrepreneurship by scientists and spurred the rise of university technology transfer offices (TTOs).[85] The Association of University Technology Managers reports that there were about 40,000 active technology licenses and options in 2012.[86]

Government subsidies are not close substitutes for market incentives for innovation. The National Science Board estimates that federal agencies provided over $132 billion for R&D.[87] Wright *et al.* find that even though corporations provide just over 5% of US university research funding, "corporate-sponsored research is surprisingly valuable for further innovation."[88] As they observe: "Data collected over 20 years at nine campuses and three national laboratories administered by the University of California show that corporate-sponsored inventions are licensed and cited more often than federally sponsored ones."[89]

Government agencies would replace decentralized markets with centralized allocation. Government agencies are not well equipped to run market places. Health insurance exchanges are an example of government market place design.[90] Government allocation of goods and services often entails high administrative costs, significant transaction costs, and allocative inefficiencies.[91] Historical evidence suggests that state and federal regulation led to considerable allocative and dynamic inefficiencies in markets for electric power, natural gas, telecommunications, railroads, trucking, and airlines.[92] Increased regulation in health care is expected to generate similar allocative and dynamic inefficiencies.[93]

Historical evidence casts doubt on prize systems as sources of invention and innovation. The advantages of prices over prizes is confirmed by extensive and careful historical analysis by Zorina Khan demonstrating that patents outperform prizes in the dissemination of new technologies.[94] According to Khan, "the historical record shows that administered prize systems tend to be associated with the potential for bias or corruption, unpredictable methods of allocation and outcomes, as well as other deficiencies attendant on a nonmarket orientation."[95]

Khan studies inventors in Britain and the US during the transition from the First to the Second Industrial Revolutions and finds that because prizes are less systematic than patents, they offer lower expected benefits for inventors.[96] Khan considers a sample of exhibits and premiums at US industrial fairs between 1837 and 1874 and finds that prize winners tended to belong to privileged social groups, with prizes awarded less systematically than patents and unrelated to various proxies for the productivity of the innovation.[97]

Khan provides a critically important historical comparison of the effects of patents and prizes on technology diffusion.[98] She compares patented inventions with inventions that were submitted for prizes at annual industrial fairs of the American Institute of New York in the 19th century. Khan finds that patents promoted much greater spatial diffusion of innovations than prizes. Additionally, Khan's research shows that patents had large and significant effects on unpatented innovations in contiguous and adjacent counties, in contrast to limited geographic effects of prize-winning inventions.[99]

Historical experience with a national prize system is instructive. The US has offered the National Medal of Science since 1959 and the National Medal of Technology and Innovation since 1980.[100] Congress extended the coverage of the National Medal of Science in 1980 to include the social and behavioral sciences.[101] The limited scope of such awards in comparison to the patent system is indicated by there having been only 487 awards of the National Medal of Science up to 2015.[102]

Markets for invention depend on the knowledge and opinions of consumers, producers, investors, inventors, and innovators. In contrast to broad participation in the market for inventions, the awarding of prizes depends on the opinions of very few decision makers. For example, a committee of 12 scientists and engineers appointed by the President evaluates nominees for the National Medal of Science.[103]

Beginning in the late 1950s, the Soviet Union instituted a system of "inventors' certificates" that involved transfer of the invention to state ownership and some limited monetary and non-monetary rewards for the inventor based on usage.[104] Compared to patent systems in market economies during the same time period, it is apparent that this approach was not successful in generating innovation.[105] In addition, the Soviet Union offered a limited honorary "prize" system. During its entire existence, the Soviet Union awarded its "Honoured Inventor of the USSR" medal only sixteen times.[106]

Prize advocates assume that central planners are fully informed about market demand and producer costs. Central planners would need to have sufficient knowledge about science and technology to design contests and to choose the best inventions. Central planners must be sufficiently informed to allocate inventions efficiently to producers. The complexities of invention and innovation create significant information challenges for market participants; such challenges are likely to be insurmountable for central planners. The dramatic differences in the historical performance of market economies and centrally-planned economies are even more pronounced in innovative industries.

Problems with central planning extend beyond asymmetry of knowledge. Prize advocates assume that governments maximize social welfare. Even if they could be fully informed, central planners need not act in the public interest. Central planners can be expected to suffer from corruption, abuse of power, discrimination, bureaucratic inefficiency, and other forms of government failure. Government agencies are likely to provide rewards to cronies of politicians, lobbying organizations, incumbent firms, political donors, voting blocs, or ideological allies. A government prize system would encourage rent-seeking to obtain prizes, diverting resources away from invention and innovation and toward political influence. Government agencies also are likely to pursue objectives other than allocative efficiency, such as subsidies for groups of voters, increases in employment, income redistribution, regional economic growth, industrial policy, and support for political causes.

Although necessarily imperfect, the patent system is less subject to corruption than a public prize system. With patents, the government establishes general rules of the game through a system of private property rights. The patent system involves the legislature, the courts, and the USPTO, which is part of the executive branch. The market for inventions determines prices for inventions and selects the best inventions and innovations. In contrast, with a system of prizes, the government micromanages innovation: it designs the contests, chooses prizes, selects inventions, and allocates technology.

A government prize system would diminish private incentives for commercialization of inventions. Kieff emphasizes the importance of markets in stimulating commercialization of inventions.[107] Public ownership or common ownership of inventions would eliminate private incentives for the commercialization of inventions, as Kieff explains.[108] Common ownership of inventions also would diminish incentives for innovation to develop products, manufacturing processes, and transaction techniques based on those inventions. Additionally, common ownership would diminish marketing of products that embody inventions.

Some advocates of government contests view the discouragement of commercialization as an advantage of a prize system. For example, Love and Hubbard assert that marketing products is a "waste,"

> "The elimination of marketing monopolies, the de-coupling of R&D incentives from prices, and the creation of an evidence-based reward system linked to changes in health outcomes will lead to significant reductions in expenditures to market products, the area of the largest waste in the current system."[109]

Contrary to this assertion, marketing and sales are important coordination mechanisms in a market economy. Marketing and sales are essential for the commercialization of inventions and the development of innovations.

Government prizes for inventors would fail to fulfill the functions of IP in product markets. Markets determine the value of goods and services through interaction of supply and demand, and the same applies to inventions. John Stuart Mill explains this clearly: "the reward conferred by it depends upon the invention's being found useful, and the greater the usefulness, the greater the reward; and because it is paid by the very persons to whom the service is rendered, the consumers of the commodity."[110]

A prize system without property rights for inventors would eliminate the allocative and dynamic efficiencies of the market for inventions. Inventors would lose innovative control over their inventions, thus eliminating incentives to allocate inventions to the highest-value uses. Lack of innovative control would eliminate incentives to develop inventions, commercialize inventions, introduce innovations based on inventions, and invest in complementary assets.[111]

The prize system lacks all of the key features of the patent system — exclusion, transferability, disclosure, certification, standardization, and divisibility. Without these fundamental elements, the market for inventions would be highly constrained and less efficient.[112] Demsetz identifies IP rights as critical for reducing transaction costs in markets for invention.[113] Epstein emphasizes the importance of IP property rights in disseminating protected information.[114]

Replacing patents with prizes would be analogous to replacing corporate securities with prizes for investors. Such investment prizes would not finance corporations because they would provide neither return of principle nor return on principle. Invention prizes would not stimulate invention and innovation because they would not provide economic returns for inventors, innovators, or investors in complementary assets. Just as investment prizes could not replace financial markets, so invention prizes cannot replace the market for inventions.

2.3.2. *Allocative Efficiency in the Market for Inventions*

The pro-prize argument maintains that a prize will perform the same functions as a market price because it will provide incentives for invention. This argument is flawed because it views market prices as *rewards for inventors* and *penalties for producers*. This view reflects a fundamental misunderstanding of markets. Prices are essential to the allocative efficiencies generated by market transactions.

More than just a choice of policy instruments, the question of public prizes replacing market prices revives the debate between competitive markets and central planning. Markets offer significant economic advantages over central planning. The efficient performance of markets is fundamental to the history and development of economic thought. The informational attributes of the price system figure prominently in the renewed interest in price theory.[115]

Prices result from market transactions and serve to guide decentralized decision-making by individuals in the market place who have the best knowledge of their own situations. As Friedrich Hayek explains, the price system is a "condensed index of relative change."[116] The price system provides communication and coordination: "In abbreviated form, by a kind of symbol, only the most essential information is passed on, and passed on only to those concerned."[117]

Markets generally promote efficiency in resource allocation and, in contrast, government agencies are not able to achieve efficient resource allocation. Although invention and innovation may exhibit economies of scale, they are not natural monopolies because there are economic benefits from applying a variety of inventions and from continual technological change.

In market exchange, both parties benefit from economic transactions — both parties receive *gains from trade* — because transactions are voluntary. Market transactions provide rewards to both buyers and sellers because they are the terms of exchange. In markets for consumer goods, buyers receive surplus from transactions equal to the benefits of consuming goods and services net of payments to sellers. Sellers receive benefits from transactions equal to payments from buyers net of the sellers' costs of providing goods and services.

Replacing the price system would cause harm to both buyers and sellers of IP by removing the transactions that generate gains from trade. Market prices of inventions provide rewards to both IP owners and IP users. In the market for inventions, exchange of IP through licensing, cross-licensing, transfers, and contracts benefits both IP owners and IP users. By exchanging IP, market participants achieve gains from trade, which increases the quality of innovation.[118] The greater the extent of the market for IP, the greater the quality of innovation.[119]

Public ownership and distribution of technology at a zero price may benefit some producers, but these benefits are only short term. Producers will suffer harm in the long term because the quality of technology will be diminished by the government prize system.

The government prize system diminishes incentives to produce new technology because improvements by inventors end when the prize is awarded. This contrasts with incentives to improve inventions for patent owners who develop their inventions after patents are granted. If investment is needed to commercialize and develop the new technology, publicly-provided access to technology will eliminate incentives to make that investment. Also, public distribution of technology will eliminate the economic returns to complementary investments. As a consequence, a prize system with publicly provided access to technology will likely reduce innovation and decrease social welfare in comparison to the market for inventions.

Another problem with the view that prices are rewards for sellers is that prices are *mechanisms of competition*. Eliminating the price mechanism for IP would harm buyers and sellers by reducing price competition. In competitive markets, buyers bid competitively to attract sellers and sellers bid competitively to attract buyers. This also applies to markets for inventions and to markets for innovative goods and services. Prices for inventions and innovations are essential to competition throughout the economy. Prices of inventions can be explicit, as is the case with patent licensing and patent transfers. Prices of inventions can be implicit, as is the case with cross-licensing, contract R&D, inventions embodied in goods and services, and securities of corporations that own inventions. Replacing market prices for inventions with government prizes would eliminate the benefits of market competition.

Competition stimulates invention and innovation when there is a market for inventions.[120] Entry of competing inventors improves the expected quality of inventions and also increases competition in royalties and the prices of patent transfers. Better inventions and lower royalties increase the returns to entry of producers, leading to increased competition and more innovation in product markets. Conversely, competition in product markets among producers that obtain technology in the market for inventions increases industry output in the product market, which in turn stimulates demand for technological inventions. This increases economic rents for inventors, which encourages entry of inventors and investment in R&D, thus increasing inventive effort and improving the expected quality of inventions.[121]

Prices in the market for inventions also are instruments of *cooperation*. Prices reflect the terms of trade between buyers and sellers. Negotiation of royalties depends not only on the features of the invention but also on the application of the invention. Patented inventions are a form of technology capital that can be used by multiple firms, in multiple locations, and in multiple productive activities.[122] Patented inventions can be applied to generate returns through licensing, cross-licensing, and sales. Patented inventions can also be applied by firms to develop innovations, including new products, production processes, and transaction methods. Patented inventions can also be applied to create new inventions.

Economic efficiency suggests that the price of an invention can vary depending on applications of the invention.

Prices in the market for inventions depend on many critical factors. Various factors such as the characteristics of trading partners affect gains from trade in the market for patents.[123] Epstein and Malherbe find that a careful economic analysis is required in calculating damages from infringement and urge caution in considering comparable royalties from other patents.[124] They point out that "For example, one patent may be economically 'strong' (in the sense that the specific technology has no close and inexpensive substitute) while another may be economically 'weak' because commercially acceptable alternatives or design-arounds are readily available."[125] Negotiated royalties depend on features of the transaction: "When a patent's value is derived from reducing manufacturing costs, the cost savings for different patents or even different applications of the same patent may not be the same. Differing degrees of licensing exclusivity, duration, field of use, and potential overlap and competition with the patent holder's own sales could influence the royalty."[126] Epstein and Malherbe also find that negotiated royalties depend on commercialization and innovation: "Patents may also differ in the amount of additional investment required to achieve commercialization, including research and development, production facilities, product testing and regulatory approvals, marketing, and acquisition of additional intellectual property rights."[127] Finally, they observe "royalties in other licenses may be part of a complex transaction that includes joint licensing of other patents (i.e., patent pooling), cross-licenses, know-how, and/or product support, as noncash features of the deal."[128]

2.3.3. *Marginal Cost Prices and Central Planning*

Inventions are costly to produce and distribute, their market returns are rivalrous, and they generally are provided in abundance by competitive markets. Prize advocates tend to assume that transaction costs are zero in markets for invention and innovation. They then suggest that because usage of inventions is non-rivalrous, there is no need for price rationing so that the efficient "marginal cost" price equals zero. This would suggest that central planners face no problems of calculating "shadow prices" because they already know that the efficient price is zero. However, because the efficient price of an invention need not equal zero, central planners would encounter problems of information gathering and processing in determining "shadow prices."

The proposed prize mechanism requires the government to subsidize the production and distribution of inventions. The government would obtain inventions through contests and make them available at a zero price to attain the desired marginal cost price.[129] This policy recommendation recalls the marginal cost controversies of public utility regulation, going back at least to Harold Hotelling.[130] As Arthur Pigou points out, the provision of public goods entails both direct costs and indirect costs caused by taxation.[131] Ronald Coase observes that government subsidies to attain marginal cost pricing would result in tax-induced distortions, inefficient resource allocation, income redistribution, and rent-seeking.[132] Such objections were important in the deregulation of electric power generation, telecommunications, and other public utilities. Coase's objections to subsidized marginal cost pricing apply directly to IP, as John Duffy points out.[133]

The prize mechanism proposals would centralize the selection of inventions and their dissemination to producers. This approach suggests that there are efficiencies from centralized management of innovation, which resembles the natural monopoly argument for government regulation of public utilities. Whenever a firm operates at an output where there are economies of scale in production, marginal cost pricing will not generate sufficient revenues to cover costs. Hotelling and others recommended government subsidies for public utilities to make up the difference between marginal and average costs.

Public policies such as government regulation should not be based on the existence of economies of scale. This is because practically any economic activity involves economies of scale. Insisting on government ownership or subsidies whenever economies of scale exist would require abandonment of a market economy entirely because economies of scale are pervasive in manufacturing, services, or distribution. Markets routinely allocate goods and services whose production and distribution feature economies of scale.

When there are economies of scale, market returns necessarily cover the average costs of production so that firms are able to break even. In competitive markets, prices tend toward average costs so that the revenues are sufficient to cover costs. Even in markets with few firms, entry and potential competition for the market drive prices toward average costs.[134]

The notion that prices of goods and services should equal marginal costs of production is itself questionable. The optimality of marginal cost pricing depends on various assumptions including a partial equilibrium optimum for a single market and an absence of economies of scale. With economies of scale, the theoretical ideal of a marginal cost pricing equilibrium that is Pareto optimal is likely to be a vacuous concept. This means that a market equilibrium solution may not exist for a general equilibrium model with economies of scale and marginal cost pricing.[135]

In practice, however, markets routinely address economies of scale with various pricing mechanisms. Prices can approach marginal pricing when necessary with two-part tariffs and other pricing mechanisms.[136] A two-part tariff involves a fixed fee that helps to cover fixed costs while allowing firms to lower per-unit fees. Markets also distribute some products such as broadcast television and Internet search using advertising revenues. Products such as cable television rely on combinations of access fees and advertising revenues. Markets for patents and other IP thus have pricing mechanisms that address efficiency without the need for government ownership or price regulation.

Even if the optimal price is close to marginal cost that does not imply that such a price can be chosen by regulatory authorities. Market forces including competition among buyers and among sellers may drive prices closer to marginal costs evaluated at market equilibrium outputs. This is very different from having regulatory agencies or courts engage in "marginal cost pricing." This would require regulatory agencies or courts to estimate the marginal cost schedule of a firm, to estimate the market demand schedule at various prices for the product in question, and then to determine the appropriate output level at which to evaluate both marginal costs and market demand. Then, the regulatory agencies or courts would need to calculate the marginal cost price at this critical output level and then adjust the price as costs and demand change over time. Such calculations are difficult, subject to error, and would need to be repeated across many goods and services.

The calculation of regulated prices created prohibitive administrative costs in natural gas production, railroad rates, and other regulated industries. The regulatory agencies had to calculate so many prices that the time needed to complete the task was nearly limitless. The costs to regulatory agencies of calculating prices of various types of IP also would pose significant administrative challenges, made all the more difficult by the complexities and uncertainties of technological change.

Centrally planned economies faced an even greater challenge. Some economists believed that if only central planners could perform the necessary economic calculations they could derive market prices. The prices would be obtained by maximizing social welfare subject to various resource and production constraints, thus yielding estimates of "shadow prices." For example, Janos Kornai and Th. Lipták applied mathematical programming to suggest methods of central planning in Hungary and other socialist economies.[137] Lange and Taylor suggested that by using "shadow prices" central planners would not need to solve millions of equations.[138] Economists in centrally-planned economies recognized the additional complications that would result for technological change.[139] Abba Lerner also advocated marginal cost pricing as optimal in planned socialist economies.[140]

Prize advocates begin with a faulty premise: if only central planners could find the right "shadow prices," they could replace the market. "Shadow prices" set by central planners cannot replicate the decisions of millions of decision makers in competitive markets. Central planners cannot replace transactions with mathematical programming. They lack the detailed information that market participants have about their own situation, as Hayek emphasized. The advantages of markets over central planning can be readily observed by comparing economic growth in the market economies in the United States, Europe, and Asia with the economic collapse of centrally-planned economies in Eastern Europe and the Soviet Union. The beneficial effects of introducing market institutions in centrally planned economics are exemplified by the ongoing economic transformation of the People's Republic of China.

Prize advocates believe that "shadow pricing" of inventions is feasible because the marginal cost is zero and therefore already known. This relieves central planners of the problem of gathering information about supply and demand and the burden of calculating "shadow prices." However, because the marginal costs of inventions are not zero, prices for inventions are just as difficult to estimate by central planners as are the prices of other goods and services. Calculating government prizes for inventions face at least the same difficulties as calculating "shadow prices" for other types of goods and services, and perhaps even greater problems as a result of scientific and technological uncertainties.

A government prize system requires central planners to design contests for inventors. Even if central planners could accurately identify a particular category of invention, central planners would need to determine what inventions should be rewarded before discoveries are made, requiring the ability to predict scientific and technological inventions before they occur. Not only would central planners lack the scientific and technological expertise, the problem is impracticable because inventors generally do not know the outcome of R&D in advance. R&D not only involves risky outcomes, it involves situations in which the inventor does not know the relative likelihood of possible outcomes and may not be able to describe fully the set of possible outcomes.[141] In contrast, market prices for patented inventions are established after inventors make the initial discoveries.

2.3.4. *Public Goods and Natural Monopoly*

The theory of public goods suggests that there are cost advantages to providing the same public good to all consumers. Usage of public goods is non-rivalrous and distribution costs are equal to zero. Providing the same public good to all consumers is efficient because production costs are not duplicated by multiple providers. If inventions are pure public goods, prize advocates suggest that it would be efficient for the market to be served by a single invention. Based on this argument, prize advocates recommend that the government should identify a "best invention" through prize contests and make this invention available to all producers at a zero price.

The economic theory of public goods is similar to the theory of natural monopoly. As William Baumol and Robert Willig observe, "the resource allocation problems that stem from fixed costs are formally identical with those that accompany public goods — both their sources and their character are the same. Thus, the rationale for public supply of public goods may be no different from that pertaining to nationalization of natural monopolies." If inventions are public goods, this argument would suggest that there is an economic rationale for either public supply of inventions or even government taking of inventions through nationalization.

The natural monopoly argument for public utility regulation is that it is more efficient for the market to be served by a single firm rather than two or more firms. The formal definition of natural monopoly refers to a static cost function.[142] The cost function exhibits the natural monopoly property if the costs of producing a particular output level by a single firm are less than the costs of producing that output by two separate firms. This definition extends readily to the costs of producing multiple products. The cost function exhibits the natural monopoly property if the costs to a single firm of producing multiple products are less than the costs of producing those products by two separate firms.

The economic analysis of public goods or natural monopoly framework does not transfer readily to invention. The standard public good or natural monopoly arguments apply to production of a homogeneous good. Suppose that the cost of producing street lighting involves a fixed cost of $100. Many consumers benefit from the same street lighting, so that it is not necessary to incur the fixed cost more than once. Such an argument would not apply to the production of inventions. Suppose that the cost of producing an invention involves a fixed cost of $100. Unlike the production of street lighting, invention is not a deterministic activity and the outcome of invention is not a homogeneous good.

Invention is not a natural monopoly. The outcome of invention is subject to considerable uncertainty that generally requires multiple inventive efforts. Far from being a generic activity, R&D involves creative effort. Invention requires not only inspiration but also many different approaches. There are many different types of R&D in technology, science, the social sciences, and other areas. Even within narrow areas of inquiry, there is significant trial and error and disagreements about how to address various research problems and what the problems being addressed are. There is considerable specialization and division of labor in R&D.

These diverse activities cannot be readily agglomerated into a single enterprise for the economy as whole. There may well be fixed costs and other sources of economies of scale in R&D. However, a central government laboratory would not be sufficient to produce all inventions for an economy. There would still be a need for many research facilities in the economy. Thus, invention should not be viewed as a natural monopoly that should be regulated or nationalized to attain zero marginal cost prices.

What about the usage of inventions after they are produced by R&D? Non-rivalrous consumption implies that the same invention can be used by multiple producers. The fixed costs of invention have already been incurred and are sunk, so that these costs need not be considered in the allocation of inventions. If there are fixed costs in the procurement of inventions from inventors or in the distribution of inventions, economic efficiency would suggest that only one invention should be used by all. That is, public good or natural monopoly arguments would suggest that only one invention should be used.

However, exploring a variety of ideas is central to invention and innovation — inventions are not homogeneous goods. The features of inventions can differ in complicated ways so that there need not be a "best" invention in a set of substitute inventions. There is often a need for multiple inventions that address the same problem.

Variety is essential to the creative process. There is a need for a variety of innovative applications, just as there is a need for many types of novels, movies, songs, or other creative works. It may be cost efficient to have only one movie that is seen by everyone, but that misses the point of arts and entertainment. Each consumer derives benefits from consuming a variety of artistic works or different sources of entertainment. Also, consumers have different preferences so that they will favor different types of artistic works and entertainment.

In the same way, any consumer may prefer to use multiple inventions that are substitutes in demand. Also, consumers may have different needs so that there cannot be just one headache remedy or just one medicine for high blood pressure. Producers differ as well so that different producers may prefer to apply different inventions in product designs, production processes, and transaction methods.

The notion that there is a best invention that should serve the entire market is a static efficiency concept. The public good and natural monopoly concepts provide static views of economic efficiency.[143] However, technological change is an inherently dynamic process. Different efficiency concepts apply because of technological change. It may no longer be efficient for a particular invention to serve the entire market.

To illustrate the problems that can arise from applying static efficiency concepts to invention and innovation, consider a situation in which technological change happens only once. Suppose that there is a set of inventions that have the same features and suppose that producers make technology decisions at the same time. Suppose also that there are fixed costs associated with distributing those inventions. It may then be efficient by standard public good or natural monopoly arguments for all producers to adopt one invention. The notion that inventions are pure public goods or natural monopolies might suggest that only one technology should be in use.

Now consider what happens when there is a second round of technological change. It may be efficient for some producers to adopt an invention in the first period and to continue using that invention in the second period. It may be efficient for other producers to wait until the second period to adopt the better technology. This implies that even though there are fixed costs of distributing inventions, it may be more efficient for there to be two inventions in use in the second period. This implies that an invention need not be a natural monopoly. Even if inventions have public good properties, it may be more efficient for multiple inventions to be in use at the same time.

In addition to technology change, consumer preferences and needs change over time. Also, changes in market demand and other market conditions will change the needs of producers. Different inventions will be required over time to produce new products, production processes, and transaction methods. Again, it may be more efficient for multiple inventions to be in use at the same time as adoption decisions may occur in different periods. Section 2.4 considers the dynamic aspects of efficiency in the market for inventions.

2.4 Patents and Incentives for Invention and Innovation

Prices in the market for inventions provide important economic signals that guide the decisions of inventors, producers, and investors. An important feature of prices in the market for inventions is that they are state-contingent. Market prices for inventions are contingent on the features of inventions and the features of substitute and complementary inventions. Because prices for inventions adjust to technological changes, which are necessarily unexpected, they provide valuable guidance for decision-making under uncertainty. This is particularly important because prices in the market for inventions are likely to change continually over the twenty year life of a patent.

2.4.1. *What is Competition?: Markets versus Tournaments*

Competition in markets differs substantially from stylized models of R&D tournaments and patent races. Prize advocates compare the reward from a prize with the reward from a market price as mechanisms for inducing R&D effort. This comparison is misleading because it fails to take into account the complexity of market competition. In contrast to prize contests, inventions do not just compete *for* the market, they compete *within* the market. In contrast to prize contests, market competition is a dynamic process that responds to new technological discoveries and new information about consumer preferences and producer costs.

In economic models of tournaments, a principal designs the R&D tournament by offering a contract to multiple agents.[144] The agents compete by investing in R&D. The principal offers a prize that is contingent on winning the R&D tournament based on a specific measure of quality. An inventor wins the prize by beating other inventors according to the quality criterion. Economic models of contests consider the problem of inducing inventors to devote effort to R&D. Even with an optimally designed contest, agents may choose inefficient effort levels. Michael Baye and Heidrun Hoppe show that R&D efforts in R&D tournaments are excessive relative to socially optimal effort levels.[145]

In models of R&D racing, inventors compete by investing in R&D with the winner being the inventor who makes the discovery first.[146] The outcome of R&D is the same for all R&D projects, with the only difference being the time it takes to make the invention. Baye and Hoppe show that models of R&D tournaments and patent races are formally equivalent under some conditions.[147]

Competition in the market for inventions differs from government contests in many different ways. First, competition in the market for inventions is dynamic. Inventors that engage in R&D take into account existing inventions developed from past R&D. Inventors also recognize that after their inventions are introduced, they will face competition from future inventions. This continual interaction and competition among inventions over time is very different from a one-shot tournament.

Second, because competition in the market for inventions is dynamic, there is no simple ranking of inventions based on fixed quality criteria as might occur in a single tournament. There may be some quality rankings among specific groups of inventions at any date, but the quality criteria keep changing as new discoveries are made and as the features of inventions change over time. The prices of inventions change continually in response to the introduction of new inventions, in contrast to the one-time prize in a tournament.

Third, in contrast to tournaments, market competition generally involves many different inventions that are imperfect substitutes in demand. Instead of a single winner of a tournament or an R&D race, inventions compete in the market by satisfying different needs of diverse producers and consumers. For example, there may be competition among different inventions that reduce the costs of production, but many of these inventions will be purchased in the market because of the different needs of producers. There may be competition among different types of medicines or medical devices without there being a single winner because of the different needs of patients. Each invention may best satisfy the needs of a segment of the market.

Fourth, in contrast to tournaments, market competition involves assembling complementary inventions. Market prices provide coordination devices that help producers to assemble groups of inventions and other complementary resources to create innovations. These innovations may be new production processes, final products, or transaction technologies. This contrasts with government contests that attempt to view inventions in isolation, somehow determining which invention is the winner. What may make a technology useful in the market is how well it interoperates with other inventions and resources. For example, an advance in computer hardware may increase the value of a particular software invention. Without knowing about the computer hardware invention, it is not possible to evaluate the software invention. Such complementarity effects are not confined to inventions but often involve other resources. For example, a decrease in the price of natural gas may increase the demand for production technologies that affect the costs of using natural gas. Without knowing the effects of changes in the price of natural gas, it is not possible to evaluate competing production technologies.

Fifth, in contrast to prizes in tournaments, the price of inventions is not an end in itself. The contest ends when the prize is awarded. However, as Kitch points out, the "rewards" view of patents is inaccurate because patents provide IP protections for investments in development and commercialization that occur after the patent is granted.[148] The market for inventions provides rewards based on the additional efforts of inventors and adopters of inventions. This includes investments in developing complementary technologies and investments in assets that will be used to apply the invention. The market for inventions includes the entire process of licensing or transferring the invention, improving the invention, and applying the invention.[149]

Sixth, in contrast to government contests, competition in the market for inventions is a learning process. In designing a contest, government agencies must specify what the rules are and the objectives of the contest *before knowing the technologies that will be discovered.* Then, government agencies must determine the criteria for choosing the best invention *before knowing how the technologies will be applied by producers.* Government agencies also must determine the best invention *before knowing how consumers will evaluate new products or transaction methods.* Government agencies must determine prizes *before knowing the value of inventions.*

In contrast, market competition takes place after inventions are made so that decision makers can respond to the characteristics of discoveries. Market competition benefits from extensive information revealed by R&D and additional information revealed by the application of inventions. Also, market competition responds to the choices of adopters as they experiment with the application of different technologies. Market competition benefits from learning about consumer reactions to new products and transaction methods. Most goods and services need market testing; who knows in advance what is the best car, the best software, or the best ice-cream?

Market competition involves the determination of prices of inventions, which provides information about the value of those inventions. As Hayek points out: "it is useful to recall that *wherever* we make use of competition, this can only be justified by our *not* knowing the essential circumstances that determine the behavior of the competitors" (emphasis in original).[150]

2.4.2. *Providing Information: Prices versus Prizes*

Both buyers and sellers benefit from the information content of prices. Prices of inventions are particularly significant because they provide convenient indicators of technological change. Prices for inventions and innovations provide extensive information to buyers and sellers. Because technology is an input to production, producers' demand for the technology is a derived demand — it depends on the demand for the producers' final products. Increases in the prices of inventions can reflect increases in consumer demand for products that are produced using the inventions or whose design is based on the inventions.

A price offers highly condensed information because just one number summarizes an enormous amount of information in a way that everyone can understand. A price describes the terms of a transaction by specifying the amount of a given currency that can be exchanged for the provision of a particular good or service. Market actors can observe the information contained in prices without having to know all the details of supply and demand. The information contained in prices is highly useful because decision-makers can compare prices of very different goods and services. Decisions makers can compare prices across periods of time, in different locations, and in different currencies. Decision-makers can use prices to aggregate or disaggregate total expenditures or total revenues corresponding to bundles of goods and services.

A key aspect of the patent system is that the market prices of inventions generally are determined *after* discoveries take place. This contrasts with the fixed nature of government prizes, which are determined by policymakers *before* discoveries take place. Market prices adjust to information about scientific and technological discoveries and convey information about those discoveries. Prizes are awards that are arbitrarily established by government agencies and do not depend on scientific and technological discoveries nor do they convey information about these discoveries. Roin (2014) points out that patents allow the rewards to owners to vary over time reflecting changes in the value of inventions, giving patents an important advantage over static "prizes" with common ownership.

After receiving a patent grant, an inventor may license the invention or transfer the invention to others. Licensing royalties and transfer prices result from transactions among market participants and reflect information about the features of inventions. Because patents cover development of inventions, market prices change continually as additional features of the patented invention emerge. Market prices of patented inventions also change continually as a result of commercialization efforts of patent owners and the emergence of new applications of the patented inventions. In addition, market prices of patented inventions change continually to reflect the development of substitute and complementary technologies.

Prices summarize market conditions and change in response to market transactions. Whether for goods and services or inventions, market equilibrium prices result from competition among buyers for scarce products and competition among sellers to provide products. Market prices can be posted by buyers or sellers, they can result from negotiation, they can be chosen by intermediaries, or they can be established though organized auctions and other bidding mechanisms. Market prices are affected by the willingness to pay of the buyers in the market place and the costs of sellers in the market place. Buyers' willingness to pay depends on their preferences, incomes, and availability of substitutes and complements. Sellers' costs depend on their technologies, costs of capital, labor, resources, and IP. The resulting market prices summarize this vast amount of information in a way that provides useful information to buyers, sellers, and other market participants.

Prices in the market for inventions reflect transactions between many types of market participants, including inventors, innovators, producers, investors, and consumers. These prices are the result of many millions of individuals engaging in search, marketing, negotiation, buying, selling, and contracting. The prices also are affected by underlying efforts in R&D, commercialization of inventions, and innovation in products, production processes, and transaction methods. Market prices also reflect the costs of complementary investments in product design, manufacturing equipment, and wholesale and retail distribution.

2.4.3. *The Effects of Technological Change on Market Prices*

Prizes are one-shot deals chosen by central planners in advance of relevant scientific discoveries and technological changes. This implies that prizes provide only limited guidance to inventors. After the contest has taken place, prizes have no information content for inventors, producers, and investors.

Prices in the market for inventions provide guidance for decision makers because prices vary in response to information about scientific and technological discoveries and economic innovations. Anticipation of these state-contingent incentives helps inventors choose R&D projects and determine the extent of effort to devote to particular R&D projects. State-contingent prices also guide IP owners and producers in developing and commercializing patented inventions.

Inventors benefit from state-contingent prices for inventions without the need to specify those contingencies in advance, as would be the case with a state-contingent contract. The state-contingent nature of market prices also implies that prices will continually change in response to inventions and innovations. Prices of patented inventions continue to vary based on discoveries and market forces. The highly complex system of state-contingent prices contrasts with a government prize system that sets a one-time fixed prize for a single winner.

Inventors are necessarily engaged in planning under uncertainty. R&D projects are subject to various forms of risk and uncertainty. The inventor is engaged in developing knowledge and so may not be able to formulate even the basic questions. When designing and conducting experiments, the inventor does not know what will be the outcome of basic research and generally does not know the likelihood of alternative outcomes. Although R&D involves extensive study, preparation, and effort, unexpected outcomes may occur that appear serendipitous and even "easy" to outside observers. In the process of conducting R&D, the inventor often acquires tacit knowledge that is difficult to codify and communicate to others.[151]

Inventors engage in multiple research tasks that are needed to formulate the problem, conduct experiments, and develop inventions based on discoveries. There can be multiple outcomes for any particular R&D project. Inventors often choose among multiple R&D projects, each of which has different sets of outcomes. Inventors make multiple decisions over time, adding and removing activities from their R&D projects. The R&D process often cannot be described in advance by a single outcome with a specific economic value.

The state-contingent nature of market prices provides important guidance for decision-making under uncertainty. The inventor's price expectations provide guidance for various types of decisions generally associated with investment projects. The inventor can choose to undertake an R&D project if the project has a positive net present value (NPV), that is, if the expected value of the project exceeds its costs. The inventor can choose among a set of projects by comparing their NPVs and the inventor can choose to allocate resources across a portfolio consisting of multiple R&D projects. If the inventor is risk averse, then the inventor can consider the expected utility of the project given the variation in prices across outcomes of R&D and the likelihood of the various states of the world. These standard aspects of financial decision-making carry over to decisions about invention and innovation.

The state-contingent nature of prices also is useful in deciding whether to invest in further development and commercialization of a patented invention. After an invention has been granted a patent, patent owners make investments in commercialization and development of innovations. Patent owners benefit from gathering additional information about the market value of the invention before choosing whether or not to develop the patented invention. The patented invention then is a "real option" for the patent owner because the owner invests only if the market value of the invention exceeds investment costs. The economic value of the patented invention takes the form of an option because the patent owner invests only if the price exceeds the cost of investment. The patent owner benefits from making decisions after learning about prices because prices convey information. As a result, the project has a greater expected value than it would if the patent owner had to make an investment decision before observing the market price.

The inventor's R&D decision-making anticipates the combination of patent protections for prospective claims and state-contingent market prices. The inventor's incentives to invent are increased by patent protections for investments that are made *after* the patent is granted. This is because exercising an option after gathering additional information increases the expected value of the invention in comparison with the expected present value of the project when investment decisions are made before gathering information.

Patents protect the inventor's IP after the patent is granted, including development of the invention and investment in commercialization and innovation. The inventor's IP is a state-contingent claim that includes both residual returns and residual control. In this way, patents as prospective claims increase incentives to invent and to innovate. This supports Kitch's observation that patents serve a valuable function by protecting the investment-backed expectations of their owners after the patent is granted.[152]

A number of studies have considered the role of real options in invention and innovation decisions.[153] Ariel Pakes and Mark Schankerman study patent renewals as options that are exercised when the value of the patent exceeds the costs of renewal.[154] Ziedonis studies corporate sponsorship contracts for university research that include an option to purchase.[155]

The state-contingent nature of market prices also serves to guide investors that provide financing for invention and innovation. Patented inventions are intangible real assets that are created through investment in R&D. Market transactions determine prices for patented inventions in a similar manner to other types of assets. Patents owned by corporations are intangible real assets that affect the market value of the firm. Patents are an important form of collateral for secured debt and companies using patents as collateral perform a significant share of R&D.[156] Stuart Graham *et al.* find that startups that patent their inventions benefit in terms of greater venture capital financing. They also find that startups funded by venture capital tend to hold more patents than startups with other types of funding.[157]

2.4.4. *Market Prices as Indicators of Technological Change*

Market prices for inventions provide highly condensed indicators of complex technological change. Prices for inventions undergo dynamic adjustments that reflect new information, competition from new technologies, and discovery of complementary technologies. After a patent is granted, the prices for the relevant inventions fluctuate over time in response to market forces and efforts to develop, commercialize, and apply the inventions. By comparing prices of inventions over time and across inventions, decision makers learn about the effects of technological change. These important properties of market prices contrast with once-and-for-all government prizes.

Some improvements in technology can be expected to reduce the quality-adjusted prices of products that embody inventions. To illustrate how prices provide condensed indicators of technological change, consider changes in the quality-adjusted prices of microprocessors. Price changes for microprocessors reflect Moore's Law, which provides a summary of the complex technological changes in microprocessors. Moore's Law predicts exponential technological change: the number of electronic components that can be put on a chip doubles every 24 months.[158] Electronic components include transistors, resistors, diodes, and capacitors.[159]

Moore's Law has accurately described this aspect of technological change in microprocessors for a period of about fifty years. Moore's Law is a very basic description of some effects of highly complex changes in technology, many of which were discovered long after the prediction. Two significant production processes for microprocessors motivate Moore's Law. First, the *diffusion and oxide-masking* process allowed the use of photographic techniques in producing semiconductors.[160] Second, the *planar* process allowed the use of lithography to make electronic connections on a flat wafer of silicon.[161]

The patenting process played a role in these critical developments according to Gordon Moore,

> "When the patent application for the planar transistor and the process for making it was being prepared for filing, having been made aware of our view of the importance of this invention, the patent attorney asked if we had thought through the implications of the invention to be sure that we were covering it sufficiently."[162]

Answering the patent attorney's question led to consideration of further developments of the invention,

> "To consider this question, Noyce assembled a meeting of the key technical people in the Research and Development Department at Fairchild to discuss how [Jean A.] Hoerni's invention might be extended. . . . During this session, Noyce described how the planar idea could be extended to make complete circuits rather [than] just individual components."[163]

The result of this discussion was a fundamental invention in microprocessor technology: "At this meeting, Noyce described all the additional features necessary to extend the planar transistor technology to make a practical structure for an integrated circuit."[164] Moore observes that Noyce obtained "a patent on the key idea of interconnection [R. N. Noyce, US Patent 2 981 877, April 25, 1961], although his insight was much broader."[165] Noyce's patent illustrates the forward-looking nature of patents, with patented claims looking ahead to the development and application of inventions.

The diffusion and planar processes not only increased the density of devices on a chip but also lowered production costs. This motivated the original prediction; Gordon Moore recalled "from where I was in the laboratory, you could see the changes that were coming, make the yields go up, and get the cost per transistor down dramatically."[166] However, Moore became concerned that the production costs of microprocessors were also growing at an exponential rate.[167]

The question to be addressed is whether quality-adjusted prices of computer chips changed systematically. As a rough illustration, I compiled a list of Intel microprocessors using the number of transistors as a measure of quality. I tried to obtain the price for the most basic version of each microprocessor in terms of processing speed so as to make consistent comparisons across microprocessors.[168]

To adjust for inflation, I list the price of the microprocessor in the year that it was introduced and convert to 2013 dollars.[169] Then, I divide the inflation-adjusted price by the number of microprocessors. This gives only a snapshot of technological change. The quality-adjusted price indicates the effects of improvements in Intel's fabrication processes (45 nm in 2008, 32 nm in 2010, 22 nm in 2012).[170] However, there were also other major technical achievements such as the three-dimensional Tri-Gate transistor introduced by Intel in its Ivy Bridge microprocessors.[171] Intel's microprocessors offered many other improvements in quality that are not reflected in my very basic method of calculating quality-adjusted prices. There is also a slight departure from the trend due to the Pentium III, which appears to be a bargain.

With these caveats in mind, the rapidly decreasing quality-adjusted prices shown in Table 2.1 give a clear indication of the many technological changes that occurred in microprocessors over the period of four decades. These prices summarize a great amount of technological and market

Table 2.1: Quality-adjusted prices of selected Intel microprocessors 1971–2012.

Microprocessor	Year of introduction	Number of transistors	Price in 2013 dollars (nominal price)	Quality-adjusted price in dollars per transistor
4004	1971	2300	172.56 (30)	0.0750
8080	1974	4500	1,701.11 (360)	0.3780
8086	1978	29,000	1,286.27 (360)	0.0443
Intel286	1982	134,000	869.06 (360)	0.0065
Intel386	1985	275,000	647.34 (299)	0.0024
Intel486	1989	1,200,000	1,690.82 (900)	$1409 \cdot 10^{-6}$
Intel Pentium	1993	3,100,000	1,415.48 (878)	$456.6 \cdot 10^{-6}$
Intel Pentium II	1997	7,500,000	724.27 (499)	$96.57 \cdot 10^{-6}$
Intel Pentium III	1999	28,000,000	334.19 (239)	$11.94 \cdot 10^{-6}$
Intel Pentium 4	2000	42,000,000	871.22 (644)	$20.74 \cdot 10^{-6}$
Intel Itanium 2	2004	220,000,000	1,445.34 (1172)	$6.570 \cdot 10^{-6}$
Intel Core 2 Duo	2006	291,000,000	612.44 (530)	$2.105 \cdot 10^{-6}$
Intel Core 2 Quad	2007	582,000,000	269.65 (240)	$0.4633 \cdot 10^{-6}$
Intel Core i3-530	2010	382,000,000	120.72 (113)	$0.3160 \cdot 10^{-6}$
Intel Core i7-377	2012	1,400,000,000	309.47 (305)	$0.2210 \cdot 10^{-6}$

Sources:

1. Year of introduction and number of transistors for selected microprocessors (4004, 8080, 8086, Intel286, Intel386, Intel486, Intel Pentium, Intel Pentium II, Intel Pentium III, Intel Pentium 4, Intel Itanium 2), http://www.intel.com/pressroom/kits/events/moores_law_40th/?iid=tech_mooreslaw+body_presskit, accessed July 10, 2014.

(Continued)

Table 2.1: (*Continued*)

2. Year of introduction and number of transistors for Intel Core 2 Duo, Intel Core 2 Quad, http://download.intel.com/pressroom/kits/IntelProcessorHistory.pdf, accessed July 10, 2014.
3. Year of introduction and number of transistors for Intel Core i3-530, Source: http://www.cpu-world.com/CPUs/Core_i3/Intel-Core%20i3-530%20CM80616003180AG%20(BX80616I3530%20-%20BXC80616I3530).html, accessed July 10, 2014.
4. Year of introduction and number of transistors for Intel Core i7-377, http://hexus.net/tech/reviews/cpu/37989-intel-core-i7-3770k-22nm-ivy-bridge/, accessed July 10, 2014.
5. Price of the 4004 is $30 for 100 to 999 units in 1971 dollars; EDN Staff, "One-Chip CPU Available for Low-Cost Dedicated Computers," January 15, 1972, http://www.edn.com/electronics-products/other/4320004/One-Chip-CPU-available-for-low-cost-dedicated-computers, accessed July 10, 2014.
6. Price of the 8080 is $360:http://www.intel.com/pressroom/kits/quickrefyr.htm, http://www.informit.com/articles/article.aspx?p=130978, http://www.scaruffi.com/svhistory/sv/chap86.html, http://en.citizendium.org/wiki/Intel_8080, http://messui.the-chronicles.org/comp/history_of_micro-computers.pdf. http://www.chips.5u.com/idxhst.html, accessed July 10, 2014.
7. Price of the 8086 is $360; http://www.techrepublic.com/blog/classics-rock/intels-8086-passes-the-big-3-0/, accessed July 10, 2014.
8. Price of the Intel286 is $360, price of the Intel386 is $299, price of the Intel486 is $900, Intel Pentium II is $499, price of the Intel Pentium III is $239, and Intel Pentium 4 is $644. "Intel introduces new and updated Pentium III processors based on 0.18-micron technology, code-named Coppermine. The processor incorporates 28 million transistors with 0.18-micron technology. Speeds and prices in 1000-unit quantities range from 500 MHz (US$239) to 733 MHz (US$776) for desktop versions." "Intel introduces the Pentium 4 processor, at speeds of 1.4 and 1.5 GHz. . . . The processor incorporates 42 million transistors in a 0.18-micron process. Code-name during development was Willamette. Prices are US$819 (1.5 GHz) and US$644 (1.4 GHz) in 1000-unit quantities." Price of the 1.4 GHz Itanium 2 processor is $1172 in 1000-unit quantities, http://processortimeline.info/proc1980.htm, accessed July 10, 2014.
9. The price of the Intel Core 2 Duo in 2006 is $530, http://www.pcmag.com/article2/0,2817,1989161,00.asp, accessed July 10, 2014. The Intel Core 2 Duo has 291 million transistors, http://download.intel.com/pressroom/kits/IntelProcessorHistory.pdf, accessed July 10, 2014.
10. Intel Core 2 Quad was introduced in 2007 and has 820 million transistors. The price of the Intel Core 2 Quad is $851 in quantities of 1,000. http://www.techspot.com/review/36-intel-core2-quad-q6600/, accessed July 10, 2014.
11. Price of the Intel Core i3-530 Processor in 2010 is $113: http://ark.intel.com/products/46472/Intel-Core-i3-530-Processor-4M-Cache-2_93-GHz, accessed July 10, 2014. The Intel Core i3-530 Processor has 382 million transistors; http://www.cpu-world.com/CPUs/Core_i3/Intel-Core%20i3-530%20CM80616003180AG%20(BX80616I3530%20-%20BXC80616I3530).html, accessed July 10, 2014.
12. Price of the Intel Core i7-3770 in 2012 is $305: http://ark.intel.com/products/family/65506/3rd-Generation-Intel-Core-i7-Processors#@Desktop, accessed July 10, 2014. The Ivy Bridge microprocessors have 1400 million transistors; http://hexus.net/tech/reviews/cpu/37989-intel-core-i7-3770k-22nm-ivy-bridge/, accessed July 10, 2014.

information. This example illustrates how prices serve as condensed indicators of technological change.

2.5 Conclusion

The America COMPETES Reauthorization Act opens the door to replacing patents and market prices with contests and government prizes. The Act gives prize authority to the heads of every government agency. Although transferring patented technology to the government is voluntary, such transfers could be required as a condition for participating in prize contests. Additionally, the government has an array of powerful instruments for inducing participation in contests, including antitrust, research grants, subsidies for research by universities, labs and corporations, tax credits and penalties for individuals and corporations, government procurement rules, and economic regulation of industry.

This raises the question of what institutions perform best in generating efficient invention and innovation. Although seemingly benign, replacing patents with contests would harm invention and innovation. In contrast to market prices for inventions, a system of government prizes with either public or common ownership of technology, would apply command-and-control to innovation. The government would determine the "shadow prices" of inventions, select the winning inventions, pay rewards to inventors, and allocate technologies to potential users. If only central planners could find the right "shadow prices," as advocates believe, they could replace market prices with government prizes, thus avoiding the need to solve "millions of equations." But the premise is inconsistent with experience in centrally planned economies.

Central planners necessarily lack the detailed private information of inventors, innovators, producers, and consumers that generate prices in the market for inventions. Government prizes would fail to reflect the extensive private information contained in market prices and would fail to adjust continually to changes in economic conditions, including technological change. Central planners cannot match the knowledge that Hayek's "man on the spot" has about the benefits and costs of goods and services. Central planners are even less equipped to match the knowledge of scientists, engineers, entrepreneurs, and managers engaged in invention and innovation. Market systems perform much better than governments in diffusing inventions and innovations.

Public contests and taxes used to finance prizes would generate deadweight welfare losses greater than any caused by market prices. The administrative costs of government control of invention, innovation, and technology diffusion would be many times market transaction costs. Governments cannot expect to improve static and dynamic efficiency of market allocation of inventions. Replacing market prices with public prizes would create the very problem they are meant to solve.

It is impossible for a few occasional contests designed by bureaucrats to replace the millions of informative signals provided at every moment by the price system. Market prices help inventors, innovators, and adopters understand consumer needs and innovative efficiency. Market prices are instruments of cooperation and competition among inventors and producers. Market prices for inventions help guide the diffusion of technology and the application of technology to innovation. Bureaucrats cannot possibly know in advance what information will be revealed by future technological advances and unfolding market prices.

Patents and competitive markets tap into a vast ocean of ingenuity. Responding to these incentives, inventors, innovators, and entrepreneurs provide the multitude of technological advances that drive the global economy. Patents and markets produce streams of patented inventions in a staggering number of areas including medicine, pharmaceuticals, biotechnology, chemistry, materials sciences, electronics, computers, and communications.

Invention and innovation are risky, costly, and very difficult. It is absurd to believe that public prizes can match even a small fraction of the rewards offered by competitive markets. Antitrust and regulations that weaken IP rights impede the operation of the market for inventions and diminish invention and innovation. Replacing market prices with government prizes would severely reduce invention and innovation and harm social welfare and economic growth.

Chapter 3

Patents and the Business Revolution

3.1 Introduction

Extensive limits on what types of inventions are eligible for patents threaten to decrease the effectiveness of the patent system. Targeted limits can have substantial impacts on invention and innovation because they necessarily occur at the frontiers of technology. Supreme Court decisions have addressed patent subject matter eligibility in software, business method inventions, medicine, and biotechnology. Patent subject matter eligibility has crucial implications for public policy toward invention, innovation, and entrepreneurship.

The debate over subject matter eligibility appears in the Supreme Court's contentious *Bilski* decision, which addresses business method inventions.[1] Business method inventions are significant because they drive what I call the "Business Revolution," which includes advances in e-commerce and applications of AI.

This chapter focuses on patent subject matter eligibility in the context of *Bilski.* The *Bilski* decision rejects the categorical exclusion of business method inventions. The Court in *Bilski* also rejects using the machine-or-transformation test as the sole criterion for a process to be patentable. The *Bilski* decision leaves room for the development of new criteria specifically limiting the patent subject matter eligibility of business method inventions. There is also uncertainty in Europe over the patentability of business method innovations.[2]

The Supreme Court builds on *Bilski* in its *Alice* decision.[3] In *Alice*, the Court addressed patents that "disclose a computer-implemented scheme for mitigating 'settlement risk' (i.e., the risk that only one party to a financial transaction will pay what it owes) by using a third-party intermediary."[4] The Court in *Alice* rejected patent subject matter eligibility because the patent claims "are drawn to the abstract idea of intermediated settlement, and that merely requiring generic computer implementation fails to transform that abstract idea into a patent-eligible invention."[5]

The USPTO has issued guidance to its patent examiners based on the "Alice/Mayo" test.[6] This test draws on the Court's *Alice* and *Mayo* decisions.[7] In *Mayo*, the Court considered "patent claims covering processes that help doctors who use thiopurine drugs to treat patients with autoimmune diseases determine whether a given dosage level is too low or too high."[8] The *Mayo* decision observes

> The Court has recognized, however, that too broad an interpretation of this exclusionary principle could eviscerate patent law. For all inventions at some level embody, use, reflect, rest upon, or apply laws of nature, natural phenomena, or abstract ideas.[9]

The Court in *Mayo* rejected the patent claims at issue because "the steps in the claimed processes (apart from the natural laws themselves) involve well-understood, routine, conventional activity previously engaged in by researchers in the field."[10]

The Court also addressed patent subject matter eligibility in *Myriad*.[11] According to the Court, "[g]roundbreaking, innovative, or even brilliant discovery does not by itself satisfy the §101 inquiry."[12] *Myriad* considers "whether a naturally occurring segment of deoxyribonucleic acid (DNA) is patent eligible under 35 U. S. C. §101 by virtue of its isolation from the rest of the human genome."[13] *Myriad* also examines "the patent eligibility of synthetically created DNA known as complementary DNA (cDNA), which contains the same protein-coding information found in a segment of natural DNA but omits portions within the DNA segment that do not code for proteins."[14] The Court held "that a naturally occurring DNA segment is a product of nature and not patent eligible merely because it has been isolated, but that cDNA is patent eligible because it is not naturally occurring."[15]

The chapter is organized as follows. Section 3.2 introduces an economic definition of business method inventions and also examines how such inventions are defined by the USPTO, the Patent Act, and the courts. Section 3.3 finds that constraining IP protections for business method inventions would adversely impact entrepreneurship and the commercialization of scientific and technological inventions. Section 3.4 argues for the patentability of business method inventions based on considerations of economic efficiency. Section 3.5 considers the critical role that business method inventions play in fostering the Business Revolution.

3.2 The Debate over Business Method Inventions

In this chapter, I conduct an economic and legal analysis of business method inventions to determine whether such inventions should be eligible for patents. The analysis suggests that there is no need for limiting criteria that apply specifically to business method inventions; general limits on patentability of inventions are sufficient. I conclude that the patent system should continue to provide IP protections for business method inventions just as it does for other types of inventions.

3.2.1. *Business Method Inventions*

The Supreme Court in *Bilski* states, "[t]he question in this case turns on whether a patent can be issued for a claimed invention designed for the business world." Questioning the patentability of business methods is a lot like trying to close the barn door after the horse has bolted. The United States has awarded business method patents practically since the establishment of the patent system in 1790.[16] In its first fifty years, the U.S. Patent Office granted forty-one financial patents covering arts of bank notes, bills of credit, bills of exchange, check blanks, detecting and preventing counterfeiting, coin counting, interest calculation tables, and lotteries.[17]

The USPTO has awarded many business method patents in a wide variety of categories, including over 100,000 patents since 1976 in Patent Class 705, "Data Processing: Financial, Business Practice, Management, or Cost/Price Determination."[18] *State Street* strengthened the patentability of business methods by the test that such inventions must produce a "useful, concrete and tangible result."[19] In the wake of *State Street*, business method patenting increased in both volume and complexity.[20] Inventive efforts in the area of business methods grew rapidly and were compared to a "flood," a "frenzy," and a "gold rush."[21] To undo patent protections for business method inventions would create substantial economic costs and would adversely impact technological change in computer hardware, software, communications, and the Internet. More than avoiding such disruptions, however, the case for patenting business method inventions rests on fundamental economic principles.

Extensive patenting of business method inventions and related legal battles have generated controversy. Some researchers blame the patent system's problems on business method inventions. James Bessen and Michael Meurer argue that the patent system is a "failure" because patents do not provide the type of clarity and protections that one might expect from physical property rights.[22] They observe that "patents on software, and especially patents on business methods (which are largely software patents), stood out as being particularly problematic."[23] Dan Burk and Mark Lemley find that business method inventions are responsible for a "crisis" in the patent system.[24] They contend that the courts should solve the problem by varying intellectual property (IP) protections across industries, with particular scrutiny of "bad patents" for software and business methods.[25]

I begin by providing an economic definition of business method inventions that serves as a guide to the IP debate. I define a *business method invention* as the discovery of a commercial technique that firms can apply to address market opportunities. This is significant because the initial implementation of a business method invention by firms is a *Schumpeterian innovation*. Business method inventions thus are the commercial discoveries and ideas that drive subsequent commercial innovation, which is the implementation of those discoveries.

The economic definition of a business method invention builds on developments in the economic theory of the firm, the economics of transaction costs, the economics of innovation and entrepreneurship, and financial economics. Entrepreneurs and managers implement business method inventions by establishing new types of firms, developing new industries, and improving the productivity and performance of established firms. Patents for business method inventions not only provide incentives to invent *before* the patent award but they also facilitate innovation that implements the invention *after* the patent award.

Based on this economic framework, I advance several arguments for the patentability of business method inventions. First, patents for business method inventions are important for entrepreneurship and for the commercialization of many scientific and technological inventions. Stuart Graham *et al.* find that entrepreneurs tend to benefit from patents which confer competitive advantage, protect technology from copying by rivals, assist in obtaining financing, and enhance the startup's reputation.[26] The work of Graham *et al.* illustrates the complex ways that IP protections for business method inventions affect subsequent innovation by entrepreneurs.

I argue further that business method inventions provide a major channel for commercialization of scientific and technological discoveries and are important for entrepreneurship. Business method inventions often contain scientific and technological discoveries and help to commercialize scientific and technological discoveries already developed. Business method inventions that commercialize information and communications technology (ICT) are often targeted toward electronic commerce (e-commerce) applications. Restrictions on patenting business methods would cause inventors to present their discoveries under various other categories and could prejudice the awarding of patents against scientific and technological discoveries that have commercial applications.

Second, I show that business method inventions should be patentable because IP protections are essential for economic efficiency. I emphasize that business method patents increase dynamic, allocative, and transaction efficiencies in the market for discoveries because they facilitate the commercialization of invention. I address concerns of critics regarding the legal and administrative costs of business method patents. I show how some critics of business method patents offer economically flawed recommendations for IP rules that would reward inventors based on the costs of invention. In contrast, maintaining patentability of business method inventions allows markets to reward inventors based on the benefits of invention.

Third, I explain that business method inventions are critical for the "Business Revolution," which represents a fundamental transformation of the economy and a major source of economic growth. The Business Revolution is changing the office, the store, and the market, just as the Industrial Revolution earlier changed the factory. Scientific and technological advances in ICT have generated changes in commerce on a scale that rivals or surpasses the Industrial Revolution. ICT advances automate practically all business transactions, thereby increasing labor productivity and efficiency in retail, wholesale, finance, and many other industries. This explains the large number of business method patent applications and awards. Removing or weakening patent protections for business method inventions potentially jeopardizes advances in e-commerce, ICT, and the Internet. The traditional machine-or-transformation test for patentability is restrictive because it does not effectively address ICT applications to business transactions. The machine-or-transformation test is more suited to the Industrial Revolution than to the Business Revolution. Introducing new specific limits on IP protections for business method inventions would constrain the Business Revolution.

3.2.2. *An Economic Definition of Business Method Inventions*

The absence of a clear definition of business method inventions poses a problem for researchers, inventors, judges, and public policymakers.[27] In questioning business method inventions generally and in suggesting the possibility of specific limitations on business method patentability, the *Bilski* Court emphasizes the need for a better understanding of this type of discovery. This section presents an economic definition of business method inventions. Next, the section considers the USPTO's definition, the guidance provided by the Patent Act, and the courts' attempts to define business method inventions.

A *business method invention* is the discovery of a commercial technique for firms to address market opportunities, such as a transaction procedure, market microstructure, financial system, operational process, or organizational form.[28] Business method inventions contribute to the establishment of new types of firms, development of new industries, and improvement in the productivity and performance of established firms. A business method invention often involves the creation and application of economic and business knowledge. A business method invention can encompass scientific and technological discoveries that implement the commercial technique. Also, a business method invention can commercialize scientific and technological discoveries developed by other inventors.

A business method invention can be transferred to other economic agents in the market for discoveries, embodied in new firms by entrepreneurs, or developed and implemented by managers of existing firms. Elsewhere, I define a *firm* as a particular type of transaction institution.[29] Firms are distinguished from other types of transaction institutions when their business objectives are separable from the consumption objectives of their owners.[30] The "separation criterion" builds on fundamental concepts in finance and neoclassical economics.[31] By creating markets and organizations and intermediating transactions, firms offer efficiencies in comparison to other types of transaction institutions.

A business method patent formalizes and codifies various aspects of the commercial discovery. Inventors can sell or license business method inventions to market intermediaries, to entrepreneurs, or to existing firms. In practice, a business method invention can be expressed as an entrepreneur's business plan for a new firm or as a manager's strategic plan for an existing business, along with accompanying technical and scientific information. Independent inventors can apply their business method inventions to become entrepreneurs and establish firms that embody the inventions. Existing firms can develop and implement business method inventions. The innovator formulates a new strategy by identifying a market opportunity and the resources needed to address that opportunity. The innovator commercializes the strategy by transferring knowledge to others or by establishing a new firm. New or existing firms obtain the resources needed to implement the strategy and to address the market opportunity.

Business method inventions provide the foundations for new industries, enhance the performance of existing industries, and drive economic growth. Business method discoveries draw on the social sciences, including economics and related fields such as finance, marketing, accounting, management strategy, and operations research. Business method inventions are not restricted to manufacturing; they can apply to all of the firm's functional areas, including marketing, sales, procurement, inventory management, R&D, customer service, accounting, and finance.

Business method inventions serve to reduce transaction costs, which constitute a major share of the economy.[32] Transaction costs are important determinants of the activities of firms, as Ronald Coase emphasized.[33] Financial innovations increase entrepreneurship and economic growth by increasing the availability of financial capital.[34] Josh Lerner points out that "financial innovations enable firms of all industries to raise capital in larger amounts and at a lower cost than they could otherwise."[35] Lerner finds that in the period from 1990 to 2002, smaller firms accounted for a disproportionate share of financial innovations and financial firms obtained limited patent protections for financial innovations.[36]

The *initial implementation* of a business method invention in the market place is a Schumpeterian innovation.[37] The business method invention is the fundamental commercial discovery that forms the basis of a Schumpeterian innovation, which is the realization of that idea in the marketplace. Identifying the underlying commercial discovery extends Schumpeter's discussion of innovation. The concept of a business method invention benefits from new developments in the theory of the firm, transaction cost economics, the economics of innovation and entrepreneurship, and financial economics. Also, the concept of a business method invention highlights the effect of IP rules on both the market for such inventions and their subsequent implementation by firms. When business method inventions are patented, their application in the marketplace is "practicing the patent." IP protections for business method inventions enhance incentives for invention and facilitate subsequent innovation.

Schumpeterian innovation is the introductory application of business method inventions by firms. Schumpeter defines innovation as "'doing things differently' in the realm of economic life."[38] For Schumpeter, economic development is "defined by the carrying out of new combinations," often through the efforts of entrepreneurs.[39] Schumpeter's "innovations in the economic system" include the "introduction of a new good," "introduction of a new method of production," "opening of a new market," "conquest of a new source of supply of raw materials or half-manufactured goods," and "carrying out of the new organization of any industry."[40]

Schumpeter emphasizes that "innovation is the outstanding fact in the economic history of capitalist society."[41]

Schumpeter distinguishes between an innovation in the commercial sense and an invention in the scientific sense: "Innovation is possible without anything we should identify as invention, and invention does not necessarily induce innovation."[42] Schumpeter observes that "Although most innovations can be traced to some conquest in the realm of either theoretical or practical knowledge, there are many which cannot." Schumpeter finds no economic distinction between the two situations because the economic effects of the innovation need not depend on its "scientific novelty."[43] An innovation can have significant economic impacts even when it lacks scientific novelty. The market value of an innovation depends on the extent to which consumers are willing to pay for the goods and services of firms that "do things differently."

Schumpeter further distinguishes between the personal features of the inventor and the innovator, pointing out that even when innovation consists of commercializing a particular invention, "the making of the invention and the carrying out of the innovation are completely different things,"

> Personal aptitudes — primarily intellectual in the case of the inventor, primarily volitional in the case of the businessman who turns the invention into an innovation — and the methods by which the one and the other work, belong to different spheres (*ibid.*).[44]

Schumpeter distinguishes between the scientist and the innovator who often is an entrepreneur or a manager of an existing firm. Schumpeter's distinction between invention and innovation has implications for the question of patentability of business methods.

What is fundamentally at issue is whether the patent system should recognize discoveries that are purely commercial, such as a new transaction procedure. This is distinguished from discoveries that involve advances in chemistry, physics, biology, engineering, and medicine. When there is an accompanying scientific or technological breakthrough, a patent could presumably be awarded for the scientific invention directly. The question of whether commercial discoveries are valuable inventions worthy of IP protections afforded to industrial discoveries stems from a long-standing debate over the relative economic value added by distribution versus production. In *The Wealth of Nations*, Adam Smith argued that both production and distribution are important: "The capital of the merchant exchanges the surplus produce of one place for that of another, and thus encourages the industry and increases the enjoyments of both."[45]

This debate is reflected in the *Bilski* Court's question about IP protections of business method inventions. Public policies that distinguish transaction technologies from production technologies are likely to generate biases that adversely affect invention and commercialization. The main implication of a more precise understanding of business method inventions is that public policies should treat them in the same way as other types of inventions.

The distinction between commerce and production has little practical basis. Public policy makers, who draw artificial distinctions between commercial and industrial inventions either to support or oppose business methods, will generate economic distortions. Courts seeking to identify differences between transactions and production would face an impossible task. As Coase demonstrated, firms determine whether to carry out a particular task by comparing market transaction costs with internal governance costs.[46] Transaction costs affect whether a task is part of a firm's production process or part of its market transactions, thus determining the boundaries of the firm. As compared with internal governance costs, relatively high market transaction costs favor vertical integration, and relatively low market transaction costs favor outsourcing.

Because firms solve Coase's "make-or-buy" problem, what might appear to be a production task in one context could appear to be a market transaction in another context. This makes the distinction between manufacturing inventions and business method inventions impractical for the patent office and for the courts. Even knowing how the firm resolves the "make-or-buy" choice, it remains difficult to distinguish in-house production from market purchases because both activities involve market transactions and internal management.[47] As Harold Demsetz observes, the tasks are highly similar:

> Hence, in-house production does not constitute a clear elimination of transaction costs. Similarly, purchasing goods from another firm, rather

> than producing these in house, involves an implicit purchase of the management services undertaken by the other firm, so management cost is not eliminated by purchasing more nearly complete goods across markets.[48]

Demsetz concludes that the correct question is not whether the transaction cost of purchase is less than the management cost of production, but rather whether the sum of management and transaction cost incurred through in-house production is more or less than the sum of management and transaction cost incurred through purchase across markets, since either option entails expenditures in both cost categories.[49]

Elsewhere, I define the scope of the firm as the combination of its market-making and organizational activities, emphasizing that firms create and manage both market and organizational transactions.[50] Therefore, the absence of an operational distinction between commerce and production suggests that business method exceptions to patents cannot be justified by economic analysis. Business method inventions should be accorded the same IP protections as other inventions.

3.2.3. *The USPTO's Definition of Business Method Inventions*

The USPTO recognizes business method inventions and necessarily implements its definition through extensive categorization. The USPTO mainly identifies business method inventions through its class 705 "Data Processing: Financial, Business Practice, Management, or Cost/Price Determination":

> This is the generic class for apparatus and corresponding methods for performing data processing operations, in which there is a significant change in the data or for performing calculation operations wherein the apparatus or method is uniquely designed for or utilized in the practice, administration, or management of an enterprise, or in the processing of financial data. This class also provides for apparatus and corresponding methods for performing data processing or calculating operations in which a charge for goods or services is determined.[51]

The USPTO's 705 class definition suggests both computer hardware and software (apparatus and method) that are used to "change" data. The class definition emphasizes applications of data processing to business management or financial data. The USPTO "scope of the class" for class 705 identifies the importance of patent claims that relate to business management and transactions involving commodities and finance.[52] The USPTO's definition under this class is by no means exhaustive because the USPTO further references twenty-eight other classes of inventions, such as electronic funds transfer.[53]

The courts have struggled to address business method inventions in part because these discoveries are intertwined with advances in ICT. If the courts or the USPTO were to rule out patenting of business method inventions, the impact would be mitigated because of these ICT connections. As John Allison and Starling Hunter point out, skilled patent attorneys can draft patents strategically to opt out of, or in to, particular categories, as occurred with software patents.[54] Patent applications for business method inventions would similarly include descriptions of production technologies and applications. This is implicitly recognized by the USPTO's 705 class. Many business method inventions could be patented as ICT inventions, but doing so would affect the disclosure function of patents.

Courts seeking to identify software inventions faced related difficulties as patent attorneys wrote in claims of machines and physical devices.[55] Julie Cohen and Mark Lemley point out that the *Diehr* decision and others in its wake created what they call "the doctrine of the magic words": "During the 1980s and early 1990s, knowledgeable patent attorneys did exactly that, claiming software inventions as hardware devices, pizza ovens, and other 'machines.'"[56] A "mathematical or 'mental process' algorithm" would qualify if the patent application contained "any physical element or step."[57]

As Scott Kieff observes, "patents are legal documents drafted by lawyers for interpretation by judges and lawyers, not technical documents evaluated by peer review."[58] From a patenting perspective, drawing a distinction between business methods and ICT inventions would be difficult in practice. Business method patents are closely tied to related advances in computer software, computer hardware, and communications technologies. If business method inventions are simply a type of computer hardware or software, then presumably they can be patented as ICT inventions.

3.2.4. *Guidance from the Patent Act in Defining Business Method Inventions*

The patent system involves all three branches of government: the Congress, the courts, and the executive branch through the USPTO, which is an agency of the Department of Commerce. Although the Patent Act does not address business method inventions specifically, it sheds some light on when such inventions might satisfy the statute.

The Patent Act describes patentable inventions as belonging to four broad categories: "Whoever invents or discovers any new and useful process, machine, manufacture, or composition of matter, or any new and useful improvement thereof, may obtain a patent therefor, subject to the conditions and requirements of this title."[59] The Patent Act indicates that "(a) The term 'invention' means invention or discovery. (b) The term 'process' means process, art, or method, and includes a new use of a known process, machine, manufacture, composition of matter, or material."[60] An invention is patentable only if it is novel and non-obvious.[61]

The Act's categories could readily include a variety of business methods as patentable inventions. Newly discovered business methods represent progress in science and the useful arts. There is nothing in the Act that specifically excludes business methods.[62] To be patentable, an invention need only satisfy one of the categories of the act — process, machine, manufacture, or composition of matter — not two or more categories. It is sufficient that a business method be a particular type of process. The common definition of a process suggests that a business method defined by a series of actions performed in a definite manner and having a particular result or outcome could be a patentable invention.[63] The *OED* defines a "method" as "a procedure for attaining an object" and "2. a. More generally: a way of doing anything, esp. according to a defined and regular plan; a mode of procedure in any activity, business, etc." A business method can be a process consisting of a plan of action in business.

Business methods could also be thought of as belonging to the category of a "manufacture." Business methods are used to produce a product, which can consist of a good or service. Such methods need not be restricted to machines or the physical transformation of inputs into outputs. After World War II, the U.S. economy began to be characterized as a "service economy." An early study found that "The United States is now pioneering in a new stage of economic development. During the period following World War II this country became the world's first 'service economy' — that is, the first nation in which more than half of the employed population is not involved, in the production of food, clothing, houses, automobiles, or other tangible goods."[64] Almost all the increase in employment between World War II and 1968 took place in services, including health care, finance, retail, and wholesale.[65]

The economy's gross domestic product (GDP) provides a useful measure of the contribution of services to the economy.[66] The GDP measures the value added of various economic activities.[67] Intermediaries in finance, retail, and wholesale and providers of business services contribute a third of U.S. GDP. The economic activities that are focused on transactions and their value added to the economy include retail trade (8 percent), wholesale trade (6 percent), finance and insurance (7.8 percent), and professional and business services and other services (12.4 percent).[68] Taken together, the transaction sector comprises 34 percent of GDP, well over one-third of total value added. Adding services from such industries as education and health care increases the contribution of services to well over half of GDP. The ICT-producing industries consist of "computer and electronic products; publishing industries (includes software); information and data processing services; and computer systems design and related services," which together contribute 7.3 percent to total GDP. The services component of ICT further increases the estimate of the contribution of services to the economy.

Restricting inventions to manufacturing without including services would exclude more than half of the economy, whether measured on the basis of employment or value added. The machine-or-transformation test would tend to limit inventions to the manufacture of products or to those services that directly rely on equipment. This would tend to exclude business methods that use software and organizational activities to provide services to consumers and businesses. The result of a narrow definition of inventions based on manufacturing of goods other than services would be a view of business based on production methods of the type observed in the Industrial Revolution. This would bias the development of inventions away from those associated with the service sector, which has come to dominate developed economies.

Business method inventions could be classified using combinations of categories, such as a process and a machine. For example, it might involve a process for providing services using ICT machines. The bundle of inventions need not rely exclusively on the machine or process components, but can include both parts of the bundle. In addressing bundles of discoveries, the Patent Act singles out a particular type of biotechnological process for special treatment.[69] For "a biotechnological process using or resulting in a composition of matter," the Act notes that when it is novel, it shall further be considered non-obvious if

> (A) claims to the process and the composition of matter are contained in either the same application for patent or in separate applications having the same effective filing date; and (B) the composition of matter, and the process at the time it was invented, were owned by the same person or subject to an obligation of assignment to the same person. (2) A patent issued on a process under paragraph (1)-(A) shall also contain the claims to the composition of matter used in or made by that process, or (B) shall, if such composition of matter is claimed in another patent, be set to expire on the same date as such other patent.[70]

The specific treatment of biotechnological inventions is interesting because it refers to a bundle of two components: a "process" and a "composition of matter."

3.2.5. *The Courts' Movement toward a Definition of Business Method Inventions*

Although the *Bilski* court is unanimous in rejecting the patent at issue in the case, the justices split three ways on the general question of patentability of business method inventions. Anthony Kennedy joined by John

Roberts, Clarence Thomas, and Samuel Alito take the position that business methods are patentable inventions. John Paul Stevens joined by Ruth Bader Ginsburg, Stephen Breyer, and Sonia Sotomayor take the opposite position against business methods. Breyer, joined by Antonin Scalia, takes what might be described as a middle position, affirming the usefulness of the "machine-or-transformation" test and expressing doubt about *State Street*'s "useful, concrete, and tangible result" approach.[71] In *Bilski*, the court seeks guidance regarding the nature of business inventions and the function of IP protections for these types of discoveries.

A decade after *State Street*, the U.S. Court of Appeals for the Federal Circuit (CAFC) attempted to close the barn door on business method patents by imposing a restrictive "machine-or-transformation" test.[72] In *Bilski*, the court reviews that decision and finds that the "machine-or-transformation test" should not be the sole criterion for evaluating the patentability of business methods. Those on the court who favor the patentability of business methods take a prospective approach, emphasizing technological change in industries such as software, biotechnology, and electronics. Those opposed to the patentability of business methods take a retrospective approach, emphasizing production and technology during the Industrial Revolution. Justice Stevens considers the intent of the framers of the Constitution regarding particular types of inventions that would be patentable. Stevens refers to inventions for actual horses (in contrast to my metaphorical characterization of business method inventions as escaping horses):

> Indeed, just days before the Constitutional Convention, one delegate listed examples of American progress in 'manufactures and the useful arts,' all of which involved the creation or transformation of physical substances. See T. Coxe, An Address to an Assembly of the Friends of American Manufactures 17–18 (1787) (listing, *inter alia*, meal, ships, liquors, potash, gunpowder, paper, starch, articles of iron, stone work, carriages, and harnesses).[73]

Previous decisions provide generic restrictions on patents that also apply to business methods. The laws of nature are not patentable even when they are used to provide customers with a new product. In *Funk*

Bros., Bond obtained US Patent No. 2,200,532 in 1940 for a method of combining compatible strains of bacteria inoculants to be applied to growing legumes.[74] Bond offered customers the convenience of buying a bundle of compatible inoculants in a single package. Bond charged the Funk Brothers Seed Company with infringement because they offered their customers a different bundle of inoculants.[75] The court stated that

> The qualities of these bacteria, like the heat of the sun, electricity, or the qualities of metals, are part of the storehouse of knowledge of all men. They are manifestations of laws of nature, free to all men and reserved exclusively to none. He who discovers a hitherto unknown phenomenon of nature has no claim to a monopoly of it which the law recognizes. If there is to be invention from such a discovery, it must come from the application of the law of nature to a new and useful end.[76]

In *Benson*, the court found that the "method for converting numerical information from binary-coded decimal numbers into pure binary numbers, for use in programming conventional general purpose digital computers, is merely a series of mathematical calculations or mental steps, and does not constitute a patentable 'process' within the meaning of the Patent Act."[77] The court rejects the argument that "a process patent must either be tied to a particular machine or apparatus or must operate to change articles or materials to a 'different state or thing.'"[78] Yet, *Benson* calls for action by Congress to determine whether computer programs are patentable.[79] Then, in *Flook*, the court extends this approach, finding that post-solution applications of a mathematical formula are not sufficient for patentability.[80]

The court ruling in *Diehr* found "laws of nature, natural phenomena, and abstract ideas" not to be patentable.[81] Mathematical algorithms are not patentable because they are abstract ideas, which would be echoed in *Bilski*. *Diehr* concerns a patent for a process for molding synthetic rubber.[82] The court cites an earlier decision regarding the patentability of a process:

> If new and useful, it is just as patentable as is a piece of machinery. In the language of the patent law, it is an art. The machinery pointed out as

> suitable to perform the process may or may not be new or patentable; whilst the process itself may be altogether new, and produce an entirely new result.[83]

Business method inventions transcend these objections in the landmark *State Street* case. *State Street* was based on U.S. Patent No. 5,193,056 whereby mutual funds could pool their assets in an investment portfolio that was organized as a partnership: "This investment configuration provides the administrator of a mutual fund with the advantageous combination of economies of scale in administering investments coupled with the tax advantages of a partnership."[84] The economies of scale derive from transaction efficiencies because an administrator can jointly manage the assets of the mutual funds. The average costs of managing each fund decline with the number of funds being managed.

The patent at issue in *State Street* contains multiple machine claims and multiple business method claims. The CAFC points out that it does not matter whether the patent is for a machine or a process because they both fit into the categories of invention.[85] *State Street* is important because the patent describes the application of computers to business. The patent claim includes "A data processing system for managing a financial services configuration of a portfolio established as a partnership, each partner being one of a plurality of funds."[86] The data processing system described would apply to most basic information technology applications, consisting of a personal computer having a central processing unit (CPU) and data storage, and various arithmetic logic circuits.

> Today, we hold that the transformation of data, representing discrete dollar amounts, by a machine through a series of mathematical calculations into a final share price, constitutes a practical application of a mathematical algorithm, formula, or calculation, because it produces 'a useful, concrete and tangible result' — a final share price momentarily fixed for recording and reporting purposes and even accepted and relied upon by regulatory authorities and in subsequent trades.[87]

State Street emphasized that "Since the 1952 Patent Act, business methods have been, and should have been, subject to the same legal requirements for patentability as applied to any other process or method."[88] *State*

Street endorses the U.S. Patent and Trademark 1996 Examination Guidelines for Computer Related Inventions, which treats business methods as any other type of claim, noting that "Whether the claims are directed to subject matter within §101 should not turn on whether the claimed subject matter does 'business' instead of something else."[89]

In emphasizing the need for a "useful, concrete and tangible result," *State Street* essentially treats business methods as any other type of invention. Additionally, *AT&T versus Excel Communications* found there to be no basis in subject matter for excluding business method patents.[90] However, the CAFC in *In re Bilski* applies the "machine-or-transformation test" in an attempt to find a technological middle ground:

> the more challenging process claims of the twenty-first century are seldom so clearly limited in scope as the highly specific, plainly corporeal industrial manufacturing process of *Diehr*; nor are they typically as broadly claimed or purely abstract and mathematical as the algorithm of *Benson*.[91]

In so doing, the CAFC goes against its prior tests, Supreme Court precedent, the Patent Act, and Congressional intent.[92]

The *Bilski* court effectively reopens the issue that might have been settled in *State Street* because it seeks to distinguish business methods from other inventions. The court emphasizes that it does not endorse *State Street*.[93] The court speculates that the *In re Bilski* decision was a way of undoing *State Street*: "The appeals court may have thought it needed to make the machine-or-transformation test exclusive precisely because its case law had not adequately identified less extreme means of restricting business method patents."[94] The court signals to the CAFC that it might develop distinctions between business methods and other inventions: "this Court by no means desires to preclude the Federal Circuit's development of other limiting criteria that further the Patent Act's purposes and are not inconsistent with its text."[95] *Bilski*'s rejection of *State Street* not only creates uncertainty for future business method inventors, it also calls into question business method patents issued since *State Street.*

Although patenting business methods is the fundamental issue, the bone of contention in *Bilski* is the machine-or-transformation test for patentability. This test may be well suited for the Industrial Revolution but not for the current Business Revolution.[96] Arguing against business method patents, Alan Durham states that to the framers of the U.S. Constitution, "useful arts" referred only to industry: "There is no corresponding evidence that the Framers intended to encourage developments in business methods, political strategies, pedagogical techniques, or similar undertakings."[97] Also, John Thomas asserts that

> By restricting patentable advances to the repeatable production or transformation of material objects and excluding subject matter founded upon the aesthetic, social observation or personal skill, the industrial application requirement would restore a sense of patentable subject matter that matches our sensibilities.[98]

Echoing the arguments of legal scholars who oppose patenting business methods, Stevens finds that for the framers of the Constitution, "the term 'useful arts' was widely understood to encompass the fields that we would now describe as relating to technology or 'technological arts'" and the "industrial, mechanical and manual arts of the late eighteenth century."[99]

Stevens argues in *Bilski* that the court's opinion "can only cause mischief" and that business methods should not be patentable: "a claim that merely describes a method of doing business does not qualify as a 'process' under §101."[100] Stevens turns to earlier patenting: "there is no basis in the text of the Statute of Monopolies, nor in pre-1790 English precedent, to infer that business methods could qualify." However, Kennedy cautions that relying only on the machine-or-transformation test "would create uncertainty as to the patentability of software, advanced diagnostic medicine techniques, and inventions based on linear programming, data compression, and the manipulation of digital signals."[101]

The argument that industrial processes should be patentable while business methods should not recalls unfortunate but long-standing social biases. Contempt for professional merchants dates back at least to ancient Greece and Rome, reflecting the fear of the newly rich on the part of those who inherited their wealth.[102] Schumpeter observes that social resentment of entrepreneurs occurs because some are successful despite the rarity and temporary nature of their success.[103] Paul Veyne also finds that resentment of success explains why commerce was "almost universally devalued until the industrial revolution."[104]

The notion that manufacturing is somehow superior to commerce and entrepreneurship also resembles Marxian criticisms of merchants, intermediaries, and business in general.[105] Countering this bias, Deirdre McCloskey provides an extended defense of "bourgeois virtues," arguing that commerce helps to promote ethical behavior: "But the assaults on the alleged vices of the bourgeoisie after 1848 made an impossible Best into the enemy of the actual Good."[106] Thomas Sowell observes that "The organizations, large and small, which produce and distribute most of the goods and services that make up a modern standard of living — businesses — have long been targets of the intelligentsia."[107]

3.3 Limiting the Patentability of Business Method Inventions Would Constrain the Commercialization of Inventions and Entrepreneurship

Narrow reliance on such criteria as the machine-or-transformation test would not only exclude many useful commercial discoveries but would also potentially exclude scientific and technological advances. Constraining patenting of business method inventions might also adversely impact entrepreneurship. Recall the economic definition of business method inventions as new commercial techniques that firms can apply to realize market opportunities. Some business method inventions are purely commercial discoveries without any associated scientific and technological inventions. However, other business method inventions commercialize scientific and technological inventions that might not otherwise leave the laboratory or the university. By identifying market opportunities and the technologies needed to address them, business method inventions provide applications for some types of scientific and technological inventions. Constraining IP protections for business methods would reduce the economic returns to commercial discoveries — affecting not only business method inventions but also the scientific and technological inventions that they commercialize. Inventors of business methods might present some types of discoveries as ICT inventions or perhaps limit the commercial claims of ICT inventions.

3.3.1. *Business Method Inventions and the Commercialization of Scientific and Technological Discoveries*

A package of Wrigley's chewing gum crossed a bar code scanner at Marsh's Supermarket in Troy, Ohio, in June 1974, beginning a major transformation of retail and wholesale transactions. The Universal Product Code (UPC) and bar code scanners are important business method inventions because they automate transactions. They replace workers' efforts with capital equipment in the supply of commercial transactions. In only two years after the first product with the UPC symbol was purchased, over three-quarters of supermarket products carried the symbol.[108] The use of UPC codes spread quickly to other consumer goods industries such as clothing, household products, and toys and to commercial and industrial products.

Joseph Woodland and Bernard Silver obtained the first patent for a bar code on October 7, 1952. Their early conception of a bar code was a drawing of a bull's-eye pattern with the thickness of the rings conveying product information.[109] The patent is for a "classifying apparatus and method," so it involved both a machine and a business method.[110] The bar code patent states that "it is the object of the invention to provide an automatic apparatus that will execute with precision and dispatch classifying orders which are given to it and will yield up the results of the classifying process in an intelligible manner."[111] The patent specifically mentions supermarkets although it is not limited to that application. The patent also includes a description of equipment to read the bar code, allowing the processing and utilization of the information it conveys.

The combination of bar coding and scanner technology provides a useful illustration of a business method invention. The invention is much more than a combination of an information storage process (the bar code itself) and a reader (the scanner). In itself, the storage-reader technology would constitute an ICT invention. However, the discovery is a business method invention because it changes the way business is conducted. The invention identifies a market opportunity and provides a commercial technique that greatly improves economic efficiency for practically any retail or wholesale transaction.

Bar codes speed customers through the checkout counter, providing convenience for consumers and increasing the productivity of cashiers. Customers receive detailed receipts that identify the products that are purchased. Product data from bar codes are used to provide marketing promotions and targeted discounts. Bar codes also reduce the cost to merchants of generating information used to track sales patterns and to update inventories. Better inventory control reduces the costs of carrying inventory and improves the match between inventories and customer demands, thus enhancing immediacy. Bar codes also lower the costs of price adjustment for retailers and wholesalers, because prices can be posted on store shelves and adjusted on the firm's cash registers and databases. Moreover, the information generated at the checkout counter changes retailers' relationships with wholesalers and manufacturers, allowing them to exchange sales data electronically. Bar coding underlies automated ordering and billing systems that are used in Internet transactions.

By the end of the 1990s, over eighty countries had organizations that issued product codes.[112] UPC codes and scanner technology, together with related advances in information technology, are used by small retailers, supermarket chains, and large discount retailers, such as Walmart, Costco, and Target. UPC codes and scanner technology also are employed by shipping firms, such as UPS and Federal Express, for tracking packages and by manufacturing companies for identifying parts, components, and materials. UPC codes and scanners also facilitate information exchange between companies.

The bar code patent illustrates how some business method inventions commercialize scientific or technological discoveries. The bar code invention includes both a business process discovery and an ICT discovery. The business process discovery is a way to utilize digital codes to identify objects. The ICT discovery is a way to represent information that can be read by a machine and the design of a machine that can read the digital code. The bar code invention is much more than either a way to index objects or an ICT discovery of a process for information storage and retrieval. It is the combination of the process for indexing objects and the system of information storage and retrieval that makes this particular business method invention so significant. Taken together, these ideas revolutionize all manner of transactions because they allow firms to automate the handling of almost any type of object, whether it is a retail or wholesale product being exchanged, a product being inventoried, a product being shipped, or an input or an output produced or used in a factory.

The commercial technique is vital to the bar code invention; without it, the ICT discovery might not be useful or interesting. Presenting the bar code invention as an ICT discovery would limit disclosure and reduce the breadth of the patent. The *Bilski* court's question about whether business methods should be patentable may reflect the relatively early state of the art of those business method inventions that involve applications of ICT discoveries. Such controversies are to be expected with new categories of technology; consider earlier debates over the patentability of computer software. In 1999, *State Street* removed the business method exception in the course of addressing controversies in software patentability.[113]

The Business Revolution, as will be shown in a later section, is driven in large part by business methods inventions that involve applications of ICT discoveries. In e-commerce, there is a wide range of hardware and software technologies that are specific to business methods.[114] An e-commerce website requires a logical design that specifies the flow of information and a physical design that identifies the software, computer hardware, and communications requirements.[115] Many large traditional retailers built their own sites that made use of their in-house IT personnel, databases, and telecommunications systems.[116] Identifying the extensive set of packaged software tools and pre-built website templates, Kenneth Laudon and Carol Traver caution that building your own e-commerce website is difficult and costly and risks duplicating what has already been invented by other firms.[117]

Some types of business method inventions involve applications of previous scientific inventions to the development of new products, services, transactions, market designs, production processes, components, materials, and organizations. Many scientific and technological inventions will not reach the market unless they are commercialized; they will remain in the laboratory or the university. Inventors and adopters will not reap the benefits of scientific and technological discoveries without the efforts of entrepreneurs and intermediaries. Developing new business methods need not require delivering scientific and technological inventions to the market place. However, the commercialization of scientific and technological inventions often requires delivery by new business methods. Therefore, constraining the development of new business methods would likely impact the commercialization of scientific and technological discoveries.

The close interconnection between business method inventions and ICT discoveries is evident from a review of the top patentees in category 705. Table 3.1 shows patentees with ten or more patents in this category.

Table 3.1: Patent ownership is determined by the first-named assignee listed on a patent. USPTO, Patent Technology Monitoring Team (PTMT), Patenting In Technology Classes, Breakout By Organization Count of 2011–2015 Utility Patent Grants, By Calendar Year of Grant With Patent Counts Based on Primary Patent Classification, Rank-Ordered Listing of Organizations Receiving 5 or More Utility Patents During the Period Having Primary Classification In Class 705, DP: Financial, Business Practice, Management, or Cost/Price Determination (Data Processing).

The following table displays first-named assignees and counts of their associated patents, as distributed by the year of patent grant.

First-named assignee	2011	2012	2013	2014	2015	Total
~INDIVIDUALLY OWNED PATENT	404	480	556	394	176	2010
INTERNATIONAL BUSINESS MACHINES CORPORATION	237	263	258	195	114	1067
GOOGLE, INC.	38	96	167	139	79	519
AMAZON TECHNOLOGIES, INC.	71	103	151	108	68	501
SAP AKTIENGESELLSCHAFT	84	91	133	80	15	403
EBAY INC.	62	64	112	93	38	369
BANK OF AMERICA CORPORATION	39	69	131	86	41	366
TRADING TECHNOLOGIES INTERNATIONAL, INC.	59	76	91	78	7	311
MICROSOFT CORPORATION	62	87	82	75	4	310
INTUIT, INC.	64	69	77	47	18	275

(*Continued*)

Table 3.1: (*Continued*)

First-named assignee	2011	2012	2013	2014	2015	Total
AMERICAN EXPRESS TRAVEL RELATED SERVICES COMPANY, INC.	76	71	67	39	15	268
JP MORGAN CHASE BANK, N.A.	44	53	78	63	10	248
UNITED SERVICES AUTOMOBILE ASSOCIATION (USAA)	57	55	70	50	15	247
ACCENTURE GLOBAL SERVICES LIMITED	52	53	42	51	13	211
AT& T INTELLECTUAL PROPERTY I, L.P.	31	48	58	48	23	208
YAHOO, INC.	36	36	49	40	21	182
HARTFORD FIRE INSURANCE COMPANY	30	40	47	51	7	175
VISA U.S.A., INC.	24	25	48	57	13	167
CHICAGO MERCANTILE EXCHANGE, INC.	25	42	50	42	2	161
HEWLETT-PACKARD DEVELOPMENT COMPANY, L.P.	47	42	37	23	12	161
ORACLE INTERNATIONAL CORPORATION	25	30	27	35	15	132
GOLDMAN, SACHS & CO.	29	32	41	16	5	123
SONY CORPORATION	21	28	24	31	17	121
VISA INTERNATIONAL SERVICE ASSOCIATION	12	18	38	36	12	116
SPRINT COMMUNICATIONS COMPANY L.P.	26	32	24	23	9	114
BGC PARTNERS, INC.	24	28	33	16	1	102
XEROX CORPORATION	18	23	27	24	9	101
MASTERCARD INTERNATIONAL, INC.	6	14	25	38	15	98
CERNER INNOVATION, INC.	19	22	24	25	4	94
WESTERN UNION COMPANY	25	12	30	20	4	91
APPLE, INC.	7	21	17	26	13	84
GENERAL ELECTRIC COMPANY	19	17	19	24	5	84

Table 3.1: (*Continued*)

First-named assignee	2011	2012	2013	2014	2015	Total
INVENTION SCIENCE FUND I, LLC	10	30	18	16	6	80
FIRST DATA CORPORATION	22	12	19	17	4	74
PITNEY-BOWES, INC.	27	12	13	6	7	65
UNITED STATES OF AMERICA, POSTAL SERVICE	12	21	13	14	3	63
VERIZON PATENT AND LICENSING, INC.	3	3	17	19	16	58
CFPH, L.L.C.	11	13	16	14	3	57
UNITED PARCEL SERVICE OF AMERICA, INC.	14	11	13	13	6	57
BOEING COMPANY	6	16	13	13	6	54
FACEBOOK, INC.	3	5	15	16	12	51
SIEMENS AKTIENGESELLSCHAFT	11	14	11	7	8	51
RICOH COMPANY, LTD.	9	15	7	9	10	50
WELLS FARGO BANK, N.A.	12	10	12	10	5	49
ALLSTATE INSURANCE COMPANY	9	9	9	19	2	48
ITG SOFTWARE SOLUTIONS, INC.	8	14	11	14	0	47
NCR CORPORATION	5	10	11	13	8	47
TARGET BRANDS, INC.	6	11	15	8	7	47
WALKER DIGITAL, LLC	16	15	14	1	0	46
SAMSUNG ELECTRONICS CO., LTD.	4	14	8	9	10	45
WALGREEN CO.	8	15	9	12	0	44
FEDERAL HOME LOAN MORTGAGE CORP.	14	10	12	6	1	43
STAMPS.COM, INC.	10	10	12	8	3	43
WAL-MART STORES, INC.	0	0	3	21	19	43
FANNIE MAE	21	6	7	7	0	41
ISLAND INTELLECTUAL PROPERTY LLC	5	9	21	6	0	41
SAS INSTITUTE, INC.	14	10	8	9	0	41
SIEBEL SYSTEMS, INC.	12	7	14	8	0	41

(*Continued*)

Table 3.1: (*Continued*)

First-named assignee	2011	2012	2013	2014	2015	Total
FMR LLC	8	9	7	14	2	40
FUJITSU LIMITED	13	8	9	9	1	40
THE NIELSEN COMPANY (U.S.), L.L.C.	3	10	16	8	3	40
ADOBE SYSTEMS INCORPORATED	5	5	6	17	6	39
AMAZON.COM, INC.	12	14	9	4	0	39
CAPITAL ONE FINANCIAL CORPORATION	7	6	13	8	5	39
METABANK	4	18	11	5	1	39
MCKESSON FINANCIAL HOLDINGS LIMITED	6	3	14	13	2	38
THE PNC FINANCIAL SERVICES GROUP, INC.	9	7	17	4	1	38
JDA SOFTWARE GROUP, INC.	4	11	14	4	4	37
CATALINA MARKETING CORPORATION	7	7	11	9	1	35
CHICAGO BOARD OPTIONS EXCHANGE, INCORPORATED	4	15	10	6	0	35
MORGAN STANLEY	16	9	5	5	0	35
SIEMENS MEDICAL SOLUTIONS USA, INC.	11	9	7	7	0	34
THE NASDAQ OMX GROUP, INC.	13	14	5	0	2	34
AT& T INTELLECTUAL PROPERTY II, L.P.	7	6	6	12	2	33
SIGNATURE SYSTEMS, LLC	3	5	18	6	1	33
AVAYA INC.	6	7	12	4	3	32
FAIR ISAAC CORPORATION	10	9	5	8	0	32
CISCO TECHNOLOGY, INC.	5	3	11	4	8	31
MICROSOFT TECHNOLOGY LICENSING, LLC.	0	0	0	0	31	31
OPEN INVENTION NETWORK, LLC	4	4	7	10	6	31
EXPERIAN INFORMATION SOLUTIONS, INC.	10	5	5	8	1	29

Table 3.1: (*Continued*)

First-named assignee	2011	2012	2013	2014	2015	Total
TOSHIBA CORPORATION	6	9	4	6	4	29
EWINWIN, INC.	1	12	7	7	1	28
QUALCOMM, INC.	3	2	7	9	7	28
BARCLAYS CAPITAL INC.	11	4	6	6	0	27
DELL PRODUCTS, L.P.	6	5	7	5	4	27
STATE FARM MUTUAL AUTOMOBILE INSURANCE COMPANY	0	0	4	11	12	27
TOSHIBA GLOBAL COMMERCE SOLUTIONS HOLDINGS CORPORATION	0	4	12	7	4	27
VERSATA DEVELOPMENT GROUP, INC.	7	8	4	6	2	27
EBS GROUP LIMITED	10	9	3	4	0	26
INTEL CORPORATION	2	6	8	6	4	26
PANASONIC CORPORATION	8	6	7	3	2	26
PAYPAL. INC.	3	6	3	2	12	26
WEST CORPORATION	3	11	6	5	1	26
AMADEUS S.A.S.	2	9	6	6	2	25
CANON KABUSHIKI KAISHA	6	6	8	3	1	24
MEDCO HEALTH SOLUTIONS, INC.	5	5	11	3	0	24
TELEFONAKTIEBOLAGET L M ERICSSON (PUBL.)	3	3	6	9	3	24
BOKU, INC.	0	3	9	7	4	23
CHARLES SCHWAB & CO., INC.	7	4	5	7	0	23
HEALTH HERO NETWORK, INC.	21	1	1	0	0	23
HITACHI, LTD	6	5	5	6	1	23
NOKIA CORPORATION	2	5	4	10	2	23
SYMANTEC CORPORATION	6	4	3	6	4	23
ALCATEL LUCENT	1	9	8	3	1	22
AMDOCS SOFTWARE SYSTEMS LIMITED	3	5	8	4	2	22

(*Continued*)

Table 3.1: (*Continued*)

First-named assignee	2011	2012	2013	2014	2015	Total
CITICORP DEVELOPMENT CENTER, INC.	4	6	9	3	0	22
CONTENTGUARD HOLDINGS, INC.	5	7	6	4	0	22
PIPELINE FINANCIAL GROUP, INC.	16	6	0	0	0	22
ACCENTURE GLOBAL SERVICES GMBH	10	5	4	2	0	21
AOL LLC	7	3	5	3	3	21
ARIBA, INC.	5	3	7	6	0	21
PRUDENTIAL INSURANCE COMPANY OF AMERICA	4	4	8	5	0	21
CITICORP CREDIT SERVICES, INC.	3	4	7	4	2	20
NINTENDO OF AMERICA INC.	2	6	5	6	1	20
AMERICAN AIRLINES, INC.	2	5	3	7	2	19
CBS INTERACTIVE, INC.	3	6	4	5	1	19
CERTUSVIEW TECHNOLOGIES, LLC	0	0	11	2	6	19
HEALTHTRIO LLC	2	6	7	4	0	19
INFOSYS LIMITED	0	1	7	8	3	19
SALESFORCE.COM, INC.	1	4	4	8	2	19
SWISS REINSURANCE COMPANY LTD.	4	7	5	3	0	19
AMERICAN WELL INC.	8	1	7	2	0	18
CA, INC.	0	0	6	7	5	18
CATERPILLAR INC.	2	8	3	3	2	18
ENPULZ, LLC	0	1	5	7	5	18
ICAP SERVICES NORTH AMERICA LLC	4	5	7	1	1	18
NEOPOST TECHNOLOGIES	9	2	3	1	3	18
TOSHIBA TEC KABUSHIKI KAISHA	3	3	7	3	2	18
VERINT AMERICAS INC.	5	7	3	2	1	18
YELLOWPAGES.COM LLC	0	0	0	5	13	18
AT& T MOBILITY II LLC	2	2	3	2	8	17
KONINKLIJKE PHILIPS N.V.	0	0	5	7	5	17

Table 3.1: *(Continued)*

First-named assignee	2011	2012	2013	2014	2015	Total
PALO ALTO RESEARCH CENTER INCORPORATED	1	4	2	8	2	17
THE CRAWFORD GROUP, INC.	1	6	6	4	0	17
TRUECAR, INC.	1	1	7	3	5	17
ALIBABA GROUP HOLDING LIMITED	1	4	2	6	3	16
CITIBANK N.A.	3	4	3	4	2	16
CONSUMERINFO.COM, INC.	2	4	3	4	3	16
DIGIMARC CORPORATION	2	4	5	3	2	16
EPIC SYSTEMS CORPORATION	2	3	4	5	2	16
HOSPIRA, INC.	3	0	5	7	1	16
INVENTOR HOLDINGS, LLC	0	0	1	14	1	16
KONINKLIJKE PHILIPS ELECTRONICS N.V.	4	6	5	0	1	16
NHN BUSINESS PLATFORM CORPORATION	6	4	2	3	1	16
RAKUTEN, INC.	0	1	2	8	5	16
RAYTHEON COMPANY	6	5	2	3	0	16
SQUARE, INC.	0	0	4	2	10	16
SYNCADA LLC.	4	2	5	5	0	16
TICKETMASTER L.L.C.	6	2	6	2	0	16
ALIGN TECHNOLOGY, INC.	7	4	1	3	0	15
CAREFUSION 303 INC.	2	3	3	4	3	15
COMPUTER SCIENCES CORPORATION	12	2	1	0	0	15
DIGITAL RIVER, INC.	2	8	3	1	1	15
EXPRESS SCRIPTS, INC.	1	4	2	7	1	15
RED HAT, INC.	1	1	5	3	5	15
UTBK, INC.	5	7	3	0	0	15
CANTOR INDEX LLC	5	2	4	3	0	14
MEDAPPS, INC.	0	14	0	0	0	14

(Continued)

Table 3.1: (*Continued*)

First-named assignee	2011	2012	2013	2014	2015	Total
PROMONTORY INTERFINANCIAL NETWORK, LLC	8	2	2	2	0	14
QURIO HOLDINGS, INC.	3	1	6	1	3	14
REARDEN COMMERCE, INC.	7	5	2	0	0	14
TEXTURA CORPORATION	6	6	1	1	0	14
THE VANGUARD GROUP, INC.	3	6	2	3	0	14
YODLEE.COM, INC.	4	5	3	1	1	14
A9.COM, INC.	2	2	4	3	2	13
ACS STATE & LOCAL SOLUTIONS, INC.	3	5	3	2	0	13
CHECKFREE CORPORATION	9	2	1	1	0	13
CORELOGIC SOLUTIONS, LLC	0	0	8	3	2	13
EXPERIAN MARKETING SOLUTIONS, INC.	2	6	2	3	0	13
FISERV INCORPORATED	0	3	3	7	0	13
FUJI XEROX CO., LTD.	2	4	1	4	2	13
GUIDEWIRE SOFTWARE, INC.	1	1	6	5	0	13
HONDA GIKEN KOGYO KABUSHIKI KAISHA (HONDA MOTOR CO., LTD.)	1	8	3	1	0	13
HUMANA INC.	1	6	2	4	0	13
INTERNATIONAL GAME TECHNOLOGY (IGT)	3	2	3	3	2	13
LG ELECTRONICS INC.	4	3	3	3	0	13
NIKE, INC.	2	1	7	3	0	13
NUANCE COMMUNICATIONS, INC.	0	2	0	7	4	13
OMX TECHNOLOGY AB	2	2	6	3	0	13
OPTUMINSIGHT, INC.	0	3	3	5	2	13
PROGRESSIVE CASUALTY INSURANCE COMPANY	1	4	4	2	2	13
SCHLUMBERGER TECHNOLOGY CORPORATION	2	3	1	5	2	13
SEIKO EPSON CORPORATION	2	7	1	2	1	13

Table 3.1: (*Continued*)

First-named assignee	2011	2012	2013	2014	2015	Total
THE BANK OF NEW YORK MELLON CORPORATION	1	7	3	2	0	13
VIRTUAL RADIOLOGIC CORPORATION	2	6	4	1	0	13
W.W. GRAINGER, INC.	1	4	4	3	1	13
CARDINALCOMMERCE CORPORATION	1	4	0	7	0	12
CONCEPT HEDGING, LLC	0	3	7	2	0	12
CREDIBILITY CORP.	0	0	4	3	5	12
DISCOVERY HOLDINGS LIMITED	3	5	3	1	0	12
E-2 INTERACTIVE, INC.	0	4	3	5	0	12
EMC CORPORATION	3	1	5	2	1	12
FUJIFILM CORPORATION	3	2	3	4	0	12
GROUPON, INC.	0	5	3	3	1	12
METAVANTE CORPORATION	2	3	2	5	0	12
MYMEDICALRECORDS, INC.	0	4	3	5	0	12
PALANTIR TECHNOLOGIES, INC.	1	1	2	3	5	12
PRICELINE.COM, INC.	3	5	1	3	0	12
SHARP KABUSHIKI KAISHA (SHARP CORPORATION)	1	7	2	1	1	12
SMART OPTIONS, LLC	0	2	2	1	7	12
SONY COMPUTER ENTERTAINMENT AMERICA LLC	0	2	3	5	2	12
TOUCHTUNES MUSIC CORPORATION	0	4	2	1	5	12
VERIZON BUSINESS GLOBAL LLC	2	5	3	2	0	12
VIDEOMINING CORPORATION	5	1	3	3	0	12
ALTISOURCE SOLUTIONS S.A.R.L.	2	3	5	1	0	11
AMERIPRISE FINANCIAL, INC.	2	2	4	3	0	11
DISNEY ENTERPRISES, INC.	2	0	2	5	2	11
MILLENNIAL MEDIA, INC. (MARYLAND)	0	0	1	7	3	11

(*Continued*)

Table 3.1: (*Continued*)

First-named assignee	2011	2012	2013	2014	2015	Total
ORACLE AMERICA, INC.	1	2	4	3	1	11
PROPULSION REMOTE HOLDINGS, LLC	0	2	4	5	0	11
SCIQUEST, INC.	3	2	1	4	1	11
SEARS BRANDS, LLC	1	1	3	3	3	11
SILVERBROOK RESEARCH PTY. LTD	7	4	0	0	0	11
STUBHUB, INC.	3	3	3	2	0	11
TERADATA US, INC.	4	4	2	1	0	11
THOMSON REUTERS GLOBAL RESOURCES	2	2	3	3	1	11
TRIZETTO GROUP, INC.	2	6	3	0	0	11
ALMOND NET, INC.	1	5	2	1	1	10
AOL ADVERTISING INC.	1	3	3	2	1	10
APOLLO ENTERPRISE SOLUTIONS, INC.	0	1	5	4	0	10
BLACKBERRY LIMITED	0	0	1	6	3	10
BRANCH BANKING AND TRUST COMPANY	1	1	4	4	0	10
BROADCOM CORPORATION	3	1	1	3	2	10
CELLCO PARTNERSHIP	0	1	2	4	3	10
COCA-COLA COMPANY	1	3	0	4	2	10
CUMMINS-ALLISON CORPORATION	3	2	3	0	2	10
EMPIRE TECHNOLOGY DEVELOPMENT LLC	0	1	2	4	3	10
GENERAL MOTORS LLC	3	2	2	2	1	10
GENWORTH FINANCIAL, INC.	5	1	4	0	0	10
HEAVY HAMMER, INC.	3	3	3	1	0	10
I2 TECHNOLOGIES US, INC.	10	0	0	0	0	10
KAPSCH TRAFFICCOM AG	1	2	4	3	0	10
KING FAHD UNIVERSITY OF PETROLEUM AND MINERALS	2	2	3	1	2	10
MONEYGRAM INTERNATIONAL, INC.	1	0	2	6	1	10

Table 3.1: (*Continued*)

First-named assignee	2011	2012	2013	2014	2015	Total
PROCTER + GAMBLE COMPANY	3	5	0	1	1	10
THE DIRECTV GROUP, INC.	2	1	2	2	3	10
THE TRAVELERS INDEMNITY COMPANY	2	3	2	3	0	10
UAT, INC.	2	4	3	1	0	10

Source: https://www.uspto.gov/web/offices/ac/ido/oeip/taf/tecasg/705_torg.htm.

The dominance of computer software and electronics companies in this list provides an indication of the technological aspects of business method patents. The legal debate about patenting business methods depends on how the USPTO and the courts treat business applications of ICT discoveries. Determining whether or not business method inventions are patentable will in turn affect the commercialization of many underlying ICT discoveries.

3.3.2. *Business Method Inventions and Entrepreneurship*

Entrepreneurs implement business method inventions by establishing new firms that use the inventions. Entrepreneurship provides an important market outlet for independent inventors who can either transfer their inventions to specialized entrepreneurs or become entrepreneurs themselves and embody their inventions in new firms. Entrepreneurship thus gives independent inventors an alternative to transferring technology to existing firms. This helps to explain Schumpeter's identification of entrepreneurs as important agents of innovation.

Elsewhere, I introduce a dynamic theory of the entrepreneur. During the period of entrepreneurship, the entrepreneur's consumption and savings decisions are difficult to separate from the business decisions of the startup.[118] This interconnection is due to financing constraints that result from asymmetric information and capital market imperfections. Separation occurs only with the end of entrepreneurship when the start-up's growth, technological development, and financing allow the launch of the new firm. I refer to this milestone as the "foundational shift."

Because of the interconnections between the entrepreneur and the startup, it is difficult in practice to distinguish the entrepreneur's IP from that of the startup.[119]

In evaluating the interactions between IP and entrepreneurship, a major study conducted by Graham *et al.* provides valuable guidance.[120] They analyze the results of the Berkeley Patent Survey of 2008 that examines 1,332 early-stage technology companies founded since 1998. To focus on innovation, they target their survey to chief executive officers (CEOs), presidents, and chief technology officers (CTOs). They discover a highly interesting connection between invention and entrepreneurship: "it is common for startups' patents to originate with founders prior to the company's founding date. Such patents may first issue to founders (as individuals, with no initial corporate assignee) and only later be assigned to the company."[121] Graham *et al.* find that patent ownership is more widespread among new firms than previously reported, although many startups do not hold patents. When startups patent, "they are often seeking competitive advantage, and the associated goals of preventing technology copying, securing financing, and enhancing reputation."[122] The main factors explaining patenting by startups include

> preventing others from copying products or services; improving the chances of securing investment; obtaining licensing revenues; improving the chances/quality of liquidity (e.g., acquisition/IPO); preventing patent infringement actions against the company; improving the company's negotiating position with other companies (e.g., cross-licensing); and enhancing the company's reputation/product image.[123]

Their study finds substantial differences in the effects of patents across the economy with patents being more common in health-related sectors (biotechnology and medical devices) and less common in software and Internet. However, startups with venture capital financing tend to hold more patents than startups with other types of funding. Startups primarily forgo patenting due to the legal costs of obtaining and defending patents, suggesting that improvements in the effectiveness of the patent system would be beneficial to entrepreneurs. Graham *et al.* also find that startups license technology from others in order to gain knowledge and settle IP disputes, highlighting the role of entrepreneurs in the commercialization and implementation of inventions.[124]

In creating startups and establishing firms, entrepreneurs commercialize both business method inventions and other types of scientific and technological inventions. Simcoe *et al.* find that "Entrepreneurs often develop innovations that are only valuable as part of a larger platform, such as the Internet, the personal computer or the cellular phone network."[125] Simcoe *et al.* show that entrepreneurial entrants' IP strategies differ from those of large established firms. Entrepreneurs may have an interest in protecting platform standards to earn rents, while larger existing firms may prefer more open standards that yield returns to their complementary assets. Their empirical results suggest that patents are important to entrepreneurs and to the division of innovation labor in markets.[126]

An inventor can become an entrepreneur and innovate by embodying inventions in new firms. Alternatively, an inventor can enter the market for ideas by transferring his invention to an intermediary, a prospective entrepreneur, or an existing firm. IP rules affect entrepreneurship in fundamental ways because they impact the inventor's choice between technology transfer and entrepreneurship. IP rules that penalize or reward one of these options will bias market outcomes and lead to economic inefficiency. The result may be too much or too little entrepreneurship, with too much entrepreneurship resulting in costly creative destruction and too little entrepreneurship reducing competition and favoring incumbent firms.

Own-use of inventions through entrepreneurship may provide the inventor with greater IP protections because there is no need to disclose the invention to potential buyers and the inventor can protect the discovery from business rivals through secrecy. The inventor encounters costs of keeping the secret and faces the risk of independent invention but benefits from avoiding copying and expropriation.[127] The alternative of entrepreneurship also raises the inventor's bargaining power in dealing with existing firms. Because the inventor can use the invention by starting a firm and competing with the existing firm, entrepreneurship provides a threat point in bargaining with the existing firm. Even if entrepreneurship does not occur at the market equilibrium, the possibility of entrepreneurship affects the incentives to invent for both the independent inventor and the existing firm.[128] When entrepreneurial entrants offer differentiated products, competition between the entrant and existing firms is mitigated, which can induce inventors to choose entrepreneurship over technology transfer.[129]

Strategic interactions between inventors and existing firms result in cooperation or competition. When an inventor and an existing firm cooperate, the inventor transfers the invention and accompanying technology to the existing firm. Alternatively, the inventor becomes an entrepreneur and establishes a firm that competes with existing firms. Entrepreneurship in existing industries entails creative destruction as the new firm competes with incumbent firms. Competition from new firms often causes existing firms to decline or to exit entirely, although some incumbent firms are stimulated by the competition. Creative destruction is socially efficient if there are net benefits from the entry and growth of new firms and the concurrent displacement of existing firms.

The relationship between IP and entrepreneurship is complex. Improvements in legal protections for IP in the market for technology transfer can reduce entrepreneurship that would occur as a means of realizing the value of IP. Without adequate IP, the risk of imitation or expropriation reduces the expected returns that the innovator could obtain by attempting to transfer the technology to the existing firm. Better IP protections increase the expected returns to contracting, making technology transfer relatively more attractive in comparison with entrepreneurship, which reduces the supply of entrepreneurs. However, IP protections reduce the need for existing firms to rely on corporate R&D, allowing them to outsource innovation to new firms. By decreasing the transaction costs of cooperation between existing firms and new firms, IP protections increase incentives for entrepreneurs to establish firms that develop, sell, and license technology. This increases opportunities for entrepreneurs who establish new firms that help to commercialize and implement business method inventions. In this way, IP protections increase the likelihood of innovative entrepreneurship. IP protections for business method inventions promote efficiency in the transfer of these discoveries and in the establishment of firms by entrepreneurs.

3.4 Efficiency Arguments in Favor of Patenting Business Method Inventions and Response to the Critics

Patenting of business method inventions serves to promote dynamic, allocative, and transaction efficiency. Concerns regarding legal and administrative costs should not be sufficient to prevent patenting of business method inventions. Many of the arguments made against business method patents are generic; they are the same as those made against patents generally. To examine whether business method inventions should be patented, it is useful to consider the purpose of patents. Administrative patent awards clearly differ from property rights for physical property such as land. Patent awards require a government agency, the USPTO, to examine the scientific and technical details of the invention. Inventors must apply for the patent and satisfy a complex administrative process. Before awarding a patent, examiners must determine whether the invention is useful, novel, and non-obvious. Patents are of limited duration, in contrast to tangible property. Patents convey a right to exclude others, but that exclusion and the application of the patented technology are subject to various legal challenges from other inventors. The patent owner must successfully defend against possible charges of infringement and must obtain redress should infringement arise. Patent litigation can involve difficult scientific and technical issues, whether or not the patent at issue involves business method inventions. This section presents efficiency arguments in favor of patenting business method inventions and responds to the academic critics of business method patenting.

3.4.1. *Patenting of Business Method Inventions Promotes Dynamic Efficiency in the Market for Discoveries*

A system of IP rights promotes *dynamic efficiency* when it generates valuable discoveries in a cost-effective manner. By providing rights to exclude others, IP rights provide incentives to inventors to engage in discovery.[130] When inventors obtain returns to invention, they have incentives to develop better inventions and supply them to the marketplace. Society benefits from valuable scientific and technological discoveries so that a system of IP rights generates social benefits.[131] The returns to inventions provide incentives to inventors to direct their talents and creative capabilities toward promising areas for discoveries and to invest costly resources in R&D, so as to generate useful inventions.

Property rights generate dynamic efficiencies because they provide incentives to invest in productive activities to supply the market place. The benefits of property rights are encouragement of production, not investment in itself — *incentives from property rights should reward outputs, not inputs*. It is well known that property rights, whether in land or technology, create incentives to make investments that may produce useful output. For example, property rights to mineral resources once produced generate investments in exploration and drilling. However, the property rights should encourage the production of mineral resources; investment in the production of resources is not an end in itself. Not all investment in drilling produces resources; dry holes are a common phenomenon. Simply investing in drilling at any random location is costly but not necessarily beneficial.

Similarly, IP rights generate dynamic efficiencies by providing incentives to produce better inventions in an efficient manner. Investment in R&D should never be the goal; it is at best a means to an end. High levels of investment in R&D projects that will not generate useful inventions are not desirable; intellectual dry holes are never valuable no matter how much it costs to drill them. Conversely, it is desirable to obtain valuable inventions even if it costs practically nothing to develop them. It is better to explore where resources are located; intellectually rich areas are valuable even when costs of production are low. Never mind that high levels of investment may fail to generate interesting or useful inventions, while inexpensive creative efforts may generate inventions of great value.

The dynamic efficiencies created by IP rights have been misunderstood or mischaracterized by some commentators. These commentators assert that the IP rights exist to promote investment in R&D, not useful inventions. Confusion between inputs and outputs is evident in the IP literature and yields precisely the wrong policy conclusions. For example, Alan Devlin and Neel Sukhatme argue for a cost-based system of property rights:

> Optimally, property rights should be awarded in a parsimonious manner, awarding deserving inventors just enough proprietary control over their

> discoveries to compensate them for the risk, capital, and opportunity cost expended ex ante.[132]

Also arguing for rewarding inputs rather than outputs, Burk and Lemley suggest that courts should distinguish among industries in providing patent protection on the basis of the costs of invention:

> The systematic variation in R&D expenditures across industries naturally affects the need for patent protection. Industries that must spend more time and money in R&D generally have a greater need for patent protection in order to recoup that investment. That doesn't mean that the patent system has no place for cheaper inventions; they may still facilitate market transactions in new innovations. But it means that certain industries have a stronger claim than others to need the incentives patents provide.[133]

Burk and Lemley maintain that because of the public-goods nature of invention, "patent protection will be more important in industries that require a large investment in R&D than in industries that don't need such an investment."[134] They also argue that "Industries that must spend more time and money in R&D generally have a greater need for patent protection in order to recoup that investment."[135] They conclude on the basis of R&D costs that patent protections should be lower in information technology (IT) than in other industries: "the appropriate policy levers for the IT industry differ rather dramatically from those that were appropriate in the biotechnology or pharmaceutical industries."[136]

The notion that patents should be based on recouping investment is a public utilities view of invention. Somehow, inventors produce inventions like an electric utility produces power, and should receive compensation from regulated rates reflecting the risk and capital. Even if the process of investment were a mechanical process similar to electric power generation, it is well known that paying for investment leads to inefficient production, high costs, and gold-plated facilities. The same is true for invention: paying for investment will inevitably lead to inefficient R&D, high costs, and gold-plated laboratories. The result of such rewards would be "big science" similar to projects sponsored by large corporations and the government. An example of such big science is the ill-fated particle accelerator known as the Superconducting Super Collider that was to have been built in Texas. Offering debatable scientific returns, the accelerator would have had a ring circumference of over 50 miles and costs that were projected at over $12 billion with the possibility of substantial cost overruns.

But R&D is the result of creative effort, not a mechanical process with results based on the size of inputs. How would policymakers determine who are "deserving inventors"? This approach to public policy quickly leads to public procurement of R&D with government officials determining who the deserving inventors are, that is, bureaucrats picking winners. The result is industrial policy with government agencies choosing the direction of R&D, the level of investment, and awarding contracts on the basis of grant proposals. The inevitable criteria for government funding will be the costs of projects, not their benefits. This contrasts with market-based rewards for R&D that are based on the benefits of projects, not their costs.

Devlin and Sukhatme not only suggest rewarding investment in R&D rather than outcomes but they also recommend disqualifying from patent protections those "inventions that are consumed by the inventors themselves."[137] They assert that "Most 'self-consumed' inventions would be crafted regardless of whether the patent system existed. That is because the innate utility of these inventions drives inventors to create them in the first place."[138] Devlin and Sukhatme recommend that the Supreme Court "should reconcile the patentable subject matter inquiry with patent law's utilitarian roots by denying patentability to internal business methods."[139] This misguided policy recommendation would not only discourage in-house R&D by existing firms but it would also discourage inventors from engaging in entrepreneurship, which would in turn discourage many inventors from inventing for the purpose of entrepreneurship. In-house R&D by firms and invention by prospective entrepreneurs certainly cover a substantial share of inventive activity.

Based on the same conceptual error — rewarding R&D investment rather than inventions — these commentators would penalize creativity and inspiration. Devlin and Sukhatme would disqualify "'eureka' inventions — those that are discovered in a flash of brilliance rather than preceded by capital-intensive endeavors. There is some reason to believe that such ad hoc discoveries, immensely valuable to society as they might be, would be invented anyway even if they did not receive patent protection."[140] Devlin and Sukhatme admit that denying IP rights based on creativity would be impractical. Imagine inventors seeking patents by demonstrating that they were not inspired when making their inventions.[141] Similarly, Burk and Lemley characterize penicillin and Post-it notes as accidental inventions that should not be patented "since there is no need to encourage investment in serendipity."[142] Such policy recommendations would rule out IP protections for the many inventions that are the result of chance discoveries by well-prepared scientists.

Devlin and Sukhatme would further disqualify, if it were feasible, "discoveries that are spurred primarily by social, rather than pecuniary, incentives. Such inventions are often discovered in academic circles, where the lure of reputational gain might obviate the need for patent protection."[143] Such IP policies would rule out the extensive patenting by academic scientists and university Technology Transfer Offices. Such restrictions on patents would eliminate incentives to invent for academics. The success of the Bayh–Dole Act (35 U.S.C. 200–212) in encouraging academic technology transfer illustrates why ruling out patents for academics would be a misguided policy.

The notion that "eureka" inventions and academic inventions should not be patentable again confuses the cost of invention with the benefits of invention. The example of graphene fits the type of invention for which Devlin and Sukhatme and Burk and Lemley would wish to deny patents. Graphene was a "eureka" invention: Andre Geim and Konstantin Novoselov's method of producing graphene was startlingly simple; the inventors applied scotch tape to graphite and pulled off a thin layer. Also, graphene was an academic discovery; Geim and Novoselov were at the University of Manchester, U.K. Although Geim and Novoselov were discouraged from patenting their invention due to legal costs and the stage of development of the technology, many other scientists and firms are likely to patent inventions based on graphene.[144]

Geim and Novoselov won the Nobel Prize for Physics in 2010 for the discovery of how to produce graphene, a sheet of carbon the thickness of one atom. The Nobel Prize was based on the amazing physical properties of graphene, that is, on the benefits of the invention.[145] Not only is graphene one of the strongest materials ever discovered but it also has important properties that promise to be highly useful in superconductors and semiconductors with applications in computer chips, video screens, and many other areas. As with many inventions, the benefits of graphene bear no relation to the costs of invention.

Arguments against various forms of patents — for self-consumption, for serendipitous discoveries, and for academic inventions — reflect the view of some that patents are unnecessary because creative people would invent anyway so that dynamic efficiency is achieved without IP. The typical evidence for such an argument is that inventions have occurred in the past without the benefit of IP protections. Noting innovation and entrepreneurship in the eighteenth century, Malla Pollack finds that "The absence of business method patents cannot be explained by an absence of entrepreneurial creativity in Great Britain during the century before the American Revolution. On the contrary, 1720 is widely hailed as the beginning of a new era in English public finance and the beginning of major innovations in business organization."[146] Sharing this view, Justice Stevens writes in *Bilski*,

> Also noteworthy is what was *not* patented under the English system. During the 17th and 18th centuries, Great Britain saw innovation in business organization, business models, and management techniques, and novel solutions to the challenges of operating global firms in which subordinate managers could be reached only by a long sea voyage. Few if any of these methods of conducting business were patented.[147]

Of course, many scientific and technological inventions occurred in the past without the benefit of patents, but this would not suggest abandonment of the patent system as a whole. The reasoning should be no different for business method inventions.

Occurrence of a class of inventions without patents does not mean that inventions in that class cannot be patented in the future. Various inventions involving the wheel occurred without patents; this does not imply that inventions of machines with wheels in them are not patentable. Conversely, past awards of patents for certain types of inventions need not indicate the need to continue awarding those types of patents. Past patents for James Watt's steam engines need not require future patents for steam-powered machines. Inventions that are novel and non-obvious in one era need not be so in another. In *Bilski*, Stevens asks, "Why start patenting business methods now when we did not patent them before?"[148] Kennedy cautions, "But times change. Technology and other innovations progress in unexpected ways."[149]

Some argue that business method patents are not necessary for dynamic efficiency because markets already reward such inventions. Lemley and Burk assert that "[C]ompanies have ample incentives to develop business methods even without patent protection, because the competitive marketplace rewards companies that use more efficient business methods."[150] However, this argument could be applied generically to any type of invention; applying this argument to business methods, however defined, is highly selective and misleading. Companies have profited from inventions in science, engineering, and manufacturing techniques, including those that satisfy the machine or transformation test, without the benefit of patents. One might argue that companies have ample incentives to develop scientific and technological inventions because the marketplace rewards new products and manufacturing processes. This type of argument would suggest eliminating practically any category of patent.

Another generic objection to business method patents is that they reduce competition by increasing the market power of patent owners.[151] This objection is not specific to business method inventions, but potentially applies to scientific or technological inventions. Limits on patent length are meant to reduce the exercise of market power by patent owners of all categories. Patents generate incentives to invent by providing economic rents to their owners; market power is inherent in the generation of rents. Without exclusivity, copying the invention would dissipate economic rents. Patents also generate incentives to invent because expropriating the inventions of others is not an option. The economic rents that go to existing patent owners generate incentives to inventors to generate substitute inventions that will improve upon and possibly replace existing inventions.

3.4.2. *Patenting of Business Method Inventions Promotes Allocative Efficiency in the Market for Discoveries*

IP rights for inventions serve to provide *allocative efficiencies* in the market for discoveries. Despite their differences from physical property, patents once awarded fulfill many of the functions of property rights. IP rights for business method inventions foster the development of markets for these types of discoveries. The right to exclude allows buyers to compete to obtain inventions and sellers to compete to provide inventions. As with other types of markets, well-functioning markets for discoveries efficiently match buyers and sellers of inventions.

Markets for discoveries facilitate the commercialization of invention, which is essential for the development of economic incentives for inventors. Economic historians have examined the effects of market demand on inventive activity and find that market demand often drives technological change.[152] Commercialization based on industrialization played an essential role in stimulating inventive activity. Kenneth Sokoloff's analysis of patents demonstrates that the growth of markets induced and accelerated inventive activity during the early industrialization of America in the period 1790–1846.[153] Market demand in the United States helped to stimulate the commercialization of British technology.[154]

The interaction of demand and supply determines the market value of inventions, as with most other goods and services. The costs of invention will affect the entry of inventors, ultimately affecting the supply of inventions. The success rate of inventors in producing different but competing inventions will also affect the supply side. Elsewhere, I show how competition among inventors dissipates rents to invention and affects the equilibrium in the market for inventions.[155] It bears emphasis that allocative efficiencies are important regardless of whether the R&D process involves a flash of insight or prolonged and difficult effort. An inventor may accidentally stumble upon an invention that changes the world, such as penicillin, while others may toil long and hard to produce useless inventions. The value of inventions to buyers, the demand side of the market, is independent of the cost to suppliers of producing those inventions.[156]

Allocative efficiency in the market for discoveries requires that inventions go to the highest-value users, that is, users with the greatest willingness to pay. Consider, for example, an inventor with a discovery that has two potential buyers who value the invention at V_1 and V_2, where $V_1 > V_2$. Because IP provides the right to exclude, the inventor can provide access to the first buyer while excluding the second buyer, thereby generating a higher benefit than if the invention were sold to the second buyer. Such allocation may take place through bargaining, auctions, intermediated exchange, and other market mechanisms. With patents, the inventor will wish to assign the patent to the first buyer. This will generate the greatest social benefits as well because the first buyer obtains the greatest benefit from the invention.

Because of the nature of inventions, it may be feasible for the inventor to license the invention to both buyers. If the buyers do not compete in activities that apply the invention, then the seller will generate the greatest value by licensing to both buyers, $V_1 + V_2$. If in contrast, the two buyers compete when they apply the invention, for example, they compete in a downstream product market, their values from licensing the invention will diminish, equaling $v_1 < V_1$ and $v_2 < V_2$. Then, the efficient outcome will be either to sell the invention to the first buyer or to license the invention to both buyers, depending on whether V_1 is greater than or less than $v_1 + v_2$. The inventor allocates the invention to the group of users that obtains the greatest value. Kenneth Arrow showed that a monopoly inventor obtains greater rents from selling to downstream firms that compete with each other than from selling to a downstream monopolist.[157] This is because competitive markets generate greater rents and these can be appropriated by the inventor. Elsewhere, I show that extending patent protections internationally increases the extent of the market and thus improves the quality of inventions and their diffusion.[158]

IP rights affect the market for discoveries because of the risk of imitation or expropriation by potential buyers. Kenneth Arrow points out that selling inventions requires revealing information to potential buyers.[159] Without adequate IP protections, revealing the invention increases the likelihood that the buyer can copy or expropriate the technology.[160] Arrow observes that without property rights "the only effective monopoly would be the use of the information by the original possessor."[161] When IP protections are limited, inventors are less likely to sell or license their inventions and correspondingly are more likely to seek alternative ways to apply their inventions.

IP protections play a critical role in the commercialization of invention. This includes both the transfer of the invention itself and complementary resources. Legal protections for knowledge include licensing contracts, patents, copyrights, trademarks, and trade secrets. Knowledge can be transferred in various forms such as prototypes, technical specifications, blueprints, chemical formulas, industrial designs, business plans, software, training, and consulting. Trademarks, copyrights, and secrecy are not sufficient to protect discoveries.[162] Although patents and trade secrets are often viewed as substitutes, they are often complementary. Karl Jorda recommends that firms use a combination of patents and trade secrets to protect particular inventions.[163] Jorda further observes that a combination of patents and trade secrets is useful for technology transfer: "Hybrid patent/trade-secret agreements are also prevalent, since patent disclosures generally cover only embryonic or early stage R&D results, which are insufficient for commercializing the patented technology, absent access to collateral proprietary know-how."[164] In considering trade secrets, copyrights, trademarks, and sui generis protections, Chad King observes that "while some of them complement patent law in protecting software-related inventions, none of them can effectively replace the vital role patent law plays in protecting software."[165] Patents are designed to encourage disclosure and exchange of technology, so suggesting that companies rely on trade secrecy is precisely the opposite of the functions of an IP system.

3.4.3. *Patenting of Business Method Inventions Promotes Transaction Efficiency in the Market for Discoveries*

Patents provide transaction efficiencies by lowering the costs of transactions in markets for discoveries. IP provides a standardized form of property that serves as a foundation for markets in knowledge, inventions, and related intellectual outputs. IP rights increase commercialization by facilitating coordination among market participants, reducing the costs of market transactions, and increasing specialization though market exchange.[166] IP rights are based on more standard common law property rights rather than specialized knowledge institutions such as legal liability rules, open source projects, and government procurement.[167]

IP rights facilitate the purchase and sale of knowledge. IP rules help to address information costs in markets for discoveries.[168] Patents provide some standardization of IP rights in terms of registration, disclosure, descriptions of inventions, and legal protections. IP rights can favor outsourcing to specialized technology suppliers.[169] Patents also provide transaction efficiencies by reducing contracting costs in transferring technology.[170] Paul Heald points out that patents function as titles to property-protecting firms that acquire technology from challenges by third parties.[171]

As already noted, the patent system provides the basis for markets for the sale and licensing of patented technologies. Without patent protections, inventors will seek other means of obtaining returns, including copyrights, trademarks, and trade secrets, that may not perform as well as patents in protecting inventions. If inventors seek these other forms of IP protections because their inventions are denied patent protections, it is likely that they involve higher transactions costs than markets for patented inventions.

Business method inventions are important features of the market for discoveries. By reducing transaction costs, IP rights facilitate the decisions of firms regarding the mix of markets and organizations. Firms establish both markets and organizations as means of coordinating transactions.[172] With well-defined rights for IP, firms need not favor market transactions or organizational transactions as the means of overcoming imperfections in intellectual property. International business strategies provide a useful illustration of the effects of imperfect IP protections. The risk of expropriation of IP in host countries has tended to favor internal allocation of IP by international businesses. Because of weak IP protections in many countries, multinational corporations tend to establish foreign divisions for production and distribution as a means of keeping IP within the company. Most international technology transfers occur within multinational corporations. As foreign protections for IP increase through greater host country legal protections and international treaties governing IP, there is a growing international market for arms-length technology transfers and technology licensing. IP protections also facilitate the growth of outsourcing of business services, manufacturing, and supply chain coordination, as businesses face less risk of technology expropriation from their business partners.

Some critics of patents have expressed concerns that IP increases the costs of coordination. Inventors incur costs of searching across patents to avoid infringement of existing patents. Companies seeking to develop new technologies or to apply existing technologies may have to obtain the consent of many patent holders, which can involve substantial transaction costs. Finally, there are substantial litigation costs involved in seeking redress from infringement and in defending against charges of infringement. However, Kieff notes that "The typical laptop computer represents a bundle of thousands of patent and other IP permissions, yet the negotiation to buy one takes only a few clicks of a mouse and costs as little as $1,000, if not less."[173] In biotech, for example, IP rights do not appear to impede the process of invention and discovery.[174] There is evidence that the patent system works very well in many industries including chemistry and biotechnology.[175]

Just as with products and financial assets, IP intermediaries reduce transaction costs in the market for IP through market-making and matchmaking activities. Patent dealers and other intermediaries invest in transaction costs needed to buy and sell IP. Additionally, patent dealers bring together inventors and potential users of technology through matchmaking. Patent dealers provide liquidity and immediacy in IP markets, thus increasing the returns to invention. Perhaps most significantly, patent dealers help to enforce property rights by investing in legal action that is not available to financially constrained inventors and entrepreneurs. James McDonough points out that even though patent dealers significantly improve market efficiency, they are inaccurately vilified as "patent trolls" by policymakers and some established firms.[176] The complaint that patent dealers do not produce or employ inventions ignores the contributions of specialized intermediaries to market efficiency.[177]

Specialized intermediaries began to create a market for patented technologies in the late nineteenth and early twentieth centuries.[178] Lamoreaux and Sokoloff observe that this important development "facilitated the emergence of a group of highly specialized and productive inventors by making it possible for them to transfer to others responsibility for developing and commercializing their inventions."[179] Patent agents and lawyers matched buyers and sellers of patent rights, reduced transaction costs, and increased the effectiveness and speed of commercialization, allowing inventors to obtain the returns from specialization in inventive activity.[180] This development helps to explain why many large firms scaled down their R&D operations and relied on licensing and contracts with inventors and smaller firms.[181]

Another objection to patents in general, and business method patents in particular, is that inventions have properties of what economists call "public goods." In particular, inventions are non-rivalrous in the sense that there can be multiple users of the same invention. Unlike eating a cake, consumption of the invention does not deplete it. Of course, if multiple firms copy an invention, they will dissipate the rents to the inventor. Competition among firms applying the same invention is of course rivalrous. The non-rivalrous nature of IP does not imply that such goods should be provided for free; there is no free lunch, and dynamic efficiency requires providing incentives to invent. To the contrary, the economics of public goods suggests instead that the supply of a public good should reflect the benefits obtained by multiple users. Private firms are capable of earning such rents by charging users for access; consider, for example, cable television. Similarly, by licensing inventions, patent owners can reap the benefits from supplying the invention to multiple users. Therefore, the public good nature of inventions suggests the use of patents to reward inventors.

3.4.4. *Addressing Legal and Administrative Efficiency: Business Method Patents are not Intrinsically Vague or Abstract*

Business methods inventions are not intrinsically vague or abstract; there is little if anything inherent about this category of inventions that distinguishes it from scientific or technological inventions. The economic definition of business methods inventions given in the previous section should help to formalize the description of such inventions. Application of economic analysis to characterizing business method inventions is useful in clarifying claims.

Opponents of business method patenting suggest that the subject matter itself generates bad patents. A common argument against business method patents and related ICT patents is that they are intrinsically vague.[182] Bessen and Meurer suggest that most business method inventions are software and present evidence that software is involved in a large share of patent lawsuits. Their empirical analysis suggests that "poor patent notice has reduced the incentives to invent."[183] Vincent Chiappetta opposes business method patenting, arguing that business methods or commercial arts are abstract although the technologies that implement those processes are not.[184] In *Bilski*, Stevens worries that "Anything that constitutes a series of steps would be patentable so long as it is novel, nonobvious, and described with specificity."[185] For Stevens, "Business methods are similarly often closer to "big ideas," as they are the basic tools of *commercial* work."[186]

Concerns over vagueness or abstraction are generic objections that are not sufficient to reject business method inventions. Such concerns would apply to many scientific discoveries that involve abstract concepts in physics, mathematics, chemistry, and biology. Those business methods that are so general and basic are ruled out by the same rules that restrict patenting of abstract ideas. Abstract ideas continue to be ineligible for patenting, so inventions that do not offer useful results and practical applications are already excluded. The claim that business methods are mere series of steps could apply to many descriptions of scientific or technological processes. There is little evidence that business methods are more or less abstract than other types of inventions. John Allison and Emerson Tiller's statistical analysis of patent quality finds any presumed inferiority of business method patents to be a "myth."[187]

Bessen and Meurer emphasize that the abstract nature of such inventions interferes with the notice function of patents and increases costly litigation.[188] They argue that the property rights function of patents fails because of the high costs of search of prior patent awards. When patent claims are vague, inventors cannot determine ex ante whether they are infringing a particular patent, or even spot the patents they might be infringing, so that the risk of patent litigation becomes a significant cost for innovators.[189] Their proposed solution to the patent notice problem is not elimination or restriction of business method patents, but rather the improvement of the system of patent claims to enhance the notice function of patents. Such improvements in the system of patent claims should help to address many concerns about patentability of business method inventions.

Another standard criticism of business method patents is that they are either obvious or not novel. A standard example is Amazon.com's one-click patent.[190] Another standard example is Priceline.com's patenting of a Dutch auction for airline tickets.[191] Rochelle Dreyfuss suggests that the transfer of business models to the Internet should only be patentable when they involve "the creation of nonobvious implementing technology."[192] Eugene Quinn concludes that "there is very little prior art being considered when the examiners assess patentability of new software and business method patent applications."[193] Jay Dratler, commenting on *State Street*, characterizes the "alleged invention" as a "pedestrian computer program" with overly broad claims: "The claims, however, were not limited to any particular programming methods; they were broad enough to cover *any* computer program used in *any* manner to control that type of business."[194]

The arguments that business methods are obvious or not novel could apply generically to any category of invention. These arguments are easily addressed; those inventions that are obvious or not novel are not patentable in general, whatever the category of invention. The question of whether the responsibility for evaluating the patentability of inventions rests with either the USPTO or with the courts is generic as well.[195] Bessen and Meurer recommend greater deference by the Federal Circuit to the USPTO and trial courts, public access to information on patent boundaries, and limits on software claims.[196] Robert Merges suggests restructuring procedures for awarding patents to improve patent quality.[197] Less scrutiny by the patent office may be efficient because litigation only occurs for patents that matter.[198] Kieff argues that less scrutiny by the USPTO under a hypothetical system of registering patents would improve incentives to provide information for inventors and competitors.[199] The issue of assignment of responsibility for evaluating inventions is not specific to business method inventions.

Whether a business method invention is a stand-alone commercial discovery or is accompanied by a scientific discovery, standard patenting procedures can be applied to evaluate the usefulness, novelty and non-obviousness of the invention. Standards for evaluating business method inventions are comparable to those that apply to more traditional scientific discoveries. Business method inventions certainly can be evaluated in terms of usefulness; economic impacts implicitly enter into consideration because the claims identify applications in the marketplace. It is feasible to determine whether or not business methods are obvious or just recitations of mathematical algorithms and laws of nature. Business methods are not new phenomena; retailing, wholesaling, banking, financial hedging, or lotteries have long existed. Therefore, the novelty of business methods can also be evaluated in comparison to previous inventions and business practices.

3.5 Business Method Inventions and the Business Revolution

The rapid growth of business method inventions reflects a major new technological area that underlies what I refer to as the Business Revolution. What distinguishes the current era from any other is that the Business Revolution involves the application of science and technology to organizations and markets rather than to production alone. The Industrial Revolution augmented and replaced human effort by machines in manufacturing, farming, and transportation. The Business Revolution, in contrast, augments and replaces physical and mental effort devoted to repetitive commercial interactions in offices, stores, and markets. While the Industrial Revolution greatly increased labor productivity in manufacturing, the Business Revolution is dramatically increasing labor productivity in transactions.

3.5.1. *The Industrial Revolution: Machines and Transformation*

Great technological advances improve the human condition when they increase labor productivity. With a given effort level, individuals can produce more products, better products, and a greater variety of products. Individuals can obtain the same goods and services with less effort, avoiding stress, strain, and drudgery. Increased productivity relaxes the tradeoff between effort and output so that individuals in an economy can be made better off by simultaneously obtaining greater output while expending less effort.

In economic terms, technical advances increase labor productivity by changing the relationship between output and productive inputs, referred to as the production function. These changes can be quantitative, with given levels of capital and labor generating greater output. Technological change is often qualitative in nature; the type of capital equipment put into use changes, with the power loom replacing the handloom. Such changes in capital equipment can increase the productivity of labor, with capital equipment acting as a substitute for labor.[200] Technological changes such as mechanization and automation require different types of labor services. The effort and skills needed to operate and maintain equipment such as power looms differ from those used in traditional weaving. As Gary Becker observes, investments in human capital, through education, training, and migration, increase labor productivity.[201] Different inputs that enter into the production function, including new materials and new sources of energy, also increase the productivity of labor.

Increases in the productivity of individuals generally increase firms' demand for labor, which in a competitive market is based on the marginal revenue produced by labor. Workers in competitive markets tend to receive wages that are at least the market value of their marginal product. Increased demand for labor increases wages and employment in a market equilibrium, which translates into greater material wealth in an economy. Higher incomes, in turn, are associated with improvements in housing, education, health, lifespan, and leisure.[202]

Technological change also affects the types of effort and skill that firms demand. Increases in the productivity of individuals potentially improve working conditions by reducing the need for physical effort in manufacturing or farming. Depending on how business is organized, new forms of production can create new difficulties. For some workers in the Industrial Revolution, the drudgery of factory work replaced the effort and difficulty of weaving cloth and spinning thread. However, the shift of employment to industry from agriculture and small-scale traditional handicrafts occurred gradually.[203] Although industrialization initially brought new work habits and longer working hours, evidence suggests that holidays and shorter hours were introduced as more workers entered industry.[204]

The Industrial Revolution refers to a broad historical period in which an important set of innovations and productivity improvements occurred, particularly in manufacturing and transportation. There is considerable debate among historians about its origins, duration, and economic implications.[205] However, the technological changes set in motion during the Industrial Revolution would result in substantial increases in economic growth.[206] Evidence suggests that these technological changes increased workers' standards of living.[207] The Industrial Revolution saw the replacement of human power by machinery and mechanical power, both relieving physical labor and boosting worker productivity.[208] The application of science and technology to manufacturing during the Industrial Revolution generated increases in prosperity and economic growth.[209] Whether or not living standards rose during the period of the Industrial Revolution itself, it is apparent that significant and unprecedented economic growth subsequently occurred during the nineteenth and twentieth centuries.[210]

Mechanization and the application of centralized power changed the manufactory to the factory.[211] Beginning in the late eighteenth century, the mechanization of spinning and weaving in the textile industry yielded significant increases in labor productivity and inspired productivity increases in many other industries. Just as windmills and water wheels had earlier relieved the drudgery of grinding grains, so the use of water power in textile mills allowed mechanization that reduced the drudgery of spinning and weaving. In the nineteenth century, the Industrial Revolution entered another phase with the development of steam-powered railroads and ships, the introduction of the internal combustion engine, and electric power. These developments not only improved transportation, but allowed for further mechanization of production that increased industrial productivity. These important developments in manufacturing and transportation, while sweeping in nature, addressed very specific types of human effort.

3.5.2. *The Business Revolution and Transactions*

The Business Revolution is the replacement and enhancement of human effort devoted to economic transactions. Transaction effort is a major category of human activity that remained largely unaffected by technological change until the late twentieth century. The mental and physical effort associated with conducting business transactions differs substantially from the physical effort required in traditional manufacturing. Beginning in the late twentieth century and continuing into the twenty-first century, technological change replaced transaction effort.

Advances in information and communication technologies (ICT) including the Internet set in motion the Business Revolution. E-commerce over the Internet connects consumers with firms and makes connections among firms. By standardizing and automating the exchange of business information, the Internet replaces human effort devoted to mundane tasks in the exchange and distribution of goods and services. The Internet offers new forms of transactions and economic institutions and promises increases in prosperity and economic growth. Mobile communications technologies and advances in network connectively further increase transaction efficiencies. These developments facilitated the sharing economy including online markets for transportation, lodging, and services.

Websites and mobile communications replace human effort required to "mind the store." Increases in business productivity reflect the substitution of capital equipment for human effort devoted to business transactions. Capital equipment includes computers and communications networks. Technological change in the generation of business transactions involves new types of capital equipment. Such technological change involves new types of human capital and transaction effort. The result is an increase in the productivity of employees and managers in generating transactions and improvements in the quality of transactions.

The Business Revolution necessarily involves new types of human capital devoted to economic transactions. Innovations in Artificial Intelligence (AI) replace and support human effort in managing business transactions. Innovations in ICT change the demand for labor and alter the types of labor skills that firms demand. David Autor, Frank Levy, and Richard Murnane find that computer capital substitutes for labor in cognitive tasks that involve explicit rules.[212] They also find that computer capital complements labor in tasks that involve "nonroutine problem solving and complex communications tasks."[213] Their analysis shows that beginning in the 1970s, "within industries, occupations, and education groups, computerization is associated with reduced labor input of routine manual and cognitive tasks and increased labor input of nonroutine cognitive tasks."[214] Evidence suggests that investment in ICT has generated value added for firms.[215] Also, investment in ICT has generated significant growth in labor productivity in service industries.[216]

The effects of the Business Revolution extend into every area of the economy. Increases in transaction efficiencies are analogous to increases in productive efficiencies in the Industrial Revolution. While the Industrial Revolution would change manufacturing and distribution, the Business Revolution is changing economic interaction among individuals, among firms, and between firms and individuals. The fundamental economic developments that spring from the Business Revolution are only beginning to be realized.

Because transactions have traditionally been labor intensive, transaction effort constituted a large share of transaction costs. Coase introduced the concept of transaction costs, which he defined as the "costs of using the market."[217] Individuals devote transaction effort to such activities as communicating, negotiating, searching for trading partners, gathering information, selecting prices, and monitoring contractual performance. Transaction costs reflected the time, skills, and disutility of effort of individuals engaged in transactions. Coase wrote his initial article introducing transaction costs in 1937; the production of transactions would remain labor intensive for most of the twentieth century.

Transaction effort occurs in routine distribution and management activities. There are numerous examples associated with the distribution of goods and services: (1) Retail and wholesale clerks expend transaction effort, including the monotony of "minding the store" when there are no customers and the routine aspects of retail transactions such as record keeping and collecting payments. (2) Purchasing agents within companies expend transaction effort in executing orders for parts, components, equipment, and services. (3) Clerical personnel within companies expend transaction effort in managing information associated with routine sales, billing, production, inventories, and accounting. (4) Clerical personnel within companies also expend transaction effort on meetings, correspondence, business forms, and basic contracts.

The contribution of an activity to GDP is a measure of its economic value added. A study by Deighton *et al.* defines the advertising-supported Internet ecosystem as "market-making and business-enabling."[218] They find that this ecosystem contributes over $1 trillion to U.S. GDP.[219] Deighton *et al.* show that this ecosystem employs 4.1 million people directly and 6.3 million people indirectly.[220]

Microeconomic studies of ICT usage and productivity effects are limited because of the evolving nature of this phenomenon. There is some evidence that computer networks increase the efficiency of businesses processes such as order taking, inventory management, accounting, and product distribution.[221] A study of the impact of computer networks in three OECD countries, Denmark, Japan, and the United States, finds that usage of computer networks increases firm-level productivity.[222] A study in the United Kingdom of computer networks in e-commerce shows increases in productivity.[223] However, the study finds that e-buying has positive impacts on output growth and e-selling has negative impacts. The problem is to separate price effects from transaction cost effects because when electronic markets increase competition and lower prices, buyers will benefit from lower expenditures and sellers will have reduced earnings.[224]

Firms are transaction institutions, often acting as intermediaries between buyers and sellers.[225] Firms handle transactions by creating and managing markets and organizations.[226] The intermediation role that firms play in the contemporary economy implies that they possess substantial transaction cost advantages over direct exchange.[227] The role of the firm in improving transactional efficiency suggests an "intermediation hypothesis," which states that increases in consumer transaction costs relative to those of the firm lead to growth of the scope of the firm. The "intermediation hypothesis" is complementary with the "internalization hypothesis," otherwise known as the "make-or-buy" choice, which suggests that firms address some types of transaction costs by vertical integration. This determines how the firm divides its scope between its market-making activities and organizational activities. The "intermediation hypothesis" suggests that, as a result of transaction costs, the extent of the market explains the establishment of firms to replace consumer organizations and direct exchange. The general theory of the firm yields useful insights that can be tested empirically using contemporary and historical data. The diversity of firms in the contemporary economy provides substantial information for studying the activities of firms.[228]

Transactions contribute a significant proportion of the economy's total value added. By improving the efficiency of these transactions, business method inventions generate the Business Revolution. Some parts of the economy are almost entirely devoted to economic transactions and provide insights into the costs of transactions. The economic activities that are focused on transactions and their value added to the economy include retail trade (8 percent), wholesale trade (6 percent), finance and insurance (7.8 percent), and professional and business services and other services (12.4 percent).[229] Taken together, industries focused on transactions comprise 34 percent of GDP, well over one-third of total value added.[230]

Standard approaches to telecommunications and the Internet focus directly on the information–communications–technology-producing industries. This consists of "computer and electronic products; publishing industries (includes software); information and data processing services; and computer systems design and related services," which contribute 7.3 percent to total GDP. Adding this group of activities would bring transactions to over 40 percent of GDP. This surprising figure excludes the contribution of transaction activities in such industries as manufacturing; agriculture; mining; construction; transportation and warehousing; utilities, educational services, health care, and social assistance; and arts, entertainment, recreation, accommodation, and food services.

Retailers include supermarkets, discount stores, department stores, general merchandise stores, specialty apparel stores, warehouse clubs, drug stores, convenience stores, and variety stores. Some sell durable goods, some sell nondurables, and some sell both. The retail sector performs a wide variety of intermediation functions including pricing, marketing, inventory holding, selection of suppliers, setting bid prices offered to suppliers, quality certification, and management of transactions. Retailers have enhanced their market-making activities through traditional Electronic Data Interchange (EDI) with their suppliers, which lowers costs and increases speed in exchanging data on sales, inventory, and marketing, as well as expediting billing and invoicing. Retailers have improved data collection and exchange through bar coding of merchandise, point-of-sale scanners, and computerized inventory tracking and reordering. Increases in information about sales allow a rapid response to changing market conditions.

Wholesalers act as intermediaries for transactions between businesses. Like retailers, they distribute goods, manage inventories, communicate price and product information, certify quality, and provide credit. Wholesalers market to retailers, search for suppliers, and handle interbusiness transactions. In addition, they increasingly provide value-added services such as packaging, labeling, bar coding, electronic data interchange, product lot tracking, inventory controls, and faster delivery.[231]

About 90 percent of firms in the wholesale sector, holding 60 percent of the market, are merchant wholesalers.[232] Their business is split about 50–50 between durable and nondurable goods. The other 40 percent of the wholesale sector is split among other intermediation arrangements. The most important of these alternative distribution arrangements include direct manufacturer–retailer transactions (retail chain stores, warehouse clubs, discount stores, and home center stores), mail order, catalog sales, manufacturer–industrial user transactions, and retail sales to industrial users.[233] Wholesalers also include manufacturer's sales branches, and agents, brokers, and commission merchants.

Financial intermediaries perform a wide array of services, including pricing of some financial assets, providing liquidity, risk allocation, allocation of financial assets over time, combining assets to reduce the transaction costs of diversification, supplying information, and managing transactions. Depository institutions intermediate between borrowers and lenders, setting rates of interest for loans and deposits, screening borrowers for creditworthiness, and monitoring their repayment performance. Securities and commodity brokers provide a range of intermediation services, including managing complex financial transactions, carrying out trades on the organized exchanges, and supplying investors with information. Insurance companies manage transactions, allocate risk, and intermediate between investors and buyers of insurance contracts.

Business and professional services include professional, scientific, and technical services; management of companies and enterprises; and administrative and support services. Many types of business services are directly or indirectly involved in managing transactions, including advertising, credit agencies, direct mail, advertising services, personnel supply services, and computer rental and leasing.[234]

Some activities in the retail and wholesale sector may be closer to production than to intermediation. Conversely, intermediation activities are present that can be difficult to discern in aggregate data on the manufacturing, agriculture, mining, construction, transportation, or public utilities sectors. Manufacturers do expend a substantial effort on marketing and sales, purchasing, personnel recruitment, financing, and technology procurement, and surely such activities account for some share of the value added by the manufacturing sector. However, the aggregate manufacturing data are focused on units of output, employees, total costs, inventories, and receipts, and do not separate out the value added by the retail, wholesale, marketing, and sales activities carried out internally by manufacturers.

Many of the companies in manufacturing, mining, construction, transportation, and public utilities sectors are vertically integrated. These companies carry out many intermediation functions that are difficult to identify from company data, including pricing, marketing, inventory management, and ordering from suppliers. This shortcoming in the manufacturing data reflects the traditional economics perspective that the firm is a manufacturer and that market allocation decisions are handled by an exogenous price system. In addition, manufacturers have significant finance and personnel requirements. They devote effort to raising capital on financial markets, communicating with investors, and issuing debt and equity. Manufacturers also invest in hiring personnel, learning about the labor market, and managing the employment relationship. Such labor market activities are explicitly recognized contributions to GDP as part of business services when they are outsourced to temporary help firms.

Similar considerations apply to companies in the mining, construction, transportation, and public utilities sectors. For example, major oil companies not only carry out mining and refining but also make complex decisions about purchases, supplies, inventories, and pricing. Transportation and logistics companies, such as UPS, manage a vast transportation market, intermediating between customers mailing packages and transportation suppliers. Intermodal trucking companies, such as J. B. Hunt Transport, perform intermediation services by coordinating transfers of shipments with rail and shipping companies. Manufacturing companies also engage in merchant activities, operating markets for goods and services and factors of production. The distinction between merchants and manufacturers is not clear-cut. In combination with managing transactions, intermediaries often transform products to add value: transporting, storing, repackaging, assembling, preparing for final use, and adding information and guaranties. Manufacturers carry out many market-making activities, intermediating between sellers of raw materials or product components and buyers of manufactured goods.

One indicator of the scope of firms' market-related activities is that about 30 percent of manufacturing employees are not classified as production workers. These employees include supervisors and sales personnel, as well as "advertising, credit, collection, installation and servicing of own products, clerical and routine office functions, executive, purchasing, financing, legal, personnel (including cafeteria, medical, etc.), professional, and technical employees."[235] For example, manufacturing includes "apparel jobbing (assigning of materials to contract factories or shops for fabrication or other contract operations); as well as contracting on materials owned by others."[236] Over 40 percent of total manufacturing payroll goes to nonproduction employees.[237]

3.5.3. *Business Method Inventions and New Transaction Techniques*

With transactions accounting for at least one-third of economic activities, greater efficiency will have great effects on economic performance and growth. The gains from the Business Revolution result from automation of transactions, more effective intermediaries, and more efficient markets. Market transactions can be classified in three categories: business to business, business to consumer, and consumer to consumer.[238] In addition, business method inventions improve the efficiency of transactions within organizations by producing more transactions for a given cost and by improving the accuracy of transactions. This section illustrates some important examples of business method inventions.

Business method and apparatus patents date back to those obtained by Herman Hollerith in 1889 for data processing based on punch cards.[239] Hollerith was both an inventor and an entrepreneur, and his Tabulating Machine Company would later be renamed the International Business Machine Corporation (IBM).[240] With the development of the computer and the growth of the Internet, business method patents have been closely associated with hardware and software used in electronic commerce.

Most of the examples given below are e-commerce applications, but many firms engage in marketing through multiple channels, operating both Internet stores and brick-and-mortar facilities. These activities can be substitutes because customers choose between online and local outlets. However, some aspects of multi-channel marketing and sales are complements. For example, customers who purchase online can receive delivery through a local store. Conversely, customers who visit a local store may place online orders there and receive delivery at home.

Business method innovations automate the store. This means that the application of ICT replaces human efforts and skill in managing retail and wholesale transactions. Computers "mind the store" for Internet websites: displaying products and prices, informing customers about product features, determining product availability, taking orders, billing and receiving payments, issuing order confirmations and receipts, keeping records of the transactions, and arranging deliveries. For example, Amazon.com, Overstock.com, and practically all other Internet retailers offer automated transactions. Amazon.com took the automation process further by offering sellers the services of "storefronts" located in a virtual marketplace.

The shopping activity itself is automated, reducing buyers' costs of locating sellers and sellers' costs of locating buyers. Shopbots offer automated comparison shopping that finds products for shoppers. Search engine firms, such as Google, Bing, and Yahoo!, automate the information-gathering process. Search services gather information from websites, images, audio, video, government documents, books, and scholarly articles. Information provision by online search engines replaces some of the routine information gathering and dissemination functions of teachers, doctors, pharmacists, attorneys, and reference librarians. Google further automated the process of using search services with a service that guesses the user's query from a few or even one key stroke, estimating that saving a few seconds of search "will add up to 350 million hours in time savings for its users over the next year."[241]

The automation of Internet advertising sales contributed to the growth of search and e-commerce generally. GoTo introduced a system for auctions of keywords, renamed Overture, that ranked an advertiser's messages based on their bids.[242] Overture provided their advertising system to many other search engines.[243] Overture obtained a patent for "A system and method for enabling information providers using a computer network such as the Internet to influence a position for a search listing on a search result list generated by an Internet search engine."[244] Yahoo! initially partnered with Overture to offer search services and paid advertising and acquired Overture in 2003 (http://www.searchenginehistory.com). Yahoo!'s service, renamed Yahoo! Search Marketing, initially ranked advertisements based on bids, and then adjusted rankings using click-through rates and quality measures with the introduction of its Panama software. Microsoft initially partnered with Overture and later established AdCenter in 2006, which featured demographic targeting and an algorithm that used cost per click and ad click-through rate.[245]

Google offered its AdWords program to sell search advertising in 2000 and in 2003 introduced AdSense, which automated the placement of advertisements.[246] Overture filed a patent infringement lawsuit against Google in 1999. In 2004, Overture, which by that time was owned by Yahoo!, settled for 2.7 million shares of Google stock.[247] Google obtained approximately three-quarters of the market for Internet advertising, followed by Yahoo! and Microsoft.[248]

Business method innovations also automate search and matching functions in business-to-business applications. For example, ChemConnect serves companies in the chemical industry with automation of transactions for materials and finished products, and transmission of information about demand, inventories, and orders. Serving 9,000 companies from over 150 countries, ChemConnect helps "customers manage and optimize complex supply chains throughout the sourcing, fulfillment, and ultimately the sales processes."[249]

Business method innovations automate specialized services that often involved highly skilled personnel. For example, travel agents provided expert help to individuals in making reservations and travel plans.

This required knowledge of travel schedules, pricing, and alternative transportation providers. Internet websites such as Expedia, Orbitz, and Travelocity provide full access to airlines, hotels, rental cars, and other travel-related services. Automated travel websites handle all of the transactions associated with displaying schedules and prices, making travel reservations, and purchasing travel services.

Business method innovations apply to many other types of specialized financial agents. Most banks offer fully automated online banking, and some banks operate exclusively online, handling many types of banking services, including loans. Automated agents sell home, auto, and life insurance. Automated payment intermediaries such as PayPal handle transactions online, and most banks offer bill payment services, including automatic bill payments and transfers. Automated intermediary services replace specialized personnel in securities brokerage (Scottrade, Charles Schwab, Etrade, OptionsHouse, TDAmeritrade, and TradeKing).

Business method innovations have succeeded in automating the services provided by a particularly skilled intermediary, the auctioneer. For example, eBay offers automated auctions in which a virtual auctioneer receives buyer bids, automatically places bids for buyers who provide maximum bids, and determines the winning buyer. MercExchange filed an infringement suit against eBay and Half.com.[250] MercExchange holds a business method patent for an electronic marketplace for used and collectible goods (U.S. Patent No. 5,845,265). The Supreme Court in *eBay* affirmed a set of general rules for injunctive relief, finding that the patent holder did not need to practice to obtain an injunction. Search engines Google, Bing, and Yahoo! hold automated "position auctions" for sellers that place advertisements with search results.

Business method innovations were instrumental to the automation of markets. Traditional financial exchanges relied on floor trading with professional traders engaged in "open outcry," often shouting, exchanging hand signals, and pushing and shoving each other in trading pits. Advances in ICT have replaced the congestion costs of floor trading with the nearly unlimited capacity, increased speed, and greater accuracy of electronic trading.[251] Traditional exchanges that were organized as mutual associations reorganized as corporations to implement the business method innovations and to raise investment capital for the new systems.[252] The traditional exchanges were associations of brokers and dealers, and the reorganized exchanges operate as joint ventures of large market-making firms and broker-dealers.[253]

Business method innovations automate the firm's organization, including its inventory management, production, financial and accounting systems, sales operations, and human resources. These processes include the traditional data management and information-processing functions within companies, as well as new support systems for online commerce for both Internet retailers and traditional retailers with online marketing channels.[254] Sikander and Sarma identify software applications in various areas of e-commerce: "authentication, authorization, caching, communication (browser-based user access, communication between applications layers, communication with back-end systems such as ERP [enterprise resource planning], payment integration, analytics systems, search engines), data access, and security."[255]

3.6 Conclusion

The debate over the patentability of business method inventions among academics and public policy makers reflects the growing economic importance of such discoveries. The surge of business method inventions and patents attests to their substantial economic benefits. Commercial discoveries significantly augment and replace human effort in business, improving the performance of firms and increasing the efficiency of economic transactions. Just as patenting and IP law adjusted to the Industrial Revolution, so the IP system must adjust to significant developments associated with the emerging Business Revolution.

Business method patents extend IP protections to commercial discoveries, which are the foundation of subsequent Schumpeterian innovation. Business method patents are helpful to entrepreneurs who often transfer their IP to the startups and new firms that they establish. Business method patents are not only useful to innovative entrepreneurs but they also assist in the commercialization of scientific and technological discoveries developed in conjunction with business methods. Additionally, business method inventions should be patentable because such inventions increase the market value of previously developed scientific and technological discoveries.

Business method inventions are a new class of discoveries because they often generate or apply advances in ICT technologies.

The question of whether business method inventions should be patentable, raised by *Bilski*, poses a challenge to the patent system. The Court views business methods as abstract ideas and the implementation of those ideas by computers as mere instructions. The Court's *Alice* decision illustrates the dangers: "the relevant question is whether the claims here do more than simply instruct the practitioner to implement the abstract idea of intermediated settlement on a generic computer. They do not."[256]

Problems with patent quality and litigation are by no means intrinsic to business method discoveries. General patenting rules, such as those requiring that inventions be useful, novel, and non-obvious, are sufficient to evaluate business method inventions. There should not be limiting criteria that apply specifically to business method inventions. Restricting IP protections for business method inventions would weaken the patent system because in practice, it is difficult if not impossible to distinguish commercial inventions from manufacturing methods. IP protections for business method inventions are important for dynamic, allocative, and transaction efficiencies in the market for discoveries. The patent system should provide IP protections to business method inventions just as it does to other types of discoveries.

Chapter 4

Patent Infringement and Reasonable Royalty Damages

4.1 Introduction

Markets for IP depend on effective legal protections for patent owners.[1] There is, however, considerable controversy in patent law regarding damages for patent infringement.[2] As Peter Menell *et al.* observe, "[o]ne of the most vexing issues in patent law is the proper measure of damages."[3] The various legal and economic methodologies for determining reasonable royalty damages produce inconsistent results.[4] These differences in measures of damages can have significant financial implications for patent owners and infringers. Measures of damages significantly affect IP licensing decisions and incentives for invention and innovation.[5]

To help resolve this controversy, I propose a *contract approach* to reasonable royalty damages for patent infringement. Royalties are the consideration in patent license contracts.[6] The only way to understand reasonable royalties as a damage remedy is within the context of a patent license contract. I introduce the concept of an "informed contract" that is based on information revealed during the period of infringement. The court constructs an "informed contract" based on evidence in the patent case, thus providing greater accuracy in determining damages. I show how addressing damages from a contractual perspective helps address many of the issues in patent disputes.[7]

There are more than 5,000 patent case filings per year in the U.S.[8] Reasonable royalty damages for patent infringement are essential to enforcing patents and compensating patent owners. Reasonable royalty damages are awarded either in addition to lost profits or instead of lost profits when there are no lost profits or lost profits cannot be measured.[9] In the U.S. from 2007–2016, firms that practice patents were involved in about four-fifths of infringement cases and received damages consisting of 21% lost profits only, 61% reasonable royalties only, and 19% a combination of lost profits and reasonable royalties.[10] The remaining one-fifth of infringement cases involved nonpracticing entities (firms, individuals, universities, and other nonprofits) that can only receive reasonable royalty damages.[11]

Determining damages for infringement has reached something of an impasse. The courts have struck down various traditional methods of calculating reasonable royalty damages such as the 25% of profits rule without identifying alternative methods.[12] The "hypothetical negotiation" approach has proven to be problematic and impractical.[13] Also, the courts have become more active as gatekeepers with increased scrutiny of expert testimony.[14] According to the Supreme Court in *Daubert*, the trial judge must decide whether an expert's "reasoning or methodology properly can be applied to the facts in issue."[15] In spite of the greater focus on evidence for reasonable royalty damages, the legal controversy has only intensified.

In my view, the patent law controversy stems from a conflict between property and tort approaches. Many advocate a property approach to infringement. Roger Blair and Thomas Cotter state "[a] substantial number of the law and economics scholars who have written on this subject appear to agree that it is generally preferable to protect intellectual property rights through the use of property, as opposed to liability, rules."[16] Stewart Sterk points out that "[a]lthough intellectual property doctrine has borrowed much from real property doctrine, it has not yet recognized the important role of negligence principles in cases where the title and scope of rights are less than crystal clear."[17] In contrast, many others argue that patent law takes a tort approach and places various limits on strict liability for infringement.[18] Ted Sichelman observes that "patent remedies mirror traditional tort law remedies by attempting to restore the patentee to the status quo ante — namely, the state of the world in which there is no infringement of the patent."[19] Keith Hylton considers enhanced damages for patent infringement and notes, "[t]he torts literature on which I rely typically examines damages awards in the context of a lawsuit between a victim and an 'injurer.'"[20]

But, a patent license agreement is a *contract*. Indeed, patent license agreements are perhaps the most common type of contract.[21] Patent license agreements are subject to contract law.[22] Patent license agreements are contracts for the purpose of commercializing inventions.[23] According to the Code of Federal Regulations,

> A patent license is, in effect, a contractual agreement that the patent owner will not sue the licensee for patent infringement if the licensee makes, uses, offers for sale, sells, or imports the claimed invention, as long as the licensee fulfills its obligations and operates within the bounds delineated by the license agreement.[24]

I argue that the court in a patent case should construct an "informed contract" based on available evidence. In practice, the court does exactly that, naturally filling in many of the terms of an "informed contract." The court's construction of an "informed contract" typically reflects what actually happened in the course of infringement.[25] The court's interpretation of the "informed contract" provides a sound economic and legal basis for determining reasonable royalty damages.

The contract approach proposed here views infringement as a failure to contract. Infringement disputes can be avoided or resolved by a patent license contract between the patent holder and the technology implementer.[26] This implies that remedies for infringement should be grounded in contract law. Remedies based on contracts apply whether infringement is intentional or inadvertent.[27] Because patent license contracts include royalties, the structure of licensing contracts helps in finding reasonable royalty damages.

4.2 The Contract Approach to Patent Infringement

I introduce a contract approach to resolving patent infringement disputes. I find that applying contract rules to patent infringement helps bridge some of the gaps left by property and tort rules. The contract approach protects the patent holder's interests and provides compensation for patent infringement. The contract approach is useful for characterizing interactions between market institutions and legal practice.

4.2.1. *Patents and Intellectual Contracts*

The contract approach offered here provides methodologies for finding reasonable royalty damages and suggests what evidence should be obtained in the patent case. Based on the contract approach, I introduce a "market value method" for calculating reasonable royalty damages. The market value of a patent or patent portfolio changes continually, just as do stock prices and the prices of other financial assets.[28] The contract approach suggests how to adjust the purchase price of the patent or the purchase price of comparable patents to calculate reasonable royalty damages. The "market value method" is based on economic analysis because it relies on market information. The "market value method" compensates the patent holder for the expected value of licensing royalties lost due to infringement. This method addresses evidence requirements because it uses observable market information and can be applied even when there are no comparable contracts. Reasonable royalty damages are calculated as a share of the market value of the patent that takes into account the number of infringers and the characteristics of "informed contracts." This method extends readily to multiple patents and patent portfolios. The "market value method" is also useful for reasonable royalty damages when there are standard essential patents ("SEPs").

Also, the contract approach is helpful in finding comparable license contracts. The contract approach suggests how to adjust royalties such that damages are compensatory. The provisions of the "informed contract" constructed by the patent case and other information about the extent of infringement, the patented technologies, and technology standards help to adjust estimates of the patent holder's opportunity costs and the infringer's benefits.

The contract approach leads to a better understanding of the economic function of patent license contracts. The contract approach provides guidance to the courts regarding the calculation of reasonable royalty damages. The contract approach preserves the injunctive relief of the property approach. The contract approach addresses compensation of the patent holder as in the tort approach. The contract approach thus complements the conflicting property and tort approaches to reasonable royalty damages and should help resolve the patent law controversy.

The contract approach completes the legal picture for several reasons. The contract approach draws upon market institutions because parties to patent license agreements generally determine royalties in the context of the overall contract. The contract approach to infringement also conforms to the statute by addressing compensation.[29] The proposed "informed contract" accounts for the economic effects of infringement and applies evidence obtained by the patent case. The contract approach builds on legal precedent by recognizing the failure to contract of the patent holder and infringer.

The "informed contract" approach differs fundamentally from the flawed "hypothetical negotiation." The "hypothetical negotiation" is the main instrument for calculating reasonable royalty damages.[30] The idealized "hypothetical negotiation" places impossible demands on the court because it requires determining the knowledge and expectations of the patent holder and infringer had they entered into a negotiation before the infringement began.[31] The "hypothetical negotiation" is likely to be inconsistent with the evidence in the patent case because the patent holder and the infringer acted in the absence of an agreement.[32] The "hypothetical negotiation" is unrealistic because it is based on the fiction of a willing licensor and a willing licensee.[33] Scott Kieff and Anne Layne-Farrar observed that infringement destroys both the patent holder's option to say "no" to a license request and the patent holder's option to say "yes" exclusively or on distinct terms to some party other than the infringer.[34] The "informed contract" should compensate the patent holder for the loss of these options.

The "informed contract" includes *ex post* information revealed by evidence in the patent case.[35] The "informed contract" is not limited by the *ex ante* knowledge of the parties at the time infringement began. The "informed contract" takes into account information revealed after infringement began, including patent validity, technology standards, market outcomes, and the extent of the infringement.

The "informed contract" provides a conceptual foundation for reasonable royalty damages. Economic analysis suggests that current information allows better estimates of damages from infringement.[36] This conforms to the legal requirement that reasonable royalties provide compensation for damages.[37] The "informed contract" is objective because it relies on evidence rather than conjectures about the subjective knowledge and perceptions of the patent holder and the infringer. As District Judge James F. Holderman states in *In re Innovatio*, "[n]onetheless, by the time the damages phase of an infringement suit arrives, the court has determined infringement and validity, thus foreclosing the hypothetical negotiator from benefiting from any uncertainty as to future court rulings."[38]

The contract approach depends on the court's *interpretation* of the "informed contract," without requiring idealized intent of the two parties.[39] In a patent case, the parties are bound by the informed contract as constructed by the court.[40] The patent case builds a contract on the basis of what actually occurred.[41] Here, actions necessarily speak louder than words. The "informed contract" depends on evidence regarding the parties' actions as discovered in the patent case. When did the infringement begin and end? Were the patents valid? How did the infringer use the IP? Was there any prior licensing and negotiation between the parties and other business relationships between the patent owner and the infringer? Did the patent owner license the IP to others? Did the patent owner have SEPs? Did the patent owner make fair, reasonable, and non-discriminatory ("FRAND") royalty commitments to standard-setting organizations ("SSOs")?

The contract approach considers reasonable royalty damages in the context of the other provisions of the "informed contract," as determined by the patent case. Instead of offering an untethered last-minute calculation of reasonable royalty damages, the contract approach builds on evidence gathered in the patent case. By the time the issue of reasonable royalty damages arises, the court and the litigants have already done much of the heavy lifting. In practice, patent license contracts involve negotiation of various provisions, including but not limited to royalties.[42] The terms of a patent license contract increase or decrease royalties depending on the economic value generated by the contract and the allocation of benefits between the patent holder and the implementer.[43] This provides guidance for the calculation of reasonable royalty damages based on the provisions of the "informed contract." The contract approach offers further guidance to the court on what additional evidence should be gathered and how it should be used to obtain reasonable royalty damages.

The patent case discovers the critical elements of the "informed contract." These include the following: (1) identification of the parties, description of their businesses and their business relationship with each other; (2) start date, duration of the agreement, and period of coverage; (3) definition of the IP; (4) grant of rights (IP limits, field of use, territory, degree of exclusivity, and improvements to the technology); and (5) compensation. Taken together, these critical elements provide a context for reasonable royalty damages.

Although an "informed contract" does not involve a "meeting of the minds," this situation is not limited to patent infringement because such a problem arises often in contractual disputes.[44] Oliver Wendell Holmes Jr. observes the following:

> [w]e talk about a contract as a meeting of the minds of the parties, and thence it is inferred in various cases that there is no contract because their minds have not met; that is, because they have intended different things or because one party has not known of the assent of the other. Yet nothing is more certain than that parties may be bound by a contract to things which neither of them intended, and when one does not know of the other's assent.[45]

Holmes points out that "[t]he parties are bound by the contract as it is interpreted by the court, yet neither of them meant what the court declares that they have said."[46] The "informed contract" in a patent case depends on the interpretation of the court, just as in other contract cases.

The contract approach yields insights into various patent damage controversies including apportionment and the royalty base, particularly the entire market value rule ("EMVR"), and the Smallest Salable Patent-Practicing Unit ("SSPPU") rule.[47] The contract approach also helps address several closely related issues arising from multiple inventions: royalty stacking, patent thickets, patent hold-up, and SEPs.

4.2.2. *The Patent License Contract versus Patent Infringement*

The contract approach to infringement is fruitful because the patent license contract and patent infringement have opposite effects. A patent license contract is a *cooperative* technology transfer that generates joint economic benefits.[48] When transaction costs are low, the patent license contract should provide incentives for efficient performance and efficient utilization of IP. The provisions of a license contract adjust for the effects of patent law and other regulatory restrictions.[49]

In contrast, patent infringement is a *non-cooperative* technology transfer that generates an externality.[50] An externality is a transfer of costs or benefits outside of a market transaction.[51] Such a technology transfer typically benefits the infringer and harms the IP owner.[52] The benefits to the infringer can be incremental profits from further invention and innovative products, production processes, and transactions that are derived from the patented technologies.[53] The harm to the patent owner can take the form of lost profits from business stealing effects and lost opportunities to license the technology to third parties.[54] The patent owner loses the royalties that would have been obtained from licensing to the firm that infringed the patent.[55]

Because patent infringement involves an externality, it is likely to be economically inefficient for the parties involved, leading to excessive or conflicting usage of the IP. The infringing firm likely will make inefficient technology adoption decisions and use substitute and complementary resources inefficiently. Put differently, the social benefits of a technology transfer are less than the private benefits of the technology transfer of the infringer. This is because the calculation of social benefits deducts the private costs of the patent owner that result from infringement.

A patent license contract between the technology provider and adopter addresses the infringement externality and can improve economic incentives. The technology user has incentives to make better adoption decisions and invest more efficiently in invention and innovation.[56] This is consistent with Ronald Coase's characterization of bargaining as an efficient means of addressing social costs.[57] Efficiency of contracting is also consistent with extensive economic analysis of negotiation with full information.[58] Technology providers and adopters generally design contracts to mitigate the effects of transaction costs and incomplete information, which can be significant for IP.[59]

Patent license contracts can solve problems stemming from patent infringement. A patent license contract provides a way of settling or avoiding a patent infringement complaint.[60] Once the infringement is discovered, the parties can then negotiate a patent license contract to resolve the disagreement. For example, Nokia and Apple settled a patent infringement dispute with a combination of patent license agreements and business contracts.[61] TiVo settled patent litigation against Samsung with a patent license agreement covering mobile, consumer electronics, and set-top box technologies.[62]

Conversely, breach of a particular restriction that is part of a patent license contract can generate either a breach of contract suit or a patent infringement claim.[63] For example, in *Tekelec*, the Fifth Circuit found Verint to have breached both a patent settlement and license contract for failing to make payments.[64] Also, Rydex successfully sued Graco for patent infringement after Graco breached their licensing contract.[65] These examples illustrate that violating a patent license agreement can be viewed either as breach of contract or as patent infringement.

Failure to complete the negotiation of a patent license contract when there is usage of the technology can result in a patent infringement complaint.[66] For example, MercExchange offered to license a patent to eBay and Half.com.[67] After some negotiation, the companies failed to reach an agreement, leading MercExchange to file a patent infringement suit against eBay and Half.com.[68] Failure to contract also resulted in Unwired Planet's patent infringement suit against Huawei.[69]

Failure to renew a patent license contract when there is usage of the technology can result in an infringement complaint. For example, Rovi, a subsidiary of TiVo, successfully filed a patent infringement complaint against former licensee Comcast before the International Trade Commission.[70]

4.2.3. *Patent License as Contract*

The contract approach is fundamental to explaining the nature of licensing royalties. The patent license agreement involves the standard contractual elements of offer, acceptance, and consideration.[71] Standard contract law applies to patent license agreements.[72] The parties choose the provisions of patent license contracts to maximize the joint value of the relationship.[73] The parties to a patent license contract choose the terms of the agreement in the context of their business relationships with each other and other businesses.[74]

A patent license contract is a cooperative agreement designed to maximize the returns to combining the licensor's technology with the licensee's technology, efforts, products, investment, and complementary assets.[75] Royalties not only serve to divide the contractual pie but they also help maximize the size of the pie.[76] Thus, patent license royalties are more than a payment for the transfer of an asset. Patent license royalties are payments to patent owners for the licensee's opportunity to use, improve, and add value to an asset.

Because patent license agreements are contracts that are specific to the licensor and the licensee, they typically must be negotiated.[77] For this reason, licensors do not announce "posted prices" for patent license agreements as sellers often do when providing standardized goods and services. This means that public policy concerns cannot be based exclusively on economic models of imperfect competition with posted prices. Instead, public policy toward patents must take into account bargaining over patent license agreements. Negotiation of patent license agreements eliminates the basis for concerns about royalty stacking and other problems typically associated with SEPs.[78]

The patent license agreement, as with many other types of contracts, involves cooperative activities that take place over time. The licensee uses the patented technology for some specified period of time and pays royalties to the licensor over time.[79] It may take time for the licensee to absorb the invention and to develop innovations based on the invention. It may take time for the licensee to obtain financing, invest in capital equipment and facilities, produce outputs, and sell and distribute products. The licensee earns revenues over some period of time and generally pays royalties based on output or sales over time.[80] As with contracts generally, patent license contracts are prospective; the parties share costs, revenues, and risks over time.[81]

Patent license agreements involve much more than renting an asset. For this reason, licensing royalties are not simply a division of the economic rents from exchange. This means that the patent license contract negotiation is about more than the choice of royalties. The parties choose contract terms that maximize the economic value of their relationship. They select contract terms to provide incentives for efficient performance. Royalty payments serve the overall purpose of the contractual relationship and should be viewed in that context. Examining the full scope of the contract negotiation gives a better idea of what are the resulting royalties and contract terms.

Some practitioners characterize the demand or "pull" for patent license contracts as having three sources: "carrots," "sticks," and "bundles."[82] "Carrots" refer to voluntarily negotiated patent license contracts based solely on the benefits of the technology to the implementer.[83] "Sticks" refer to patent license contracts negotiated under the threat of litigation.[84] Niklas Östman observes, "[p]atent licenses are not your normal products. In fact they are extremely unusual as products. I have heard patent licenses be characterized as offering 'peace of mind', 'insurance against being sued', 'freedom of operation', 'access to technology' and many other things, including 'relief from fear and pain.'"[85] Finally, "bundles" refer to contracts that combine patent license contracts with other non-patent inducements including various goods and services.[86]

Legal penalties for infringement are necessary but not sufficient for patent license contracts to have market value just as property rights are necessary but not sufficient for an asset to have market value.[87] The threat of legal penalties only exists if firms infringe, that is, if there is some demand for inventions protected by patents.[88] This means that the patent is valid and the implementer obtains benefits from using the technology.[89] Implementers benefit from using the technology whether infringement is intentional or inadvertent.[90] The market value of patent license contracts reflects the benefits to implementers, whether license contracts are "carrots," "sticks," or "bundles."[91]

The actual or implicit threat of litigation thus does not imply that royalties are the result of legal penalties. Companies have the option of using alternative technologies and can take steps to reduce the likelihood of inadvertent infringement.[92] The threat of litigation does not mean that patent owners making license offers are engaging in "hold-up" because patents must be both valid and infringed.[93] Implementers have the option of negotiating in good faith and avoiding "hold-out."[94]

There is considerable evidence that patented technology provides economic value.[95] There are many patent license contracts between patent holders and implementers.[96] At the same time, patent litigation is a very rare event.[97] Ron Katznelson examines the period from 1923–2013 and finds that patent lawsuits filed in U.S. District Courts as a fraction of U.S. patents in force are less than one-third of 1% for all years.[98] Because litigation is both risky and costly and because it may be difficult to detect infringement, law suits involve only a small proportion of patents.[99]

Some view SEPs as "sticks" because implementing the standard requires practicing the patents.[100] SEPs, however, can be "carrots" because they offer access to technology that contributes to the innovations represented by the standard.[101] A producer need not implement a particular standard when there are multiple standards that compete in the marketplace. The producer will implement the most attractive standard in terms of technological benefits and market returns. Implementing the standard is a non-patent inducement to license the patent. SEPs can be demanded as part of "bundles" because the licensee obtains a valuable patented technology and the ability to implement the standard.[102]

SEPs are also "carrots" because there can be other SEPs that are competitive substitutes.[103] Royalties are competitive even after the standard is chosen.[104] SEPs are also "carrots" because not all patents declared to be SEPs are necessary for the standard.[105] Robin Stitzing *et al.* find systematic over-declaration of SEPs.[106] They demonstrate empirically that in telecommunications, economic models explaining patent value are not sufficient to explain the technical essentiality of SEPs.[107]

Contracts between patent holders and implementers can include both licenses and other products.[108] Östman notes,

> [y]ou can also combine patent licenses with other things like access to source code, other technology implementations, documentation, trade secrets or even product support. The classic example being the pharma industry, where patents are licensed in a big package together with the underlying research, clinical studies, FDA approvals, trademarks and even production knowhow.[109]

For example, Nokia established contracts with Xiaomi, Apple, and Samsung covering a combination of patent licensing and business relationships.[110]

"Bundles" do not indicate that the patent license contracts have no market value. Rather, patent licenses are bundled with other business transactions because they are complementary and the parties benefit from broader contracts.[111] Company managers who negotiate "bundles" determine royalty payments within the context of business relationships.[112]

The patent holder has an interest in the technology adopter succeeding in the marketplace.[113] For example, Suzanne Harrison and Patrick Sullivan consider how companies engage in strategic technology transfers involving both IP and a company's non-IP intangibles.[114] They refer to non-IP intangibles as "I-stuff," which includes "tacit knowledge, know-how, relationships as well as the non-legally protected and codified knowledge of the firm."[115] Harrison and Sullivan quote Jeff Weedman, Vice President at Procter & Gamble:

> [p]art of my unit's I-stuff is found in the way we approach a business or licensing negotiation with an external organization. When we sit down to 'negotiate,' we don't spend a lot of up-front time talking about the royalty rates or what should be the value to you and the value to me. The most productive thing we talk about is how we can marry our capability and yours to build the most value. We consciously focus the conversation on how we can make the pie bigger.[116]

Patent license agreements often arise at the intersection of invention and innovation.[117] Technology providers supply inventions created through research and development ("R&D"). Technology adopters extend the inventions, apply the inventions to create innovations, and use the inventions to generate economic value.[118] Technology adopters absorb knowledge, design products, develop transaction methods, implement production techniques, and obtain complementary assets.[119]

The traditional view of patent license agreements is that licensing royalties exist only to compensate inventors for their costs of invention or for the contributions of their inventions to society.[120] This backward-looking approach to royalties derives from the traditional characterization of patents as rewards for inventors who successfully conclude their R&D efforts.[121]

Patents, however, generate dynamic efficiencies by providing incentives for invention, innovation, and technology adoption. Patents serve to protect the returns to *future* investments in developing the inventions, creating innovations that apply the invention, and using the inventions to generate economic value.[122] Patents have an important forward-looking role in protecting incentives for inventors to improve and commercialize their inventions.

Patent holders commercialize their IP by contracting with technology adopters. Inventors provide their inventions to firms who can use the inventions and develop innovations based on the inventions. The market for inventions includes a variety of transactions including patent license contracts, cross-licensing agreements, patent transfers, and financing of invention and innovation.[123] As Scott Kieff observes,

> [t]his commercialization approach sees property rights in IP serving a role akin to beacons in the dark, drawing to themselves all of those potential complementary users of the IP-protected-asset to interact with the IP owner and each other. This helps them each explore through the bargaining process the possibility of striking contracts with each other.[124]

Kieff points out that patents "facilitate investment in the complex, costly, and risky commercialization activities required to turn nascent inventions into new goods and services."[125]

Patents are the basis of what I have termed the "market for innovative control."[126] The market for inventions is not simply a market for future returns but also a market for rights to control innovation that is based on the inventions. Through patent license agreements, a licensor delegates some innovative control to the licensee.[127] The licensee has decision-making authority to apply and extend the inventions subject to restrictions in the licensing contract.[128] The patent license contract grants to the licensee rights to practice the invention and develop innovations based on the invention.[129] Licensing royalties not only reflect returns to inventors but are also based on the returns to managing the adoption and application of inventions.[130]

The technology transfer addressed by a patent license agreement must add economic value. This means that the technology adopter's usage of the technology generates economic value. The technology adopter creates value by applying the technology to produce goods and services, develop production processes, or implement business methods. For the technology transfer to create economic value, the technology adopter's benefits from the technology transfer must be greater than the technology provider's costs resulting from the transfer.

4.2.4. *The Informed Contract*

The "informed contract" provides a guide for the finder of fact in determining reasonable royalty damages. The "informed contract" is based on the actions of the patent holder and the infringer during the period of infringement rather than the presumption of a willing licensor and a willing licensee. The "informed contract" builds on relevant information revealed during the period of infringement. This allows the court to base reasonable royalty damages on evidence from the patent case. The court constructs an "informed contract" on the basis of information observed after infringement began. This improves estimates of damages to the patent holder from infringement. The burden on the court is reduced because the patent case already gathers much of the relevant information.

Uncertainty is a key issue in the determination of reasonable royalty damages.[131] The "informed contract" bases reasonable royalty damages on information obtained after uncertainty is resolved. The court takes an objective approach based on *ex post* information rather than a subjective approach based on *ex ante* information. In contrast, the "hypothetical negotiation" requires the court to make assumptions about the knowledge, beliefs, and expectations of the parties before information was revealed.[132] The court's task is impossible because parties' knowledge, beliefs, and expectations are unobservable and intangible.

The "hypothetical negotiation" approach requires the court to ignore much of the relevant information. This approach is necessarily speculative because it must imagine an agreement that would have occurred prior to infringement.[133] The "hypothetical negotiation" approach thus provides an inaccurate picture of the patent holder's damages. Reasonable royalty damages under the "hypothetical negotiation" approach are likely to be inconsistent with the evidence in the patent case.

The "informed contract" constructed by the court generally should not be the same as the contract that the two parties would have negotiated at the time the infringement occurred. Both the patent owner and the infringer have engaged in economic activities in the absence of a contract. These activities are likely to differ from the activities both parties would have undertaken if they had entered into a contract. This is because a contract provides incentives that affect the business decisions of the licensor and the licensee.[134]

Contracts differ from immediate exchange such as the sale of products or assets.[135] Contracts involve incentives for performance over time.[136] The object of contract negotiation generally is to maximize the joint returns from exchange.[137] In the same way, a patent license agreement differs from an immediate exchange such as a patent transfer.[138] Rather, a patent license involves incentives for performance over time.[139] The purpose of a patent license agreement is to induce efficient technology adoption by the potential licensee.[140] Also, a patent license agreement should induce efficient invention, innovation, and other profit-maximizing actions by the licensee.[141]

Negotiation of a patent license agreement thus involves much more than simply determining what a willing buyer will offer and a willing seller will receive. License royalties are more than transfer payments for instantaneous exchange. Rather, license royalties are structured to provide incentives for efficient performance over time.[142] Royalties reflect the efforts of the parties to maximize the returns from investment.

The license agreement specifies royalties within the context of other contract provisions.[143] This implies that to determine reasonable royalties, the patent case should construct an "informed contract." The provisions of the "informed contract" should affect how the court estimates reasonable royalty damages.

The terms of the "informed contract" depend on the observed actions of the parties and the interpretation of the court. The "informed contract" lacks intent on the part of the patent owner because the patent owner did not agree to the infringement and related activities of the infringer. The "informed contract" also lacks intent on the part of the infringer whether or not the infringement was intentional. This implies that the "informed contract" can differ from what would have been negotiated by the parties at the time infringement began.

If the infringement was inadvertent, the infringing firm made economic decisions without recognizing the effects of using a patented technology. The infringing firm made technology adoption decisions without taking into account the cost of royalty payments and the benefits and costs of using the patented technology. The infringing firm may not have explored the costs and benefits of adopting and applying alternative technologies. The infringing firm chose products, production processes, and transaction methods without adjusting for royalty payments or contractual restrictions on using the patented technology. The "informed contract" must adjust for the actions of the infringing firm and their effects on the patent holder.

If the infringement was intentional, the infringing firm's actions are likely to differ substantially from those actions if there had been a contract with the patent owner. The infringer did not intend to negotiate a contract and need not have chosen the particular terms of the forgone contract. Intentional infringement includes the possibility that the infringer engaged in licensing negotiations without intending to reach an agreement or engaged in hold-out to delay or prevent an agreement. Again, the court must adjust the provisions of the "informed contract" to address the actions of the infringing firm and their effects on the patent holder.

The court constructs an "informed contract" to remedy the failure to contract. Infringement represents a failure to contract whether the infringer's action was inadvertent or intentional. Infringement may be inadvertent because the infringer was unaware of the patented technology. Alternatively, the infringer may have avoided searching for patented technology, neglected to obtain licenses from patent owners, refused to negotiate a licensing agreement, or copied the technology deliberately. Deliberate infringement, however, can be difficult to prove and, as noted previously, may only trigger enhanced penalties with egregious behavior.[144]

The parties can fail to contract even after a patent suit is filed. The parties have the option of resolving the dispute through a contract either before or during the patent case.[145] In practice, the advantages of negotiation and the costs of the legal system provide incentives for the parties to resolve patent disputes outside the courtroom. Only a small share of patent suits reaches the end of trial. Jean Lanjouw and Mark Schankerman find that once patent suits are filed, about 95% are settled before the end of trial and most are settled before trial begins.[146]

Constructing an "informed contract" can involve considerable difficulties. It is widely acknowledged that the courts have difficulty enforcing observable contracts.[147] Transaction costs limit the efficiency of negotiated contracts, including the design of contingent contracts.[148] Even negotiated contracts are subject to mistakes by the parties.[149] The parties negotiating a patent license agreement face various types of uncertainty. There is uncertainty regarding whether or not the patents are valid and whether or not the patents are included in technology standards. There is also market uncertainty that may affect the returns to the technology implementer and the opportunity costs of the patent owner.

The contract approach to patent infringement offered here suggests an alternative interpretation of the *Georgia-Pacific* factors. *Georgia-Pacific* is not controlling law in the Federal Circuit or in the Supreme Court. The widely cited *Georgia-Pacific* case provides a "comprehensive list of evidentiary facts relevant, in general, to the determination of the amount of a reasonable royalty for a patent license."[150] The *Georgia-Pacific* factors are very useful because they describe the negotiation of royalties in the context of patent license contract provisions, rather than simply the division of rents from exchange.[151] *Georgia-Pacific*, however, is flawed because it requires turning back the clock before infringement and maintains the fiction of a willing licensor and a willing licensee.[152] This can be remedied by using the *Georgia-Pacific* factors in the context of an "informed contract."

Basing the "informed contract" on the facts of the case means that the patent case takes into account information revealed after infringement. In *Panduit*, Judge Howard Markey emphasizes that determining reasonable royalties depends on the facts of the case.[153] This requires a modification of the "hypothetical" negotiation at least where infringement is deliberate.

> On the date a patent issues, a competitor which made no investment in research and development of the invention, has four options: (1) it can

> make and sell a non-infringing substitute product, and refrain from making, using, or selling a product incorporating the patented invention; (2) it can make and sell the patented product, if the patent owner be willing, negotiating a license and paying a reasonable (negotiated) royalty; (3) it can simply take the invention, running the risk that litigation will ensue and that the patent will be found valid and infringed, or (4) it can take a license under option (2) and thereafter repudiate its contract, challenging the validity of the patent. Determination of a reasonable royalty, after election of option (3), cannot, without injustice, be treated as though the infringer had elected option (2) in the first place.[154]

Judge Markey points out the speculative nature of the "hypothetical negotiation":

> Determination of a "reasonable royalty" after infringement, like many devices in the law, rests on a legal fiction. Created in an effort to "compensate" when profits are not provable, the "reasonable royalty" device conjures a "willing" licensor and licensee, who like Ghosts of Christmas Past, are dimly seen as "negotiating" a "license." There is, of course, no actual willingness on either side, and no license to do anything, the infringer being normally enjoined, as is Stahlin, from further manufacture, use, or sale of the patented product.[155]

The "informed contract" approach suggested here is consistent with some aspects of *In re Innovatio* and *LaserDynamics*.[156] Judge James F. Holderman in *In re Innovatio* approaches the "hypothetical negotiation" from an *ex post* perspective, taking into account information revealed since infringement.[157] Judge Holderman points out that "[a]t the time of the hypothetical negotiation, the parties in actuality would not have known whether a given patent is valid or infringed, and the alleged infringer would have had the option of contesting these issues in court."[158] Judge Holderman further observes, "[s]tated another way, the hypothetical negotiator could no longer leave the negotiating table to contest liability in court, and could no longer demand the benefit of uncertainty about a court's rulings."[159]

Judge Holderman cites *Lucent Technologies*, "the hypothetical negotiation also assumes that the asserted patent claims are valid and infringed," explaining that this is "because no hypothetical negotiation would have taken place if it were otherwise. The patent infringer gets no discount on its licensing fee because of uncertainty about its liability that has since been cleared up by litigation."[160] This differs from the *ex ante* negotiation in the absence of infringement that is envisaged in *Lucent Technologies*.[161]

The "informed contract" approach provides a context for the reasonable royalties damage remedy. Total compensatory damages should adjust for imperfections in enforcement and risks associated with the legal process. This is necessary to avoid incentives to infringe and to mitigate incentives for hold-out in patent license negotiations. Compensation should not exceed damages to avoid incentives for excessive use of the legal system. The court can grant injunctions if necessary to fully compensate the patent holder and to prevent future infringement.[162] In addition to compensatory damages, the court can award legal costs to the patent owner.[163] If compensatory damages are not sufficient to address injuries, the courts can provide enhanced damages when there is egregious behavior by an infringer.[164]

4.2.5. *Comparison to the Property Approach to Patent Infringement*

To understand the contribution of the contract approach offered here, it is useful to review the property approach to licensing and infringement. Property-based damages for patent infringement are similar to remedies for breach of a patent license contract: an injunction, compensatory damages, and attorney fees.[165]

This suggests that reasonable royalty damages for infringement should include expectation damages for breach of the "informed contract."[166] The patent owner should also receive injunctive relief and attorney's fees where necessary to compensate for infringement.

Property rules for technology offer the many advantages of the power to exclude.[167] If effectively enforced, property rules provide incentives for market transactions such as patent licensing and patent transfers. Competitive markets serve to promote economically efficient licensing royalties and prices for patent sales.[168]

By protecting IP, patents support what I have called "the market for innovative control."[169] Patent ownership not only generates economic returns but also provides control over how inventions are used.[170] This means that markets for licensing and transferring patents not only allocate rents from invention but also allocate control over innovation based on invention.[171] Patents provide a highly effective system of IP rights that includes exclusion, transferability, disclosure, certification, standardization, and divisibility.[172] These features generate transaction efficiencies by improving the allocation of IP and inducing investment in invention and innovation.

With protections for IP rights, payments for using patented technologies are market determined, reflecting competition among IP owners to supply technology and competition among IP adopters to obtain technology.[173] Market pricing of technology reflects the knowledge of many market participants, which is inevitably superior to the knowledge of courts or government regulators. Market allocation of technology offers efficiencies in specialization and division of creative and productive labor, allocation of technology to the highest-value users, and dynamic efficiencies in promoting R&D.[174]

Property protections are sufficient for economic efficiency when there is knowledge of prior art, detection of infringement, and effective enforcement.[175] With IP rights, injunctions and penalties help reduce hold-out in patent license negotiations and deter patent infringement.[176] Problems arise, however, when there are imperfections in knowledge of prior art, detection, and enforcement. Courts must still determine damages when infringement occurs.[177] Viewing either royalties or damages as payment for the use of property generally does not fully reflect the role of licensing agreements in creating inventions, developing innovations based on inventions, and promoting technology adoption.

The contract approach to infringement is complementary to enforcement of IP rights. Injunctive relief for infringement provides incentives for firms to enter into licensing contracts with patent holders. If patent holders make patent license offers to technology adopters, patent holders run the risk that adopters will engage in hold-out, that is, they may seek to delay negotiation as a means of reducing royalty payments. The possibility of injunctions provides incentives for adopters to negotiate with patent holders rather than engaging in hold-out. Damages for infringement and compensation for legal costs also provide incentives for infringers to avoid engaging in hold-out. Conversely, limitations on infringement damages, injunctive relief, or compensation for legal costs provide incentives for hold-out and infringement.

4.2.6. *Comparison to the Tort Approach to Patent Infringement*

An advantage of the contract approach over the tort approach is that the contract approach identifies the harm from infringement as a failure to contract. This allows a determination of reasonable royalty damages on the basis of an "informed contract." The failure to contract also implies that courts should consider injunctive relief, which can differ from tort approaches. The contract approach is consistent with the tort approach in that it provides compensation for harm to the patent owner caused by infringement.

Tort liability rules are problematic because they often *prevent* the patent holder from excluding access to technology.[178] This contrasts sharply with IP rules, which give patent owners the rights to exclude others from using, making, or selling the invention.[179] Tort liability rules prevent exclusion because infringers can obtain access to the technology simply by paying its market value if liability is established.[180] Richard Epstein observes that in general, property rules dominate liability rules when the objective is "to preserve the stability of possession and social expectations that are necessary for the growth of any complex social order."[181]

The tort approach applies liability rules to infringement.[182] Liability rules are useful when there is imperfect enforcement of property rights because they compensate patent owners for damages and damage payments may reduce infringement.[183] With liability rules, however, courts seeking to determine damages for infringement face the usual constraints on information and expertise. Courts may not accurately estimate lost profits and reasonable royalty damages in comparison to royalties and transfer prices established by efficient markets. Without the possibility of injunctions, the parties may not have sufficient incentive to enter into settlement negotiations. Remedies for patent infringement should provide incentives for efficient contracts between licensors and licensees.[184]

The tort approach and liability rules are increasingly prominent because courts have placed greater emphasis on damages for infringement and stricter limits on injunctions.[185] In *eBay*, the Supreme Court emphasizes that permanent injunctive relief in patent cases requires satisfying the four-factor test, and in particular, showing that damage remedies are inadequate compensation for infringement.[186]

The main purpose of damages is to compensate the patent owner for infringement rather than deterring infringement or punishing the infringer.[187] Over the last half century, damages for infringement have been based on the forgone royalties or the lost profits of the patent owner.[188] 35 U.S.C. § 284 states, "[u]pon finding for the claimant the court shall award the claimant damages adequate to compensate for the infringement, but in no event less than a reasonable royalty for the use made of the invention by the infringer, together with interest and costs as fixed by the court."[189]

Reasonable royalty damages are based on harm to the patent owner.[190] Reasonable royalty damages consider the gains of the infringer only as a means of estimating harm to the patent owner.[191] Prior to *Aro*, however, "judges, lawyers, and academics took for granted that a patentee could recover the infringer's profits."[192] Gain-based remedies refer to restitution damages and disgorgement damages.[193] Under the restitution remedy, the infringer's gain from using the invention would provide a form of relief to the patent owner.[194] Interestingly, some commentators refer to restitution as an implied contract or a quasi-contract.[195]

4.3 The Patent License Contract and the Patent Case

The contract approach contributes to an understanding of reasonable royalty damages for patent infringement. Contract negotiation addresses economic factors that increase or decrease reasonable royalty damages. Reasonable royalty damages should be based on the terms of the "informed contract." The economic benefits and costs of the "informed contract" provide an economic foundation for determining compensatory damages. The contract approach is consistent with the combination of an injunction, damages, and attorney's costs.

4.3.1. *The Framework of a Patent License Contract*

To better understand the patent case, it is useful to consider a list of patent license contract provisions.[196] The elements of a patent license contract affect the benefits of the agreement for the licensor and the licensee.[197] The provisions of a patent license contract also affect the compensation arrangements chosen by the parties.[198] In a similar manner, the provisions of the "informed contract" will help determine reasonable royalty damages for infringement.

Although patent license contracts typically are confidential, it is nonetheless feasible to observe many license agreements.[199] The EDGAR database of the U.S. Securities and Exchange Commission ("SEC") includes many patent license agreements, although confidential portions of these agreements are redacted.[200] The International Trade Commission ("ITC") also includes patent license contract filings, although confidential portions of these agreements are redacted.[201]

The framework of a patent license agreement includes the following six critical elements. The list does not describe in detail provisions such as treatment of confidential information, representations and warranties, disclaimers and limitations of liability, conflict resolution, contract termination and renewal, and enforceability.[202]

4.3.1.1. *Identification of the Parties, Description of their Businesses and their Business Relationship with Each Other*

Patent license contracts reflect the characteristics of the particular licensor and licensee.[203] Each patent license agreement includes rights and obligations specific to the combination of the licensor and licensee.[204] This explains why there generally is no standard patent license contract.[205] The terms of the contract depend on the properties of the technology that is being transferred.[206] The terms of the contract also depend on the applications of the technology by the licensee.[207] The license agreement includes "recitals" that detail developments leading up to the contract such as whether the contract was a settlement of an infringement dispute.[208]

The contract terms including royalties will be tailored to the particular characteristics of the licensor and licensee and will reflect their business relationship. The licensor and the licensee may have other business relationships that are connected to or extend beyond the licensing agreement. These include complementary knowledge transfers from the licensor to the licensee that enhance the value of the patented technology to the licensee resulting in higher royalties for the licensed technology. The licensor may be supplying products to the licensee so that the licensing terms may adjust depending on the value of the business relationship to the licensor and the licensee. For example, Qualcomm supplies modem chips such as Snapdragon for mobile phones to phone manufacturers such as Apple, Asus, LG, Samsung, and Sony.[209] Qualcomm also licenses its patents to those manufacturers and requires patent licences as a condition for the purchase of its chips.[210]

4.3.1.2. *Start Date, Duration of the Agreement, and Period of Coverage*

The start date and duration of the agreement are important for determining performance and the basis for compensation. The duration of the agreement and period of coverage limit the grant of rights to the licensee. The duration of the agreement and period of coverage provide an indication of the activities of the licensee in terms of application of the technology by the licensee. During the time period specified by the contract, the licensee may develop products, production processes, or transaction methods that apply the technology.[211]

The duration of the agreement also provides information about the time period during which the licensee produces output or makes sales that are the basis for royalties to be paid to the licensor.[212] The license contract may also specify how the parties may terminate the agreement. Additionally, the license contract specifies a period of coverage of the patented technology that may differ from the duration of the agreement.[213] Coverage can include compensation for infringement that occurred prior to the start of the licensing agreement.[214] The agreement may also include compensation for use of the patented technology that may extend beyond the term of the licensing agreement.

4.3.1.3. *Definition of the IP*

Perhaps the most important aspect of the patent license contract is identification of the IP covered by the agreement. This part of the agreement specifies what patents are covered by the license and may identify particular claims within patents. Contracts also cover patent portfolios consisting of many individual patents.[215] Because technological change occurs during the contract, the agreement may include new patents that will be added to those portfolios. The contract may include patent families across countries including the United States, the European Union, China, Japan, and Korea.[216] The agreement may also specify other types of IP that are covered by the agreement, including patent applications, trademarks, copyrights, trade secrets, and know-how. In cross-licensing contracts, the contract specifies all of the IP that is covered by the agreement.[217]

4.3.1.4. *Grant of Rights (IP Limits, Field of Use, Territory, Degree of Exclusivity, and Improvements to the Technology)*

The Code of Federal Regulations states "the licensing of a patent transfers a bundle of rights which is less than the entire ownership interest, e.g., rights that may be limited as to time, geographical area, or field of use."[218] The grant of rights imposes limitations that affect the benefits of the transaction for both the licensor and the licensee. The grant of rights may place limitations on both parties in cross-licensing contracts.[219]

For convenience and to mitigate transaction costs, patent licenses may include the entire patent portfolio of the licensor.[220] Alternatively, the patent license may be limited to specific patents and even to specific claims within the patents covered by the agreement.[221] The license agreement may place "field-of-use" restrictions on the licensee's ability to make, use, or sell products using the patented technology.[222] Also, the license agreement may limit the geographic area in which the licensee may use the patented technology.[223]

The license agreement also specifies the degree of exclusivity.[224] The license may be exclusive to the licensee and the licensor may not practice the invention or grant licenses to others.[225] A sole license allows the licensor and the licensee to practice the patent.[226] A nonexclusive license allows the licensor to practice the patent and to license the patent to others.[227] The degree of exclusivity may affect product market competition between the licensor and the licensee and among licensees. The grant of rights also may include a release if the license is part of a settlement of an infringement dispute.[228]

The licensing contract addresses the effects of inventive activities that improve the features of the technology.[229] Either the licensor or the licensee may make improvements in the technology. If the licensor makes improvements in the technology, the licensing contract can specify whether the licensee will be able to use those improvements.[230] The licensee would benefit from these additional improvements, which may be reflected in higher royalties.[231] The license contract determines whether or not to grant the licensee a right to modify the invention and specifies who owns the IP resulting from the modification.[232] Cameron and Borenstein point out that "[l]icensee improvements may be a far more contentious matter to negotiate than licensor improvements. If the licensee intends to actually modify the technology in order to create improvements, the license grant must provide that right."[233] Cameron and Borenstein also point out that the licensing agreement may require the licensee to disclose improvements.[234] If the licensee benefits from ownership of improvements, this may be reflected in higher royalties for the licensed technology.

4.3.1.5. *Compensation*

Royalty payments and other contract terms are jointly determined by the contracting parties. The licensor and the licensee choose royalty payments in the context of other aspects of their business relationship. The royalty payments in the contract are jointly determined with the other provisions of the contract. For example, when the parties are engaged in cross-licensing, there is an adjustment of net payments to reflect the net benefits of the parties.[235] When infringement occurs, however, the infringer is not granting cross-licenses to the patent holder. This means that all other things being equal, the "informed contract" would have greater royalties than a licensing contract with cross-licensing.

To illustrate how compensation is determined within the context of the contract provisions, consider, for example, a patent license agreement between a patent holder Interdigital Technology Corporation ("ITC") and an adopter Samsung Electronics Co., Ltd. ("SEC Group").[236] The contract identifies the parties and describes their businesses.[237] The contract specifies the license grant: "a non-exclusive, worldwide, royalty bearing, perpetual license for the life of and under the Licensed Patents ... to make, have made, use, sell, lease or otherwise dispose of" various time-division multiple access ("TDMA") technologies.[238] The contract specifies running royalty payments per unit of products, in this case subscriber units or infrastructure units.[239] The contract refers to the calculation of royalties based on the manufacture, sale, lease, and/or use of the units of products.[240] The contract provides for advance payments of royalties.[241] The contract has a "no stacking" provision for the two types of products sold by the adopter.[242] The contract also provides for cross-licensing of patents from SEC Group to ITC.[243]

4.3.2. *Patent Pools and the Patent License Contract*

The basic framework of a patent license agreement applies even to licensing contracts offered by patent pools. This is important because patent pool contracts are the exception that proves the rule. Patent pool royalty rates are generally "posted prices" that are publicly announced and the contract itself also is posted and applied to all technology users.[244] These contracts are not negotiated with licensees, which serves to reduce the transaction costs of widespread adoption and application of the technology.[245] Standardized royalties and contract terms, however, reflect internally negotiated agreements among members of the patent pool rather than negotiation between patent owners and technology adopters.[246]

Even with standardization of royalties and contract terms, patent pool license agreements have complex provisions.[247] Patent pool royalties should be viewed in the context of the overall licensing agreement. With suitable adjustments for differences in contract provisions, patent pool contracts can provide comparable license contracts.

Because the agreement is a patent pool license, it typically does not address complementary knowledge transfers.[248] The antitrust guidelines toward IP, however, state concerns that

> a pooling arrangement that requires members to grant licenses to each other for current and future technology at minimal cost may reduce the incentives of its members to engage in research and development because members of the pool have to share their successful research and development and each of the members can free ride on the accomplishments of other pool members.[249]

Consider for example, MPEG LA's MPEG-2 Patent Portfolio License (hereafter "MPEG-2 contract").[250] The license contract offered by the pool covers SEPs and has helped to establish a technology standard.[251] According to the patent pool MPEG LA, "[w]ide acceptance of the MPEG-2 Patent Portfolio License has helped produce the most widely employed standard in consumer electronics history."[252]

4.3.2.1. *Identification of the Parties, Description of their Businesses and their Business Relationship with Each Other*

The MPEG-2 contract begins with identification of the parties.[253] Because the agreement is standardized, it does not specify the business relationship between the parties. The contract identifies the licensors, for example, "Alcatel Lucent, a corporation of France, having a principal place of business in Paris, France."[254] The agreement also limits the business relationships: "Nothing in this Agreement shall be construed to create a principal-agent relationship, partnership or joint venture between the parties, or give rise to any fiduciary duty from one party to the other party."[255]

4.3.2.2. *Start date, Duration of the Agreement, and Period of Coverage*

Section 6 of the MPEG-2 Patent Portfolio License specifies the term and termination: "[t]his agreement shall expire on termination of all MPEG-2 Patent Portfolio Patents."[256] The contract provides for termination for material breach by the licensee.[257]

4.3.2.3. *Definition of the IP*

The MPEG-2 Patent Portfolio License "provides access to patents that are essential to the MPEG-2 Video and Systems coding standards used in set-top boxes, DVD players and recorders, TVs, personal computers, game machines, cameras, DVD Video Discs and other products."[258] The first "whereas" statement identifies the relevant technology standard, "SO/IEC JTC 1 and The International Telecommunications Union have jointly adopted an international standard relating to video data compression and data transport, formally known as ISO/IEC 13818-1 and 13818-2, and referred to in this Agreement as the 'MPEG-2 Standard.'"[259]

4.3.2.4. *Grant of Rights (IP Limits, Field of Use, Territory, Degree of Exclusivity, and Improvements to the Technology)*

The MPEG-2 contract spells out the grant of rights.[260] Section 4.2 of the contract sets forth the licensing administrator grant.[261] For example, for MPEG-2 Decoding Products, the contract reads as follows:

> [T]he Licensing Administrator hereby grants to Licensee a royalty bearing worldwide, nonexclusive, nontransferable sublicense under all MPEG-2 Patent Portfolio Patents to make, have made, use, and Sell or offer for Sale MPEG-2 Decoding Products (i) that bear the brand name that Licensee owns or otherwise has the right to use at Licensee's discretion or (ii) Sold without a brand name if the decision to do so is at the discretion of Licensee.[262]

The whereas clauses also state the following with regard to the grant of rights:

> WHEREAS, each Licensor hereby commits on behalf of itself and its Affiliates to make available licenses and/or sublicenses under any and all MPEG-2 Essential Patents licensable or sublicensable by the Licensor and its Affiliates to any individual, company or other entity desiring such a license and/or sublicense on fair, reasonable and nondiscriminatory terms and conditions;
>
> WHEREAS, each Licensor has granted the Licensing Administrator a worldwide, nonexclusive license and/or sublicense under all MPEG-2

Essential Patents licensable or sublicensable by the Licensor to allow the Licensing Administrator to grant worldwide, non-exclusive sublicenses under all such MPEG-2 Essential Patent(s) under the terms hereof;

WHEREAS, the Licensors desire to make available through the Licensing Administrator license rights under their and their Affiliates' respective MPEG-2 Essential Patents in a single sublicense for the convenience of any individual, company or other entity desirous of acquiring such rights, thereby avoiding the need of such individual, company or other entity to obtain a separate license from each of the Licensors under its MPEG-2 Essential Patent(s);

WHEREAS, the Licensing Administrator desires to grant MPEG-2 Patent Portfolio Licenses to all individuals, companies and other entities desiring such a license under the terms and conditions set forth herein;

WHEREAS, nothing in this Agreement precludes the respective Licensors from licensing or sublicensing rights under individual MPEG-2 Essential Patent(s) to make, use, sell, or offer to sell products or processes including but not limited to the rights licensed in the MPEG-2 Patent Portfolio License.[263]

The agreement states the following:

Licensee shall promptly identify to the Licensing Administrator each Patent(s), except for MPEG-2 Patent Portfolio Patents of the Licensors, licensable or sublicensable by Licensee or its Affiliate(s), if any, which Licensee believes in good faith to be an MPEG-2 Essential Patent(s) within fourteen (14) Days of execution of this Agreement.[264]

4.3.2.5. *Compensation*

Section 3 of the MPEG-2 contract covers royalty and payments.[265] The contract specifies the royalty base and the level of payments in terms of number of units sold.[266] For example, Section 3.1.1 addresses the MPEG-2 Decoding Product.[267]

Upon the Sale of each MPEG-2 Decoding Product Manufactured or Sold in a country in which one or more MPEG-2 Patent Portfolio Patent(s) is in force, the royalty for the sublicense granted pursuant to Section 4.2.1 shall be four United States Dollars (U.S. $4.00) per MPEG-2 Decoding Product Sold prior to January 1, 2002; two and one

> half United States Dollars (U.S. $2.50) per MPEG-2 Decoding Product Sold between January 1, 2002 and the later of December 31, 2009 or the execution date of this Agreement (in which case as provided below, the applicable royalty is Two United States Dollars ($2.00) per MPEG-2 Decoding Product as of the later of such dates) but not later than December 31, 2015; two United States Dollars ($2.00) per MPEG-2 Decoding Product Sold between the later of January 1, 2010 and the execution date of this Agreement (failing which the applicable royalty continues to be two and one half United States Dollars (U.S. $2.50) per MPEG-2 Decoding Product through such execution date) but not later than December 31, 2015; and $0.50 per MPEG-2 Decoding Product Sold after December 31, 2015 with right of voluntary termination on thirty (30) Days' written notice unless and until an election is made to the Licensing Administrator in writing for a royalty of $0.35 per MPEG-2 Decoding Product, MPEG-2 Encoding Product (pursuant to Section 4.3.1.2 below) or Consumer Product (pursuant to Section 4.3.1.3 below) Sold after December 31, 2015 in which case a right of voluntary termination shall not be available until on or after January 1, 2018 on thirty (30) Days' written notice.[268]

4.3.3. *The Framework of the Patent Case*

The patent case proceeds through a number of standard phases: the early case, preliminary injunction, discovery, claim construction, summary judgment, pretrial, the trial, and the post-trial.[269] At each stage, the patent case collects and records information about the parties. The patent case also gathers information about the technology. Patent cases may involve many patents and large numbers of patent claims.[270] The courts engage in claim construction to interpret the meaning of patent claims and evaluate validity and infringement.[271]

The patent case also constructs an "informed contract" when there are SEPs. In *Microsoft v. Motorola*, United States District Judge James L. Robart outlines the case as follows:

> The court's analysis proceeds in six parts. First, the court introduces the parties and their relation to one another. Second, the court provides background on standards, SSOs, and the RAND commitment. Third, the court develops a framework for assessing RAND terms. Specifically, the

> court adopts a modified version of the Georgia-Pacific factors to recreate a "hypothetical negotiation" between the parties. See Georgia-Pacific Corp. v. United States Plywood Corp., 318 F. Supp. 1116 (S.D.N.Y. 1970). Importantly, the court determines that the parties in a "hypothetical negotiation" would set RAND royalty rates by looking at the importance of the SEPs to the standard and the importance of the standard and the SEPs to the products at issue. These considerations are central to the court's analysis. Fourth, after establishing a framework for assessing RAND terms, the court introduces the H.264 Standard and Motorola's H.264 SEPs, analyzing each patent in turn and setting out the portfolio's relative importance to the H.264 Standard and to Microsoft's standard-using products. Fifth, the court introduces the 802.11 Standard and Motorola's 802.11 SEPs and analyzes each 802.11 Patent using the same framework. Sixth, the court uses all of the foregoing information, along with comparables suggested by the parties, to determine an appropriate RAND royalty rate for Motorola's SEPs.[272]

The components of a patent case roughly correspond to the elements of an "informed contract." The patent case thus collects information that describes various aspects of the "informed contract." Many of the terms of the "informed contract" are set in stone because infringement already has occurred. By the time of the patent case, the actions of the infringer and the patent owner have filled in much of the patent license contract. The court discovers and interprets many of the elements of the "informed contract" in the course of resolving the infringement dispute. The court determines royalties in the context of the overall patent case, so that the court determines royalties in the context of an "informed contract."

The patent case can be compared to the basic elements of an "informed contract" identified in the previous sections. The evidence gathered by the patent case provides information that constructs the provisions of a patent license contract.

4.3.3.1. *Identification of the Parties, Description of Their Businesses and their Business Relationship with Each Other*

The patent case specifies the parties to the "informed contract" and their business relationship. The patent case describes the identities and characteristics of the licensor and licensee. We can observe the industries in which the licensor and licensee operate. We know whether or not the licensor practices the patent and we may be able to observe whether or not the patent owner makes use of the patented technology. We also know whether or not the licensor has licensed the patent to others.[273]

4.3.3.2. *Start Date, Duration of the Agreement, and Period of Coverage*

The patent case determines the starting date and the duration of the "informed contract." The date that infringement began determines the starting date of the forgone license contract.[274] The duration of the infringement specifies the duration of the forgone license contract.

4.3.3.3. *Definition of the IP*

The infringement litigation determines the IP that is being transferred by the "informed contract." This is because the litigation determines the IP that is infringed, including particular patents, trade secrets, and other technology. Determining the patents at issue and the specific claims within patents is of critical importance in infringement disputes.[275] Litigants and the courts devote effort to selecting what patents and specific claims within those patents will be part of the infringement case. Menell *et al.* identify many legal strategies for claim winnowing and claim construction.[276] They point out, "[c]onstruing patent claim terms has long been a key aspect of patent litigation and arises in almost every patent case."[277] The district judge has responsibility for claim construction.[278]

4.3.3.4. *Grant of Rights (IP Limits, Field of Use, Territory, Degree of Exclusivity, and Improvements to the Technology)*

The actions of the infringer and the patent owner during the period of infringement determine the rights granted by the "informed contract." The rights granted by a patent license agreement are the main purpose of the contract.[279] The infringer may have made, used, sold, or imported products or production processes based on the patented invention. In this way, the actions of the infringer determine some of the rights granted by the forgone license contract.

The actions of the patent owner determine the type of the "informed contract." If the patent owner does not use or license the technology, the "informed contract" is exclusive. If the patent owner licenses the technology to others, the "informed contract" is nonexclusive. If the patent owner uses the technology but does not license it to others, the "informed contract" is a sole license.

The infringer's actions during the period of infringement determine various restrictions in the "informed contract." These restrictions include the industry and territory in which the technology adopter will operate. The descriptions of the business activities of the infringer indicate the restrictions in the "informed contract." Also, the infringer's relationships with customers and suppliers may indicate whether or not the infringer has shared the technology with third parties, including sub-licensing. This determines whether the forgone license contract granted sub-licensing rights to the licensee.

4.3.3.5. *Compensation*

The business activities of the infringer during the period of infringement determine some critical aspects of consideration in the "informed contract." In particular, it is possible to observe the infringer's number of units sold, prices received, sales revenues, costs, and profits. These provide a basis for determining some aspects of royalty payments in the "informed contract." Royalty payments may be defined in terms of the units sold or sales revenue of the technology adopter. Although the patent case generally focuses on specific patents or patent claims, the IP being infringed is often part of a portfolio. Compensation should reflect the fact that patent licensing often involves entire portfolios rather than individual patents or specific claims.

4.3.4. *Contrast with Hypothetical Negotiation*

The "informed contract" approach proposed here modifies the "hypothetical negotiation" approach by recognizing what actually occurred during the period of infringement. In contrast, the Federal Circuit Bar Association Model Patent Jury Instructions emphasize expectations of the patent holder and infringer for calculating damages:

> A reasonable royalty is the amount of royalty payment that a patent holder and the alleged infringer would have agreed to in a hypothetical negotiation taking place at a time prior to when the infringement first began. In considering this hypothetical negotiation, you should focus on what the expectations of the patent holder and the alleged infringer would have been had they entered into an agreement at that time, and had they acted reasonably in their negotiations.[280]

However, these jury instructions then depart from expectations by recognizing that the patent is valid and infringed, something that may not have been known at the time infringement began.

> In determining this, you must assume that both parties believed the patent was valid and infringed and that both parties were willing to enter into an agreement. The reasonable royalty you determine must be a royalty that would have resulted from the hypothetical negotiation, and not simply a royalty either party would have preferred. Evidence of things that happened after the infringement first began can be considered in evaluating the reasonable royalty only to the extent that the evidence aids in assessing what royalty would have resulted from a hypothetical negotiation. Although evidence of the actual profits an alleged infringer made may be used to determine the anticipated profits at the time of the hypothetical negotiation, the royalty may not be limited or increased based on the actual profits the alleged infringer made.[281]

Consistency requires that the estimation of damages should also recognize the infringer's actual profits after infringement began. This provides a consistent basis for estimating reasonable royalty damages when there is insufficient evidence about lost profits and lost licensing opportunities.

Using the information obtained from the patent case, including the infringer's actual profits, vastly improves the estimate of damages. This better fulfills the purpose of the damage estimate, which is used to compensate the patent holder. The profits of the infringer during the period of infringement are readily obtained and provide the best foundation for calculating damages when the patent holder's lost profits and opportunity costs from technology transfer are not available.

The infringer's profits and other events during the period of infringement provide a better guide than the court's conjectures regarding the expectations of the patent holder and the infringer. What is already an impossible task becomes even more unrealistic when the court asks the jury to imagine what the expectations of the patent holder and the infringer were some years in the past. This requires the jury to forget what actually happened and to form beliefs about how the patent holder and the infringer might have seen the future. It is difficult enough for an individual to understand his own current expectations about the future, let alone his past expectations. By eliminating this philosophical problem, the "informed contract" greatly simplifies the problem of estimating damages.

4.4 Reasonable Royalty Damages

Based on the contract approach outlined here, this section introduces a "market value method" for calculating reasonable royalty damages. The "market value method" does not require information about comparable licensing contracts. Conversely, when information on comparable licensing contracts is available, the contract approach provides guidance on selecting comparable licensing contracts and inferring reasonable royalty damages from those contracts.

4.4.1. *The Market Value Method*

Courts in patent cases may face the difficult task of determining reasonable royalty damages when there are no comparable patent license contracts. Even if there are comparable license contracts, the royalties on those contracts may be confidential. Then, the court must estimate reasonable royalty damages using other information. The market value of a patent or patent portfolio provides information that is useful for determining reasonable royalty damages. An advantage of using market prices of patents is that they embody expectations about earnings without having to make arbitrary estimates of expected royalties.

4.4.1.1. *Calculating Reasonable Royalty Damages*

The "market value method" offered here determines reasonable royalty damages using the estimated market price of a patent. The market price of a patent generally is the best indicator of the economic value of the patent.[282] This approach is consistent with Judge Richard Posner's decision in *Apple v. Motorola*, "[f]or example, a party may use the royalty rate from sufficiently comparable licenses, value the infringed features based upon comparable features in the marketplace, or estimate the value of the benefit provided by the infringed features by a comparing the accused product to non-infringing alternatives."[283]

The purchase price of a patent provides valuable information. As Gregory Leonard and Stephen Rusek observe,

> The purchase of a patent is just another type of market transaction. As such, the purchase of a patent should also be accorded substantial consideration in a damages analysis. Of course, as with any potentially comparable market transaction (including an existing license), it may be necessary to make adjustments to account for any significant dissimilarities in the underlying economic conditions between the market transaction and the hypothetical transaction.[284]

Bruce Burton and Scott Weingust note that

> With some frequency, attorneys, businesspeople and damages experts have attempted to meaningfully compare the purchase price of a patent to the damages being sought by the plaintiff associated with the same patent in patent infringement litigation ("litigation damages value"). Courts have also been asked to consider whether the purchase price of an allegedly infringed patent should somehow limit the amount of patent damages that can be sought as a result of the infringement of that same patent.[285]

Among a number of cases, they cite the example of *Spectralytics*: "In this suit, the defendants argued that the relatively low purchase price for the allegedly infringed patent should preclude plaintiffs from asking for a 5 percent royalty, which, when applied to the relevant royalty base, caused damages to greatly exceed the prior purchase price of the patent."[286]

If there is no observable market price for a patent, it may be possible to estimate the price of the patent based on the market prices of comparable patents. The market prices of comparable patents yield information about the effects of patent characteristics on market value, including the type of technology, the age of the patent, and whether the patent reads on a standard.

The market value of a patent equals the total expected discounted stream of returns from owning the patent. This follows from standard economic analysis of the market value of durable assets.[287] The stream of returns from patent ownership should be discounted at the risk-adjusted interest rate.

The market value of a patent is based on the patent holder's benefits from residual returns and innovative control.[288] The patent holder's benefits include the returns to own-use and the returns to licensing the patent to others over the life of the patent. The returns to own-use include the returns obtained by practicing the patent and excluding others from making, using, selling, or importing the invention.[289] The returns to licensing include royalties and other compensation from entering into patent license contracts net of transaction costs and administrative costs.

The "market value method" does not require information about comparable licenses. This method applies in the absence of licensing of the patent at issue. If the patent owner intended to practice the patent without licensing, the market value method also takes into account the effect of infringement on benefits from own-use. If the patent owner has lost profits from competition, these may be evaluated separately from reasonable royalties.

The "market value method" extends readily to a group of patents because the market prices of the patents can be added to each other. Also, the market value method extends to patent portfolios when there are market prices for the portfolios.

Suppose that the benefits of patent ownership are from licensing royalties. Royalties from a patent license contract equal the expected discounted stream of royalty payments. Then, the market price of a patent equals total licensing royalties across patent licenses over the lifetime of the patent. The market price of a patent equals the total of the expected discounted streams of royalty payments. This implies that we can infer the total expected discounted streams of royalty payments by observing the market price of the patent.

The greater the demand for the patent, including demand for licensing the patent, the greater is the market value of the patent. Because technology has public good features, there can be multiple users of the same technology.[290] Increases in the number of potential users for a patented technology can increase the market value of the patent.[291] For example, the development of the Internet of Things ("IoT") increases the market value of various patents by increasing the number of users and applications of the patented technologies.[292]

For purposes of illustration, suppose that the patent holder does not practice the patent and enters into patent license contracts. Let R denote the present value of total market equilibrium royalties for a particular patent license contract and suppose that contracts continue for the remaining lifetime of the patent. Let V denote the estimated market price of the patent and let T denote licensing and legal costs. Suppose that patent license contracts are symmetric and let N denote the market equilibrium number of licensees. Suppose also that the number of licensees remains constant over the remaining life of the patent. Then, the market value of the patent equals the number of licensees multiplied by market equilibrium royalties net of licensing and legal costs, $V = N \cdot R - T$. This means that the market equilibrium royalty equals the market value of the patent plus licensing and legal costs divided by the number of licensees, $R = (V + T) \div N$. So, we can infer the market equilibrium royalty from the market price of the patent and the number of licensees.

The market value method calculates reasonable royalty damages as the estimated market price of the patent plus licensing and legal costs allocated among infringers. When infringement is symmetric and there are N infringers, reasonable royalty damages are given by $R = (V + T) \div N$. This method of calculating reasonable royalty damages compensates the patent holder for infringement. Infringement deprives the patent holder of the expected returns from patent ownership, including own-use and licensing royalties.

For example, if two firms infringe a patent valued at \$3 million and licensing and legal costs are \$1 million, reasonable royalty damages would be \$2 million per firm. If say four firms infringed a patent portfolio valued at \$60 million, with licensing and legal costs of \$12 million, then reasonable royalty damages would be \$18 million per firm.

If the patent holder is not practicing the patent and has not licensed the patent, compensation should equal the estimated market value of the patent plus licensing and legal costs divided by the number of infringers. Recovering damages from each infringer will recover no more than the market value of the patent plus licensing and legal costs.

If there is only one infringer and the patent owner is not licensing the patent, then the estimated market value of the patent plus licensing and legal costs provides a measure of reasonable royalty damages. A patent transfer is analogous to an exclusive license agreement for the life of the patent. Infringement by a sole infringer then corresponds to a patent transfer or an exclusive license contract. Infringement deprives the patent holder of the sale of the patent or the returns from an exclusive license contract. So, reasonable royalty damages should equal the market value of the patent plus licensing and legal costs, $R = (V + T)$.

The patent holder's returns can differ across patent license contracts depending on the characteristics of the licensee and the provisions of the patent license contracts. For purposes of illustration, suppose that the patent license contracts are for the remaining life of the patent. If the patent holder practices the patent, the patent holder's benefits can be represented by a stream of royalty payments. Consider N licensing agreements with royalties R_i indexed by i. Then, the market value of the patent equals the sum of royalties net of licensing and legal costs, $V = \sum_{i=1}^{N} R_i - T$. Then, each royalty can be expressed as a share of the market value of the patent plus licensing and legal costs, $R_i = s_i(V + T)$, where the shares sum to one, $\sum_{i-1}^{N} s_i = 1$.

When there are multiple infringers, their shares of the market value of the patent may differ. Then, reasonable royalty damages equal the estimated market price of the patent plus licensing and legal costs multiplied by the infringer's share, $R_i = s_i(V + T)$. The shares can be calculated on the basis of the provisions of the informed contracts for the various infringers. For example, if there are two infringers, one of which has infringed on the patent for twice as long as the other, all other things equal, reasonable royalty damages for that infringer would be two-thirds of the market value of the patent plus licensing and legal costs. If there are two infringers and one produces twice as much final output as the other, then all other things equal, reasonable royalty damages for that infringer would again be two-thirds of the market value of the patent plus licensing and legal costs.

If the patent holder practices the patent, a similar approach can be used to assign shares of the market value of the patent plus licensing and legal costs to the patent holder and the infringers. Then, reasonable royalty damages again equal an infringer's share of the market price of the patent plus licensing and legal costs. Suppose that the patent holder practices the patent and there is one infringer, then if the patent holder and the infringer are comparable firms, reasonable royalty damages might be half of the market price of the patent plus licensing and legal costs.

4.4.1.2. *Adjusting Estimates of Market Value*

The contract approach emphasizes the importance of taking into account new information in calculating reasonable royalty damages. The market value of the patent changes to reflect various economic developments that affect the value of own-use and license royalties.

Market prices vary over time depending on changes in supply and demand. Market prices tend to reflect information available to market participants. The market prices of patents vary continually over time just as do prices of financial assets.[293] The book value of a patent need not provide an accurate estimate of its market value. In other words, the market value of a patent is the current price not the past purchase price.[294] It is necessary to adjust the purchase price of a patent or the prices of comparable patents to reflect new information.

A number of events are likely to raise the market value of a patent. First, the market value of a patent is likely to increase when a patent is found to be valid and infringed.[295] The market value of the patent could increase in comparison to the original purchase price, often by a substantial amount. Calculating reasonable royalty damages would require an adjustment of the purchase price to reflect this information. If the patent price reflected a likelihood of 50% that the patent was valid, a finding that the patent was valid could double the patent price. The contract approach suggests that estimates of the market price of the infringed patents should use prices of comparable patents that also are found to be valid and infringed.

Second, the price of a patent will contain a premium if it is an SEP. This requires an upward adjustment in the purchase price of a patent if it becomes an SEP. The court should use the market prices of comparable SEPs when determining reasonable royalty damages for infringement of SEPs. When comparing the price of an SEP to a patent that is not an SEP, it is necessary for the court to make an upward adjustment to the price of the benchmark patent. Just as patents that are found to be valid and infringed command a premium, so too should SEPs command a premium. This is because a patent that is an SEP is likely to be more valuable than a patent that is not an SEP, all other things being equal.[296] The premium is due to the value of the technology represented by an SEP. The premium does not result from the SEP being incorporated into a standard or because the SEP has an SSO seal of approval.

SEPs tend to be more valuable than other patents because SSOs have incentives to choose valuable technologies as the basis for standards.[297] SEPs are often more valuable because they provide benefits to the industry and allow the industry to achieve the best standard.[298] The market prices of SEPs take into account the patents' contribution to the industry technology and ultimate customer benefits.[299] Not all patents declared to be SEPs are actually essential and not all technologies need be adopted to satisfy the standard.[300] The market price of the SEP provides an indication of the incremental contribution of the patented invention to industry technology and customer benefits.

Third, the market price of a patent will increase when demand for the technology increases. There may be new developments in products that use the patented technology. There may be changes in expectations about future technological change. The development of complementary technologies may also raise the demand for the patent technology at issue. Demand increases require an upward adjustment in the past purchase price of the patent or upward adjustments in the prices of comparable patents.

Fourth, the market price of a patent will decrease when the technology becomes obsolete, particularly when inventors develop substitute technologies. This requires a downward adjustment in the purchase price of the patent to reflect current market value. Alternatively, it is necessary to take into account technological change and obsolescence when considering comparable patents.

Fifth, the market price of the patent depends on various other factors such as the age of the patent.[301] The patent price may be low due to restrictions on licensing or cross-licensing as part of the sales contract.[302]

The market value of a patent is affected by competition among buyers and among sellers.[303] Even if there was limited competition in buying or selling a particular patent, the patent transfer price still results from an agreement between a willing buyer and a willing seller. The purchase price will not exceed the buyer's net benefits and will be greater than the seller's opportunity costs. Patent ownership is not concentrated because there are many patent owners. Also, patent adoption is not concentrated because there are many potential purchasers of patents.

The market value of the patent may be affected by the number of infringers. More infringers can reduce the value of the patent by increasing competition in the product market and dissipating returns to the invention.[304] Alternatively, more infringers can increase the value of the patent by employing the technology in production, selling products that use the patented technology, and combining the patented invention with complementary assets.[305]

4.4.1.3. *Estimating the Market Value of a Patent*

Estimates of the market value of a patent should be based on economic considerations. The main economic approaches to estimating the market prices of patents are (1) prices in patent transfers, (2) the intangible asset value of the patent to the firm, and (3) the patent holder's renewal decisions.[306]

The market price of a transfer provides the most accurate indication of the market value of a patent.[307] The market for patents yields information on the characteristics of patents that are bought and sold. The characteristics of patents affect the likelihood that those patents will be transferred, including the age of the patent, the size of the buyer's patent portfolio, and the technological fit of the patent in the buyer's portfolio.[308] There are market prices for some patent portfolio transactions. For example, the Rock Star Alliance acquired the Nortel LTE portfolio for $4.5 billion and Google obtained a portfolio of LTE patents from Motorola Mobility for $5.5 billion.[309]

If the market price of a patent or patent portfolio is not available, the price can be inferred from observed prices of comparable patents. This requires adjustment of the prices of comparable patents to reflect differences between the patents at issue and comparable patents. For example, patents should have a price premium if they are found to be valid and infringed. Patents that are SEPs should command a premium in comparison to patents that are not SEPs. Other factors that potentially affect market value include the age of the patent, forward and backward citations, patent families, and the type of technology.

There are various indicators of patent value that can be used to estimate patent value. This would require a regression analysis to explain variations in the market value of the patent. The regression analysis takes the market value of the patent as the dependent variable and various indicators of patent value as the independent variables.[310]

A number of empirical studies examine the determinants of market prices observed in auctions conducted by the Ocean Tomo company.[311] Timo Fischer and Jan Leidinger consider how the market value of patents depends on forward citations, size of the patent family, and the number of distinct IPC classes to which the patent is assigned.[312] Cristina Odasso *et al.* also use Ocean Tomo data and examine the effects on patent value of the number of claims, forward and backward citations, the size of the patent family, and the technological congruence of the lot being auctioned.[313] Katherine Sneed and Daniel Johnson also look at the market value of patents and examine the effects of such factors as patent scope, family size, forward and backward citations, number of claims, public or private ownership, and the number of inventors.[314] Shyam Nair *et al.* use USPTO information about the patents as predictor variables including age, generality, originality, forward and backward citations, and technology field.[315]

The main issue is obtaining prices of patents. This is becoming more feasible with the expansion of the market for patent transfers. The

United States Patent and Trademark Office has a database that records over 7.2 million patent assignments involving over 12.2 million patents.[316] This database can be used to obtain information about what patents are transferred.[317] The SEC provides information about reported patent sales and acquisitions.[318] The global market for patents is expanding as well.[319]

There are various private sources of information about patent transfers. According to a report by Richardson *et al.* "[w]e are currently tracking $11 billion of patent packages, across over 3,500 packages with more than 86,000 assets. Through assignment data, we see that $2.3 billion of that market has sold. However, this number likely underestimates the total sales because not all assignments are recorded."[320] AST launched IP3 2017 (Industry Patent Purchase Program), "a fixed price, fixed term, collaborative patent buying program."[321] IAM Magazine established IAM Market that brings together patent buyers and sellers.[322] ICAP Patent Brokerage, which refers to itself as the "world's largest neutral patent intermediary," operates patent auctions.[323]

Some patent transfers involve entire patent portfolios. For example, a consortium consisting of Apple, EMC, Ericsson, Microsoft, Sony, and Research In Motion bought a portfolio of patents in 2011 from the bankrupt Nortel Networks for $4.5 billion.[324] The Nortel Networks portfolio consisted of 6,000 patents and patent applications.[325] In 2012, Kodak sold its digital imaging patent portfolio to a consortium of twelve companies for $525 million.[326] Some firms specialize in purchasing patents and patent portfolios. For example, Intellectual Ventures has acquired 95,000 patents and patent applications.[327]

Corporations report the value of their intangible assets including patents in their balance sheets. For example, IBM reports its patents and trademarks as an intangible asset class, and specifies the gross carrying amount, accumulated amortization, and net carrying amount.[328] The company further reports the acquisitions of intangible assets including patents, which provides some information about its market transactions and indicates the market value of patents involved in those transactions.[329] IBM earned 8,088 patents in 2016, becoming the first company to earn more than 8,000 patents in one year, and has earned 97,040 total patents since 1993.[330] IBM reports its royalty-based, custom development income, and sales and other transfers of intellectual property.[331] IBM states in its annual report, "[s]ome of IBM's technological breakthroughs are used exclusively in IBM products, while others are licensed and may be used in IBM products and/or the products of the licensee."[332]

Various economic studies estimate the value of the firm's group of patents by considering the contribution of the firm's intangible IP assets to the value of the firm.[333] Firms report the value of their intangible assets including patents, as in the IBM example. Also, the market value of a firm's patents can be inferred from the market value of the firm by subtracting the value of the firm's tangible assets and non-patent intangible assets. For example, James Besen obtains upper-bound estimates of the expected discounted value of the firm's future patent returns using regressions on Tobin's Q, which is the ratio of the firm's market value to the replacement costs of its assets.[334] Akcigit *et al.* look at the firm's market value in relation to the characteristics of its patent portfolio including a measure of technological distance of the patent portfolio and the firm.[335]

A similar approach to estimating patent value as an intangible asset infers patent value from the effects of patent announcements on the market value of the firm. Leonid Kogan *et al.* estimate the market value of patents from the increase in the market value of a company following the announcement of new patents owned by that company.[336] They find the median value of a patent to be $3.2 million, which they note is comparable to estimates from survey data.[337]

Many studies estimate the market value of patents using information on patent renewals. The appeal of renewal data is that it provides a lower bound for patent value because patent holders will not renew unless they expect the value of the patent to cover the costs of renewal.[338] Empirical analysis shows that there is a concentration of high-value patents in the upper tail of the distribution.[339] Nicolas Van Zeebroeck considers the market potential of a patent.[340] Estimates based on patent renewals, however, do not accurately indicate the extent to which the value of patents exceeds the costs of renewal. For purposes of determining reasonable royalty damages, analysis of renewal data can provide some useful guidance on the lower bound of patent valuation. Such estimates miss the critical upper tail of patent value that may be significant in patent cases involving important patents.

Some studies use survey data based on the evaluation of patent value by patent holders or by experts. Informal reports may be significantly different from market value.[341] Large-scale surveys provide insights into how patent holders subjectively view the value of their patents and what factors influence value, but have limited application for determining the value of specific patents or patent portfolios.[342] Alfonso Gambardella *et al.* examine survey data to determine the value of patents as measured by the price at which patent owners are willing to transfer the patent to others.[343] This is an indicator of the market value of the patent, which could involve both use of the patent by the firm that owns the patent and licensing revenues. They find that that country, technology, and patent class fixed effects explain less than 12% of the variation in patent value.[344] Gambardella *et al.* refer to this result as a "measure of our ignorance" about the determinants of patent value.[345]

There are various other approaches to estimating the market value of patents.[346] Estimates of the market value of patents based on the discounted cash flow of returns to patent ownership may be useful because companies report their licensing revenues. The firm's set of patents, however, is subject to change so it may be difficult to associate returns from licensing to particular groups of patents. Also, the cash flow may reflect the firm's investment in complementary assets and sales efforts.[347] Estimates of the market value of a patent should not be based on arbitrary rules of thumb because such estimates will not reflect economic evidence. In addition, valuation methods based on the costs of R&D are not useful because the market value of any type of good or asset need not be related to the costs incurred to produce it.

Additional study of the determinants of the market value of patents is needed. A better understanding of the determinants of the market value of patents should be useful in estimating the market value of patents and patent portfolios that have not been traded. This would be helpful in applying the proposed market value method because it would help to identify comparable patents and patent portfolios and also to adjust the observed prices of those patents to obtain estimates of the value of the infringed patents.

4.4.2. *Comparable Patent License Contracts*

The contract approach helps the court estimate the patent holder's economic costs due to infringement. The costs of infringement include lost profits resulting from competition with the infringer. The costs of infringement also include the costs of foregone licensing opportunities and other damages to the patent holder. Estimating royalties for the "informed contract" should begin with identifying comparable license contracts. Reasonable royalty damages equal royalties in comparable contracts with adjustments for differences in contract terms and technology.

4.4.2.1. *Calculating Reasonable Royalty Damages from Comparable Licenses*

The patent case determines reasonable royalty damages on the basis of evidence. The best way to measure the patent holder's economic costs of infringement is to consider royalties on comparable patent licenses when such information is available. This important principle is reaffirmed in *Ericsson*, "the fact that a license is not perfectly analogous generally goes to the weight of the evidence, not its admissibility."[348]

The best measure of economic value of a good is its market price.[349] The market price of a good reflects both the demand and supply of the good.[350] With negotiation between a buyer and seller, the exchange price reflects the buyer's benefits and the seller's costs from the exchange and accounts for market alternatives available to the buyer and seller. Prices resulting from bilateral negotiation are market prices.

The imputation of economic value when market prices are not available is a classic economic problem.[351] A solution to this problem is to infer market prices for a good from the market prices of related goods. It may be possible to infer the price of a good from a substitute good by estimating the economic value to consumers of differences in the features of the two goods. The additional expenditures associated with product differences are referred to as *compensating variation*.[352] For example, a particular good may have different prices at two locations. It may be possible to estimate the price of the good at one location from the price of the good at the other location. When the good is mobile and transportation costs are known, the possibility of arbitrage implies that the price difference must be less than transportation costs.[353] For goods that are not mobile, differences in the costs of inputs may be useful in inferring a relationship between prices at two locations. When inputs are mobile, this will limit differences in the prices of the goods at the two locations.[354]

If comparable patent license contracts exist, the royalties in those contracts can be used to estimate reasonable royalty damages. Royalties on comparable patent license contracts provide the best indicators of the market prices of the technology. The court can determine reasonable royalty damages by adding other costs from infringement to market royalties on comparable contracts.

Comparable patent licenses can involve patents other than the infringed patents. The licenses, however, should be for similar technology if not the technology itself. The court in *LaserDynamics* faults an expert witness for not relying on licenses for the patent itself.[355]

The contract approach helps in the search for comparable patent license contracts. A patent license contract differs from the exchange of an asset where the buyer's benefit and the seller's cost are fixed at a certain level. In the exchange of an asset, the negotiation between the buyer and the seller is only about the price.[356] In contrast, the provisions of a license contract affect the adopter's willingness to pay and the provider's willingness to accept. Royalties and the other terms of the contract are part of a contract negotiation.[357] This means that royalties and the other terms of the contract are jointly determined; royalties are not the cause of other contract terms nor are other contract terms the cause of particular values of royalties.

The parties to a patent license contract choose contract provisions and engage in economic activities to maximize the economic value of the contract.[358] Negotiation generates an efficient outcome when transaction costs are low, as Ronald Coase emphasized in his discussion of bargaining when there are social and private costs.[359] The parties adjust the terms of the contract to account for benefits, costs, and legal constraints.

The "informed contract," however, reflects decisions made by the patent holder and infringer in the absence of negotiation. It follows that the "informed contract" is likely to differ from an efficient contract. Reasonable royalty damages are thus likely to differ from a "hypothetical negotiation." So, the provisions of comparable contractual agreements are likely to differ from the terms of the "informed contract." The patent holder's damages may be greater than or equal to the royalties in a comparable contract.

It generally will be necessary to modify the royalties on comparable licenses to estimate reasonable royalty damages. The court should consider compensating variation in royalties to account for the effects of contract provisions on the economic costs to the patent holder. It is necessary to adjust market royalties for contract features such as the royalty base, the duration of the agreement, additional knowledge transfers, investment by the licensee, and degree of exclusivity.

As already noted, the contract approach suggests the need to use information revealed during the period of infringement. The actions of the parties determine many of the provisions of the informed patent license contract. The provisions of the informed patent license contract affect the calculation of reasonable royalty damages. For example, royalties should be greater for exclusive contracts than they would be for nonexclusive contracts.

Patent license contracts present additional complications because they are often the subject of bilateral negotiation and royalties depend on the unique characteristics of the licensor–licensee pair and the provisions of the contract.[360] The patent case constructs many of the contract terms so that comparable licenses should approximate those provisions. Comparable contracts should be those with provisions similar to those of the "informed contract." It may be necessary to adjust royalties from comparable licenses that differ from the "informed contract." Some contractual provisions benefit the licensor and others benefit the licensee and may systematically increase or decrease license royalties.

The "informed contract" approach presented here suggests that the best comparable contracts are those in which the parties agree that the patent is valid and the licensee is making use of the patented technology. This implies that the court should adjust the royalties on benchmark patent licenses that have not been found to be valid and infringed.

Jonathan Masur argues that when using comparable patents that have not been found valid and infringed, the court should make an upward adjustment in royalties.[361] Alternatively, he suggests that courts should use comparable licenses that accurately reflect the finding that a patent was valid and infringed or modify comparable licenses accordingly.[362] When using a comparable patent license that has not been found to be valid or infringed, the court should multiply royalties from comparable contracts by 1/z where z is a probability that represents the parties' expectations that a patent would be found to be valid and infringed. Thus, if the parties to a comparable license contract negotiated royalties expecting that a patent will be found to be valid and infringed with a probability of say 25%, the court should multiply those royalties by a factor of four. This adjusts for expectations of the parties in a "hypothetical negotiation" prior to the determination that the particular patent is valid and infringed.[363]

It is not necessary, however, for the court to make the full adjustment for the probability that a patent is found valid and infringed. Litigation costs help to deter infringement and induce adopters to license patents. This increases negotiated royalties and offsets some of the effects of uncertainty about whether a patent will be found to be valid and infringed. Thus, if negotiated royalties equal damages multiplied by the likelihood the patent is found valid and infringed plus legal costs L, it follows that $R = zD + L$. For example, if anticipated damages are 100 and legal costs are forty, then when z equals 25%, the corresponding royalty would equal sixty-five. So, damages would involve an adjustment to the benchmark royalty of 100/65, which is about one and a half.

Litigation costs are substantial. An AIPLA survey compares average litigation costs to the amount in controversy.[364] For an amount in controversy less than $1 million, legal costs through trial are $873,000.[365] For an amount in controversy between $1 million and $10 million, legal costs through trial are $2.2 million.[366] For an amount in controversy between $10 million and $25 million, legal costs through trial are $3.5 million.[367] Finally, for an amount in controversy greater than $25 million, legal costs through trial are $6.3 million.[368] This suggests that adjustments of benchmark royalties to take into account the determination that a patent is valid and infringed need not reflect the full effects of uncertainty.

Some commentators recommend that "naked licenses" should be used as comparable licenses in calculating reasonable royalty damages.[369] This recommendation is based on the erroneous idea is that removing contractual provisions would help to estimate royalties. This is inconsistent with the contract approach because infringement is not a "naked license." Rather, infringement generates harm to the technology provider and benefits to the technology adopter that differs from a "naked license." The economic benefits and costs of infringement are comparable to a more complex licensing arrangement that is consistent with the patent case.

The term "naked license" indicates a basic or simple license that allows usage of the technology with no transfers of additional IP.[370] Even the most basic license, however, is likely to have contract terms beyond royalties.[371] Additional contract terms are necessary to spell out the details of the business relationship over time and to address various contingencies.

The patent owner has an interest in managing how the IP is used in the marketplace, making a "naked license" unlikely for patent agreements. In trademark licensing, a "naked license" refers to an absence of formal quality controls by the licensor over the licensee.[372] Even if the licensor trusts the licensee to maintain product quality and the licensee does provide product quality, the courts view a "naked license" as abandonment of a trademark, resulting in the loss of a trademark.[373] In the same way, the courts should reject the notion of a "naked license" as the basis for royalties in patent disputes.

The contract approach presented here addresses important legal issues regarding expert testimony and the rules of evidence. After *Lucent Technologies* and *ResQNet*, experts must place royalties in comparable contracts in some context.[374] The provisions of patent license contracts provide the context for royalties. The provisions of comparable patent license contracts should be compared to the provisions of the "informed contract" examined by the court.

4.4.2.2. *Comparable Licenses with Technology Standards and SEPs*

Technology standards affect the use of comparable license contracts for the determination of reasonable royalty damages. If the patents at issue are SEPs, it is useful to consider royalties for license contracts that also involve SEPs. If the patents at issue are SEPs, the royalties on comparable license contracts for patents that are not SEPs should be adjusted upward to account for the additional economic value generated by SEPs. Finding comparable license contracts should take into account differences in SEPs and possible over-declaration of SEPs.[375]

The standard does not make the technology; it is the technology that makes the standard. Technology standards create value for industries by allowing companies to coordinate their inventive and innovative efforts.[376]

SSOs provide mechanisms for reducing coordination costs and also facilitate the exchange of information among industry members.[377] As noted previously, SSOs choose SEPs because of the contribution of the patented inventions to the value of the technology.[378] The economic value of the technologies underlying the standard is what drives the market value of standardized products.[379]

FRAND commitments for SEPs raise fundamental issues with regard to comparable license contracts. Addressing these issues depends on whether the legal interpretation of FRAND commitments should rely on property, tort, or contracts.

One view of FRAND commitments is based on contract law because there is an agreement between the SEP holder and the SSO. Gregory Sidak characterizes FRAND commitments as contracts.[380] He observes that the SEP holder satisfies the FRAND obligation by making a FRAND offer to a potential licensee.[381] Sidak concludes that "[t]here is no intellectually rigorous basis for creating the legal presumption that an SEP holder's request for an injunction either breaches its FRAND commitment or violates antitrust law."[382]

Another view of FRAND commitments is based on property and tort law. Jay Kesan and Carol Hayes argue for property and tort approaches to FRAND commitments and against contract principles because they are concerned that contractual obligations may not accompany patent transfers.[383] They oppose injunctions for SEPS on that basis: "Through application of theoretical insights concerning property rules and liability rules, we established why a FRAND commitment should be understood as a waiver of the right to seek an injunction for infringement of an SEP."[384]

The contract approach to reasonable royalty damages introduced here supports a contract view of FRAND obligations. The patent holder makes a contractual commitment to the SSO regarding negotiation of royalties for SEPs. The patent holder's FRAND obligations are satisfied by the choice of compensation provisions in patent license contracts.

FRAND obligations are consistent with injunctions. The question of whether or not injunctions are justified in a particular patent case depends on the negotiation of patent license contracts. Judge Posner in *Apple v. Motorola* points out that FRAND commitments do not preclude the use of injunctions: "an injunction may be justified where an infringer unilaterally refuses a FRAND royalty or unreasonably delays negotiations to the same effect."[385] The Court of Justice of the European Union in *Huawei v. ZTE* emphasizes that the actions of both the patent owner and the infringer determine the availability of injunctive relief.[386] Holders of SEPs must alert infringers and make license offers to infringers willing to enter into a patent license contract on FRAND terms.[387]

Patent license contracts play an important role in *Huawei v. ZTE*.[388] Holders of SEPs that make contract offers to license the SEPs on FRAND terms may pursue an injunction without violating competition law.[389] According to Sir Robin Jacobs and Alexander Milner, "[b]roadly the position is that competition law merely bolsters existing FRAND commitments (to grant licences on Fair Reasonable and Non-Discriminatory terms) and compels owners of SEPs to offer to grant licences on such terms."[390]

Injunctions may not be necessary when comparable license agreements allow the determination of reasonable royalty damages. Judge Posner in *Apple v. Motorola* observes, "Motorola's FRAND commitments, which have yielded many license agreements encompassing the '898 patent, strongly suggest that money damages are adequate to fully compensate Motorola for any infringement."[391]

To apply comparable contracts in determining reasonable royalty damages, it is necessary to determine whether or not the patent holder in those contracts has made FRAND commitments. Then, it is necessary to determine whether or not the patent holder in the patent case has SEPs that are subject to FRAND commitments. The royalties for the comparable contract may need to be adjusted accordingly if the patents differ in terms of FRAND commitments.

Patent license contracts play an important role in patent disputes involving SEPs. A patent license contract may insulate patent owners from disputes regarding whether license terms meet a FRAND commitment. In *Unwired Planet*, Justice Colin Birss states, "[i]f parties agree license terms then their rights and obligations under the ETSI FRAND undertaking will be discharged and replaced by their contractual rights under the license."[392]

Unwired Planet finds that FRAND commitments apply to royalties that are agreed to under patent license contracts rather than to royalty offers by either technology providers or technology adopters.[393] Justice Birss writes,

> [t]herefore it makes much more sense to interpret the ETSI FRAND obligation as applicable primarily to the finally agreed terms rather than to the offers. In other words, it is an obligation to enter into FRAND licenses. The same logic also applies to implementers: an obligation on implementers to make FRAND *offers* as opposed to enter into FRAND licenses would have them paying rates higher than the FRAND rate.[394]

Reasonable royalties for SEPs should consider comparable contracts for SEPs that were negotiated after the relevant standards were established. The Federal Trade Commission argues instead that reasonable royalty damages for SEPs should be based on royalties that would have been negotiated before the standard chosen.[395] Critiquing the FTC report, Richard Epstein *et al.* argue in contrast that

> if the FTC's bargain prices were always available to infringers through the courts — or worse yet, were used as a standard to accuse negotiated license terms retroactively of being 'unreasonable' — the result would be the destruction of private bargains and the generation of government-sponsored hold-up that would substantially reduce the returns to innovators and adopters alike.[396]

4.4.2.3. *Adjusting for the Provisions of the Patent License Contract*

The *structure of royalty payments* refers to the various royalty provisions in the licensing contract. A particular level of total royalties is consistent with different combinations of running royalties and lump-sum fees.[397] Also, a particular level of total royalties is consistent with different combinations of royalties and outputs or sales levels.[398] Running royalties and lump-sum fees are building blocks that are used to construct total royalty payments.[399]

The various provisions of the patent license contract affect the economic benefits of the technology adopter and the economic costs of the technology provider. These provisions affect how the parties allocate the economic value of the contract through royalties. Various economic factors affect the structure and level of royalty payments.

Patent license agreements often involve the entire patent portfolio, for convenience and lowering transaction cost. Some bundling occurs for the usual reasons that firms bundle complements, or substitutes, or both. Some bundling occurs to address asymmetric information about the technology being offered and the needs of the licensee.[400] Patent license contracts bundle patents even when the parties are aware that the licensee would only use some subset of the available technology.

A patent case, however, generally extracts particular patents or even specific claims from patents.[401] This can affect the court's search for comparable licenses. This suggests that the court should use the full portfolio in the search for comparable license agreements if contracting parties typically do not extract particular patents or specific claims.

Reasonable royalty damages generally should be increased in comparison with contracts that bundle patent licenses with other products. This is because the infringing firm does not purchase the products that are bundled with the patent license. Varner observes,

> [a] patent license also may specify that a royalty will be reduced if the licensed product is combined with another product. Combination product royalty reductions are a way to apportion a licensed patent's value in the event that a licensed product is later combined into a single saleable unit with another product that is not covered by the patented technology.[402]

In the absence of bundling, the royalty would be increased.

The technology adopter's economic benefits are equal to the value obtained by using the patented technology in combination with other technologies minus the net benefits of using the substitute technology in combination with other technologies. Let P represent the value of using the patented technology in combination with other technologies. This is the present value of the technology adopter's stream of profits during the period of infringement. Profits are the technology adopter's revenues minus any relevant costs, including production, marketing and sales, additional R&D, and transaction costs. Let A represent the adopter's opportunity cost. The adopter's opportunity costs are the returns to applying the best alternative technology available at the time infringement began. This is the best alternative technology that would have been available to the parties negotiating a licensing contract. By using the best alternative technology in combination with other technologies, the technology adopter would have obtained value P^A and paid royalties R^A for access to the alternative technology. Then, the adopter's opportunity costs are the net returns that the technology adopter would have obtained from using the best alternative technology, $A = P^A - R^A$.

Then, the adopter's economic benefits can be written as $B = P - A$. Alternatively, the technology adopter's economic benefits equal the incremental contribution of the invention plus royalties on the best alternative invention, $B = P - P^A + R^A$.

Let C represent the patent holder's opportunity costs. These costs of providing the technology are contingent on the terms of the patent licensing contract. These costs are the technology provider's willingness to accept payment for the technology. Total opportunity costs are the discounted stream of opportunity costs during the term of the contract. These costs include returns to licensing to other potential technology adopters that might have occurred. These costs also can include lost profits due to competition from the technology adopter.

The economic value of the contract equals the economic benefits of the technology adopter of using the technology minus the economic costs of the patent holder of providing the technology, $B - C$. A voluntary technology transaction could only occur only if the licensee's economic benefits are greater than the licensor's economic costs, $B > C$. Royalties allocate the economic value of the contract between the two parties. The technology adopter's economic benefits from using the patented invention B provide an upper limit to the range of reasonable royalty damages. The technology provider's economic costs of supplying the invention provide a lower limit to the range of reasonable royalty damages. If the informed contract has economic value, that is, if economic benefits exceed economic costs, this specifies a range for licensing royalties, $C \leq R \leq B$.

Reasonable royalty damages, however, may exceed the infringer's benefits. This is because the infringer obtained the technology without cost and thus made business decisions without taking into account the market value of the patented technology. Without taking into account running royalties, an infringer might have expanded output beyond the efficient level for those royalties. It is possible that the infringer's economic returns were not sufficient to cover the market value of the patented technology. Faced with paying the market value of the patented technology, the infringer would not have entered into a licensing contract. Infringement may also impose various other costs on the patent holder such as legal costs and the costs of monitoring infringement.[403]

As already stated previously, royalties in patent license agreements are not just fixed payments for use of the inventions.[404] Rather, they are combinations of payments consisting of running royalties, lump-sum license fees, and payments contingent on milestones attained by the licensee.[405] There may also be maximum or minimum limits on payments as a share of profits, maintenance fees, and compensation in the form of equity in the licensee's firm. Running royalties typically are based on sales.[406] If running royalties are *specific*, running royalties consist of a royalty r multiplied by the number of units sold Q. Total royalty payments with specific running royalties are $R = F + rQ$, where F is a lump-sum fee. If running royalty payments are *ad valorem*, they are a share s of the licensee's revenues PQ, where P is the sales price. Total royalties with ad valorem running royalties are $R = F + sPQ$.

The structure of the royalty payments often depends on the particular characteristics of the licensor and the licensee including in what industry the firms operate.[407] The extent of competition and ease of entry in the downstream industry may affect the structure of royalty payments. If the downstream industry resembles the economics textbook description of "perfect competition," it may not be possible for licensees to pay fixed fees because competition and entry would drive down the profits of licensees.[408] Accordingly, licensors would rely on running royalties based either on revenues or on units sold.[409] Conversely, if the downstream industry resembles a textbook "monopoly," the licensor can charge a lump-sum royalty either up front or on an annual basis.[410] Using a lump-sum royalty in licensing to a monopolist avoids the distortionary effects of double marginalization, which would occur because the monopolist would increase final product prices to reflect the higher per-unit costs that would result from a running royalty.

If the downstream industry, however, lies between the extremes of "perfect competition" and "monopoly," some combination of running royalties and lump-sum royalties may be feasible. I show elsewhere that when there is imperfect competition in the downstream industry, an inventor may rely on both running royalties and lump-sum royalties.[411] I also show that when there is imperfect competition in the downstream industry, and there is competition among inventors offering substitute inventions, the patent license may involve both running royalties and lump-sum royalties.[412] This is because competition limits profits in the downstream industry, which in turn limits lump-sum royalties so that the licensor uses a combination of running royalties and lump-sum royalties.

Eric Stasik surveys announcements of royalty rates by licensors and finds that royalties are shares of sales of the final product, in this case, mobile telephone handsets.[413] Stasik cautions, "[i]t is necessary at this point to clarify that an 'announced' royalty rate may be significantly different than the 'actual' royalty rate resulting from a bi-lateral negotiation."[414] Even though these are likely to be opening bids in negotiations, the final outcome also appears to be royalties based on shares of sales revenues. Stasik cites a study by Kearsey and Goldstein showing that for 3G technology, "[i]ndividual patent owners usually charge between 0.5 and 4 percent on essential patents," again in terms of shares of final sales revenues.[415]

Thomas Varner finds that royalty rates for patent license contracts are among the lowest rates observed in IP license agreements.[416] Varner's 2010 study examines royalty rates for a wide variety of IP license contracts, including "joint venture agreements, product bundling or re-branding agreements, distribution agreements, settlement agreements, manufacturing and supply agreements, employment agreements, and acquisition agreements."[417] Varner in a 2011 study focuses on patent licensing royalties including fixed fees, running royalties, and equity.[418] Varner considers both licensing of "patents-plus-know-how" and "bare patents" and finds that practically all contracts for "patents-plus-know-how" have running royalties and about 85% of contracts for "bare patents" have running royalties.[419] Varner finds that running royalties are based on sales revenue for about 90% of license contracts, with most of the rest of running royalties relying on units of output sold.[420]

Mariko Sakakibara examines the structure of royalties in Japanese patent license contracts.[421] The contracts involve both running royalties and lump-sum payments.[422] She finds that royalties are affected by the profitability of underlying patents, the reservation price of licensors, and the relative bargaining power of licensors and licensee.[423] Sakakibara conducts a regression analysis to examine how various determinants affect royalties in patent license contracts.[424] The regressions consider the effects on licensing royalties of the following sets of factors: the attributes of licensors, the attributes of licensees, the attributes of licensor–licensee pairs, the attributes of contracts, and the attributes of traded patents.[425]

Sakakibara addresses the structure of royalty payments by considering both running royalties and lump-sum royalties, controlling for the effects of sales in examining the determinants of running royalties.[426] Also, she controls for the length of the contract and whether or not the contract is exclusive.[427] Sakakibara considers the attributes of licensors and licensees in terms of whether they are large or small firms and whether they are companies or research organizations.[428] She finds that larger licensors tend to receive lower running royalties and larger licensees tend to have higher running royalties.[429] Royalties are decreasing in the age of patents being licensed, perhaps reflecting the effects of technological change on obsolescence of inventions.[430] Royalties are increasing in patent effectiveness, measured by survey analysis within industry categories.[431]

An empirical analysis of the market for technology conducted by Pere Arqué-Castells and me demonstrates that technology transactions take into account both the technology provider's lost profits from business stealing and the technology adopter's increased profits from business creation.[432] The study finds that market proximity and technological proximity can increase the likelihood of a match between a technology provider and a technology adopter.[433] Market proximity and technological proximity increase the economic value of the contract.[434] As a consequence, market proximity and technological proximity may increase royalties in the forgone contract. This suggests that market proximity and technological proximity should increase reasonable royalty damages.

The structure of royalty payments is particularly significant because of their incentive effects. An important function of the royalty structure is to provide incentives for the licensee to invest efficiently in applying the invention and to share information about the profitability of using the invention.[435] The royalty structure also may provide incentives for the licensor to provide know-how to the licensee. Economic studies have examined how asymmetric information and incentives affect the structure of royalties in patent license contracts.[436] Deepak Hegde, for example, explores how tacit knowledge affects the structure of royalties in licensing contracts, including royalty rates, lump-sum fees, milestones, and minimum payments.[437]

4.4.2.4. *The Georgia-Pacific Factors*

The contract approach introduced here suggests that the *Georgia-Pacific* factors are useful only if they correspond to the information revealed by the patent case. In *Ericsson v. D-Link*, the court observes that "the district court included all 15 *Georgia-Pacific* factors in its damages instruction — over objection — without considering their relevance to the record created at trial."[438] Events such as technology standardization and FRAND obligations affect the applicability of the factors: "[i]n a case involving RAND-encumbered patents, many of the *Georgia-Pacific* factors simply are not relevant; many are even contrary to RAND principles."[439]

The "informed contract" approach provides guidance on using the *Georgia-Pacific* factors.[440] The *Georgia-Pacific* factors have been applied widely.[441] Although these factors focus on the provision of evidence, they are significant because they characterize the economic basis for reasonable royalty damages in the context of a contract. The *Georgia-Pacific* factors suggest how comparable contracts can be used to estimate reasonable royalty damages.[442]

Georgia-Pacific quotes a Supreme Court decision:

> [i]n fixing damages on a royalty basis against an infringer, the sum allowed should be reasonable and that which would be accepted by a prudent licensee who wished to obtain a license but was not so compelled and a prudent patentee, who wished to grant a license but was not so compelled.[443]

Georgia-Pacific also cites *Faulkner v. Gibbs*, 199 F.2d 635, 639 (9th Cir. 1952): "[t]he primary inquiry, often complicated by secondary ones, is what the parties would have agreed upon, if both were reasonably trying to reach an agreement."[444] *Georgia-Pacific* refers to this as the willing buyer and willing seller rule, but also as "a willing licensor and a willing licensee."[445]

The *Georgia-Pacific* factors view royalties in the context of an overall contractual agreement. The first two factors take into account the market alternatives available to both parties.[446] The first factor considers the royalties that the patent owner may have received from alternative licensees: "The royalties received by the patentee for the licensing of the patent in suit, proving or tending to prove an established royalty."[447] As already noted, this approach should be followed if there is information about the royalties that the patent owner would have received.[448]

The second factor considers market alternatives that may be available to the adopter or comparable royalty rates paid by the adopter: "The rates paid by the licensee for the use of other patents comparable to the patent in suit."[449] As already noted, if this information is not available, it may be possible to use the market value of comparable patents.[450]

The *Georgia-Pacific* factors three through seven explicitly identify the contractual provisions of the patent license contract: the nature and scope of the license, the licensor's conditions on restrictions of licensing to others, the commercial relationship between the licensor and the licensee, the value of the invention in generating sales, and the duration of the license.[451] These factors are important aspects of patent license contracts and are very likely to be specified in the patent case.[452] These factors are important determinants of reasonable royalty damages for infringement.

Factor three refers to "[t]he nature and scope of the license, as exclusive or non-exclusive; or as restricted or non-restricted in terms of territory or with respect to whom the manufactured product may be sold."[453] Thus, royalties should be increased the greater the scope of the "informed contract" and the greater the territory covered by the infringer. Factor four refers to "[t]he licensor's established policy and marketing program to maintain his patent monopoly by not licensing others to use the invention or by granting licenses under special conditions designed to preserve that monopoly."[454] Royalties should be increased to the extent that the patent owner would have chosen not to license to others or would have granted few licenses to others to preserve the patent holder's market power.

Factor five is "[t]he commercial relationship between the licensor and licensee, such as, whether they are competitors in the same territory in the same line of business; or whether they are inventor and promoter."[455] If the patent owner and the infringer are competitors, royalties in patent license contracts should be increased in comparison with the situation in which the patent owner and the infringer are inventor and promoter, respectively. Factor six refers to "[t]he effect of selling the patented specialty in promoting sales of other products of the licensee; the existing value of the invention to the licensor as a generator of sales of his non-patented items; and the extent of such derivative or convoyed sales."[456] Factor seven specifies "the duration of the patent and the term of the license."[457]

The next three factors take into account the market value of the patent holder's IP.[458] These factors will affect the market price of the patent in patent transfers and royalties in patent license contracts.[459] These factors are as follows: "8. The established profitability of the product made under the patent; its commercial success; and its current popularity."[460] "9. The utility and advantages of the patent property over the old modes or devices, if any, that had been used for working out similar results."[461] "10. The nature of the patented invention; the character of the commercial embodiment of it as owned and produced by the licensor; and the benefits to those who have used the invention."[462]

The eleventh factor addresses the actions of the technology implementer: "The extent to which the infringer has made use of the invention; and any evidence probative of the value of that use."[463] The greater the usage of the invention, the higher should be reasonable royalty damages.

The twelfth factor concerns the markdown of the infringer's profit: "The portion of the profit or of the selling price that may be customary in the particular business or in comparable businesses to allow for the use of the invention or analogous inventions."[464] This factor directly addresses the infringer's profit.[465] The share should not be too high to allow the infringer's business to operate. It may be useful to consider customary profit shares in the particular industry if evidence permits without resorting to an arbitrary rule of thumb.

The thirtieth factor also concerns the markdown of the infringer's profit: "The portion of the realizable profit that should be credited to the invention as distinguished from non-patented elements, the manufacturing process, business risks, or significant features or improvements added by the infringer."[466] This addresses the question of apportionment that will be addressed further. The fourteenth *Georgia-Pacific* factor refers to the testimony of qualified experts.[467] The "informed contract" approach presented here suggests that courts modify the fifteenth and final *Georgia-Pacific* factor, which describes the "hypothetical negotiation."[468]

4.4.3. *The Infringer's Benefits: The "Bottom-Up" and "Top-Down" Approaches*

Up to this point, the discussion has focused on reasonable royalty damage calculations based on the patent holder's economic costs. The market value method and the comparable license method provide estimates of the patent holder's opportunity costs. Now, the discussion shifts to consideration of damage calculations based on the infringer's benefits. Many patent cases apply some version of either the "bottom-up" or the "top-down" approaches, both of which base reasonable royalty damages on the benefits of the infringer.[469]

4.4.3.1. *The Infringer's Benefits*

If reasonable royalty damages do not exceed the infringer's benefits, then reasonable royalty damages can be calculated on the basis of the infringer's benefits.[470] This approach tends to depart from economic and legal analysis. The main problem with basing reasonable royalty damages on the benefits to the infringer is that it may not account for the value of the patent holder's IP.[471] The patent holder's damages from infringement may exceed the infringer's benefits so that calculating reasonable royalty damages as a share of the infringer's benefits may fail to provide full compensation for the patent holder.

In a patent license contract negotiation, recall that royalties are in a *range* between the opportunity costs of the patent holder and the economic benefits of the technology adopter, $C \leq R \leq B$.[472] The opportunity costs C of the patent holder are lost profits, lost licensing revenues, and other licensing costs.[473] The economic benefits B of the technology adopter are the adopter's profits net of the returns to using alternative technologies.[474] The patent holder's opportunity costs and the adopter's benefits depend on the provisions of the contract. Negotiated royalties also depend on the provisions of the contract.

Negotiated royalties are a *point* within this range. This means that negotiated royalties can be viewed in two equivalent ways: either as a markup of the patent holder's opportunity costs, $R = YC$, or as a markdown of the technology adopter's benefits, $R = XB$.[475] For any given royalty, the markup would be equal to the markdown multiplied by the ratio of the adopter's benefits to the provider's opportunity costs, $Y = X (B/C)$.[476]

The question is whether reasonable royalty damages can be determined on the basis of the infringer's benefits. If reasonable royalty damages were the result of a "hypothetical negotiation," and the outcome of the negotiation could be determined with some precision, then expressing royalties based on the patent holder's opportunity costs or the infringer's benefits would be equivalent. The infringer's profits, however, are an imperfect measure of damages to the patent holder because there was no licensing agreement. The result resembles a disgorgement remedy rather than full compensation of the patent holder.

As our discussion has emphasized, characterizing the "hypothetical negotiation" is practically impossible. The court generally cannot be expected to determine the knowledge and expectations of the parties. The "hypothetical negotiation" presumes a willing licensor and a willing licensee, which may be inaccurate.[477]

The "bottom-up" or the "top-down" approaches fail to fully compensate the patent holder when the market value of the patent holder's IP exceeds the infringer's benefits.[478] Also, markdowns of the infringer's benefits tend to be arbitrary and disconnected from market value.[479] Such markdowns may not accurately account for the market value of the patent holder's IP.[480]

Shares of the infringer's benefits tend to be arbitrary and are usually based on counting patents.[481] This is often a problem with SEPs because many patents that are declared essential may not be necessary to meet technical standards.[482] Calculating reasonable royalty damages based on counting patents waters down the contribution of technologically important patents, which can result in incomplete compensation for patent holders' IP.[483] Judge Holderman cautions in *In re Innovatio*: "[t]he court agrees that the profit margin on an accused product is not always dispositive for determining a RAND rate."[484]

4.4.3.2. *The "Bottom-Up" Approach*

The "bottom-up" approach calculates reasonable royalty damages as a share of the infringer's benefit.[485] This means that reasonable royalty damages are a share of the adopter's incremental returns, which is profit minus the returns to using alternative technologies, $B = P - A$.[486]

The "bottom-up" approach appears in various court decisions including *Microsoft v. Motorola*.[487] Jason Bartlett and Jorge Contreras refer to the "bottom-up" approach as a "recipe for inconsistency."[488] Many advocate this approach because it takes into account the incremental contribution of the patented technology to the infringer.[489] When there are SEPs, the application of the "bottom-up" approach to a FRAND royalty "begins by identifying the set of alternatives that would have been available prior to standardization and then determining the incremental value, if any, of the SEPs relative to those alternatives."[490]

If the alternative A is a close substitute, the net returns are close to the infringer's profit from applying the patented invention P.[491] If the alternative is not a close substitute, the net returns are much smaller than the profits from using the patented invention P.[492] To implement this approach, the patent case must measure the benefits of the alternative technologies net of royalty costs of those alternatives, $A = P^A - R^A$.[493]

The problem with the "bottom-up" approach is that it requires information that is generally unobservable and difficult to estimate.[494] The infringer's profits P^A from the alternative technologies are difficult to estimate because the technological alternatives are not fully specified and the infringer's profits from using those technologies are not observable.[495] In addition, it may be difficult to determine royalties R^A on the relevant alternatives because the technologies are not specified and also there may not be observable royalties on these technologies.[496] Judge Holderman in

In re Innovatio points out that finding the net benefits from alternative technologies requires accounting for royalty costs of those alternatives: "patented alternatives are also able to command a royalty, because it is unlikely that the market would drive the price of all patented technology to zero."[497]

This issue arose in *Panduit.*[498] The presence of a substitute was not sufficient for the infringer to avoid paying reasonable royalty damages.[499] The court suggested that the technology adopter had ignored the substitute for years while selling the infringing product.[500] This suggested that the alternative was not a close substitute.[501] As the court noted, "[t]here are substitute products for virtually every patented product; the availability of railroads and box cameras should not of itself diminish royalties payable for infringement of the right to exclude others from making and selling the Wright airplane or the Polaroid camera."[502]

In *Georgia Pacific*, the court arrived at a markdown of profit of 22.36% by subtracting the infringer's usual profit as a share of the selling price equal to 9% from the infringer's actual profit as a share of the selling price.[503] This provided a way of estimating the incremental contribution of the patented technology to the infringer's profit, thus giving an estimate of reasonable royalty damages.[504] The estimate of the incremental contribution of the patented technology was based on a change in profits as a share of the selling price that was presumably due to infringement.[505] Reasonable royalty damages then would be calculated by multiplying the change in the share of the selling price by the infringers' total revenues during the infringement period.[506] *Georgia Pacific* effectively implemented the "bottom-up" approach by using the change in profits to indicate the incremental contribution of alternative technologies.[507]

With multiple inventions, further difficulties arise because the total of the incremental contributions of various technologies can be greater than or less than the total value produced by using those technologies.[508] This depends on whether the technologies are what I term "innovative complements" or "innovative substitutes."[509] Then, mechanically attributing royalties to various technologies based on incremental contributions will result in total royalties that are greater than or less than their total benefit.[510] Contract negotiation resolves these problems in the market place.[511]

The problem of calculating the infringer's incremental benefits is exacerbated with technology standards. As Judge Robart observes in *Microsoft*, "[i]n practice, approaches linking the value of a patent to its incremental contribution to a standard are hard to implement."[512] Generally, this means that it may not be feasible to observe the infringer's alternative returns, which requires obtaining information on profits without the infringed technology and royalties on alternative technologies.[513]

4.4.3.3. *The "Top-Down" Approach*

Another method of determining reasonable royalty damages is the "top-down" approach.[514] The "top-down" approach appears in *In re Innovatio* and *TCL Communications v. Ericsson.*[515] According to this approach, the royalty is based on obtaining an "aggregate royalty burden" and apportioning that total royalty among multiple technologies.[516] With SEPs, the aggregate royalty burden is some share of the infringer's profits due to the technology standard.[517]

The "top-down" approach might not fully compensate the patent holder for infringement for several reasons. The infringer's profit can be less than the harm to patent holders from infringement. The share of the infringer's profit used to calculate the "aggregate royalty burden" can be less than the harm to patent holders from infringement. Even if the "aggregate royalty burden" is sufficient to compensate patent holders for infringement, the apportionment of the "aggregate royalty burden" may not correspond to the harm to individual patent holders.

The "top-down" approach avoids calculating reasonable royalty damages as a markdown from the technology adopter's economic benefits B, which requires estimating the incremental contribution of alternative technologies. The "top-down" approach is preferable to the "bottom-up" because the incremental contribution of the technology is often difficult or impossible to determine.[518]

The "top-down" approach requires estimating a markdown x of the infringer's profits during the period of infringement. Then, the aggregate royalty burden R for a technology adopter with profit P is given by $R = xP$.

The market value method introduced earlier gives an economic implementation of the "top-down" approach.[519] To illustrate the application to the "top-down" approach, suppose that there is only one patent holder. Setting aside licensing costs, reasonable royalty damages are equal to the estimated market value of the patent divided by the number of infringers, $R = V/N$. Then, the profit share necessary to realize the same reasonable royalty damages would be equal to the market value of the patent divided by the number of infringers multiplied by one over the infringer's profit, $x = (V/N)(1/P)$. This approach can be applied if the market value per infringer is less than the infringer's profit.

The market value method can be used to obtain an economic implementation of apportionment. Setting aside licensing costs, suppose that there are two patent holders each with a portfolio of SEPs. For ease of discussion, suppose also that each patent holder licenses to the same number of licensees. Reasonable royalty damages are based on the market value of the patent divided by the number of infringers for each patent holder. This is equal to $R^1 = V^1/N$ for the first patent holder and $R^2 = V^2/N$ for the second patent holder. Then, the "aggregate royalty burden" is the sum of the two reasonable royalty damages, $R = R^1 + R^2$. To calculate the apportionment ratios for each patent holder, divide each royalty by the "aggregate royalty burden". Because the number of licensees is the same for each patent holder, the apportionment ratios equal $V^1/(V^1 + V^2)$ and $V^2/(V^1 + V^2)$. To obtain each royalty, multiply the "aggregate royalty burden" by these shares. Based on the market value method, apportionment of the "aggregate royalty burden" should be based on each patent holder's share of the total market value of the SEPs.

We can compare the "bottom-up" and the "top-down" approaches. The profit share is necessarily greater than the share of benefits because profits are lower than benefits.[520] The share x of the infringer's returns depends on how close a substitute is the best alternative technology.[521] The greater the value of using the best alternative technology and the lower the royalty on the best alternative technology, the smaller the plaintiff's share of the defendant's return.[522]

Suppose, for example, that the value generated by the best alternative technology net of royalties is 90% of the value generated by using patent owner's invention, A = 0.90V. Suppose also that reasonable royalty damages are 70% of the patent infringer's economic benefits. Then, reasonable royalty damages are given by a markdown x = 7% of the infringer's profit, R = 0.70(P – A) = 0.70(0.10P) = 0.07P. To take another example, suppose that the value generated by the best alternative technology net of royalties is 50% of the value generated by using patent owner's invention, A = 0.50P. Suppose also that reasonable royalty damages are 50% of the patent infringer's economic benefits. Then, reasonable royalty damages are given by a markdown x = 25% of the infringer's profit, R = 0.50(0.50P) = 0.25P.

The share x of the infringer's profit depends on a number of factors. First, the share x depends on the characteristics of the patented technology.[523] Second, the share x depends on the contribution of the patented technology to the infringer's profit.[524] Third, the share x depends on the provisions of the patent license contract.[525]

The profit share x should depend on evidence rather than an arbitrary profit share. This is reflected in the debate over the well-known "25 percent rule."[526] As noted in *Uniloc*,

> [t]his court now holds as a matter of Federal Circuit law that the 25 percent rule of thumb is a fundamentally flawed tool for determining a baseline royalty rate in a hypothetical negotiation. Evidence relying on the 25 percent rule of thumb is thus inadmissible under Daubert and the Federal Rules of Evidence, because it fails to tie a reasonable royalty base to the facts of the case at issue.[527]

Gregory Leonard and Lauren Stiroh observe that the 25 percent rule "takes no account of the importance of the patent to the profits of the product sold, the potential availability of close substitutes or equally non-infringing alternatives, or any of the other idiosyncrasies of the patent at issue that would have affected a real-world negotiation."[528]

The problems encountered with applying the "top-down" rule can be illustrated by *In re Innovatio*.[529] The court began with the chipmaker's average profit from the sale of a Wi-Fi chip and calculated a markdown percentage.[530] The markdown percentage was based on an estimate of the profit contribution of SEPs multiplied by the number of Innovatio's

802.11 standard-essential patents divided by the number of a subset of 802.11 standard-essential patents.[531]

The problem in *In re Innovatio* arises from the estimate of the profit contribution of SEPs.[532] According to Leonard and Lopez,

> [t]his approach involves first determining the aggregate royalty burden that could be charged for all SEPs. The aggregate royalty burden is then divided among all SEPs, taking into account differences in the relative value of those SEPs. A RAND royalty for a particular set of SEPs is an apportionment of the aggregate royalty burden.[533]

Based on expert testimony, the court in *In re Innovatio* determined the contribution of SEPs to an infringer's profit based on an estimate of the relative value of patents in the electronics industry.[534] The relative value of patents was based on a study using renewal fees by Schankerman who found that 10% of patents generated 84% of value in the electronics industry as compared to other patents.[535] The court erroneously interpreted this to imply that the top 10% of patents contributed 84% of an infringer's profits.[536] The court then multiplied by the ratio of the number of an infringer's profits to 10% of the relevant number of patents.[537] This approach presumed that the patents that were infringed made the same contribution to an infringer's profits as the relative values of the top 10% of patent values in the electronics industry.[538]

There are a number of economic and legal problems with this approach. Recall that patent values calculated from renewal fees understate the upper tail of the distribution, so the contribution of the highest-value patents is understated.[539] Even so, the contribution of a particular patent to an infringer's profit is different from the distribution of patent values in an industry.[540] For example, an infringer may only use one patent and that patent may be unimportant to the industry but very important to the infringer. Also, the infringement may be very damaging to the patent holder.

In *TCL v. Ericsson*, Judge James V. Selna applied the "top-down method."[541] The court first determined a total reasonable royalty rate for the relevant SEPs that apply to the technology standard.[542] Then, the court apportioned the total royalty to the SEP holders, which gave a share of the infringer's profits.[543] Finally, the court obtained reasonable royalty damages by multiplying the profit share by the infringer's profits.[544]

Judge Selna determined the total reasonable royalties citing a press release before the relevant technology standard was established:

> Industry leaders NTT DoCoMo, Ericsson, Nokia and Siemens today reached a mutual understanding to introduce licensing arrangements whereby essential patents for W-CDMA are licensed at rates that are proportional to the number of essential patents owned by each company. The intention is to set a benchmark for all patent holders of the W-CDMA technology to achieve fair and reasonable royalty rates.[545]

Judge Selna cited a later announcement by the company: "Ericsson believes the market will drive all players to act in accordance with these principles and to a reasonable maximum aggregate royalty level of 6–8% for handsets."[546] Ericsson argued that applying announced royalty rates would be inaccurate because the prices of mobile phones had decreased.[547] Judge Selna rejected this argument on the grounds that the company's announcement was not explicitly contingent on any final output price.[548]

Next, the court in *TCL v. Ericsson* apportioned the total royalty using the ratio of the number of the patent holder's SEPs to the number of patents in the standard.[549] Judge Selna stated, "[t]he Court adopts a simple patent counting system which treats every patent as possessing identical value."[550] The economic value of patents varies considerably, so this calculation may fail to compensate the patent holder for the quality of the IP.[551] The numerical calculation also ignores the problems associated with declaration of SEPs that may not be essential.[552]

The general problems of the "top-down" approach are compounded by incorrect estimates of the infringer's profits. For example, in *TCL v. Ericsson*, the court applied an international average royalty rate and then adjusted for regional markets rather than obtaining accurate measures of the infringer's profits.[553] Applications of the "top-down" approach that do not fully account for the infringer's profits are more likely to provide incomplete compensation for the patent holder's IP.[554]

4.4.4. *Resolving Controversies over Reasonable Royalty Damages*

This Section addresses some controversies in the calculation of reasonable royalty damages. The discussion considers the selection of the rate base for applying reasonable royalty damages. Then, the discussion examines policy concerns of royalty stacking, patent hold-up, and SEPs and shows that these concerns are unfounded and based on an incorrect analytical model that is nearly 200 years old. The discussion also considers problems associated with using bargaining power in examining reasonable royalty damages. Also, the discussion considers how reasonable royalty damages affect incentives for hold-out and infringement.

4.4.4.1. *The Royalty Base*

From an economics perspective, the choice of a royalty base is arbitrary because the problem is to determine the damages caused by infringement.[555] What matters is the total value of reasonable royalty damages. Reasonable royalty damages then can be recovered as a proportion of any particular royalty base. In practice, however, this has proven to be a contentious issue.[556]

Differences in the royalty base in patent license contracts are due to considerations related to the effect on incentives for the investment and sales for the licensee.[557] Also, the division of royalties between lump-sum and running royalties depends on market structure in the final product markets as already noted.[558] The royalty base in practice also depends on what types of sales and profit information can be monitored and verified by the licensor.[559]

In *Ericsson*, the U.S. Court of Appeals for the Federal Circuit found that "[w]hat is taken from the owner of a utility patent (for purposes of assessing damages under § 284) is only the patented technology, and so the value to be measured is only the value of the infringing features of an accused product."[560] The Court of Appeals implicitly recognized the arbitrary nature of the royalty base in its instructions for experts:

> Logically, an economist could do this in various ways — by careful selection of the royalty base to reflect the value added by the patented

> feature, where that differentiation is possible; by adjustment of the royalty rate so as to discount the value of a product's nonpatented features; or by a combination thereof. The essential requirement is that the ultimate reasonable royalty award must be based on the incremental value that the patented invention adds to the end product.[561]

The "market value method" or comparable license contracts provide indicators of the effects of infringement as noted earlier.[562] These values can be assigned to various royalty bases.

The Entire Market Value Rule ("EMVR") limits the use of the market value of final products in valuing the contribution of patented inventions.[563] The typical argument against royalties using final product prices incorrectly maintains that this approach does not identify the contribution of an invention.[564] For example, Brian Love argues that using market value "systematically overcompensates patentees who own patents covering only one component of a larger, complex device. As a result, the doctrine has become a means for patentees to capture value that they did not create, at the expense of innovative infringers, other patentees, and society at large."[565]

For many comparable contracts, however, including patent pools, royalties are based on final product sales.[566] This generally is an indication that downstream markets are competitive.[567] Also, basing royalties on final product sales is convenient and tends to reduce transaction costs. It is generally feasible to monitor product sales, which provides a measure of the use of the patented invention.

In *VirnetX*, the U.S. Court of Appeals for the Federal Circuit pointed out that "[n]o matter what the form of the royalty, a patentee must take care to seek only those damages attributable to the infringing features."[568] The principle of attributable damages can be traced to the Supreme Court case *Garretson v. Clark* in 1884.[569] In *VirnetX*, for example, the Appeals Court stated,

> Indeed, the Supreme Court long ago observed that a patentee must in every case give evidence tending to separate or apportion the defendant's profits and the patentee's damages between the patented feature and the unpatented features, and such evidence must be reliable and tangible, and not conjectural or speculative; or he must show, by equally reliable

> and satisfactory evidence, that the profits and damages are to be calculated on the whole machine, for the reason that the entire value of the whole machine, as a marketable article, is properly and legally attributable to the patented feature.[570]

The notion that royalties should be based on the Smallest Salable Patent-Practicing Unit ("SSPPU") arose in *Cornell University*.[571] Judge Rador compared the relative sizes of the components of the final product:

> [T]he claimed invention is a small part of the IRB [instruction reorder buffer], which is a part of a processor, which is part of a CPU [central processing unit] module, which is part of a "brick," which is itself only part of the larger server. For some general context, this server is larger than even very large home refrigerator units; the CPU "brick" is longer and thinner than the ordinary masonry brick; the IRB is a thin wafer device approximately two inches wide and three inches long.[572]

Of course the physical size of a product or a component has little if anything to do with the market value of that product or component. The market value of a patented invention and its contribution to the market value of final product generally cannot be inferred from physical descriptions of components.

According to the *Cornell University* decision, "the processor is the smallest salable patent-practicing unit."[573] The court in *Cornell University* benefits from the fact that the technology adopter Hewlett-Packard did sell some processors a la carte, although it primarily sold servers and workstations.[574] If there is a well-established market for a component containing the patented invention, then the market price of the component is useful for determining the value of the patented invention.

The modularity of the final product, however, should not be used as a mechanism for arbitrarily reducing reasonable royalty damages. The existence of components containing the invention without a well-established market for the components would not provide an accurate basis for estimating damages from infringement.[575] The result would provide inadequate compensation for patent holders. Reducing damages from infringement based on modularity would create significant inefficiencies if it were to discourage modularity in product design.[576] Modularity is an important source of market value because it allows specialization and division of labor in the production of parts and components.[577]

The royalty base should not be used to increase or decrease reasonable royalty damages. The royalty base is useful in deriving the corresponding level of total royalties in comparable license contracts. The royalty base, however, need not provide information about damages caused by infringement.

4.4.4.2. *Royalty Stacking, SEP Hold-up, and the Cournot Effect*

The contract approach has important implications for reasonable royalty damages when there are multiple inventions. The problem of multiple inventions has generated antitrust policy concerns about the determination of royalties in patent license contracts.[578] Decisions in various patent cases reflect these concerns.[579] These concerns are based on a fundamental misconception about royalties. Negotiation of patent license contracts should eliminate concerns about royalties with multiple inventions.

These public policy concerns include royalty stacking, patent thickets, patent hold-up, the tragedy of the anti-commons, and SEPs. Although these public policy concerns appear to be very different, they have a common source in economic theory. That source is the Cournot complementary monopolies model, which predicts that multiple input monopolists will set input prices above what a monopolist would choose for a bundle of those inputs.[580] This is a familiar theoretical prediction in economics known as the "Cournot Effect."[581]

Elsewhere, I show that the "Cournot Effect" is based on the assumption that complementary input monopolists choose "posted prices."[582] This means that the input monopolists announce prices that they will charge to downstream producers.[583] This conduct generates a "free rider problem" because each of the input monopolists fails to recognize the negative influence that raising their price has on the profits of the other input monopolists.[584] The result is that total input prices are greater than what a bundled monopoly would offer to downstream producers.

The "Cournot Effect," however, does not apply to patent license agreements because these are contracts that are negotiated by the licensor and the licensee.[585] Negotiation between licensors and licensees rules out the "Cournot Effect." As a result of negotiation, patent holders obtain shares in the profits of downstream producers.[586] When patent holders choose the number of license contracts to offer producers, they recognize the effects of their offers on the profits of a producer and they have incentives to avoid raising royalties excessively.[587] This eliminates the "free rider problem" and results in total royalties that do not exceed the bundled monopoly royalty.

This suggests that the courts should not be concerned about royalty stacking in practice because patent license contracts tend to be negotiated. Royalties determined in the marketplace through negotiation should not generate concerns about excessive royalties. The courts, however, still should verify that the court's own apportionment of royalties is not excessive. Judge Robart in *Microsoft v. Motorola* expressed concern about royalty stacking:

> [t]hus, the fee that results from a hypothetical RAND negotiation is necessarily informed by the court considering the entire world of known SEPs relevant to a given standard. That ultimate sum must be the aggregate licensing fee of all essential patents calibrated against the principle that license fees should not be stacked in such a way that makes implementation of the standard prohibitively expensive.[588]

Judge Robart used patent pool licenses as comparable license contracts.[589] To address RAND royalty issues, Judge Robart determined the upper bound for royalties for Motorola's H.264 SEP portfolio based on "the highest fee discussed during formation of the MPEG LA EL264 patent pool."[590] The court further concluded that "the value to Motorola ... would be not only royalties received, but also access to the intellectual property, which equals an amount of twice the royalties received."[591]

Judge Robart also found that despite its shortcomings, the Via Licensing 802.11 pool was an "indicator of a RAND royalty rate for Motorola's 802.11 SEP portfolio."[592] He noted that "royalties in the Via Licensing 802.11 pool are shared among licensors according to a

Worldwide Revenue Sharing Algorithm. The algorithm divides revenue between licensors based on the relative number of patents each has contributed, adjusted by a country-weight factor."[593]

Judge Selna argued in *TCL v. Ericsson* that royalties for SEPs should be those established before the adoption of the technology standard.[594] He suggested that statements made by SEP owners before standards were established were designed "to induce people to adopt and invest in each standard when the risk of hold-up was low," thus "providing the SEP owners with incentive to be reasonable with their overall expectations and greatly reducing the risk of hold-up and royalty stacking."[595]

Policy concerns about hold-up and royalty stacking are founded on incorrect economic analyses of the market for patent licenses.[596] Recognizing economic incentives and market institutions eliminates the "Cournot Effect." This removes justifications for relying on patent license royalties chosen before technology standards are established. Patent license royalties for SEPs should be increased to reflect the establishment of the relevant technology standards. Courts determining reasonable royalty damages for infringement should use royalty rates that reflect the market value of SEPs and the damages to patent holders.

4.4.4.3. *Relative Bargaining Power and Reasonable Royalty Damages*

It often is suggested that the relative bargaining power of the parties determines royalties.[597] This runs the risk of circular reasoning; relative bargaining power determines the division of surplus and the division of the surplus indicates relative bargaining power. The two methods of calculating reasonable royalty damages, comparable license contracts and the market value method, avoid having to speculate on bargaining power.

It is helpful to understand bargaining power in the context of contract negotiation. One view is that bargaining power reflects the costs of not reaching an agreement.[598] The opportunity costs of the two parties summarize the costs of not reaching an agreement.[599] So, opportunity costs narrow the range of possible royalty payments. This does not explain fully, however, how to divide the economic value of the contract, which already reflects opportunity costs. As already noted, the opportunity costs of the infringer are often difficult if not impossible to observe.[600] Also, if the patent holder's opportunity costs were observable, they would be used as the basis for estimating reasonable royalty damages rather than the infringer's profit.

Some commentators advocate using basic economic models of bargaining to obtain royalties for the forgone licensing contract.[601] For example, Choi and Weinstein suggest using the Nash bargaining solution to calculate reasonable royalty damages.[602] The Nash bargaining solution is an even split of the surplus from the contract that is derived based on a set of desirable characteristics of a bargaining solution.[603] Then, royalties evenly divide the net benefits from exchange.[604] It follows that royalties are given by the average of economic benefits of the licensee and economic costs of the licensor, $R = (B + C)/2$.[605]

In *VirnetX*, however, the U.S. Court of Appeals for the Federal Circuit criticizes applications of the Nash bargaining solution that are not tied to evidence.[606] The court stated, "the invocation of a 50/50 starting point based on the Nash Bargaining Solution is akin to the '25 percent rule of thumb' that we rejected in *Uniloc* as being insufficiently grounded in the specific facts of the case."[607] This model was rejected under the *Daubert* standard.[608] Thus, it is not possible to use arbitrary bargaining solutions to specify reasonable royalty damages.

A related approach would be to include the transaction costs of bargaining, either in terms of the costs of making offers or the time involved in making offers because the parties discount the future returns to reaching an agreement. This also generates a particular division of the economic value of the contract that depends on the costs of negotiation.[609] If the parties engage in alternative offers bargaining, the outcome depends on which party makes the first offer.[610] The division of the surplus occurs because the parties seek to avoid the costs of making additional offers. The party making the first offer can obtain a larger share of the surplus by making an offer such that the other party is indifferent between accepting that offer and continuing to bargain, which leads to a bargaining equilibrium in which just one offer is made. Again, in the context of determining damages, it is generally necessary to examine whether such a negotiation would apply to the facts of the case.

4.5 Conclusion

The contract approach to reasonable royalty damages presented here is firmly grounded in economic analysis. Improving the economic analysis and factual basis for reasonable royalty damages enhances efficiency in the enforcement of IP rights. This should improve incentives for invention and innovation. Better enforcement of IP rights should also improve incentives for patent holders and technology adopters to engage in efficient negotiation.

I argued that the patent case already constructs an "informed contract." The provisions of the "informed contract" depend on the evidence presented in the patent case regarding the actions of the patent holder and the infringer. The "informed contract" also takes into account information revealed since infringement began. For example, the "informed contract" takes into account increases in the value of patents that are found to be valid and infringed.

The "informed contract" thus provides an evidence-based approach to finding reasonable royalty damages. The "informed contract" should replace the popular but problematic "hypothetical negotiation" approach. The "informed contract" approach avoids the "willing licensor and licensee" Ghosts of Christmas Past that Judge Markey cautioned against in *Panduit*.[611]

The proposed contract approach suggests two primary options for determining reasonable royalty damages depending on the nature of the evidence. The court should apply the "market value method" introduced here if there is insufficient evidence about comparable license contracts. The "market value method" assigns shares to each infringer of the market price of the patent plus licensing and legal costs. Alternatively, the court should determine royalties by considering comparable license contracts with adjustments based on the provisions of the informed contract.

Both of these approaches are based on market prices and reflect the economic value of the informed contract. The court should add price premia to the market value of patents or to comparable royalties if the patent is found to be valid and infringed and if the patent is an SEP.

The analysis identified problems with the alternative "top-down" and "bottom-up" methods that are based on the profit shares of the infringer.

These approaches are problematic if they involve *ad hoc* calculations of profit shares that are not based on market prices. When patents are SEPs, these calculations are subject to additional inaccuracies because they are sensitive to declarations of essentiality and incomplete evaluations of technology standards.

The contract approach addresses the debate over whether to apply property and liability rules to patent infringement. The contract approach is consistent with injunctive relief and provides additional information about reasonable royalty damages. The contract approach adjusts reasonable royalty damages based on the provisions of the "informed contract" and compensates the patent holder for infringement. The contract approach addresses issues related to SEPs and FRAND commitments by accounting for their effects on the market value of patents and the provisions of comparable license contracts. The contract approach to finding reasonable royalty damages helps resolve the patent law controversy.

Chapter 5

Patent Licensing: Intellectual Contract and Intellectual Law

5.1 Introduction

Patent holders often realize the market value of their IP through licensing contracts. This Chapter introduces the concept of Intellectual Contract (IC) to advance and broaden the legal analysis of technological change and intangible assets. Remedies for infringement can be viewed as Intellectual Tort (IT). IC, IT, and IP are becoming increasingly important given the rate and direction of technological change and greater focus on intangible assets. The principles of common law still apply to intangible assets.[1] However, IC, IT, and IP lack a framework that addresses the important additional implications of technological change and intangible assets.

This Chapter introduces a framework that I refer to as "Intellectual Law" to reflect major developments in legal practice and economic activity. Intellectual Law is central to myriad legal cases, including over 5,000 patent case filings per year in the U.S.[2] Copyright infringement cases in Federal District Court numbered 5,042 in 2015 and 3,944 in 2016.[3] Trademark infringement cases totaled 38,486 between 2009 and 2017, with 8,502 of those cases overlapping with commercial claims.[4] Litigation in federal courts involving trade secrets has also increased.[5] All areas of IP are expanding rapidly; the US Patent and Trademark Office (USPTO) has granted over 10 million patents and handled over 9 million trademark applications or registrations.[6] One estimate puts the value of IP in the US at over $5 trillion.[7]

Conceptual legal frameworks must catch up with fundamental technological change. Major technological developments include dramatic increases in digital connectivity and interoperability as well as significant advances in Information and Communications Technology (ICT).[8] These technological shifts drive the Business Revolution and the Fourth Industrial Revolution (4IR).[9] Important innovations that involve digital connectivity and interoperability include the Internet of Things (IoT), artificial intelligence (AI), cloud computing, data analytics, mobile communications, autonomous vehicles, additive manufacturing, and virtual reality.[10]

Achieving digital connectivity involves the formation of networks with many companies providing network components and connecting devices to the network, including mobile communications and autonomous vehicles. Companies require contracts to coordinate digital connectivity. As Spulber and Yoo observe, "networks come from supply decisions by network providers, interconnection between networks, demand decisions by network customers, and supply decisions by providers of complementary services."[11] The many types of access to networks, including retail, wholesale, interconnection, platform, and unbundled access, generally require contracts between firms.[12]

Firms also share knowledge through the formation of innovation networks.[13] The modular organization of production means that many firms are involved in the production of components and assembly of the final product.[14] Innovative products that contain new types of components and introduce inventions require knowledge of the technology of each component and knowledge about how to combine these technologies.[15] Complex innovations in particular require the combination of many new technologies.[16] Firms must make contractual agreements to obtain the components and to make sure they interoperate effectively. Firms creating complex innovations thus require contracts to coordinate inventive and innovative activities.

This Chapter argues there is a need for a general Intellectual Law framework that approaches IC, IT, and IP consistently and sheds light on their interactions. The proposed new framework of Intellectual Law will contribute to Science and Technology Law.[17] The purpose of the framework is to approach scientific issues and technological change in a more integrated fashion. Practitioners and scholars should avoid the costs and effort of reinventing the wheel when encountering each new technological development.

IP differs from traditional property because of differences between intangible and tangible assets. These differences affect the completeness, excludability, and transferability of intangible assets. ICs differ fundamentally from traditional contracts because ICs must handle problems that arise in inducing cooperative investment in intangible assets. ITs differ from traditional torts because of the additional difficulties in determining validity and infringement of IP and finding remedies for infringement.[18]

Intellectual Law has become essential because technological change has increased the economic importance of intangible assets relative to that of tangible assets. Investment in knowledge is a major driver of economic growth.[19] The U.S. national income accounts began to recognize R&D investment as part of Gross Domestic Product (GDP) as of 2013.[20] Private industry invests about two-thirds of annual R&D expenditures in the U.S., which amounted to over $527 billion in 2017.[21] U.S. investment in intangible assets exceeds $1 trillion per year, with a capitalized value of over $6 trillion.[22] Intangible assets constitute about 85% of the total market value of the S&P 500 companies.[23]

This Chapter devises the concept of Intellectual Contract to characterize an agreement to create, develop, share, or apply intangible assets involved in technological change. An IC has the standard contract features of offer, acceptance, and consideration, but differs from contracts that involve tangible assets. ICs include agreements related to traditional types of IP, that is, trade secrets, patents, trademarks, and copyrights. However, ICs also include non-traditional intangible assets such as knowledge, discoveries, inventions, innovations, and adoption of innovations that are not covered by standard IP. ICs not only include the upper tail of inventions covered by IP and IT, but step in to cover the lower tail of ideas not covered by IP. ICs make adjustments to contracts to address the particular problem of creating and using knowledge. Technological change favoring intangible assets and interoperability makes ICs highly valuable and perhaps more commonly used than traditional contracts. The many types of IC identified here play an increasingly important role in fostering technological advances.

IC rules help resolve the debate over whether IP or IT is best for protecting the interests of inventors. Technological change requires cooperative investments in invention, innovation, and adoption. ICs protect the expectation interests of parties engaged in technological change: employer and employee, firm and subcontractor, and licensor and licensee. ICs not only protect inventors who make discoveries but also innovators who apply those discoveries and adopters who demand innovations. ICs generate gains from trade that increase joint benefits for inventors, innovators, and adopters. When there are gains from trade, the inventor's returns from entering into an IC are greater than returns from either their own use of IP or an assignment to others. Because of gains from trade, ICs increase the benefits of inventors beyond what can be achieved with only IP and IT. Legal protections for inventors, innovators, and adopters thus cannot be based solely on a combination of IT and IP. Greater emphasis on IC rules by the courts within the Intellectual Law framework proposed here would address problems with both IT and IP.

I also devise the new term Intellectual Tort to designate liability rules governing the taking or infringement of intangible assets. IT includes misappropriation of trade secrets, and infringement of patents, trademarks, and copyrights. I argue that IC rules help disentangle IT rules from IP rules and overcome the shortcomings of IT rules. Many practitioners and scholars emphasize liability protections against infringement.[24] Daniel Crane introduces the term "Intellectual Liability" to identify the shift toward liability protections: "Instead of speaking about 'intellectual property,' it may be more appropriate to speak about 'intellectual rights' consisting in part of intellectual property rights and in part of intellectual liability rights."[25]

Damage remedies based on IT, however, can fail to fully compensate IP owners or to deter infringement. In contrast, IC rules support agreements between IP owners and users that can both prevent infringement and resolve infringement disputes without the need for courts to determine compensation. When infringement does occur, the courts can use IC rules as a framework for calculating reasonable royalty damages, as I argue in the previous chapter.[26] Thus, IC rules complement IT rules by helping deter infringement and determine reasonable royalties that are compensatory.

Technological change is altering the nature of contract. ICs provide agreements needed to achieve technological change, both within the firm and among firms. I suggest that ICs have five important features that distinguish them from standard contracts involving tangible assets.

First, ICs address the lack of completeness in ownership of intangible assets. An important strength of ICs is that they help protect the vast set of property interests that standard IP does not cover. The four main categories of IP — trade secrets, patents, trademarks, and copyrights — do not fully cover commercial, scientific, and technological creations. IP is subject to challenges of validity and imperfect enforcement against infringement.[27] Additionally, IP typically has significant registration requirements in comparison to tangible property.[28] USPTO patent and trademark applications must satisfy various regulatory criteria, which entail substantial legal costs in addition to the filing fees.[29] The U.S. Copyright Office registers copyrights subject to various restrictions on types of works of authorship and subject matter.[30]

Second, ICs remedy problems of exclusion of access to intangible assets because ICs help determine how parties will share the returns and control over intangible assets. Without contracts, it can be difficult to protect intangible assets. The law treats tangible and intangible properties differently because IP limits exclusivity, transferability, and duration of ownership.[31] Various court cases, statutes, and administrative decisions have weakened legal protections for IP. Although the Patent Act gives patents "the attributes of personal property," these protections are incomplete.[32] The Supreme Court ruled unanimously in *eBay Inc. v. MercExchange, L.L.C.* that "the creation of a right is distinct from the provision of remedies for violations of that right."[33] Physical barriers provide limited protection because knowledge is readily transferable and easy to imitate or appropriate. Secrecy may not be feasible because offering IP for sale or license requires disclosing the knowledge. Using IP within an organization and with business partners also requires continual sharing of knowledge.

Third, ICs handle non-rivalrous usage of intangible assets, a problem that generally does not arise with tangible assets. Intangible assets can provide services to multiple users at once.[34] ICs such as license and cross-license agreements provide access to intangible assets for multiple users and handle in-kind exchanges of access to intangible assets. ICs can bundle intangible assets such as licenses for patent portfolios, as well as bundle intangible assets with tangible assets, goods, and services. ICs also can unbundle intangible assets by specifying conditions of use through the grant of rights.

Fourth, ICs address problems in designing incentives for what I refer to here as "exploratory performance." An IC must monitor and reward the agent's performance in exploring uncharted waters. By its very nature, technological change is a leap into the unknown. Economic analysis identifies agency costs that arise from difficulties in observing an agent's hidden actions or hidden information.[35] Contracts must be based on performance because outputs are observable and verifiable while inputs are not. The design of an IC, however, encounters difficulties in determining performance targets and observing performance. It is hard to know what the outcomes of invention, innovation, and technology adoption will be. This presents a greater challenge than traditional agency costs. This also makes it difficult to determine the intent of the parties as well as to find remedies for breach of contract. ICs provide incentives for exploration by rewarding measures of performance that are observable and verifiable rather than inventive effort.

Fifth, ICs provide mechanisms for addressing fundamental uncertainty associated with invention, innovation, and adoption. Technological change involves particular types of statistical, discovery, creativity, and market uncertainty. This uncertainty distinguishes ICs from standard contracts involving routine activities and risky investments in tangible assets. Fundamental uncertainty generates benefits from contingent contracting.[36] An IC must address the well-known tradeoff between the benefits and costs of contingent contracts.[37] Contract law and the costs of contracting provide incentives for simple contract forms.[38] ICs offer basic mechanisms such as royalties and options that address the uncertainties of technological change.[39]

I identify five main types of ICs: employment, outsourcing, joint venture and consortium, license, and platform. Firms enter into employment contracts with scientific and technical personnel who conduct invention and innovation within the firm. Firms use outsourcing contracts with specialist firms and supply chain management companies that develop inventions and innovations. Firms form joint venture and consortium contracts to establish research joint ventures (RJVs) and R&D consortia. Joint venture and consortium contracts allow firms to share the costs, risks, and outputs of invention and innovation. Firms create license contracts for usage of patents, trademarks, copyrights, and business knowledge. Finally, firms apply platform contracts that bring together providers and adopters of technology. Firms enter into platform contracts with for-profit intermediaries and with cooperative institutions such as patent pools and other Collective Rights Organizations (CROs).[40]

5.2 Intellectual Law

Developing the Intellectual Law framework requires a coherent treatment of invention, innovation, and technology adoption. However, legal protections for intangible assets are a mixture of property and tort. Applications of property and tort to intangible assets fail to address consent in a consistent way. As a consequence, these protections fail to perform effectively both property and tort functions. Recognizing the widespread use of various forms of ICs would help bring consistency to Intellectual Law because it addresses the key question of consent for agreements involving intangible assets. Courts can apply ICs to improve legal protections for the creation and application of intangible assets.

5.2.1. *The Conflict between IT and IP*

Guido Calabresi and Douglas Melamed distinguish between property and tort in terms of who has consent.[41] Protections are based on property if the owner's consent to sell is necessary for transfers.[42] Protections are based on tort if the taker's consent to buy is sufficient for transfers.[43] This is because someone taking the asset determines whether they want to pay compensation by choosing to infringe. The liability rule effectively removes the owner's consent to sell, whether or not the taking is intentional.[44] The distinction between property and tort rules provides clarity for tangible assets that may be absent for intangible assets.

Legal protections for intangible assets — currently based on a haphazard combination of IT and IP — are incomplete because they do not address consent in a consistent way. Protections for intangible assets are based partly on IT because damage remedies remove the IP owner's consent to sell an intangible asset. Damage remedies make the infringer's consent to buy sufficient for ongoing transfers. Based on this perspective, some have characterized patent infringement as a "strict liability" tort.[45] Following this approach to patent infringement, various limitations on strict liability would further reduce protections for inventions.[46] Protections for intangible assets are based partly on IP because the IP owner has some rights to exclude and so must consent to license or sell an intangible asset.[47] However, IP rights often limit exclusivity, again removing the IP owner's consent to sell.[48]

The Supreme Court's unanimous *eBay* decision illustrates the mixture of property and tort approaches.[49] Problems arise because the Court did not address *consent* in a consistent way. The *eBay* decision has created some confusion by conflating IT and IP.[50] The Court in *eBay* weakens IP in comparison to tangible property by reducing the consent of the IP owner as seller.[51] The infringer's consent as buyer can dominate the IP owner's consent as seller, converting property remedies to tort remedies.

The *eBay* decision limits injunctions for intangible assets by applying the four-factor test for issuing injunctions to patent infringement.[52] The first factor, irreparable harm, is a particularly high hurdle for the IP owner. Second, requiring the IP owner to show that remedies are inadequate compensation is an additional burden that replaces IP with IT rules. Third, consideration of the balance of hardships between plaintiff and defendant differs substantially from property rights in tangible assets. Consideration of the balance of hardships combines the IP owner's consent as seller with the infringer's consent as buyer. Finally, the public interest criterion places IP rights in a different category from tangible property.

Andrew Beckerman-Rodau observes that *eBay* is "part of a broad attack on the current U.S. patent system."[53] David McGowan argues that the Court in *eBay* "reversed the longstanding presumption in favor of permanent injunctive relief for proven patent infringement."[54] Evidence suggests that post-*eBay* district courts continue to grant permanent injunctions.[55] Injunctions are more likely when the IP owner competes with the infringer.[56]

Richard Epstein argues against exclusively using damages for infringement of IP in the absence of the possibility of injunctive relief.[57] Infringement would then function as a viable option for the infringer, potentially leading to excessive infringement.[58] Epstein compares damages for infringement to the general problem of damages for breach of contract.[59] He criticizes the "efficient breach" approach when expectation damages are the only remedy for breach of contract.[60] Without the possibility of injunctive relief, expectation damages function as an option for the party contemplating breach, which may reduce incentives to contract.[61]

The courts' standard approach to resolving patent infringement disputes further illustrates the mixture of property and tort. Courts typically apply the "hypothetical negotiation" approach to calculating reasonable royalty damages.[62] The hypothetical negotiation approach combines property and tort because it tries to imagine both what a willing licensor would accept and what a willing licensee would accept.[63] The acceptance of the willing licensor is the property side of the law and the acceptance of the willing licensee is the tort side of the law. So, the hypothetical negotiation tries to simultaneously satisfy property and tort remedies.

The hypothetical negotiation, however, may fail to satisfy both property and tort remedies. One reason for this is that the hypothetical benefit to the infringer may be less than the hypothetical harm to the patent holder. If the infringer's benefit from adopting the technology is less than the patent holder's cost of providing the technology, there is no basis for an economically efficient transaction. The transaction would yield negative net benefits.

If the infringer's benefit from adopting the technology is less than the cost to the patent holder of providing the technology, there is no royalty that would support an exchange. The patent holder would not give consent as seller for any royalty that does not cover the cost of providing the technology because the royalty would not be compensatory. So, the hypothetical negotiation would not protect property interests.

Conversely, the infringer would not consent as buyer to any royalty that would be greater than the benefits of implementing the technology. The patent holder thus would not be compensated for the damages from infringement. So, the hypothetical negotiation would not satisfy tort requirements.

Further, the hypothetical negotiation also fails to provide either property or tort remedies because it undertakes the impossible task of determining the property owner's expectations and the infringer's expectations before infringement occurs.[64] This requires knowledge not available to either the patent holder or the infringer, let alone the court. The passage of time and the resolution of uncertainty will change the infringer's benefit from infringement and the patent holder's damages from infringement. Damages based on the hypothetical negotiation are unlikely to reflect either the patent holder's cost as seller or the infringer's benefit as buyer.

The courts apply two damage calculations that are subject to similar problems.[65] First, the "bottom-up" approach calculates reasonable royalty damages as a share of the infringer's benefit based on the incremental value of the patents to the infringer.[66] This approach requires not only determining the infringer's direct valuation of the patented technology but also the valuation of the best alternative.[67] Second, the "top-down" approach is based on marking down the infringer's profit and apportioning that profit among multiple technologies.[68] The top-down approach appears in *In re Innovatio* and *TCL Communications v. Ericsson.*[69]

Both of these damage calculations are based on the infringer's benefits.[70] The two methods represent tort solutions to patent infringement because they are sufficient to insure the infringer's consent as buyer for ongoing infringement. These methods may not necessarily be compensatory, however, because the awarded damages may be less than the patent holder's costs — even if the patent holder's costs are less than the infringer's benefits. These methods are a shift from IP to IT because they tend to remove the owner's consent as seller.

5.2.2. *Untangling IT and IP*

IC rules provide guidance in untangling IT and IP. Private agreements should be more efficient than outcomes created by courts because the parties know more about their situation than do the courts. Transaction costs can reduce the efficiency of private agreements, but such costs tend to be lower than litigation costs.

The courts can untangle IT from IP by separating compensation from injunction. An IC protects the expectations of the parties to the agreement. If an IC is breached, it is necessary to compensate the injured party for harm caused by the breach. The courts should at least provide compensation to owners of IP for infringement that has already occurred. The damages to IP owners should include all of the economic costs due to the infringement, including transaction costs. The damages can also be tripled if the infringer engaged in "egregious infringement behavior."[71]

The courts should not necessarily rely on compensation for infringement that has not yet occurred. Forward-looking damages give the infringer consent as the buyer and remove the owner's consent as the seller. This approach weakens IP and leads to an inefficient appropriation of technology. Instead, courts should impose an injunction when necessary to prevent future infringement.[72] This restores the consent of the owner of the intangible asset.

An injunction not only mitigates future harm but also provides incentives for the parties to negotiate an IC. If the benefit to the infringer is greater than the cost to the owner, the parties benefit from an IC; an injunction should thus lead to an IC. If the benefit to the infringer is less than the cost to the owner, then the parties will not benefit from an IC, but an injunction will stop the infringement. Injunctions protect the IP rights of the owners of the intangible assets by restoring their consent as seller.

Infringement is technology transfer in the absence of an IC. Infringement represents a failure to contract, whether or not infringement is intentional.[73] Failure to reach a contractual agreement combined with continued usage of the intangible asset is likely to lead to an infringement dispute. An IC prevents the infringement dispute and can also resolve an infringement dispute after it has already begun.

IC rules also help calculate damage remedies for infringement. Rather than imagining the situation of the parties before infringement began, it is necessary to determine the actual harm from infringement. As I discuss in detail elsewhere, the court in a patent case gathers evidence that fills in many of the terms of a patent license agreement.[74] The evidence includes the identity of the parties, their business relationship, and the nature of the IP being transferred. The evidence indicates the extent of the infringement and helps determine the harm to the owner of the intangible assets.

In infringement disputes, courts should construct what I have referred to in the previous chapter as an "informed contract."[75] This approach is consistent with IC rules and replaces the flawed hypothetical negotiation. The informed contract builds on the information revealed by the patent case to estimate the harm to the patent holder. The patent holder's lost profits and reasonable damages should be based on infringement that actually occurred. Courts should not attempt the impossible task of constructing imagined expectations for a negotiation that did not occur.

In determining damages for infringement, the IC approach suggests that courts should use royalties from comparable ICs. These royalties from comparable license contracts should be adjusted based on information revealed by the patent case. In particular, royalties should reflect the increase in market value of a license for a patent found to be valid and infringed upon. Royalties for Standard Essential Patents (SEPs) should reflect the added market value of the patent license that is revealed by inclusion of the patent in technology standards chosen by a Standard Setting Organization (SSO). Other characteristics of patents can raise or lower the market value of licenses and can be used to adjust royalties from comparable licenses.

If there are no comparable patent licenses, reasonable royalty damages can be estimated by using the market prices of patents. I have spelled out the "market value method" of calculating reasonable royalty damages.[76] The market prices of patents provide information about expected returns from own-use and total royalties from multiple licensing agreements. These can be apportioned among infringers to determine the royalties that would have been received but for the infringement.

IT, or liability for infringement, does not offer sufficient legal support for technological change. IT does little to deter infringement of ideas and provides no guidelines for cooperative agreements. Technological change cannot depend only on compensating patent holders for infringement. Although recovery of lost profits or reasonable royalty damages may serve as remedies for infringement, this is not sufficient to induce cooperative investment in creating and applying new ideas. IP protections are necessary to preserve incentives to form ICs, thus protecting expectation interests.

5.2.3. *ICs and the "Market for Innovative Control"*

IC rules help resolve the ongoing debate over whether IP or IT provides the best protections for inventors. The protection of the interests of inventors depends on the combination of property, tort, and contract rules. ICs generate gains from trade for all parties, thus enhancing the benefits for inventors beyond what IP and IT protections can provide. ICs complement IP and IT protections by supporting commercialization and cooperative investment.

ICs are the main transaction method for what I have termed the "market for innovative control."[77] ICs allocate both returns from intangible assets and rights of control over innovation using those assets. ICs protect the continual stream of discoveries and extensive sharing of knowledge required for cooperative investment. ICs involve investment in disembodied technology as well as technology embodied in goods and services. The characteristics of technological change suggest increased usage of ICs in comparison to standard contracts. Investment continues to shift away from tangible assets and toward intangible assets. Virtual inventions and innovations represent a shift away from hardware innovations and toward software innovations.[78] For example, improvements in products, production processes, and business methods may take the form of software upgrades rather than new equipment with improved capabilities. Such innovation will take the form of intangible assets. Technology transfers and upgrades will require ICs that protect expectation interests and IP.

Technological change that increases connectivity and knowledge sharing may require new types of contract provisions. Innovations in IoT involve a significant increase in connectivity among firms as well as between firms and customers. The International Telecommunications Union (ITU) defines the IoT as follows: "A global infrastructure for the information society, enabling advanced services by interconnecting (physical and virtual) things based on existing and evolving interoperable information and communication technologies."[79] According to the ITU, "The IoT is expected to greatly integrate leading technologies, such as technologies related to advanced machine-to-machine communication, autonomic networking, data mining and decision-making, security and privacy protection, and cloud computing, with technologies for advanced sensing and actuation."[80] The ITU identifies various types of business roles in IoT, including providers of platforms, networks, devices, and applications.[81] These business roles are likely to require ICs.

Advances in AI also suggest greater use of ICs. Employees and managers working with AI will jointly generate knowledge and inventions. It will be necessary to specify how to monitor and reward the performance of employees and managers who interact with AI systems. It will also be necessary to determine inventions and innovations created by employees that work with AI systems. Related considerations apply to contractual relationships between firms that involve AI systems. It may be necessary to specify performance in terms of both the activities of individuals and AI systems.

The market for innovative control depends on the broad framework of Intellectual Law. Protections for IP rights and other aspects of IP improve the efficiency of transactions in the market for innovative control.[82] Extending and enhancing these traditional protections, ICs allocate residual returns and residual control rights from IP and support cooperative investment in invention, innovation, and adoption. ICs are important for innovation by established firms and entrepreneurs because they protect the expectation interests of inventors, innovators, and adopters. ICs thus support cooperative agreements to develop and apply technology. These agreements increase the benefits of inventors beyond what they could obtain through own-use and transfers of inventions. So, ICs promote the interests of inventors beyond what property or liability rules alone could achieve.

Efficient economic activity depends on a combination of contractual agreements and property rights. Contractual agreements require well-defined property rights for tangible assets that provide completeness, exclusivity, and transferability. In turn, owners of tangible property, including land, structures, inventory, and capital equipment, cannot realize the full economic value of those assets simply from own-use and transfer of assets to others. Property owners need contracts that support cooperation over time and investment in tangible assets. A market system requires contracts for employment, production, construction, procurement, distribution, and finance.

Technological change also depends on a combination of contractual agreements and property rights. IP provides the foundation of the market for innovative control by improving efficiency and gains from trade from ICs. However, even a well-functioning IP system is not sufficient to protect the interests of inventors, innovators, and adopters. Owners of IP cannot rely only on own-use and transfers of IP. ICs allocate both residual returns and residual rights of control over how inventions are developed and applied to generate innovations. Through ICs such as licensing agreements, patent holders and technology adopters determine how technology will be applied. Firms require ICs to form agreements with employees, suppliers, partners, distributors, investors, and customers.

ICs differ from standard contracts because the characteristics of intangible assets differ from those of tangible assets. Firms form ICs with managers and specialized employees to carry out invention, innovation, and adoption. Firms form ICs with other firms to outsource R&D and to share inventions and innovations. The development and application of inventions and innovations require cooperative investment to create and develop intangible assets. ICs realize many benefits that are beyond the reach of own-use or immediate exchange of intangible assets.

An IC involves those intangible assets associated with invention, innovation, and adoption. Not all intangible assets are related to technological change.[83] According to the International Accounting Standards (IAS) 38, "An intangible asset is an identifiable non-monetary asset without physical substance. Such an asset is identifiable when it is separable, or when it arises from contractual or other legal rights. Separable assets can be sold, transferred, licensed, etc."[84] The legal rights and obligations in a contract are also intangible assets, but not all contracts are ICs.[85]

The market for innovative control allocates both returns of innovation and control over innovative investment decisions. The market for technology resembles the stock market, which allocates both residual returns and residual rights of control over corporate investment decisions. The market for innovative control includes licensing and cross-licensing agreements for IP and specialized agreements to develop and apply inventions and innovations over time. The market for innovative control also includes the transfer of intangible assets and the sale of inventions and innovations that are embodied in goods and services. The market for innovative control further includes mergers and acquisitions (M&A) that transfer ownership of corporations' intangible assets. The market for innovative control also encompasses financing of invention and innovation, including venture capital.[86]

Despite its limitations, IP improves transaction efficiencies in the market for innovative control. In addition to exclusivity and transferability, IP reduces transaction costs and improves the efficiency of contracts by offering disclosure, certification, standardization, and divisibility.[87] IP provides a basis for licensing, cross-licensing, and other ICs. IP supports ICs involving the joint development and allocation of inventions and innovations.

Robert Merges emphasizes the general contributions of property to contracting, and these contributions are particularly applicable to IP.[88] Merges points out that property provides "precontractual liability," which protects the disclosure of information before a contract is formed.[89] Merges further observes that property provides "enforcement flexibility" after a contract is formed.[90] Merges emphasizes the importance of this interaction between contract and property with modular production and specialized firms.[91]

IP enhances coordination in contractual relationships. Scott Kieff emphasizes that patents "facilitate investment in the complex, costly, and risky commercialization activities required to turn nascent inventions into new goods and services."[92] Kieff observes that "This commercialization approach sees property rights in IP serving a role akin to beacons in the dark, drawing to themselves all of those potential complementary users of the IP-protected-asset to interact with the IP owner and each other."[93] Kieff argues that the coordination provided by IP leads to contracts: "This helps them each explore through the bargaining process the possibility of striking contracts with each other."[94]

IP generates economic benefits by supporting market transactions rather than simply own-use of intangible assets. A report by the Economics and Statistics Administration and the USPTO frames the benefits of IP in terms of economic activities:

- Providing incentives to invent and create;
- Protecting innovators from unauthorized copying; Facilitating vertical specialization in technology markets;

- Creating a platform for financial investments in innovation;
- Supporting entrepreneurial liquidity through mergers, acquisitions, and IPOs;
- Supporting licensing-based technology business models; and
- Enabling a more efficient market for trading in technology and know-how.[95]

Notice that each of these economic activities is based on parties forming ICs, including invention, innovation, finance, licensing, and transactions in the market for technology.

Conversely, IP owners rely on ICs for the development, commercialization, and application of intangible assets. The increasing importance of technological change in the economy has generated a burgeoning market for innovative control.[96] Owners of intangible assets not only obtain a stream of returns but also have rights of control over inventions, innovations, and adoption. The market value of intangible assets is the present value of the stream of returns and control rights.

IC relationships provide mechanisms of commercialization for IP holders. Raymond Nimmer points out that "commercialization, which depends on contractual relationships, constitutes one of the core mechanisms by which information is developed and distributed. It is a central part of intellectual property law 'bargain' and should be recognized as such."[97] Nimmer observes, "Only the most naive observer, or one with a clear political agenda, can look at the intellectual property laws and their history and suggest that policy in the property sphere trumps or precludes the influence of contract."[98] For example, contracts such as online "click-wrap" agreements provide "private ordering" for information and knowledge sharing.[99]

Because antitrust policy generally targets anti-competitive conduct rather than ownership rights, antitrust policy toward innovation correspondingly targets anti-competitive conduct rather than ownership of intangible assets. The Department of Justice (DOJ) Antitrust Division and the Federal Trade Commission (FTC) both recognize that IP owners depend on contracts to realize the benefits from intangible assets.[100] The title of the DOJ and FTC policy thus addresses a type of IC rather than IP: "Antitrust Guidelines for the Licensing of Intellectual Property."[101]

Further, the Antitrust Guidelines acknowledge the central importance of contracts when dealing with IP: "The owner of intellectual property has to arrange for its combination with other necessary factors to realize its commercial value."[102]

ICs and IP perform different economic functions, although both have present values. An IC can be described as a joint investment project that generates a stream of returns over time and is subject to uncertainty. An immediate exchange of IP involves the transfer of a bundle of rights that generates a stream of returns over time that is subject to uncertainty. In both cases, the stream of returns over time refers to the stream of revenues minus costs at each date.

An IC provides a mechanism for cooperation over time to implement technological change. An IC spells out the performance of activities involved in technological change. Adjusting investment over time in light of new information increases the expected value of investment projects in comparison to projects that do not adjust investment levels.[103]

As with contracts generally, an IC protects the expectation interests of the parties and provides incentives for investment. Because contracts are voluntary, the parties only enter into an IC if they anticipate benefits from the bargain. To benefit from the bargain, both parties must receive gains from trade. The terms of the contract allocate gains from trade and define future performance.

The parties' expectation interests refer to the anticipation of benefits in the future. A contract protects a party's expectation interests if the party realizes the value of the contract, even if the promised performance does not occur. The legal use of the term "expectation" refers to the parties' present value of future benefits from the contract. However, this can differ from the use of the term "expectation" in the fields of probability and statistics.

The present value of a contract depends on the discount rate and expectations about uncertain outcomes. In the absence of uncertainty, the total benefits of an IC equal the present value of the stream of future returns discounted using the appropriate rate of interest. The parties to an IC will divide the present discounted value of the stream of future returns. The benefits of owning IP also equal the present discounted value of the stream of future returns obtained by using and licensing the IP. In a competitive market, the price of the IP should equal the present discounted value of the stream of future returns. When uncertainty is present, estimating the benefits of an IC and the benefits of owning IP involves expectations about the resolution of uncertainty. Combined, the discounting of future benefits and the expectation of the outcome of uncertainty generate an expected present discounted value.[104]

An IC enhances the value of IP because cooperation generates gains from trade. The parties create additional economic value relative to own-use or an immediate exchange of intangible assets. An IC protects the expectation interests of both parties. Let V denote the present value of the discounted stream of net benefits expected by parties forming an IC. Let U denote the total opportunity costs of the parties, which equals the present value of the discounted stream of expected benefits forgone. Then, $V–U$ denotes total gains from trade for the two parties entering an IC.

Licensing agreements are a form of IC covering the usage of all types of intangible assets: patents, trademarks, copyrights, and trade secrets. Suppose that V is the net benefit of the licensee and suppose also that the IP holder derives no additional benefits from the agreement. The benefit V includes the returns to investment by the licensee in applying the technology and returns to investment in complementary assets net of the costs of investment. Suppose that the licensee has no opportunity costs and U is the opportunity cost of the IP owner. The licensee pays compensation R that represents the present value of the expected stream of royalty payments to the IP owner, which is less than the benefit of the licensee and greater than the opportunity cost to the IP owner. License royalties divide gains from trade $V–U$.

Expectation damages for breach of a patent license contract are based on the royalties that the licensor would have received had the contract been honored by the licensee. Expectation damages for breach of contract generally protect the plaintiff's expectation.[105] Economic analysis suggests that expectation damages for breach of contract generate efficient performance decisions and also induce efficient reliance investment.[106]

By protecting expectation interests, an IC provides incentives to invest efficiently in invention, innovation, and adoption. Expectation damages provide incentives for efficient investment in developing the invention and in complementary assets as well. This is because parties choose investment levels that maximize expected returns net of the costs of investment. Maximization of expected returns net of the costs of investment means that investment is chosen such that the expected marginal return to investment equals the marginal cost of investment. With only partial protections for expectation interests, a party to the contract may not receive all of the expected returns to investment. This implies that a party to the contract may not receive the expected marginal returns to additional investment. This provides incentives for a contracting party to choose an amount of investment below the efficient level. Consequently, a contracting party would not choose an amount of investment that maximizes expected returns net of the costs of investment. So, protection of expectation interests is necessary for parties to obtain the greatest possible gains from trade. ICs thus provide dynamic efficiencies that protect and increase benefits to inventors, innovators, and adopters.

IC rules are consistent with property protections for intangible assets. There are two main forms of legal protection for patent holders. Federal law protects the patent holder from infringement of IP rights by enforcing exclusion.[107] State law protects patent holders from infringement that results from breach of contract.[108] Phillip Jones points out that "the licensor may have the option to seek a remedy for a license restriction breach under the contract or from a patent infringement suit."[109] Jones concludes that "[i]n fact, a licensor may be able to obtain the same range of remedies in state court for the breach of a license agreement that the licensor would be able to obtain in federal court for patent infringement under 35 U.S.C. §§ 283–85 (i.e., an injunction, compensatory damages, and attorney fees)."[110]

To illustrate how expectation damages affect breach decisions in patent license contracts, suppose that a licensor expects to receive a payment of R from the licensing agreement. For ease of discussion, suppose that the licensor does not have any lost profits and does not incur any licensing costs, although the discussion can readily be generalized without changing the conclusions. Expectation damages for a licensee breach of contract restore the licensor to the position he would be in if the contract had been honored. This implies that damages D equal the payment R that the licensor would have received.

The damages remedy affects the licensee's contract breach decision. Suppose that after the licensing contract is signed, the licensee develops an alternative invention that generates net benefits Z. Alternatively, Z could represent the market value of a new alternative invention net of royalty payments. The licensee will breach the contract if and only if the benefits of switching to the alternative technology net of switching costs and contract damages are greater than the net benefits of honoring the contract. This means that breach occurs if and only if the benefits of adopting the new technology net of damages $Z–D$ are greater than the benefits $V–R$ of the patented technology net of royalties.

Expectation damages equal the payment that the licensor expected to receive. Netting out the damage payment and the corresponding royalty payment, this implies that breach occurs if and only if the value Z obtained from applying the alternative technology is greater than the value V from the patented invention. This means that with expectation damages, breach of the licensing contract should occur if and only if breach is efficient, that is, if Z is greater than V. So, expectation damages for breach of licensing agreements provide incentives for efficient technology adoption decisions.

When expectation damages are sufficient to protect the expectation interests of the parties, the parties choose the terms of the agreement to maximize the present value of expected benefits. Also, the parties choose their investments to maximize the present value of total expected benefits. In this way, an IC increases the benefits of IP owners in comparison with immediate exchange and own-use alone.

5.2.4. *ICs and the Nature of the Firm*

ICs are critical building blocks in the formation of innovative firms. ICs are essential to the "creative destruction" that takes place when innovative entrants compete with incumbent firms. Innovative firms contract with specialized researchers within the firm to develop and manage intangible assets. Innovative firms contract in the market with firms that create, own, or apply intangible assets. Innovative firms use ICs with customers, suppliers, partners, and distributors to introduce new products, production processes, transaction methods, and organizational structures. Innovative firms use ICs to provide multi-sided platforms that offer market-making and intermediary services to customers and suppliers.

Contracts are central to the formation of firms. The firm involves both internal and external contractual relationships.[111] The firm's collection of internal and external contracts depends on the relative efficiency and transaction costs of these types of contracts. Steven Cheung interprets Ronald Coase's analysis of the firm in terms of contract: "It is not quite correct to say that a 'firm' supersedes 'the market.' Rather, one type of contract supersedes another type."[112]

A major purpose of the firm is to organize and manage the market for contracts. In my book, *The Theory of the Firm*, I show that "[t]he firm is an intermediary in the market for contracts."[113] Entrepreneurs establish firms when the benefits of intermediated contracts exceed the benefits of direct exchange: "Firms offer advantages over bilateral contracts through market making and coordination across multiple contracts."[114]

IC relationships are essential to the creation of new types of firms. As I discuss in my book, *The Innovative Entrepreneur*, entrepreneurs innovate to overcome the innovative inertia of incumbent firms.[115] Entrepreneurs also innovate to overcome friction in the market for inventions that limit transfers of their technology to incumbent firms.[116] Innovative entrepreneurs develop a complex set of contractual relationships, necessarily including ICs, to create startups and establish firms.

Contracts have well-known transaction costs, including the costs of search, negotiation, moral hazard, adverse selection, monitoring performance, and enforcement of contract terms. ICs have additional transaction costs, including difficulties in pricing IP and the costs of bundling IP with other goods and services.[117] Because of the fundamental uncertainty involved in technological change, ICs have additional costs of forming contingent agreements and monitoring outcomes. Uncertainty associated with invention, innovation, and adoption is likely to be much greater than with contracts involving tangible assets.[118]

The firm's outsourcing decisions concerning invention and innovation also depend on the relative costs of forming and monitoring an employment IC versus an outsourcing IC. The tradeoff between governance costs and market transaction costs for ICs is related to Coase's analysis of the scope of the firm's activities and the make-or-buy decision.[119] Coase's analysis applied to technological change suggests that the firm will expand its inventive and innovative activities as long as incremental governance costs are less than the transaction costs of outsourcing these activities.[120]

The trade-off between governance costs and transaction costs has important implications for innovative firms. The use of ICs both within the firm and among firms affects the direction of technological change. The reductions in the extent of vertical integration of the firm affect how R&D is organized in the economy. This is reflected in the design of products and production processes. Firms have reduced vertical integration by creating modular products and outsourcing contracts for innovation.[121]

The increasing importance of invention and innovation requires new types of intangible assets and organizations.[122] Implementing technological change requires contractual agreements. Connecting individuals and firms in new ways requires more than networks of innovative technologies with digital links; it is also necessary to connect individuals and firms with networks of contracts that support the formation of these new technological networks. Individuals and firms need legal agreements for cooperative development of virtual inventions and innovations, and to help develop interconnectivity and interoperability of technologies. Individuals and firms also need contracts that support data sharing and investment in data gathering and analytics.

Technological change leading to vertical disintegration requires coordination through ICs between many vertical levels of suppliers. Various technological developments cut across industries, leading to greater reliance on outsourcing and licensing agreements. Technological changes that cross industries include AI, IoT, and ICT.[123]

IC necessarily accompanies the growth of R&D outsourcing and the formation of innovation networks. Firms substitute networks of contracts for vertical integration.[124] Contracts among firms substitute for contracts within the firm. Matthew Jennejohn observes, "[w]here property rights no longer control, contracts substitute. In light of these developments, contract's place as one of capitalism's fundamental building-blocks takes on even greater importance."[125]

Many types of invention and innovation require coordination of activities across firms. This is reflected in the increasing importance of technological standards. There are over one thousand standard setting organizations (SSOs) that establish quality and interoperability standards in practically every industry.[126] Changes in technology standards provide an important indication of innovation.[127] Standards include "variety control, usability, compatibility, interchangeability, health, safety, protection of the environment, product protection, mutual understanding, economic performance, trade."[128] For example, the International Organization for Standardization (ISO) has published over 21,000 international standards,[129] playing an important role in the formation of global supply chains. The management literature refers to the extensive technological interdependence among firms as innovative "ecosystems."[130]

5.3 Intellectual Contract

Intellectual Law offers a framework for addressing intangible assets in a comprehensive manner. This section examines some of the main differences between IC and standard contracts; it also sets out five basic principles of IC. IC involves agreements that resolve some of the incompleteness of IP. IC also helps remedy difficulties in exclusion of access to intangible assets. IC provides agreements when there is non-rivalrous usage of intangible assets. IC provides incentives for exploratory performance. Finally, IC addresses problems of contingent contracting when agreements are subject to fundamental uncertainty.

5.3.1. *ICs and Incompleteness of IP*

IP suffers from weak enforcement as well as the inherent limitations of government grants and registration. A well-functioning system of property rights requires completeness, exclusivity, and transferability. ICs provide protections for intangible assets based on agreements between inventors, innovators, and adopters. This compensates for incompleteness of legal protections for intangible assets. An advantage of ICs is that they do not require government approval of the IP defined through the agreement. The transaction costs of IC are likely to be substantially lower than costs associated with government administration. Contractually defined protections are tailored to the particular benefits and costs of the contracting parties and the characteristics of the technology.

The Constitution frames protections for inventors in terms of exclusive rights for writings and discoveries.[131] Patent holders have the right to exclude others from making, using, offering to sell, selling, or importing any patented invention.[132] State governments and all three branches of the federal government are involved in defining and enforcing IP rights.[133] IP policies include legislative limitations on IP, executive policies toward IP — particularly involving the USPTO and antitrust agencies — and judicial decisions on IP. Many practitioners and scholars emphasize the importance of IP protections for inventors.[134]

IP protections for commercial, scientific, and technological creations are far from complete however. IP provides protections in four categories: patents, trademarks, copyrights, and trade secrets.[135] The WIPO Convention's definition of IP is more inclusive because it identifies "scientific discoveries" and "all other rights resulting from intellectual activity in the industrial, scientific, literary or artistic fields."[136]

In contrast to tangible property, patents and trademarks require government grants.[137] The USPTO not only registers the property right but also defines and certifies the features of the intangible asset.[138] At the USPTO, professional patent examiners review applications for patents and examining attorneys review applications for trademarks.[139] For inventions to be "patentable," they must satisfy criteria such as first-to-file, novelty, and non-obviousness.[140] For trademarks to be "registrable," there cannot be a "likelihood of confusion" with existing trademarks or pending applications.[141] The chance that a trademark is "registrable" also depends on the category it belongs to: fanciful or arbitrary, suggestive, descriptive, or generic.[142]

There are also limitations for copyright. In fiscal year 2016, the U.S. Copyright Office issued over 414,000 registrations out of 468,000 claims for registration.[143] The U.S. Copyright Office limits types of works and applies subject matter criteria, governed by statute: "In no case does copyright protection for an original work of authorship extend to any idea, procedure, process, system, method of operation, concept, principle, or discovery, regardless of the form in which it is described, explained, illustrated, or embodied in such work."[144]

IP offers weaker protections for inventors than protections for traditional property rights. In contrast to tangible property, patents limit the time period of exclusive rights. The regulatory time limit is a form of incompleteness. Richard Epstein argues that limiting the time period of exclusive rights transforms tangible property rules to intangible property rules.[145] Epstein suggests that limiting the time period for exclusion, use, and disposition is similar to other limits placed on property generally, including the law of private and public necessity and antitrust limitations on collusion.[146]

Subject matter limitations are another major form of incompleteness for IP.[147] The subject matter limitations for patentability under the statute specify "any new and useful process, machine, manufacture, or composition of matter."[148] The Supreme Court in *Bilski* questioned whether business method inventions should be patentable.[149] The decision cast doubt on many existing business method patents and the full range of commercial inventions, including Internet commerce software applications.[150] The Supreme Court decision in *Mayo* raised issues about biotechnology inventions by diagnostic tests for administering pharmaceuticals.[151] The Court rejected the invention using a two-step test that first determined whether the invention consisted of "abstract ideas, laws of nature, or natural phenomena," then examined whether the invention would "transform the nature of the claim" into something patentable.[152] The Supreme Court applied the two-step test in *Alice* to reject a business invention for intermediated settlement.[153]

IP also provides incomplete protections because patents do not cover many incremental inventions.[154] The costs and difficulties in obtaining and maintaining a patent can be very high.[155] This inevitably generates an expected value threshold for patent protections. An inventor will not apply for a patent unless the expected value of patenting the invention exceeds the costs of obtaining the patent. Consequently, patent protections are incomplete because they do not cover inventions with expected values below the threshold.

ICs help protect discoveries in the lower tail of the distribution of the market value of inventions. IP tends to cover the upper tail of inventions and other intangible assets.[156] Let C represent the expected legal costs and fees of obtaining and maintaining IP such as patents. Let Y be the market value of the IP, including own-use by the IP holder, if found to be valid by the courts. Let P be the likelihood that IP is found to be valid by the courts and survives administrative challenges. Then, it is not worthwhile obtaining IP if the expected benefits PY are less than the expected costs C. This type of IP is the lower tail of the net value distribution of intangible assets. Yet, incremental discoveries are generated routinely and are highly important within the firm. There are many discoveries in the lower tail of the distribution of the market value of inventions.[157]

In addition, patent application criteria and uncertainty in review by patent examiners limit coverage for inventors. Many discoveries may be original but not meet formal IP criteria, including those based on laws of nature, non-obviousness, and usefulness.[158] These considerations eliminate property protections for inventions that do not pass through formal review and meet the regulatory criteria. The risks of the review process further increase the expected value threshold for patent protections.[159] Fewer inventors seek patent protections which further increases the incompleteness of IP.

IP protections also are incomplete because of costs and inaccuracies in the legal and regulatory systems. Patent holders face costs of detecting and monitoring infringement.[160] The legal costs of obtaining compensation for infringement are significant. Additionally, patents are subject to costly legal challenges in terms of validity and infringement. Unavoidable legal errors, inconsistencies, and technical issues further limit IP protections for some useful and original inventions. Patents are also subject to challenge at the Patent Trial and Appeal Board (PTAB) within the USPTO, which may also be subject to error.[161] Taken together, these costs and risks create another type of value threshold for patent protections. Patents with an expected value below this threshold will not have IP protections.

Stronger protections for trade secrets address some of these limitations. More companies rely on protections from trade secrets and trademarks than from copyrights and patents.[162] Trade secrets do not require formal government grants of IP.[163] Ivan Png points out that "trade secrets can be unlimited in time, are not limited by particular technical standards, and do not require disclosure. Moreover, the scope of trade secrecy is much broader, extending to work in progress as well as completed innovations."[164] Individual states' adoption of the Uniform Trade Secrets Act (UTSA) has increased protections for inventors and innovators.[165] Png finds that state adoption of the UTSA has tended to increase R&D.[166]

Although trade secrets cover works in progress, they are not sufficient to protect the continual sharing of information within and among firms. Many lower tail discoveries must be disclosed to employees and the firm's customers, suppliers, and partners.[167] ICs overcome some of the limitations of trade secret protections. IC protections, such as non-disclosure agreements (NDAs), address the need to share various trade secrets in employment and outsourcing.[168]

ICs help protect cooperative use of knowledge and intangible assets not covered by formal IP. Technological change involves repeated interactions over time between a firm and its employees and among firms. This interaction involves continual sharing of small increments of knowledge. The formal apparatus of IP cannot protect such small increments of knowledge because IP is geared to larger increases in knowledge. This is because the sharing of small increments of knowledge is often informal and incomplete. Also, the costs of obtaining government grants of IP are necessarily prohibitive for small increments of knowledge. Continual sharing of knowledge may involve relational contracts because of the need for trust and implicit agreements that cannot be achieved with IP.

5.3.2. *ICs and Excludability of IP*

Parties can form ICs to allocate ownership of intangible assets and to specify how those assets will be used. These private agreements depend on contract rules and private negotiation. ICs resolve problems related to the excludability of intangible assets. The parties to an IC can choose the desired extent of exclusion. The effectiveness of IP should be considered in combination with ICs.

Legal barriers limiting access to IP substitute for the lack of physical barriers. It is more difficult for IP owners to limit, deter, and monitor access to intangible assets in contrast to tangible assets.[169] Peter Menell notes that "even if someone claims to own the knowledge, it is difficult to exclude others from using it. Intellectual property law is an attempt to solve that problem by legal means."[170] R&D can generate positive externalities because knowledge can be costless for others to learn and distribute, while it can be costly for IP holders to monitor usage by others. Positive externalities from R&D are often referred to as R&D "spillovers."[171]

The debate over patent scope considers the effects of legal exclusion on sequential invention and innovation. Robert Merges and Richard Nelson argue that patent scope should be narrow so as to encourage rivalry among inventors.[172] They express concerns that narrow patents will favor pioneer inventors and block competing inventors.[173] Advocates of narrow patent scope argue that exclusion creates monopoly rents for patent holders.[174] The advantages of not protecting patent holders' investments in developing an invention are inducing investment in developing and applying the invention by later inventors.[175]

Others argue that patent scope should be sufficiently broad to help inventors develop their own inventions without incursion by later inventors.[176] Broader patent protections encompassing future development encourage inventors to invest in improving and commercializing their patented inventions.[177] Broader patent protections also support investment in creating the initial invention and encourage disclosure of inventions.[178] Also, broader patent protections allow patent holders to choose the mix of own-use and outsourcing efficiently based on the relative economic returns to these activities.

With positive externalities from R&D, the social benefits of the initial invention are greater than the private benefits to the initial inventor. With broader patent scope, there is greater protection for IP rights of inventors and correspondingly fewer R&D spillovers. Conversely, with narrower patent scope, there is less protection for IP rights of inventors and correspondingly more R&D spillovers.

The problem of patent scope is thus similar to the problem of social cost. The social costs of an activity are defined as the total of private costs.[179] The social costs of an activity exceed the private costs to the owner of an activity when the activity imposes costs on others.[180] The costs or harm imposed on others are referred to as a negative externality if the costs are not part of a market transaction between the parties. Coase showed that private negotiation achieves efficiency regarding the extent of negative externalities when transaction costs are low and few parties are involved.[181] Coase emphasized that the assignment of property rights does not affect the efficiency of the outcome because the negotiating parties maximize their joint benefits.[182] If the party creating harm has property rights, the party suffering harm will pay them to stop.[183] If the party suffering harm has property rights, the party creating harm will be forced to pay compensation.[184] The extent of the activity will be such that the marginal private benefit to the party causing harm will equal the marginal damage to the party suffering harm.[185] The only effect of the initial assignment of property rights is distributional because the party with property rights will benefit at the expense of the party without property rights.[186]

When transaction costs are low and few parties are involved, the parties are able to attain an efficient outcome regardless of the assignment of property rights.[187] However, when transaction costs are high and many parties are involved, the assignment of property rights can affect the outcome.[188] This is because frictions may prevent or distort bargaining, thus preventing the parties from attaining an efficient outcome. It is then more efficient to assign property rights so as to minimize transaction costs. For example, there may be a few firms engaged in the activity that causes harm and many individuals suffering harm from the external effects of the activity. It is then more efficient to assign property rights to those suffering harm.

ICs can address the problem of patent scope and the effects of positive externalities from R&D. When transaction costs are low and few parties are involved, contract negotiation should attain the efficient outcome regardless of patent scope. If patent scope is narrow, the party benefitting from the initial invention can pay the inventor to conduct R&D. If patent scope is broad, the party benefitting from the initial invention can pay the inventor to use the invention, thus providing additional incentives for the inventor. The parties will reach an efficient agreement regardless of the initial assignment of IP rights.

ICs may not fully remedy the problem of patent scope when transaction costs are high and many parties are involved. In this situation, the choice of patent scope does affect economic efficiency. It is necessary for patent policy to assign property rights that achieve the right mix of initial and sequential invention. This suggests the need for broader patent scope because licensing the invention to later inventors should involve lower transaction costs than providing subsidies to potential initial inventors. As Merges points out, many potential buyers and high transaction costs suggest the need for stronger IP to support contracts.[189]

The length of patent life affects the initial inventor's returns from transferring or licensing the patent to the second inventor.[190] Also, the scope of the patent affects the extent to which sequential invention requires the second inventor to acquire or license the intangible assets of the first inventor.[191] ICs allow the allocation of returns among sequential inventors. Nancy Gallini argues that shorter lived, broad patents promote diffusion of inventions but longer lived, narrow patents lower R&D costs.[192] Amy Landers recommends that in patent disputes, courts should consider sequential invention and defines apportionment as "an examination of the differences between the infringed claim and the prior art in a manner analogous to the identification of the differences between the claimed invention and the prior art in the non-obviousness analysis."[193]

ICs also provide an important mechanism for addressing positive externalities in R&D.[194] Firms can internalize these benefits through licensing or cross-licensing agreements. Firms can also internalize positive externalities by creating RJVs and R&D consortia. Companies forming RJVs may employ covenants not to compete (CNCs) to coordinate their R&D activities. This type of CNC is a form of IC. CNCs date back over three centuries.[195] Sarath Sanga points out that corporate joint ventures involve an inherent fiduciary conflict between each company's duty to its own interests and its duty to the interests of a partner.[196] Sanga argues that this conflict of interests is resolved not only by operating the joint venture as a separate entity but also through the use of a CNC.[197]

ICs address problems arising from insufficient exclusivity of IP. Firms must disclose IP within their organizations. Firms licensing IP must disclose the features of the invention. Kenneth Arrow observed that offering inventions for sale or license involves revealing the secret.[198] Inventors must disclose their technology in order to obtain a patent. Trademarks and copyrighted works only have value if used openly.

ICs also help control technology transactions that occur when employees who switch jobs convey knowledge and inventions from their previous employer to their new one. Ronald Gilson includes legal frameworks as a source of agglomeration economies driving places like California's Silicon Valley.[199] Gilson emphasizes the importance of CNCs that facilitate employee job switching while protecting a company's intangible assets.[200] These types of CNCs also function as ICs.

Legal barriers provide weaker protections for intangible assets than for tangible assets. ICs remedy weaknesses in legal protections for IP. Infringement of a patent occurs when someone "without authority makes, uses, offers to sell, or sells any patented invention, within the United States or imports into the United States any patented invention during the term of the patent..."[201] An IC specifies who will make, use, offer to sell, or sell an invention, and places additional limitations on use and the amount of compensation. Enforcement of the agreement provides protections of the contracting parties' expectations.

5.3.3. *ICs and Non-Rivalrous Usage of IP*

Non-rivalrous usage of intangible assets distinguishes ICs from standard contracts involving tangible assets. ICs handle the non-rivalrous usage of intangible assets by facilitating allocation and sharing among multiple adopters. ICs support cooperation in developing and combining intangible assets. For example, a patent holder can grant access to an invention to multiple users by offering multiple patent license contracts.

ICs help define the characteristics and boundaries of intangible assets. Agreements between inventors, innovators, and adopters specify the features of technology being shared or transferred. Contracts adjust to the benefits and costs of the parties to the agreement and the needs of the industries in which they do business.

Some argue that IP should not receive the same legal protections as tangible property because of extensive interdependence associated with information. For example, Menell asserts, "Intellectual property has never fit the real property mold particularly well and the inherent attributes of intellectual resources as well as the increasingly interdependent nature of information ecosystems points away from the [property rights movement's] PRM's conception of property."[202]

Yet, as Polk Wagner observes, even open-source advocates seek control: "[D]espite rhetoric to the contrary, it seems quite clear that the 'open' in open source is actually rather tightly controlled, albeit in the name of generally greater access along certain philosophically-favored dimensions."[203] Polk points out that even open-source advocates turn to contracts for coordination:

> It should come as no surprise that participants in open source development efforts recognize the need for external coordination, chiefly attempting to accomplish this through the licensing of intellectual property rights to the software. Such licenses are not trivial; perhaps the best known open source license, the GNU General Public License (GPL), has been noted as an aggressive approach to both contract and copyright law, purporting to bind all subsequent users of the software to the terms of the original license.[204]

Transactions among inventors, innovators, and technology adopters depend on effective IC rules. ICs that protect the expectation interests of investors generate the benefits of interdependence in markets for invention. IP provides the foundation for the market for inventions.[205] ICs realize the benefits of coordination among creators and IP users. ICs provide parties with mechanisms to benefit from non-rivalrous usage of intangible assets.

5.3.4. *ICs and Incentives for Exploratory Performance*

An IC must solve the critical problem of designing incentives for what I refer to as exploratory performance. With technological change, the characteristics of the outcomes of invention, innovation, and technology adoption are likely to be unknown. The uncertainty involved is more complex than a lottery over known outcomes.

Uncertainty about the characteristics of outcomes increases transaction costs of contracting.[206] This distinguishes ICs from standard contracts involving tangible assets. Difficulties in specifying performance will also affect the incentives of parties involved in contract negotiation.[207]

An IC must specify the bargain when the characteristics of outcomes are unknown. With unknown outcomes, it becomes difficult to specify what performance is being offered and what performance is being accepted. The problems of defining and verifying performance make it difficult to determine the intent of the parties.

Almost all invention, innovation, and technology adoption involves delegation, whether it be to specialized personnel, managers, or firms.[208] So, an IC is likely to be subject to the two main forms of agency costs resulting from moral hazard and adverse selection.[209] A moral hazard problem arises when the employee's actions are imperfectly observable or verifiable.[210] Then, the IC must be based on some measure of performance generated by the employee's actions. Because there is a tradeoff between the cost of inducing action and the benefits of the action, the agent's action will differ from what would be chosen with observable actions.[211] The agent may not choose an efficient level of effort or investment.[212] Here, an efficient level of effort or investment refers to actions that maximize the joint benefits of the contracting parties. If the agent's activity is subject to additional uncertainty, it is not possible to infer the agent's effort from the resulting output. Contracts must therefore provide incentives to the agent or partner to generate effort or investment. Contractual incentives are based on the measure of performance and reward hidden actions indirectly.

An IC is also likely to be subject to adverse selection. An adverse selection problem arises if the employee has hidden information.[213] Even if the agent's action is observable and legally verifiable, the other party will not know what would have been the most efficient action. To address this problem, it is necessary to reward the agent's performance. There is a tradeoff between the cost of inducing the agent to tell the truth and benefits of obtaining an accurate report.[214] To induce truth telling, it may be necessary to allow a distortion of the agent's effort away from the efficient level of effort.[215]

Contracting costs associated with exploratory performance may differ from the agency costs associated with moral hazard and adverse selection. An IC can address the problem of determining exploratory performance when there is a general measure of benefits for one of the parties.[216] For example, a firm can base the rewards for specialized R&D personnel on the overall performance of the firm. This can be achieved by providing stock options for both managers and specialized R&D personnel.[217] Software companies provide long-term incentive contracts, such as stock options, to engineers and programmers involved in invention and innovation.[218] Firms making substantial investments in R&D may engage in greater delegation of authority and provide more stock options as incentives for non-executive employees.[219] Companies are also significantly increasing the use of long-term incentive contracts for managers of R&D units.[220]

The problem of rewarding exploratory performance is related to the issue of rewarding agents when the contract cannot be based on the principal's objective. Difficulties in measuring performance limit reliance on monitoring employees.[221] However, "high-powered" incentives directly tied to individual performance are often problematic. For example, rewarding R&D personnel based on the number of patents may generate lower-quality patents than rewards based on overall performance of the firm.[222] Even if the profit or stock price of the firm is observable, it can be difficult to anticipate the relationship between the benefits to the firm and the outcome of invention, innovation, or technology adoption.

Measuring performance may be problematic when basic inventions must undergo extensive development. This can generate delays in realizing the benefits of scientific and technological discoveries. Basic inventions often do not generate market returns without commercialization.[223] Obtaining rewards from inventions generally requires application in innovative products, production processes, and transaction methods.[224]

Another important aspect of ICs is that specialized research personnel engaged in exploratory performance may respond well to intrinsic motivation.[225] When R&D employees respond to intrinsic motivation, they may have an increased willingness to take risks.[226] Risk taking may be desirable in R&D because employees may pursue projects involving greater creativity and may devote more effort to experimentation.[227] Companies can design contracts and rewards that emphasize intrinsic motivation.

Kevin Murdock argues that the pharmaceutical company Merck's Mectizan Donation Program illustrates contracting with intrinsic motivation.[228] Merck developed the drug Mectizan as a cure for river blindness and offered the drug to potential users for free.[229] The Mectizan Donation Program states that it is "the longest-running drug donation program for Neglected Tropical Diseases," with over 300 million treatments per year for river blindness (onchocerciasis) and lymphatic filariasis elimination.[230] According to Murdock, a firm and its research personnel derive gains from trade when employees have intrinsic motivation.[231] Although the Mectizan project had negative financial returns for Merck, the firm benefitted because its research employees worked harder on other projects.[232] With intrinsic motivation, a firm realizes benefits from joint enforcement of multiple implicit contracts.[233]

Richard Gruner argues that patents encourage inventors to "dream big" and complete their projects.[234] He identifies some psychological aspects of invention and innovation that can generate errors:

> At least four psychological factors make it difficult for inventors to produce successful inventions based on distinctively new designs. These include: 1) difficulties in projecting the capabilities of new technologies in ways that point to new and distinctively different product designs; 2) divergences in the knowledge and experience of product inventors and product users, causing inventors to imperfectly understanding the functional needs and problems of potential invention users; 3) gaps in knowledge and experience of product inventors concerning the contexts where new inventions will be produced, supplied, and used, and; 4) inabilities of inventors to fully imagine the impacts of new inventions in use and the relative happiness of users with new inventions compared with alternative means for producing similar practical results.[235]

Gruner suggests changes in patent laws that would provide incentives for inventors that overcome these psychological problems.[236] However, it is unlikely that patent law can be fine-tuned to address problems of inventor imagination.

In contrast, private ordering through contract terms can avoid the problems of a one-size-fits-all system of government grants. Patent examination rules are legal standards applied by patent examiners.[237] In contrast to these legal rules, firms can be flexible and adaptable. Firms can adjust contract terms depending on the industry, the product, the type of technology, and even the capabilities of individual researchers. Firms can also vary contract terms over time in response to changes in competition, scientific discoveries, regulation, and consumer demand.

Through the use of ICs, firms are able to design contracts that improve incentives for exploratory performance for employees, managers, and subcontractors. Firms can induce exploratory performance by offering basic rewards contingent on the overall financial performance of the firm. Firms can coordinate invention, commercialization, and innovation to provide rewards for exploratory performance. Firms can offer a combination of extrinsic rewards and intrinsic motivation to help induce creative performance. Firms can design ICs that help inventors overcome psychological barriers to creativity.

5.3.5. *ICs and Fundamental Uncertainty*

Technological change involves fundamental uncertainty that may not be present in most standard contracts.[238] ICs provide basic mechanisms such as royalties and options that address fundamental uncertainty.[239] Even when parties to a contract face risk with a known likelihood of events, it is difficult and costly to form contingent contracts.[240] With fundamental uncertainty, contingent contracting becomes more difficult — to the point that any IC will likely be incomplete. Contract law tends to limit contractual constraints on renegotiation and therefore favors simpler contract forms.[241]

Parties forming ICs encounter various forms of fundamental uncertainty that I refer to as statistical, discovery, creativity, and market uncertainty. Statistical uncertainty describes researchers' uncertainty about the outcome of their experiments. Researchers typically design experiments and gather the data generated by those experiments. Researchers usually do not know the characteristics of the population from which the data were drawn, which is typically expressed as the lack of knowledge about the form of the probability distribution regarding some features of the population.[242] Researchers may not know anything about the form of the distribution, or researchers may know something about the form of the distribution but not specific parameter values of the distribution. This lack of knowledge can affect researchers' decisions in many different ways.[243]

Researchers use statistical inference to characterize the probability distribution that generates the data.[244] Given samples drawn from an unknown population distribution, researchers make inferences about what is the form of the distribution.[245] Statistical inference may take the form of estimation, construction of intervals that reflect a particular level of confidence, and hypothesis testing.[246]

Even if researchers learn something about the population distribution, they still may not know the distribution with certainty.[247] Thus, the process of experimentation and statistical inference does not fully eliminate uncertainty. The uncertainty can be described using probability, but even these probabilities may not be known with accuracy.[248]

Discovery uncertainty refers to lack of knowledge about the future discoveries of other researchers. This reflects not only uncertainty about the outcome of particular experiments but also uncertainty regarding the types of experiments undertaken by other researchers and professional interactions among researchers. Researchers benefit from the past discoveries of others. As Isaac Newton wrote, "If I have seen further, it is by standing on the shoulders of giants."[249] However, new discoveries will support or refute past discoveries. This effect compounds the statistical uncertainty researchers face when carrying out a particular project because the outcome of many other projects will impact the value of their work.

Science proceeds through discoveries that may confirm, extend, or refute previous discoveries. Thomas Kuhn argues that the development of scientific knowledge depends on a series of contentious revolutions.[250] Each area of scientific inquiry goes through phases associated with dominant conceptual paradigms during which "normal-scientific research is directed to the articulation of those phenomena and theories that the paradigm already supplies."[251] As Kuhn observes,

> Discovery commences with the awareness of anomaly, i.e., with the recognition that nature has somehow violated the paradigm-induced expectations that govern normal science. It then continues with a more or less extended exploration of the area of anomaly. And it closes only

> when the paradigm theory has been adjusted so that the anomalous has become the expected.[252]

Israel Scheffler questions the revolution metaphor, emphasizing instead the scientific evaluation of evidence: "The *quality* of scientific deliberations makes for a special and rare form of argumentation. It demands responsibility to the evidence, openness to argument, commitment to publication, loyalty to logic, and an admission, in principle, that one may turn out to be wrong."[253]

Whether through contentious revolutions or reasoned debate, new scientific discoveries cause researchers to reevaluate past discoveries. It is not feasible for ICs to address such complex contingencies. ICs for delegated or cooperative research are necessarily incomplete. IC design and legal rules thus need to provide general incentives for performance under discovery uncertainty.

Creativity uncertainty refers to the lack of knowledge about what other inventors and innovators will develop. It is difficult, if not impossible, to predict the outcomes of invention and innovation.[254] The limitless variety of creativity that is evident in the arts, such as music or literature, extends to invention and innovation in commerce, science, and technology. The creations of inventors and innovators inspire future creativity, further complicating uncertainty.

The creativity of inventors and innovators affects the economic value of past inventions and innovations. Inventions and innovations generate technological change that can enhance or diminish the past contributions of inventors, innovators, and adopters. Just as with discovery uncertainty, it is difficult, if not impossible, for an IC to address contingencies based on the creativity of other inventors and innovators. IC rules must therefore address the complexities of inventor and innovator creativity.

The creativity of other economic actors affects the expectation interests of parties to an IC in unpredictable ways. Advances in technology can serve as complements for existing technology and improve the performance of existing inventions and innovations. For example, advances in software can improve the demand for computer hardware.[255] Conversely, advances in technology can be substitutes for existing technology, leading to its obsolescence. For example, smart phones have displaced basic mobile phones. This corresponds to Joseph Schumpeter's concept of "creative destruction."[256]

The novel and non-obvious criteria for the patentability of an invention illustrate creativity uncertainty.[257] Novelty and non-obviousness are fleeting. An invention is a new and useful production process, machine, manufacturing technique, or composition of matter.[258] Patents are granted for novel inventions, but novelty is not a guarantee of market value because new technologies can readily supersede a patent long before it expires.[259] Obviousness is also subject to fundamental uncertainty. Based on experiments, Gregory Mandel observes,

> The results are dramatic: the hindsight bias prejudices patent decisions far more than anticipated. Not only are patent decisions routinely and unintentionally made in contradiction to patent doctrine, but even more significantly, patent law itself is incoherent. Judges, jurors, and patent examiners seemingly lack the cognitive ability to make decisions in the manner that patent law currently requires.[260]

Private agreements fill in many of the gaps left by public awards of IP and judicial decisions on patent validity. IC rules and the design of agreements can address the creativity effects of technological change. ICs reflect the parties' expectations and respond to their perceptions of what is new or obvious. The parties to an IC are better placed to evaluate how the creativity of others will affect their economic benefits. ICs handle much of what happens after the grant of IP.

Market uncertainty refers to unknown demand and costs, which can be heightened by the effects of technological change. We do not know what the demand for inventions will be in advance, particularly when the inventions have not been fully developed or tested. It is difficult, if not impossible, to predict the demand for innovations because they are new to the market. Some innovations, such as smart phones, diffuse rapidly and change the economy, and yet other innovations may be unsuccessful. It is also difficult for companies to estimate how adopting innovations will affect their costs and revenues. Additionally, companies face difficulties predicting competitor innovations and the effects that those innovations will have on market outcomes.

Market uncertainty represents fundamental uncertainty. It is difficult to determine market demand and supply because knowledge about demand and costs is dispersed among individual consumers and firms. Friedrich Hayek observes that society's economic problem is "the utilization of knowledge not given to anyone in its totality."[261] Hayek emphasizes that "the sort of knowledge with which I have been concerned is knowledge of the kind which by its nature cannot enter into statistics and therefore cannot be conveyed to any central authority in statistical form."[262] For Hayek, prices help to coordinate transactions by making the best use of dispersed knowledge.[263] The price system is essential as an adjustment mechanism: "It is, perhaps, worth stressing that economic problems arise always and only in consequence of change."[264]

Hayek argues that market uncertainty presents even greater difficulties than scientific uncertainty.[265] This is because market outcomes are fleeting and lack the relatively greater stability of scientific discoveries:

> The difference between economic competition and the successful procedure of science is that the former exhibits a method of discovering particular temporary circumstances, while science seeks to discover something often known as "general facts," i.e., regularities in events, and is concerned with unique, particular facts only to the extent that they tend to refute or confirm its theories.[266]

Because of market uncertainty, Hayek observes that "competition is important primarily as a discovery procedure whereby entrepreneurs constantly search for unexploited opportunities that can also be taken advantage of by others."[267]

The need to coordinate transactions becomes even more important when dealing with invention, innovation, and adoption. Market uncertainty has greater effects with technological change because inventions and innovations are untested. This makes ICs the essential means of addressing dispersed knowledge and adjusting to technological change.

5.4 Intellectual Contract Types

ICs protect the expectation interests of parties involved in technological change, including inventors, innovators, and adopters. This section considers various types of IC, including employment contracts, outsourcing contracts, licensing contracts, research joint ventures, and intermediary and collective rights organizations.

5.4.1. *Employment Contracts*

Companies hire specialized personnel to carry out invention, innovation, and adoption. Employment contracts between firms and specialized personnel are an important form of IC. Firms use ICs with managers and employees to create new products, production processes, transaction methods, and organizations.[268]

Most R&D is a delegated activity. R&D refers to basic research, applied research, and experimental development.[269] R&D is the process of discovery and knowledge creation. Designing employment contracts for delegated R&D can be challenging because R&D generates both explicit and tacit knowledge. Tacit knowledge can be difficult and costly to observe, transfer, and reproduce.[270]

Annual expenditures on R&D in the US exceed one-half trillion dollars.[271] Industry provides the main source of this funding ($347.7 billion); the other sources are the federal, state, and local governments ($140.2 billion), academia ($19.3 billion), and non-profits ($20.3 billion).[272] R&D is performed primarily by industry ($366.8 billion), with other R&D being carried out by academia ($75.2 billion), government agencies ($62.7 billion), and non-profits ($22.8 billion).[273]

Just as firms have production functions for goods and services, firms also have production functions for knowledge.[274] The knowledge production function describes how a firm uses R&D investment and employment to create intangible assets. The knowledge production function applies to creation of knowledge by a single firm or by groups of firms.[275] Firms produce intangible assets including various types of IP: patents, trademarks, copyrights, and trade secrets. Intangible assets also include reports of research results, statistical studies, scientific journal articles, software, blueprints, and invention prototypes. Firms produce inventions by employing researchers who have particular skill, judgment, motivation, creativity, and education. Firms invest in laboratory facilities and equipment. A firm may also apply a stock of intangible assets and licensing to produce intangible assets.

Employment contracts protect the interests of managers and employees who devote effort to R&D. Employment contracts must provide incentives for researchers to devote efficient effort to R&D, to make efficient decisions, and to report information accurately.[276] Also, ICs for invention must address who owns the resulting inventions if R&D is successful.

Employment contracts also protect the expectation interests of employers. Firms provide wages and salaries, employee benefits, and training; invest in intangible assets, capital equipment, facilities, and complementary resources; and engage in procurement, marketing, sales, production, and distribution. Employment contracts must provide incentives for firms to hire specialized personnel and invest in technological change.

Companies commonly have significant numbers of employment contracts with research personnel. The Business R&D and Innovation Survey (BRDIS) estimates that there are about 1.5 million R&D workers in the U.S.;[277] these employees include scientists, engineers, R&D managers, and support staff.[278] Brandon Shackelford and Francisco Moris state,

> Scientists and engineers are the researchers responsible for the design and creation of experiments, theories, and new products, processes, or methods. Technicians and other support staff typically work under the supervision of scientists and engineers and perform tasks such as computer programming, carrying out experiments, preparing statistical analysis, and clerical support and report writing.[279]

According to Donald Hecker,

> High-technology occupations are scientific, engineering, and technician occupations, the same group of occupations used to define high-tech industries in this and earlier studies. They include the following occupational groups and detailed occupations: computer and mathematical scientists, Standard Occupational Classification (soc) 15-0000; engineers, soc 17–2000; drafters, engineering, and mapping technicians, soc 17–3000; life scientists, soc 19–1000; physical scientists, soc 19–2000; life, physical, and social science technicians, soc 19–4000; computer and

information systems managers, soc 11–3020; engineering managers, soc 11–9040; and natural sciences managers, soc 11–9120.[280]

The use of ICs for in-house R&D and outsourcing is not a new phenomenon. David Mowery examines industrial research between 1900 and 1940 and observes the growth of R&D both within manufacturing companies and in a network of independent research organizations.[281] Mowery finds that "[r]ather than functioning as substitutes, the independent and in-house research laboratories were complements during this period, exhibiting a division of labor in the performance of research tasks."[282] Division of labor in the performance of research tasks among firms allows firms to specialize and gain greater expertise in particular areas of invention and innovation.[283]

Innovative firms must hire and motivate highly skilled managers and employees.[284] Companies engaged in technological change offer specialized employee contracts and human resources management (HRM) policies.[285] ICs for R&D managers and employees are likely to differ from other types of employment contracts. Pedro Ortín Ángel and Lluís Santamaria Sánchez argue that firms' HRM practices must adapt to the particular needs of their R&D departments.[286] They conduct case studies that examine various HRM practices in R&D, including the delegation of authority to specialized personnel, the provision of managerial support, the formation of multidisciplinary teams, internal and external networking opportunities, adjustment of recruitment policies, job rotation, career development, and compensation.[287] Kathryn Martell and Stephen Carroll suggest firms' incentives for R&D personnel follow "promotion and pay policies that are congruent with employee expectations and company goals."[288]

Firms apply ICs to address the assignment of IP generated through the employment relationship. This represents a historical shift toward greater use of contracts.[289] Catherine Fisk notes, "The law of employee inventions is an unstable mixture of the two bodies of law, the former honoring the rights of the *inventor* as employee, the latter being skeptical of the rights of the *employee* as inventor."[290] From 1830 to 1930, Fisk recounts the change in law from an IP regime, in which the employee owns inventions, to a combination of employment contracts that assign inventions to the employer and state laws that include "shop rights" for employers.[291]

Robert Merges examines the role of IP in employment contracts.[292] Merges observes that "[o]wnership is too blunt an instrument to be an effective inducement to employee-inventors."[293] Based on economic analysis, Merges argues that "the law properly allows employers to take ownership of their employees' inventions."[294] Employment contracts provide rewards for employees, specify employee duties, and allocate inventions:

> [E]mployers have broad powers — consistently upheld by the courts — to claim employee inventions by contract. In addition, these contracts usually impose several related duties on employees, including (1) a duty to assign patent applications and patents to the employer, (2) a duty to assist in the patent prosecution, and (3) a general duty to cooperate in the perfection of the employer's rights in the invention.[295]

Merges also considers three types of default rules under state law.[296] First, when employees engage in "invention for hire," the firm owns the invention.[297] Second, when non-R&D employees engage in firm-related invention, the employee may own the invention, while the firm obtains a royalty-free license as a "shop right."[298] Third, when employees engage in independent invention, they generally own the invention.[299] Regarding employee exit, Merges concludes, "both the default rules and the interpretation of post-employment contracts favor ex-employees."[300]

Employment contracts with specialized researchers are subject to asymmetric information. The firm may not be able to fully observe the employee's knowledge and skills. Also, it may be difficult for the firm to observe the experimental design and research activities of specialized employees. Then, ICs are subject to Principal–Agent problems in contract design.[301] Companies design ICs to provide performance incentives to specialized managers and employees engaged in invention and innovation.[302]

5.4.2. *Outsourcing Contracts*

Companies also use ICs to outsource invention and innovation to specialized research firms. Shackelford and Moris observe that the scientific R&D services industry is "dominated by contract research organizations that assist pharmaceutical, biotechnology, and medical device companies with clinical trials management."[303] They find that the R&D services industry "employs relatively more technicians and support staff as a share of its domestic R&D employment than do most other industries."[304] Firms contract with "star scientists" for access to knowledge and IP.[305] In-house R&D is complementary to outsourcing R&D because internal knowledge helps the firm absorb external knowledge.

ICs that outsource R&D to a specialized research firm may face problems of moral hazard and adverse selection.[306] The firm may compensate the specialized research firm based on some measure of invention or innovation, including revenues or profits.

Many companies outsource various invention and innovation activities.[307] Paul Trott and Dap Hartmann find that "R&D departments have long recognised the importance of information and knowledge beyond their own organizations."[308] Companies rely on many types of strategic alliances, including "licensing, supplier relations, outsourcing, joint venture, collaboration (non-joint ventures), R&D consortia, industry clusters, and innovation networks."[309] Henry Chesbrough and others describe a trend toward increasing R&D cooperation among firms as "open innovation."[310]

It is estimated that companies obtain about half of their innovations from outside sources.[311] Contracting to obtain R&D services from other firms is complementary to the firm's internal R&D.[312] For example, internal R&D increases a firm's absorptive capacity for external knowledge.[313]

About four-fifths of world trade moves through a global supply chain involving networks of suppliers, distributors, and intermediaries.[314] The organization of production through global supply chains often involves contracts for outsourcing invention and innovation to supply chain managers and specialized research companies.[315] For example, pharmaceutical companies outsource clinical trials to Contract Research Organizations (CROs).[316]

5.4.3. *Joint Venture and Consortium Contracts*

Firms use contracts to form RJVs and R&D consortia.[317] These are important types of IC. As with any joint venture, the RJV can take the form of a jointly owned corporation, partnership, or contract without equity.[318] RJVs and consortia allow companies to cooperate in R&D while continuing to compete in product markets.[319] Joint ventures are an alternative to expansion of the firm through growth or mergers and acquisitions (M&A).[320] Klaus Gugler and Ralph Siebert find that in the semi-conductor industry, RJVs tend to achieve greater efficiency gains than M&A.[321]

Firms form R&D joint ventures and consortia to share the costs and risks of R&D.[322] By combining projects, the R&D joint venture can realize economies of scale in R&D, including specialization of function and division of labor for researchers. The firms may benefit from combining complementary skills and knowledge in R&D. Firms may also cooperate in R&D because it may be difficult to exclude access to each other's R&D. By combining R&D projects, the firms will appropriate the benefits of the knowledge created, thus internalizing potential spillovers that would result from separate projects.[323] The RJV may also facilitate various business relationships, including agreements between suppliers and customers.[324]

The partners in an RJV may not be able to observe each other's R&D efforts or knowledge, which would lead to moral hazard and adverse selection problems. Addressing these problems requires dividing the benefits of the partnership based on some measure of performance. It may not be feasible to design an IC that induces sufficient R&D effort to maximize the joint benefits of the parties.[325] Licensing arrangements affect the incentives of partners to share IP with the RJV.[326]

The National Cooperative Research Act (NCRA) of 1984 and the National Cooperative Research and Production Act (NCRPA) in 1993 limit antitrust liability for members of R&D consortia.[327] These consortia report their membership to the Department of Justice (DOJ) and the Federal Trade Commission (FTC).[328] From 1984 to 2008, 942 joint ventures registered with the antitrust agencies.[329] The RJV may reduce competition between the partners but increase competition between the partners and other firms in the industry.[330]

Almost all joint ventures, even if they are not RJVs, involve parent companies licensing or transferring technology to the venture.[331] Kurt Saunders cautions that negotiation and planning of the RJV should address the disclosure, ownership, use, and management of IP contributed to or created by the venture.[332] The RJV agreement should also address the rights and duties of the partners and the joint venture regarding protection of IP, as well as infringement and misappropriation.[333] RJVs can provide contractual protections for intangible assets when there are insufficient patent protections.[334]

5.4.4. *License Contracts*

ICs include IP license contracts. These types of contracts have a number of common features.[335] The license contract describes the business relationship between the parties.[336] The license contract specifies the period of time for the grant of rights to the licensee and lists the IP that is covered by the agreement.[337] The contract may place various restrictions on the grant of rights.[338] The Code of Federal Regulations states, "the licensing of a patent transfers a bundle of rights which is less than the entire ownership interest, e.g., rights that may be limited as to time, geographical area, or field of use."[339] The licensing contract addresses IP issues that arise when either of the parties makes improvements to the technology.[340] The contract also specifies the IP holder's compensation, including the way that royalties are calculated.[341]

Most IP license contracts are specific to the business relationship between the licensor and the licensee.[342] This implies that most IP license contracts require bilateral negotiation that tailors the agreement to the needs of the relationship.[343] License contracts offered by patent pools are an exception because they have standardized provisions and royalties.[344]

An IP license contract is designed to maximize the joint returns of the licensor and licensee.[345] The most basic license gives the licensee access to the licensor's intangible assets.[346] These licenses can serve to avoid litigation or resolve a dispute over IP.[347] More complicated ICs involve additional business arrangements, including invention, innovation, investment, marketing, and complementary assets.[348]

License contracts may provide incentives for inventors to develop and transfer the invention and for adopters to apply the invention. The Principal–Agent problem involving hidden action or hidden information arises in licensing contracts.[349] Richard Jensen and Marie Thursby study university licensing agreements and find most include both fixed fees and royalties; many also include sponsored research clauses and equity.[350] The university licensing agreement with potential licensees involves a stage in which researchers continue to develop an invention.[351] This is a moral hazard problem because research efforts are not observable to the licensee. The licensing contract includes running royalties intended to induce inventor effort and lump-sum royalties that reflect potential earnings from commercialization of the invention.[352] Daniel Elfenbein considers university licensing agreements and observes the incidence of royalties based on sales, lump-sum license fees, milestones, maintenance fees and minimums, and equity.[353]

Inventors often have tacit knowledge that is complementary to their intangible assets. Inventors incur costs of codifying and communicating their knowledge to technology adopters.[354] When it is very costly to transmit the inventor's knowledge, the inventor may have an advantage in applying that knowledge in comparison to technology adopters. Technology adopters may have advantages in applying the technology resulting from their own knowledge and complementary assets. This can overcome the problem of transmitting the inventor's tacit knowledge, resulting in technology transfers.[355] Deepak Hegde explores how tacit knowledge affects the structure of royalties in licensing contracts, including royalty rates, lump-sum fees, milestones and minimum payments.[356]

5.4.5. *Platform Contracts*

Firms and cooperative organizations help establish and manage the market for innovative control.[357] Firms and cooperative organizations use platform contracts to reduce transaction costs for both technology providers and technology adopters. Intermediary firms offer transaction efficiencies by market making, matching buyers and sellers, and reducing adverse selection and moral hazard.

Almost all markets are established by profit-maximizing firms acting as intermediaries.[358] Firms provide intermediary services as market makers by purchasing and reselling goods and services.[359] Such firms include retailers, wholesalers, and financial brokers.[360] Market makers clear markets by balancing purchasing and sales and by posting and adjusting prices.[361] Firms also provide intermediary services by acting as match-makers, bringing buyers and sellers together.[362] Market makers and match-makers establish the rules of markets, referred to in finance as "market microstructure."[363] The Internet has given rise to platforms, which are digital market places. Intermediary firms that operate digital markets include Amazon, eBay, and Alibaba.

In the market for innovative control, just as in markets generally, there are intermediaries that improve the efficiency of transactions.[364] By handling a high volume of transactions, intermediaries benefit from economies of scale and scope.[365] These economies are due to benefits from sharing fixed costs across many units of output or across multiple products.[366] Economies of scale and scope also result from specialization of function and division of labor among the employees of intermediary firms. A centralized intermediary can realize economies of scale and scope in the management of IP, keeping track of patent renewal fees, monitoring infringement, and defending patents against infringement. The centralized intermediary can provide convenience by licensing patent portfolios as bundles.

Intermediary firms also improve transaction efficiencies by centralizing transactions.[367] Buyers and sellers derive convenience from "one-stop-shopping." A buyer can have access to the products of many sellers and a seller can reach many buyers, but any buyer or seller need only transact with the intermediary. In markets for innovative control, a licensee can obtain licenses for the technology of many licensors and a licensor can provide licenses to many sellers.

There are also transaction efficiencies from platforms that provide centralized contract negotiation.[368] This is because buyers and sellers need only negotiate with the intermediary. This dramatically decreases the number of transaction relationships in comparison to the large number of bilateral transactions needed with decentralized contracting. With centralized contracting, agreements and compensation can be standardized. This allows licensors and licensees to have standardized contracts with the intermediary. This is particularly important in industries that have complex innovations requiring a combination of many different IP licenses.

IP intermediaries use ICs to address non-rivalrous consumption. The same technology can be used simultaneously by many firms to produce new inventions and to develop innovative products, production processes, and transaction methods. IP intermediaries provide central hubs to realize the returns from contracts with many adopters.

IP intermediaries address transaction costs in patent transfers and patent licensing.[369] According to an FTC study of "Patent Assertion Entities," about half of the companies in the study used patent acquisition contracts that shared licensing revenue with the inventor or employer of the inventor.[370] The companies in the study acted as intermediaries between patent holders and licensees.[371]

Some companies acquire patents and provide a "one-stop-shopping" platform for licensees. Consider, for example, the patent intermediary Avanci:

> Avanci has created the first platform for IoT manufacturers to license crucial, standard-essential wireless technologies with an emphasis on fair, transparent pricing. Avanci's pricing model offers flat rate royalty calculations that streamline licensing and enable predictable costs to help IoT developers capitalize on a dynamic market opportunity.[372]

Avanci emphasizes the benefits of "one-stop-shopping" and the implications of connectivity:

> Products with wireless connectivity require access to thousands of patented inventions, created by many inventors. Avanci is bringing together standard-essential wireless patents that represent the most advanced wireless technology in the world, in an efficient, one-stop marketplace. So, instead of going to each technology owner to request, negotiate and pay for a license, makers of products for the Internet of Things can get the technology they need in one place.[373]

Avanci points out that transaction efficiencies increase incentives for innovation:

> By providing licenses to essential wireless technology at fair rates, Avanci is helping ensure companies who need connectivity for their

products can access it easily, and those creating wireless technology can share it as widely as possible. And both are incentivized to never stop innovating.[374]

IC intermediaries also include cooperative non-profit institutions such as patent pools and other Collective Rights Organizations (CROs).[375] By offering transaction efficiencies, such private contracting institutions help to avoid antitrust scrutiny and government-mandated licensing.[376] Robert Merges argues that "[t]he high costs of contracting — both among members, and between members and users — drive the right holders to pool their property rights in a collective organization."[377]

Patent pools act as intermediaries and provide transaction platforms for patent holders and licensees.[378] Patent pools reduce the transaction costs of combining licenses for complementary inventions.[379] For example, MPEG LA, LLC provided a "one-stop-shopping" platform for licensing patents covering the international digital video compression standard MPEG-2.[380] MPEG LA operated licensing programs covering "thousands of patents owned by hundreds of patent holders in nearly 100 countries with over 6,000 licensees."[381]

5.5 Conclusion

It has long been observed that "possession is nine-tenths of the law," although there is much more to law than property. Similarly, discussions of knowledge and technological change tend to focus on IP. Yet, there is much more to Intellectual Law than IP.

The Intellectual Law framework introduced in this chapter provides a comprehensive framework for dynamic efficiencies in technological change. The present discussion emphasizes that IC rules play an important role in Intellectual Law. ICs protect the expectation interests of those who invest in technological change. ICs allow variation in investment over time as parties make discoveries. IC law provides the basis for creating, developing, sharing, and applying intangible assets needed for technological change. IC rules enhance the economic contributions of both IP and IT rules.

IP provides the foundation of the market for innovative control, but IP is not sufficient for technological change. IP is incomplete and provides limited exclusivity. IP can be subject to public policy shocks that tend to weaken protections for inventors, innovators, and adopters. Also, the IT protections for inventors shift consent from IP owners to infringers. This suggests the need to reconsider the IP versus IT controversy in the context of contributions made by IC.

Technological change requires agreements that induce future performance. Cooperative investment generates invention, innovation, and technology adoption. Firms make these investments based on agreements with employees, suppliers, partners, investors, and customers. Technological change based on IC rules promotes economic development and drives economic growth.

ICs differ from standard contracts in various ways. ICs realize the benefits from non-rivalrous usage of technology through such mechanisms as licensing, cross-licensing, RJVs, R&D consortia, and one-stop-shopping platforms. ICs provide incentives for exploratory performance. ICs induce effort and revelation of information by rewarding performance using measures related to technological change. In contrast to contracts for the routine production of goods and services, ICs consider fundamental uncertainty. ICs must handle problems arising when contracting parties' efforts and information are unobservable and unverifiable. Such contracting difficulties are more likely to occur with invention and innovation than with more routine activities. ICs provide incentives for invention, innovation, and adoption. ICs achieve gains from trade in technology, thus increasing the rewards of IP holders beyond what they could achieve through IP alone.

The rate and direction of technological change have increased the shift toward IC. Greater connectivity and exchange of data among firms requires agreements for discovery and sharing knowledge. Increased emphasis of software over hardware means that inventions and innovations are virtual, further increasing the importance of intangible assets. The development of AI requires agreements between firms and employees and among firms to address new forms of knowledge creation. The technological development of the economy is transforming contracts and generating the need for a framework of "Intellectual Law."

Conclusion

Obtaining a patent is challenging. The process begins long before the patent application. Invention generally requires knowledge, talent, and creativity. Individuals often spend many years in extensive education and training, particularly in the fields of science, technology, engineering, and mathematics (STEM). Companies invest considerable resources in invention. R&D is risky and need not be successful.

Even if an inventor is successful, the patenting process can be costly and time consuming. There are no guaranties that the proposed invention will satisfy the requirements that it be useful, novel, non-obvious, and eligible subject matter. Legal costs easily run into thousands of dollars.[1] There are also fees for application and patent renewal.[2]

After inventors obtain patents, they must invest further in developing the invention. Then, to realize any benefits from the patent, inventors must invest in commercializing the invention through own-use and licensing, or transfer the patent to others. Developing and commercializing the patented invention entail additional technical and market risks. Patented technologies compete with other inventions and may become obsolete. Innovators may not adopt the patented technologies. After they are granted, patents are subject to legal challenges of validity and post-grant review. Patent holders seeking returns to their efforts face a barrage of criticism from companies, academics, and public policy markets.

And yet, inventors continue to seek patents. Patent holders license patents and transfer patents in the market for inventions. Innovative companies introduce new products, production processes, and transaction methods based on patented inventions. Entrepreneurs establish new firms that embody patented technologies. Standards organizations modify or replace technology standards to keep pace with these changes. Patent holders declare their technologies as essential to technology standards. Consumers adopt new products that use patented technologies.

If anything, technological change seems to accelerate. The only explanation is that inventors obtain benefits sufficient to cover the costs of invention. The economy as a whole benefits from these new technologies. It is as if inventors were guided by an invisible hand to benefit others in the society, as Adam Smith argued for business in general.

Why does the patent system work? The patent framework is deceptively simple. Expert patent examiners screen applications to satisfy general criteria. Patents are only granted for a limited term and require inventors to disclose information. Patents only offer "the right to exclude others from making, using, offering for sale, or selling the invention throughout the United States or importing the invention into the United States."

The answer is that the patent system helps protect ideas that translate into patented inventions. Protection of ideas gives inventors incentives to engage in R&D. Patent protections also help inventors to develop those ideas further after the patent is grated. The patent system provides protections for innovations that apply patented inventions.

But, patents do much more than offering basic protections for IP. Patents contribute to the foundation of the market for inventions. Patents improve transaction efficiency through information and standardization. These transaction efficiencies allow markets to form and operate that could not otherwise do so. Patent holders and technology implementers can negotiate mutually beneficial contracts that transfer technology. Recognizing this, the USPTO launched an IP Marketplace Platform called "Patents 4 Partnerships" "that brings together those who have technologies and want to make them available for licensing and those who have an interest in and the ability to commercialize the technologies."[3]

The market for inventions is a "market for innovative control." Commercializing patents not only yields a stream of revenues but also allows the inventor to exercise control over how the patent is used.

The market value of patents includes both residual returns and residual rights of control over innovation.

Patents foster the development of a market by allowing a separation of the idea from the inventor. What typically begins as the inventor's tacit knowledge becomes an asset that can be licensed and transferred to others. This allows specialization and division of labor in invention, innovation, and technology adoption. Inventors can more readily commercialize their ideas. Companies can manage and apply their IP and markets can effectively allocate that IP.

Some critics of the patent system suggest replacing the market for inventions with government contests. They argue that patents give inventors monopolies and that patent royalties are monopoly prices. These accusations have little economic foundation. Patents give inventors innovative control over their inventions, but do not confer economic monopolies. Patents do not restrict entry or competition in product markets. Companies may offer any product using any technology that does not infringe on the new technology offered by the patent holder.

Patents also do not restrict entry or competition in the market for inventions. The contribution of inventors is incremental, simply adding to what already exists. The entry of new inventions can only increase competition in the market for inventions. Patented inventions must still compete with existing technologies and future technologies. Ideas are limited only by creativity, imagination, and the expanding frontiers of knowledge.

Advocates of government contests suggest that wining inventors be given prizes in return for their technologies. The government would then provide those technologies freely to companies. Prizes would be paid for by general taxation. A few government prizes cannot compete with the market for inventions. Government bureaucrats cannot possibly choose winning technologies. They cannot substitute for the knowledge of millions of individuals and companies, as Hayek understood.

Technological change heightens the problems of centralized decision-making. Invention, innovation, and technology adoption involve exploring unknown territory. Technological change is a significant challenge that usually requires going beyond existing knowledge and understanding. Government selection and allocation of technology cannot substitute for dispersed learning and interaction. A few contests cannot pose the questions let alone determine the answers.

The market for inventions provides the flexibility needed for technological change. The same patent system that saw the Industrial Revolution addressed the opening of the Space Age, the computer revolution, the Internet, and mobile communications. Patents are able to handle autonomous vehicles, the Internet of Things, cloud computing, artificial intelligence, and biotechnology.

The patent system itself must remain flexible to continue promoting innovation. Patents are necessarily on the technology frontier because inventions must be novel and non-obvious. Technological change requires that there not be excessive or arbitrary limits on patent eligible subject matter. As the *Mayo* decision points out, all inventions involve "laws of nature, natural phenomena, or abstract ideas." Advances in computer software and business methods are critical for e-commerce, the IoT, payment systems, and AI. These developments are related to the Business Revolution that I described in Chapter 3. The patent system should also be flexible toward advances in medicine and biotechnology, recognizing the need for diagnostic techniques, vaccines, pharmaceuticals, gene editing, and medical equipment.

Patents provide a legal framework for the enforcement of IP rights. Reasonable royalty damages serve to compensate patent holders for infringement. It is important that damages for infringement reflect the economic harm from infringement. There has been considerable debate about what should be the proper approach to determining reasonable royalty damages. In Chapter 4, I proposed that reasonable royalty damages should be based on a contract approach. Applying this approach, the court constructs an "informed contract" based on evidence in the patent case. The contract approach avoids the inherent difficulties courts face in constructing a hypothetical negotiation. The contract approach helps resolve some of the conflicts between property and tort approaches to reasonable royalty damages. Applying the contract approach to reasonable royalty damages would help compensate patent holders for patent infringement.

In Chapter 4, I introduced a "market value method" for calculating reasonable royalty damages. The market value of a patent is the current price of the patent in the market. The market value of a patent reflects the present discounted value of the flow of earnings that could be obtained from the patent including own-use and royalties. When the market value of a patent is known, it can be used to infer these earnings. The market value of a patent or group of patents can thus be used to determine reasonable royalty damages in patent disputes. The market value of a patent can be observed from transfers, including negotiated transfer prices, auctions for patents, internal transfers within corporations, and asset transfers involved in M&A. When the market value of a patent cannot be observed directly, it may be possible to estimate market value using prices of comparable patents and other market data.

The demand for patent protection is a derived demand that originates with the final consumer. Consumers benefit from new products, production processes, transaction methods, and new business strategies. Adoption by individuals and companies creates demand for innovation. Innovative companies and entrepreneurs in turn generate demand for inventions. Inventors can respond to this demand effectively only if they have patents and other IP rights.

Patents are helpful at each step of the way, supporting invention, innovation, and adoption. Intangible assets, including patents, now constitute most of the market value of corporations. This suggests the need for the law to address the importance of intangible assets. I refer to this legal framework as Intellectual Law. Intellectual Property and what I refer to as Intellectual Tort receive much of the attention. I introduced the concept of Intellectual Contract to describe agreements that help commercialize patents and other IP. As intangible assets become even more prominent, business agreements will further employ Intellectual Contracts.

Technological change is essential for economic growth and development. Maintaining and strengthening IP rights enhances economic growth and development. Patents help motivate companies and entrepreneurs to invest in intangible assets and to bring innovations to market. Patents stimulate employment and the rise of new industries. Patents support innovations in products, production, and transactions that improve the well-being of consumers. The widespread and significant benefits of technological change make a strong case for patents.

Endnotes

FM

1. https://www.uspto.gov/patents-application-process/patenttrialand appealboard.
2. *eBay Inc. et al. v. MercExchange, L. L. C.*, 547 U.S. 388 (2006).

Chapter 1

1. Press Release, The United States Patent and Trademark Office, first U.S. patent issued today in 1790 (July 31, 2001), http://www.uspto.gov/news/pr/2001/01-33.jsp.
2. *Ibid.*
3. https://www.uspto.gov/about-us/news-updates/united-states-issues-patent-number-10000000.
4. https://www.uspto.gov/about-us/news-updates/united-states-issues-patent-number-10000000.
5. *See* https://www.uspto.gov/about-us/news-updates/united-states-issues-patent-number-10000000. *See* also https://10millionpatents.uspto.gov/docs/patent10million.pdf.
6. U.S. Const. art. 1, § 8, cl. 8.
7. D. F. Spulber, Market Microstructure: Intermediaries and the theory of the firm (Cambridge: Cambridge University Press 1999); D. F. Spulber, The Theory of the firm: Microeconomics with endogenous entrepreneurs, firms, markets, and organizations (Cambridge: Cambridge University Press, 2009); D. F. Spulber, The Innovative Entrepreneur (Cambridge: Cambridge University Press, 2014).

8. I discuss the market for inventions and examine some of the implications of transaction costs and other market frictions for invention and innovation in Spulber, The Innovative Entrepreneur, *supra* note 7.
9. J. Bessen and M. J. Meurer, Patent failure: How judges, bureaucrats, and lawyers put innovators at risk (New Jersey: Princeton University Press, 2008).
10. D. L. Burk and M. A. Lemley, The patent crisis and how the courts can solve it (Chicago: University of Chicago Press, 2009).
11. M. Boldrin and D. K. Levine, The case against patents, *J. Econ. Persp.* 27, 3, 18 (2013).
12. Editorial Board, Abusive and frivolous patent suits, *N.Y. Times* (April 6, 2014), http://www.nytimes.com/2014/04/07/opinion/abusive-and-frivolous-patent-suits.html?_r=0.
13. Fed. Trade Comm'n, The evolving marketplace: Aligning patent notice and remedies with Competition (March, 2011), available at http://www.ftc.gov/sites/default/files/documents/reports/evolving-ip-marketplace-aligning-patent-notice-and-remedies-competition-report-federal-trade/110307 patentreport.pdf.
14. *See, e.g.*, *Mayo Collaborative Services v. Prometheus Laboratories, Inc.*, 566 U.S. 10 (2012); *Ass'n for Molecular P. v. Myriad, S. Ct.* 133, 2107 (2013); *In re Bilski*, F.3d 545, 943 (Fed. Cir. 2008). Judge Moore lamented this state of events. *CLS Bank Int'l v. Alice Corp. Pty. Ltd.*, 717 F.3d 1269, 1313 (Fed. Cir. 2013) ("Dissenting-in-part opinion filed by MOORE, Circuit Judge, in which RADER, Chief Judge, and LINN and O'MALLEY, Circuit Judges, join. I am concerned that the current interpretation of § 101, and in particular the abstract idea exception, is causing a free fall in the patent system. The Supreme Court has taken a number of our recent decisions and, in each instance, concluded that the claims at issue were not patent-eligible. *See Bilski, Prometheus, Myriad* (under consideration). Today, several of my colleagues would take that precedent significantly further, lumping together the asserted method, media, and system claims, and holding that they are all patent-ineligible under § 101.").
15. *See* K. E. Noonan, *Thoughts on the USPTO's Patent Eligibility Guidelines (and What to Do About Them)*, Patent Docs: Biotech & Pharma Patent Law & News Blog (March 18, 2014), http://www.patentdocs.org/2014/03/thoughts-on-the-usptos-patent-eligibility-guidelines-and-what-to-do-about-them.html (discussing concerns about executive branch opposition to patents); Lisa L. Mueller, *The Thorny Problem of Patentable Eligible*

Subject Matter: An Introduction, Nat'l L. Rev. (April 15, 2014), http://www.natlawreview.com/article/thorny-problem-patentable-eligible-subject-matter-introduction.

16. K. High, *Patent Reform Movement Shines a Light on Economic Development Opportunities*, Huffington Post (March 28, 2014), http://www.huffingtonpost.com/kristal-high/patent-reform-movement-sh_b_5048578.html.
17. A. Kamdar, *The Patent Reform We Need to See from the Senate*, Electronic Frontier Foundation (March 31, 2014), https://www.eff.org/deeplinks/2014/03/patent-reform-we-need-see-senate.
18. I develop a formal model of the market for inventions with endogenous R&D and entry of inventors and producers. D. F. Spulber, Competing inventors and the incentive to invent, *Indus. & Corp. Change* 22, 33 (2013); D. F. Spulber, How do competitive pressures affect incentives to innovate when there is a market for inventions? *J. Pol. Econ.* 121, 1007 (2013); *see also* A. Arora, A. Fosfuri and A. Gambardella, Markets for technology and their implications for corporate strategy, *Indus. & Corp. Change* 10, 419 (2001) (discussing empirical studies of the market for inventions); A. Arora, A. Fosfuri and A. Gambardella, Markets for technology: The economics of innovation and corporate strategy (Cambridge: MIT Press, 2001) (discussing empirical studies of the market for inventions).
19. A. A. Alchian, *Property Rights*, *in* Concise Encyclopedia of Economics (D. Henderson ed., 2008), available at http://www.econlib.org/library/Enc/PropertyRights.html (pointing out that the three aspects of property rights are exclusion of access, control over how the asset will be used, and transfer of the asset to others).
20. The concept of the market for innovative control is analogous to the market for corporate control. On the market for corporate control, *see* H. G. Manne, Mergers and the market for corporate control, *J. Pol. Econ.* 73, 110 (1965) ("A fundamental premise underlying the market for corporate control is the existence of a high positive correlation between corporate managerial efficiency and the market price of shares of that company." p. 112); *see also* M. C. Jensen and R. S. Ruback, The market for corporate control: The scientific evidence, *J. Fin. Econ.* 11, 5 (1983) at 5 ("We define corporate control as the rights to determine the management of corporate resources") and D. F. Spulber, Discovering the role of the firm: The separation criterion and corporate law, *Berkeley Bus. L. J.* 6, 298 (2009).
21. *See* S. C. Myers, Financial architecture, *Eur. Fin. Mgmt.* 5, 133 (1999) (discussing financial separation and entrepreneurship); S. C. Myers, Outside

equity, *J. Fin. Econ.* 55, 1005 (2000) (discussing financial separation and entrepreneurship); D. F. Spulber, The Theory of the Firm, *supra* note 7 (discussing financial separation in the theory of the firm); D. F. Spulber, *Discovering the Role of the Firm: The Separation Criterion and Corporate Law*, supra note 20 (discussing financial separation in the theory of the firm); and Spulber, The Innovative Entrepreneur, *supra* note 7 (discussing financial separation in the theory of the innovative entrepreneur).

22. *See* S. J. H. Graham, R. P. Merges, P. Samuelson, and T. Sichelman, High technology entrepreneurs and the patent system: Results of the 2008 Berkeley patent survey, *Berkeley Tech. L. J.* 24, 1255 (2009).
23. This follows Stewart Myers's distinction between "assets in place" and "growth opportunities." S. C. Myers, Determinants of corporate borrowing, *J. Fin. Econ.* 5, 147 (1977).
24. *See* B. N. Roin, Intellectual property versus prizes: Reframing the debate, *U. Chi. L. Rev.* 81, 999 (2014) (providing an overview and discussion of the literature based on the "rewards" view of patents); *see, e.g.*, J. E. Stiglitz, Economic foundations of intellectual property rights, *Duke L. J.* 57, 1693 (2008); C. Shapiro, Patent reform: Aligning reward and contribution, *Innovation Pol. & Econ.* 8, 111 (A. B. Jaffe, J. Lerner and S. Stern eds., 2008).
25. *See* F. Hayek, The use of knowledge in society, *Am. Econ. Rev.* 35, 519 (1945); F. Hayek, The pretence of knowledge, *Swedish J. Econ.* 77, 433 (1975).
26. Spulber, *Competing Inventors and the Incentive to Invent*, *supra* note 18; Spulber, *How Do Competitive Pressures Affect Incentives to Innovate when There Is a Market for Inventions? supra* note 18.
27. G. S. Rich, Laying the ghost of the "Invention" requirement, *AIPLA Q.J.* 1, 26, 26 (1972) (emphasis in original).
28. H. Demsetz, Information and efficiency: Another viewpoint, *J. L. & Econ.* 12, 1, 14 (1969). For a more skeptical view of the market for ideas, *see* J. S. Gans & S. Stern, Is there a market for ideas? *Indus. & Corp. Change* 19, 805 (2010).
29. Patents add enforcement flexibility because infringement suits are an alternative to breach of contract. R. P. Merges, A transactional view of property rights, *Berkeley Technology L. J.* 20, 1477 (2005).
30. E. W. Kitch, The nature and function of the patent system, *J. L. & Econ.* 20, 265 (1977). Kitch also states "the view of the patent system offered here conceives of the process of technological innovation as one in which resources are brought to bear upon an array of prospects, each with its own

associated sets of probabilities of costs and returns. By a prospect I mean a particular opportunity to develop a known technological possibility." *Ibid.*, p. 266; *see also* Y. Barzel, Optimal timing of innovations, *Rev. Econ. Stat.* 50, 348 (1968).

31. *But see* R. P. Merges & R. R. Nelson, On the complex economics of patent scope, *Colum. L. Rev*. 90, 839 (1990). I respond to their arguments later in the present chapter.
32. F. S. Kieff, Property rights and property rules for commercializing inventions, *Minn. L. Rev*. 85, 697 (2001).
33. *Ibid.*, p. 703.
34. Kieff, Property rights and property rules for commercializing inventions, supra note 32; *see* H. E. Smith, Intellectual property as property: Delineating entitlements in information, *Yale L.J.* 116, 1742 (2007); D. F. Spulber, Should business methods be patentable? *J. Legal Analysis* 3, 265 (2011); J. E. Daily & F. S. Kieff, Anything under the sun made by humans: Patent law doctrines as eendogenous institutions for commercializing innovation, *Emory L.J.* 62, 967 (2013).
35. Kieff, Property rights and property rules for commercializing iinventions, supra note 32, p. 710.
36. R. A. Epstein, The disintegration of intellectual property — A classical liberal response to a premature obituary, *Stan. L. Rev*. 62, 455, 458 (2010).
37. *Ibid.*, p. 459.
38. H. E. Smith, Institutions and indirectness in intellectual property, *U. Pa. L. Rev*. 157. 2083, 2095 (2009).
39. H. E. Smith, Exclusion versus governance: Two strategies for delineating property rights, *J. Legal Stud*. 31, S453 (2002).
40. *Patents*, United States Patent & Trademark Office, http://www.uspto.gov/patents.
41. *Ibid.* The USPTO also grants design patents "to anyone who invents a new, original, and ornamental design for an article of manufacture" and grants plant patents "to anyone who invents or discovers and asexually reproduces any distinct and new variety of plant." *Ibid.*
42. *Nonprovisional (Utility) Patent Application Filing Guide*, United States Patent & Trademark Office, http://www.uspto.gov/patents/resources/types/utility.jsp#heading-1.
43. R. D. Katznelson, A century of patent litigation in perspective (November 17, 2014). Available at SSRN:http://ssrn.com/abstract=2503140 or http://dx.doi.org/10.2139/ssrn.2503140.

44. This does not include the years since the America Invents Act, which increased the number of suits by separating defendants. There was a brief spike approaching 1.5 percent during the 1960s. *Id.*
45. *See*, e.g., J. Bessen & M. J. Meurer, The direct costs from NPE disputes, *CORNELL L. Rev*. 99, 387 (2014). Commenting on that study, D. L. Schwartz and J. P. Kesan, Analyzing the role of non-practicing entities in the patent system, *CORNELL L. Rev*. 99, 649 (2014), point out that about 75% of alleged litigation costs are actually transfers (licensing, settlement, and judgment).
46. *See,* e.g., Bessen & Meurer, Patent Failure, *supra* note 9; Burk & Lemley, Patent Crisis and How the courts can solve it, *supra* note 10.
47. K. A. Hassett and R. J. Shapiro, What ideas are worth: The value of intellectual capital and intangible assets in the American economy, (2014), Sonecon, Washington, D.C., http://www.sonecon.com/docs/studies/Value_of_Intellectual_Capital_in_American_Economy.pdf, Accessed January 2015.
48. G. de Rassenfosse, A. Palangkarya, and E. Webster, How do patents facilitate trade in technology? Testing the appropriation and disclosure effects (Melbourne Inst. *Appl. Econ. & Soc. Res.*, Working Paper, 2014).
49. L. Branstetter, R. Fisman, and C. F. Foley, Do stronger intellectual property rights increase international technology transfer? Evidence from U.S. firm-level panel data, *Q.J. Econ.* 121, 321 (2006).
50. P. J. Heald, A transaction costs theory of patent Law, supra note 104.
51. *See* B. Z. Khan and K. L. Sokoloff, History lessons: The early development of intellectual property institutions in the United States, *J. Econ. Persp.* 15, 233 (2001); N. R. Lamoreaux and K. L. Sokoloff, Intermediaries in the U.S. market for technology, 1870–1920, in Finance, intermediaries, and economic development 209 (S. L. Engerman, P. T. Hoffman, J.-L. Rosenthal and K. L. Sokoloff eds., 2003).
52. B. Z. Khan, The democratization of invention: Patents and copyrights in american economic development, 314, 1790–1920 (Cambridge University Press 2005).
53. *Ibid.,* p. 221.
54. B. Z. Khan, Selling ideas: An international perspective on patenting and markets for technological innovations, *Bus. Hist. Rev.* 87, 39, 1790–1930 (2013).
55. *Ibid.*
56. A. Barinka, IBM wins most U.S. patents for 21st year in a row, Bloomberg (January 14, 2014), http://www.bloomberg.com/news/2014-01-14/ibm-wins-most-u-s-patents-for-21st-year-in-a-row.html.

57. The World Intellectual Property Organization observes a significant increasing in patent applications by universities and public research organizations. World Intellectual Property Organization, World Intellectual Property Report: The Changing Face of Innovation (WIPO 2011).
58. USPTO Patent Technology Monitoring Team (PTMT), U.S. patent statistics chart calendar years 1963–2019, https://www.uspto.gov/web/offices/ac/ido/oeip/taf/us_stat.htm.
59. Boldrin and Levine, The case against patents, *supra* note 11.
60. J. R. Commons, Institutional economics, *Am. Econ. Rev*. 21, 648, 648 (1931).
61. Kieff, Property rights and property rules for commercializing inventions, *supra* note 32.
62. D. F. Spulber, Tacit knowledge with innovative entrepreneurship, *Int'l J. Indus. Org*. 30, 641 (2012).
63. *See* 18; A. Arora, A. Fosfuri, and A. Gambardella, Markets for technology, *supra* note 18; A. Gambardella, P. Giuri, and A. Luzzi, The market for patents in europe, *Res. Poli.* 36, 1163 (2007) (conducting empirical studies of the market for inventions); J. S. Gans, D. H. Hsu, and S. Stern, The impact of uncertain intellectual property rights on the market for ideas: Evidence from patent grant delays, *Mgmt. Sci.* 54, 982 (2008) (conducting empirical studies of the market for inventions); A. Arora and A. Gambardella, Ideas for rent: An overview of markets for technology, *Indus. & Corp. Change* 19, 775 (2010) (conducting empirical studies of the market for inventions); C. J. Serrano, The dynamics of transfer and renewal of patents, *RAND J. Econ.* 41, 686 (2010) (conducting empirical studies of the market for inventions); A. Galasso, M. Schankerman, and C. J. Serrano, Trading and enforcing patent rights, *RAND J. Econ.* 44, 275 (2013) (conducting empirical studies of the market for inventions); S. Kamiyama, J. Sheehan, and C. Martinez, Valuation and exploitation of intellectual property, *OECD Sci. Tech. & Indus.*, Working Paper No. 2006/05, 2006) (discussing empirical studies of the market for inventions); S. Athreye and J. Cantwell, Creating competition? Globalisation and the emergence of new technology Producers, *Res. Pol'y* 36, 209 (2007) (discussing empirical studies of the market for inventions); I. Troy and R. Werle, Uncertainty and the market for reform, *Max Planck Inst. Stud. Soc'y*, Working Paper No. 08/2, 2008) (discussing empirical studies of the market for inventions); J. S. Gans and S. Stern, Is there a market for ideas, *supra* note 28 (discussing empirical studies of the market for inventions).

64. D. F. Spulber, Market microstructure, *supra* note 7; D. F. Spulber, The theory of the firm, *supra* note 7; D. F. Spulber, The innovative entrepreneur, *supra* note 7.
65. D. F. Spulber, Market microstructure, *supra* note 7.
66. *Ibid.*, D. F. Spulber, The innovative entrepreneur, *supra* note 7.
67. Patent ownership also is comparable to incorporation of companies, which provides information about the name, purpose, and location of the company.
68. D. W. Elfenbein, Publications, patents and the market for university inventions, *J. Econ. Behav. & Org.* 63, 688, 691 (2007).
69. F. S. Kieff, Property rights and property rules for commercializing inventions, *supra* note 32; F. S. Kieff, The case for registering patents and the law and economics of present patent-obtaining rules, *B.C. L. Rev.* 45, 55 (2003).
70. F. S. Kieff, The case for registering patents and the law and economics of present patent-obtaining rules, *supra* note 69.
71. F. S. Kieff, Property rights and property rules for commercializing inventions, *supra* note 32.
72. D. Hegde and H. Luo, Imperfect information, patent publication, and the market for ideas, (*Harv. Bus. Sch.*, Working Paper No. 14-019, 2013).
73. *See* G. Biglaiser, Middlemen as experts, *RAND J. Econ.* 24, 212 (1993); G. Biglaiser and J. W. Friedman, Middlemen as guarantors of quality, *Int'l J. Indus. Org.* 12, 509 (1994); G. Biglaiser and J. W. Friedman, Adverse selection with competitive inspection, *J. Econ. & Mgmt. Strategy* 8, 1 (1999); D. F. Spulber, Market microstructure and intermediation, *J. Econ. Persp.* 10, 135 (1996); D. F. Spulber, Market microstructure, *supra* note 7.
74. *See* M. A. Lemley, Rational ignorance at the patent office, *Nw. U. L. Rev.* 95, 1495 (2001); J. R. Thomas, The responsibility of the rulemaker: Comparative approaches to patent administration reform, *Berkeley Tech. L.J.* 17, 727 (2002); A. B. Jaffe and J. Lerner, Innovation and its discontents: How our broken patent system is endangering innovation and progress, and What to Do About It (New Jersey: Princeton University Press 2004); M. A. Lemley and K. A. Moore, Ending abuse of patent continuations, *B.U. L. Rev.* 84, 63 (2004).
75. R. D. Katznelson, Bad science in search of "Bad" patents, *Fed. Cir. B.J.* 17, 1 (2008). R. D. Katznelson critiques statistical methods used in two studies: C. Martinez and D. Guellec, Overview of recent changes and comparison of patent regimes in the United States, Japan and Europe, in patents, innovations and economic performance: OECD conference proceedings (*Org.*

Econ. Co-operation & Dev. 127, 2004) and P. H. Jensen, A. Palangkaraya and E. Webster, Disharmony in international patent office decisions, *Fed. Cir. B.J.* 15, 679 (2005).

76. C. Martinez and D. Guellec, Overview of recent changes and comparison of patent regimes in the United States, Japan and Europe, *in* patents, innovations and economic performance: OECD conference proceedings (*Org. Econ. Co-operation & Dev.* 127, 2004); P. H. Jensen, A. Palangkaraya and E. Webster, Disharmony in international patent office decisions, *Fed. Cir. B. J.* 15, 679 (2005).
77. Katznelson, Bad science in search of "bad" patents, *supra* note 75, p. 29.
78. R. P. Merges, As many as six impossible patents before breakfast: Property rights for business concepts and patent system reform, *Berkeley Tech. L. J.* 14, 577 (1999) (combining a discussion of the USPTO patent examination process with a presumption that software and business method inventions will lead to bad patents, although these are entirely different questions).
79. Spulber, Should business method inventions be patentable? *supra* note 34.
80. J. R. Allison and E. H. Tiller, The business method patent myth, *Berkeley Tech. L. J.* 18, 987 (2003).
81. Kieff, Property rights and property rules for commercializing inventions, *supra* note 32 (suggesting that a rush to file under the first-to-file rule can lead to inadequate disclosure, resulting in patents being more likely to be found invalid and reducing incentives for commercialization).
82. *See* Manual of Patent Examining Procedure (MPEP), United States Patent & Trademark Office, http://www.uspto.gov/web/offices/pac/mpep/index.html.
83. *United States Code Title 35 — Patents*, United States Patent & Trademark Office, http://www.uspto.gov/web/offices/pac/mpep/consolidated_laws.pdf.
84. *301 — Ownership/Assignability of Patents and Applications*, United States Patent & Trademark Office, http://www.uspto.gov/web/offices/pac/mpep/s301.html.
85. *Ibid.*
86. *Ibid.*
87. C. McCaffrey, The virtues of virtual marking in patent reform, *Nw. U. L. Rev.* 105, 367 (2011).
88. G. T. Willingmyre, Patent challenges for standard-setting in the global economy: Lessons from information and communications technology, *Nat'l Acad. Sci.* 1, 10 (2012), http://sites.nationalacademies.org/PGA/step/IPManagement/.

89. *Ibid.*, p. 16.
90. The patent owner does not grant rights of control because the patent owner is subject to whatever legal and regulatory restrictions might apply. The patent owner thus exercises residual rights of control in commercializing and developing the patented invention.
91. Kitch, The nature and function of the patent system, *supra* note 30.
92. Spulber, Competing inventors and the incentive to invent, *supra* note 18; Spulber, How Do Competitive pressures affect to innovate when there is a market for inventions? *supra* note 18.
93. Although the emphasis here is on development of the invention, the framework is sufficiently general to include randomness in the legal and regulatory process. This could include randomness in the legal patent validity as discussed in M. A. Lemley and C. Shapiro, Probabilistic patents, *J. Econ. Persp.* 19, 75 (2005).
94. M. Ceccagnoli, A. Gambardella, P. Giuri, G. Licht, and M. Mariani, Sant'Anna School. Advanced Studies, Study on evaluating the knowledge economy — What are patents actually worth? The value of patents for today's economy and society: Final report for Lot 1 (2005), http://ec.europa.eu/internal_market/indprop/docs/patent/studies/patentstudy-report_en.pdf; A. Gambardella, P. Giuri, and M. Mariani, Sant'Anna School Advanced Studies, Study on evaluating the knowledge economy — What are patents actually worth? The value of patents for today's economy and society: Final report for Lot 2 (2006), http://ec.europa.eu/internal_market/indprop/docs/patent/studies/final_report_lot2_en.pdf; P. Giuri, M. Mariani, S. Brusano, G. Crespi, D. Francoz, A. Gambardella, W. Garcia-Fontes, A. Geuna, R. Gonzales, D. Harhoff, K. Hoisl, C. L. Bas, A. Luzzi, L. Magazzini, L. Nesta, Ö. Nomaler, N. Palomeras, P. Patel, M. Romanelli, and B. Verspagen, Inventors and invention processes in Europe: Results from the PatVal-EU survey, *Res. Pol'y* 36, 1107 (2007).
95. B. N. Anand and T. Khanna, The structure of licensing contracts, *J. Indus. Econ.* 48, 103 (2000).
96. A. Arora, M. Ceccagnoli, and W. M. Cohen, Ideas for rent: An overview of the market for technology, in financing innovation in the United States, 1870 to the Present 365–403 (N. R. Lamoreaux and K. L. Sokoloff eds., Cambridge: MIT Press 2007).
97. This is according to the World Intellectual Property Organization. World Intellectual Property Organization, World Intellectual Property Report, *supra* note 57, p. 9.

98. C. A. Cotropia, J. P. Kesan, and D. L. Schwartz, Unpacking Patent Assertion Entities (PAEs), *MINN L. REV.* 99, 649 (2014).
99. *See* T. Yanagisawa and D. Guellec, The emerging patent marketplace (OECD Sci., Working Paper No. 2009/09, 2009), available at http://dx.doi.org/10.1787/218413152254; A. Hagiu and D. B. Yoffie, The new patent intermediaries: Platforms, defensive aggregators, and super-aggregators, *J. Econ. Persp.* 27, 45 (2013).
100. *See* J. F. McDonough, The myth of the patent troll: An alternative view of the function of patent dealers in an idea economy, *Emory L.J.* 56, 189 (2006).
101. *See* D. F. Spulber, Market microstructure: Intermediaries and the theory of the firm, *supra* note 7.
102. *On market intermediaries, see* D. F. Spulber, Market microstructure: Intermediaries and the theory of the firm, id. *See also* S. K. Shrestha, Trolls or market-makers? An empirical analysis of nonpracticing entities, *COLUM. L. Rev.* 110, 114, (2010) p. 160 "NPEs can serve a valuable role in enhancing innovation by identifying and acquiring high value patents and thereby funding and encouraging some of the most successful inventors."
103. *See* A. Hagiu and D. B. Yoffie, The new patent intermediaries: Platforms, defensive aggregators, and super-aggregators, *J. Econ. Perspect.* 27, 45 (2013).
104. *See* A. Arora, Contracting for tacit knowledge, *J. Dev. Econ.* 50, 233 (1996); A. Arora and R. P. Merges, Specialized supply firms, property rights and firm boundaries, *Indus. & Corp. Change* 13, 451 (2004); and P. J. Heald, A transaction costs theory of patent law, *OHIO STATE L.J.* 66, 473 (2005).
105. Serrano, The dynamics of the transfer and renewal of patents, *supra* note 63.
106. C. Arthur, "Nortel patents Sold for $4.5 bn," *The guardian*, July 1, 2011, http://www.theguardian.com/technology/2011/jul/01/nortel-patents-sold-apple-sony-microsoft.
107. D. F. Spulber, *Innovation and international trade in technology*, *J. Econ. Theory* 138, 1 (2008); D. F. Spulber, The quality of innovation and the extent of the market, *J. Int'l. Econ.* 80, 260 (2010).
108. J. Bena and K. Li, Corporate innovations and mergers and acquisitions, *J. FINANCE* 69, 1923 (2014).
109. *See* D. J. Teece, Profiting from technological innovation: Implications for integration, collaboration, licensing, and public policy, *Res. Pol'y* 15, 285 (1986) (discussing the importance of complementary assets in innovation);

D. J. Teece, Reflections on "Profiting from Innovation," *Res. Pol'y* 35, 1131 (2006) (considering the extensive follow-on literature on complementary assets).

110. U.S. Patent No. 8,615,473 (filed August 24, 2012).
111. M. R. Dickey, Mind-Blowing facts about Amazon's giant shipping operations, *Bus. Insider*, *Nov.* 26, 2012, http://www.businessinsider.com/amazon-fulfillment-center-tour-2012-11?op=1.
112. Myers, Financial architecture, *supra* note 21, p. 134.
113. *Ibid.*, *see also* S. C. Myers, Outside equity, *J. Fin.* 55, 1005 (2000).
114. Graham, Merges, Samuelson, and Sichelman, High technology entrepreneurs and the patent system, *supra* note 22.
115. P. Arqué-Castells, How venture capitalists spur invention in Spain: Evidence from patent trajectories, *Res. Pol'y* 41, 897 (2012).
116. *Ibid.*
117. I. Fisher, The nature of capital and income (Macmillan, 1906); I. Fisher, Rate of interest: Its nature, determination and relation to economic phenomena (Macmillan, 1907); I. Fisher, The theory of interest: As determined by impatience to spend income and opportunity to invest it, (Macmillan, 1930).
118. *See* Spulber, The Innovation entrepreneur, *supra* note 7.
119. N. Myhrvold, Funding eureka! *Harv. Bus. Rev.* 1, 3 (March 2010).
120. The market value of the asset can be represented by a random variable V that is distributed according to a probability distribution $F(V)$. The random variable V can be viewed as an *investment project*. The probability distribution of the value of the asset $F(V)$ can be generalized in various ways. The outcome of the investment project can depend on the level of investment and random shocks.
121. Myers, Determinants of corporate borrowing, *supra* note 23.
122. *See* The economic valuation of patents: Methods and applications (F. Munari and R. Oriani eds., Edward Elgar Publishing 2011) (discussing the financial valuation of patents); W. J. Murphy, J. L. Orcutt, and P. C. Remus, Patent valuation: Improving decision making through analysis (Wiley, 2012) (discussing the financial valuation of patents); B. H. Hall, The stock market's valuation of R&D investment during the 1980's, *Am. Econ. Rev.* 83, 259 (1993) (discussing the stock market value of R&D investment); B. H. Hall, G. Thoma, and S. Torrisi, The market value of patents and R&D: Evidence from European firms, *Acad. Mgmt. Ann. Meeting Proc.* 8, 1 (2007) (discussing the stock market value of R&D investment).
123. Barinka, IBM wins most U.S. patents for 21st year in a row, *supra* note 56.

124. C. A. Robbins, Measuring payments for the supply and use of intellectual property, *in International Trade in Services and Intangibles of the Era of Globalization* 139–171 (M. Reinsdorf and M. J. Slaughter eds., Chicago: University of Chicago Press 2009).
125. D. S. Abrams, U. Akcigit, and J. Popadak, Patent value and citations: Creative destruction or strategic disruption? (University of Pennsylvania, NBER Working Paper No. 19647, 2013).
126. Myers, Determinants of corporate borrowing, *supra* note 23.
127. *Ibid.*
128. *Ibid.*
129. M. C. Jensen and W. H. Meckling, Theory of the firm: Managerial behavior, agency costs and ownership structure, *J. Fin. Econ.* 3, 305 (1976).
130. J. Poblete and D. F. Spulber, The form of incentive contracts: Agency with moral hazard, risk neutrality, and limited liability, *RAND J. Econ.* 43, 215 (2012).
131. J. Poblete and D. F. Spulber, Managing innovation: Optimal incentive contracts for delegated R&D with double moral hazard, Euro. Ec. Rev. 95, 38 (June 2017).
132. C. Corrado, C. Hulten, and D. Sichel, Intangible capital and U.S. economic growth, *Rev. Income & Wealth* 55, 661 (2009).
133. The exception is regulated utilities. *See* K. A. Hassett and R. J. Shapiro, What ideas are worth: The value of intellectual capital and intangible assets in the american economy, *supra* note 47.
134. *See* The laws that govern the securities industry, U.S. securities and exchange commission, http://www.sec.gov/about/laws.shtml.
135. *Patents*, United States Patent & Trademark office, http://www.uspto.gov/patents.
136. *See* Roin, Intellectual property versus prizes, *supra* note 24 (overviewing and discussing the literature that discusses "prizes" for inventors).
137. Spulber, Should business method inventions be patentable? *supra* note 34.
138. Kitch, The nature and function of the patent system, *supra* note 30.
139. Merges and Nelson, On the complex economics of patent scope, *supra* note 31.
140. *Ibid.*, p. 870; *see also* R. P. Merges and R. R. Nelson, On limiting or encouraging rivalry in technical progress: The effect of patent scope decisions, *J. Econ. Behav. & Org.* 25, 1, 22 (1994) ("Inventors are coming up with inventions that the broad prospect holder is challenging in court. The danger is that competitors will be harassed out of the field. There is every reason to

believe that this would diminish not only the energy devoted to developing the prospect but also cut down on the diversity and creativity of the development.").

141. *See* Merges and Nelson, On the complex economics of patent scope, *supra* note 31.
142. A. Mossoff, The rise and fall of the first american patent thicket: The sewing machine war of the 1850s, *Ariz. L. Rev.* 53, 165, 205 (2011).
143. G. Selgin and J. L. Turner, Strong steam, weak patents, or the Myth of watt's innovation-blocking monopoly, exploded, *J.L. & Econ.* 54, 841, 841 (2011).
144. R. D. Katznelson and J. Howells, Inventing-around edison's incandescent lamp patent: Evidence of patents' role in stimulating downstream development and competition 1 (Working Paper, 2012), available at http://j.mp/Inventing-around-Edison.
145. R. D. Katznelson and J. Howells, The Myth of the early aviation patent hold-up — How a U.S. government monopsony commandeered pioneer airplane patents, *Indus. & Corp. Change* 24,1 (2015) (manuscript at 3), available at http://icc.oxfordjournals.org/content/early/2014/03/03/icc.dtu003.full.pdf.
146. J. Howells and R. D. Katznelson, The coordination of independently-owned vacuum tube patents in the early radio alleged patent "Thicket" (Working Paper, 2014), available at http://papers.ssrn.com/sol3/papers.cfm?abstract_id=2450025.
147. M. A. Lemley, The Myth of the sole inventor, *Mich. L. Rev.* 110, 709 (2012).
148. Lemley, The Myth of the sole inventor, *supra* note 147.
149. Lemley argues that inventors may be racing for patents even if racing is not observed: ("[E]ven among the majority of cases in which we have no evidence of an explicit race, that doesn't mean that there was no race.") *Ibid.*, p. 751. The notion that the function of the patent system is racing is a variant of the "rewards" view of patents, as inventors race to obtain the patent. Although racing may occur, the market foundation role presented here emphasizes the competition in the market for inventions, which occurs after patents are granted.
150. J. Howells and R. D. Katznelson, A critique of Mark Lemley's "The Myth of the Sole Inventor" (Working Paper, 2011), available at http://papers.ssrn.com/sol3/papers.cfm?abstract_id=2123208.
151. Howells and Katznelson, A critique of Mark Lemley's "The Myth of the sole inventor," *supra* note 150.

152. *Ibid.* (manuscript p. 14) (emphasis in original).
153. Lemley, The Myth of the sole inventor, *supra* note 147, p. 711.
154. Shapiro, Patent reform, *supra* note 24, p. 117; *see also* Lemley, The Myth of the sole inventor, *supra* note 147.
155. Shapiro, Patent Reform, *supra* note 24, p. 117.
156. *See*, e.g., *ibid.* Shapiro recommends applying the "independent inventor defense" in infringement cases, which would eliminate or substantially weaken the exclusion function of patents. *Ibid.*, p. 131.
157. *See*, e.g., J. Farrell, J. Hayes, C. Shapiro, and T. Sullivan, Standard setting, patents, and hold-up, *Antitrust L.J.* 74, 603 (2007).
158. D. F. Spulber, Innovation economics: Technology standards, competitive conduct and economic performance, *J. Competition L. & Econ.* 9, 777 (2013).
159. Stiglitz, Economic foundations of intellectual property rights, *supra* note 24, p. 1700 (emphasis in original).
160. *Ibid.*, p. 1706.
161. Troy and Werle, Uncertainty and the market for reform, *supra* note 63 (manuscript p. 20).
162. Spulber, Market microstructure, *supra* note 7.
163. K. J. Arrow, Economic welfare and the allocation of resources for invention, in *The Rate and Direction of Inventive Activity* p. 609, 615 (New Jersey: Princeton University Press, 1962); *see also* W. D. Nordhaus, Invention Growth, and Welfare: A Theoretical Treatment of Technological Change (Cambridge: MIT Press 1969); W. D. Nordhaus, The optimum life of a patent: Reply, *Am. Econ. Rev.* 62, 428 (1972); F. M. Scherer, Nordhaus' theory of optimal patent life: A geometric reinterpretation, *Am. Econ. Rev.* 62, 422 (1972); R. Gilbert and C. Shapiro, Optimal patent length and breadth, *RAND J. Econ.* 21, 106 (1990).
164. Boldrin and Levine, The case against patents, *supra* note 11, p. 7.
165. J. S. Mill, Principles of political economy, with some of their applications to social philosophy (W. J. Ashley ed., Longmans, Green & Co. 7th ed. 1909) (1848); G. S. Rich, The relation between patent practices and the anti-monopoly laws, *J. Pat. Off. Soc'y* 24, 241 (1942); G. S. Rich, Are patent rights grants of monopoly?, *W. New Eng. L. Rev.* 5, 239 (1993); Kitch, The nature and function of the patent system, *supra* note 30; E. W. Kitch, Elementary and persistent errors in the economic analysis of intellectual property, *Vand. L. Rev.* 53, 1727 (2000); Spulber, Innovation economics, *supra* note 158. J. S. Mill observes that "the condemnation of monopolies ought not to extend to patents." F. Machlup and E. Penrose, The patent

controversy in the nineteenth century, *J. Econ. Hist.* 10, 1, 7 (1950) citing John Stuart Mill, *Principles of Political Economy, with Some of Their Applications to Social Philosophy,* p. 932 (W. J. Ashley ed., Longmans, Green & Co. 7th ed. 1909) (1848).

166. Stiglitz, Economic foundations of intellectual property rights, *supra* note 24, p. 1706.
167. Shapiro, Patent reform, *supra* note 24, p. 112.
168. Nordhaus, Invention growth, and welfare, *supra* note 163; Nordhaus, *The Optimum Life of a Patent*, *supra* note 163.
169. Spulber, Competing inventors and the incentive to invent, *supra* note 18; Spulber, How Do Competitive pressures affect incentives to innovate when there is a market for inventions? *supra* note 18.
170. Heald points out that even with vertical integration, IP protections from patents lower costs in comparison to maintaining trade secrets, see Heald *supra* note 104.
171. E. Chamberlin, *The Theory of Monopolistic Competition* (Cambridge: Harvard University Press, 1933).
172. Consider Chamberlinian competition among inventors who enter the market to supply different inventions. Suppose that an inventor incurs fixed costs k to produce a new invention, to obtain a patent, and to commercialize the invention. Suppose that an inventor incurs a distribution cost c to license the invention to each licensee, which can be positive or equal to zero. Inventors offer an up-front fixed-fee royalty of R to each licensee. Let $D(R)$ be the total number of adopters per invention at a symmetric equilibrium when all inventors offer the same royalty. Let $D'(R)$ be the slope of each inventor's demand when all inventors offer the same royalty. Given the royalties charged by other inventors, each inventor chooses a royalty that maximizes profit taking as given by the royalties set by other inventors. For each inventor, the marginal revenue from licensing equals the cost of licensing to an adopter, c, $D(R; n) + RD'(R) = c$. Inventors conduct R&D and continue to enter the market until each inventor earns a zero profit. The royalty per license equals the average cost of invention and licensing, $R = k/D(R) + c$. Together, these conditions determine the royalty charged by each inventor and the number of inventors that enter the market for inventions.
173. A. Layne-Farrar, J. Padilla, and R. Schmalensee consider competition from substitute inventions within categories of complementary technologies. A. Layne-Farrar, J. A. Padilla and R. Schmalensee, Pricing patents for licensing in standard-setting organizations: Making sense of FRAND commitments, *Antitrust L. J.*, 74, 671 (2007).

Chapter 2

1. America Creating Opportunities to Meaningfully Promote Excellence in Technology, Education, and Science (American COMPETES Reauthorization) Act, Pub. L. No. 111–358, 104 Stat. 3958 (2011). The Act was signed into law by President Obama on January 4, 2011.
2. *Ibid.,* p. 3989.
3. *Ibid.,* p. 3991.
4. *Ibid.*, p. 3990–91 ("The Federal Government may not gain an interest in IP developed by a participant in a competition without the written consent of the participant.").
5. Practically any federal agency in the executive branch can offer prizes including, for example, the Department of Energy, the Department of Education, the National Aeronautics and Space Administration, and the National Oceanic and Atmospheric Administration.
6. Section 105 of America COMPETES Reauthorization Act ("Support for a prize competition under this section, including financial support for the design and administration of a prize or funds for a monetary prize purse, may consist of Federal appropriated funds and funds provided by the private sector for such cash prizes.").
7. *The Competitiveness and Innovative Capacity of the United States*, prepared by the U.S. Department of Commerce in consultation with the National Economic Council, January 2012, Washington, D.C., available at http://www.commerce.gov/sites/default/files/documents/2012/january/competes_010511_0.pdf, accessed February 21, 2015.
8. *Ibid.*, pp. 3–7 ("The Office of Innovation and Entrepreneurship at the Department of Commerce, in conjunction with its National Advisory Council on Innovation and Entrepreneurship (NACIE) is working to improve commercialization through its i6 Challenge Grants, a competition that funds the best ideas for technology commercialization.").
9. *Ibid.*, pp. 3–7 ("Additional initiatives in this area include a joint effort by the Administration, the Association of American Universities, and the Association of Public and Land-grant Universities to encourage university leaders to work more closely with industry, investors, and agencies to increase entrepreneurship, encourage more collaboration between universities and industry, and increase economic development.").
10. *Ibid.,* pp. 5–14.
11. *See* K. L. Judd, The Welfare Cost of Factor Taxation in a Perfect-Foresight Model, *J. Pol. Econ.* 95, 675 (1987) (discussing estimates of deadweight

welfare losses from taxes). *See also* M. Feldstein, Tax Avoidance and the Deadweight Loss of the Income Tax, *Rev. Econ. & Stats*. 81, 674 (1999).

12. *See* H. Demsetz, Information and Efficiency: Another Viewpoint, *J.L. & Econ.* 12, 1 (1969); F. S. Kieff, Property Rights and Property Rules for Commercializing Inventions, *Minn. L. Rev*. 85, 697 (2001); B. Z. Khan, *The Democratization of Invention: Patents and Copyrights in American Economic Development, 1790–1920*, Cambridge, MA: NBER, 2005; R. A. Epstein, The Disintegration of Intellectual Property — A Classical Liberal Response to a Premature Obituary, *Stan. L. Rev*. 62, 455 (2010); and D. F. Spulber, 2015, How Patents Provide the Foundation of the Market for Inventions, *J. Competition L. & Econ*. 11, 2 (2015).
13. D. F. Spulber, Competing Inventors and the Incentive to Invent, *Indus. & Corp. Change* 22, 33 (2013) and D. F. Spulber, How Do Competitive Pressures Affect Incentives to Innovate when there is a Market for Inventions?, *J. Pol. Econ*. 121, 1007 (2013).
14. F. A. Hayek, translation by M. S. Snow, Competition as a Discovery Procedure, *Q. J. Austrian Econ.* 5(3), 9 (2002) (presenting a translation from German of F. A. Hayek's "Der Wenbewerb als Entdeckungsverfahren," a 1968 lecture sponsored by the Institut für Weltwirtschaft at the University of Kiel).
15. E. W. Kitch, The Nature and Function of the Patent System, *J.L. & Econ.* 20, 265–267 (1977).
16. *See* Spulber, *supra* note 13.
17. F. Machlup and E. Penrose, The Patent Controversy in the Nineteenth Century, *J. Econ. Hist*. 10, 1 (1950) (examining the debates in the nineteenth century and showing that the idea of government prizes is not new).
18. *See* G. Becker, *On Reforming the Patent System-Becker*, The Becker–Posner Blog: A Blog by Gary Becker and Richard Posner, July 2013, http://www.becker-posner-blog.com/2013/07/ ("Narrowing the type of innovations that can be patented is a more challenging task than reducing patent length. The first step is to recognize that many innovations presently cannot be patented. A major example is the inability to patent scientific theories and concepts, such as Einstein's theory of relativity, Darwin's theory of evolution, or Keynes' model of the macro economy. The presumption in excluding basic scientific knowledge from the patent system is that the cost of restricting open access to such discoveries far exceeds any gains in encouraging the development of scientific concepts through granting temporary monopolies to the creators.").

19. M. Wei, Should Prizes Replace Patents? A Critique of the Medical Innovation Prize Act of 2005, *B.U. J. Sci. & Tech. L.* 13, 25–45 (2007) (suggesting that a "prize system could be used to supplement and close the gaps of both the patent regime and current NIH funding").
20. P. Moser and T. Nicholas, Prizes, Publicity, and Patents: Non-Monetary Awards as a Mechanism to Encourage Innovation, *J. Indus. Econ.* 61, 763 (2013).
21. F. S. Murray, S. Stern, G. Campbell, and A. MacCormack, "Grand Innovation Prizes: A Theoretical, Normative, and Empirical Evaluation," *Research Policy* 41(10), 1779–1792t (1791).
22. L. Brunt, J. Lerner, and T. Nicholas, Inducement Prizes and Innovation, *J. Indus. Econ.* 45, 657 (2012).
23. E. G. Weyl and J. Tirole, Market Power Screens Willingness-to-Pay, *Q. J. Econ.* 127, 1971 (2013).
24. B. N. Roin, Intellectual Property versus Prizes: Reframing the Debate, *U. Chi. L. Rev.* 81, 999, 1078 (2014). *See also Ibid.*, p. 1003 (adding that "Among scholars and policymakers, there is a broad consensus that without government intervention, private industry would significantly underinvest in the R & D of new ideas and expressions").
25. *Ibid.*, p. 1017.
26. A. Kapczynski, The Cost of Price: Why and How to Get Beyond Intellectual Property Internalism, *UCLA L. Rev.* 59, 970–1027 (2012) (arguing for prizes based on the view that the government should redistribute resources including information, stating that "IP rations access via the price mechanism, and so it distributes resources in a way that is sensitive to the background allocation of resources. Yet the background allocation of resources may be unjust", p. 996). *See also* M. Abramowicz, Perfecting Patent Prizes, *Vanderbilt L. Rev.* 56, 115, 126 (2003) ("With a carefully designed prize system, even if an individual decisionmaker makes an error or is influenced by political considerations in calculating a prize, these flaws will not affect the decisions that matter, those made in anticipation of the eventual governmental awards."); A. Kapczynski and T. Syed, The Continuum of Excludability and the Limits of Patents, *Yale L.J.* 122, 1900, 1907 (2013) (also advocating prizes due to deadweight welfare loss but suggesting that "prizes can help promote important but highly nonexcludable innovations that would be neglected by the patent system"); D. G. Lichtman, Pricing Prozac: Why the Government Should Subsidize the Purchase of Patented Pharmaceuticals, *Harvard J.L. & Tech.* 11, 123 (1997); S. P. Calandrillo, An

Economic Analysis of Intellectual Property Rights: Justifications and Problems of Exclusive Rights, Incentives to Generate Information, and the Alternative of a Government-Run Reward System, *Fordham Intell. Prop. Media and & Ent. L.J.* 9, 301 (1998); J. Barry, When Second Comes First: Correcting Patent's Poor Secondary Incentives Through an Optional Patent Purchase System, *Wisconsin L. Rev*. 2007, 585 (2007); and S. Levmore, The Impending iPrize Revolution in Intellectual Property Law, *B.U. L. Rev*. 93, 139 (2013).

27. On replacing patents with government prizes, *see* B. D. Wright, The Economics of Invention Incentives: Patents, Prizes, and Research Contracts, *Am. Econ. Rev.* 73, 691 (1983); M. Kremer, Patent Buyouts: A Mechanism for Encouraging Innovation, *Q. J. Econ.* 113, 1137 (1998); S. Shavell and T. Van Ypersele, Rewards versus Intellectual Property Rights, *J.L. & Econ.* 44, 525 (2001); S. Scotchmer, *Ideas and Incentives*, Cambridge, MA, MIT Press, 2004; N. Gallini and S. Scotchmer, Intellectual Property: When Is It the Best Incentive System?, in *Innovation Policy and the Economy*,Vol. 51, A. B. Jaffe, J. Lerner, and S. Stern (eds.), Cambridge, MA: MIT Press, 2002, available at http://www.nber.org/chapters/c10785; H. Hopenhayn, G. Llobet, and M. Mitchell, Rewarding Sequential Innovators: Prizes, Patents, and Buyouts, *J. Pol. Econ.* 114, 1041 (2006); and V. V. Chari, M. Golosov, and A. Tsyvinski, Prizes and Patents: Using Market Signals to Provide Incentives for Innovations, *J. Econ. Theory* 147, 781 (2012). For some economists, the patent system is a "major wound" that should be abolished, *see* M. Boldrin and D. K. Levine, The Case against Patents, *J. Econ. Perspectives* 27(1), 3, 18 (2013); and M. Boldrin and D. K. Levine, *Against Intellectual Monopoly*, Cambridge: Cambridge University Press, 2013 would leave in place some government subsidies.
28. M. Polanvyi, Patent Reform, *Rev. Econ. Studies* 11, 61, 65 (emphasis removed).
29. http://www.nobelprize.org/nobel_prizes/economic-sciences/laureates/ (indicating that the full name of the prize is the Sveriges Riksbank Prize in Economic Sciences in Memory of Alfred Nobel), accessed June 10, 2014.
30. *See* K. J. Arrow, Economic Welfare and the Allocation of Resources for Invention, in *The Rate and Direction of Inventive Activity*, Vol. 615, National Bureau of Economic Research, 1962 (suggesting that the Soviet Union offers an example of such a system of prizes).
31. J. E. Stiglitz, A Better Way to Crack It, *New Scientist*, September 2006, p. 20.
32. J. E. Stiglitz, Economic Foundations of Intellectual Property Rights, *Duke L.J.* 57, 1724 (2008). *See also* J. E. Stiglitz, Intellectual Property Rights,

the Pool of Knowledge, and Innovation, NBER, Working Paper No. 20014, March 2014, available at http://www.nber.org/papers/w20014.pdf?new_window=1.

33. B. N. Roin, Intellectual Property versus Prizes: Reframing the Debate, *U. Chi. L. Rev.* 81, 999, 1017–1018 (2014) (observing in his overview of the literature that "the primary benefit of a prize system has typically been viewed as its ability to avoid the deadweight loss associated with patents").
34. Eric de Laat correctly highlights this tradeoff by considering both the social costs of taxation and the possibility that market price distortions can be less than monopoly levels. De Laat views the choice of prizes and patent duration as problems of mechanism design under asymmetric information. *See* E. A. A. de Laat, Patents or Prizes: Monopolistic R&D and Asymmetric Information, *Int'l J. Indus. Org.* 15, 369 (1996). However, such a complex policy would be very costly for government agencies because it would require incentive mechanisms to vary with different demand and cost conditions. Patents have the advantage of being standardized without the complexities of mechanism design by government agencies.
35. Chari *et al.*, *supra* note 27, p. 787.
36. *Ibid.*
37. *Ibid. See also* Shavell and van Ypersele, *supra* note 27 (conceding that governments may lack the necessary information but argue that government prizes will dominate market prices if there is not too much uncertainty).
38. Shavell and van Ypersele, *supra* note 27.
39. *Ibid.*, p. 544.
40. Kremer, *supra* note 27, p. 1137.
41. *Ibid.*
42. *See*, e.g., *Ibid.*, p. 1140 ("To see that financing research with monopoly profits not only is not first best, but is generically less efficient than financing research through tax revenue, consider the problem of a social planner choosing a tax to finance research. The principles of Ramsey taxation should clearly guide the planner's decision, and it is highly unlikely that the optimal tax will be a several thousand percent tax on the patented good. Yet financing research by giving monopoly rights to inventors is equivalent to such a tax.").
43. *See*, e.g., Calandrillo, *supra* note 26, p. 337 ("Work incentives will be subject to some distortional effect if overall tax rates rise, but that is probably far less of a problem than the distorted purchasing decisions made today when the prices of informational works grossly exceed marginal cost.");

N, Gallini and S. Scotchmer, Intellectual Property: When is it the Best Incentive System?, *Innovation Pol'y & Econ.* 2, 51, 54 (2002) ("Monopoly pricing is equivalent to taxing a single market, which is generally thought to impose greater deadweight loss than the broad-based taxation that generates general revenue.").

44. M. Abramowicz, Perfecting Patent Prizes, *Vand. L. Rev.* 56, 1, 62 (2003) ("In the absence of a consensus that in our actual tax system increases in taxes will decrease tax distortions, it thus would be hazardous to disregard the concern about the potentially distortionary effect of increased income taxes.... One possible response to the distortionary effect might be to tax specifically those who benefit from a patent prize system in a particular context.").
45. D. J. Hemel and L. L. Ouellette, Beyond the Patents–Prizes Debate, *Tex. L. Rev.* 92, 303, 315 (2013).
46. C. E. Bohanon, J. B. Horowitz, and J. E. McClure, Saying Too Little, Too Late: Public Finance Textbooks and the Excess Burdens of Taxation, *Econ J. Watch* 11, 277, 278 (2014).
47. *Ibid.*, p. 279.
48. *Ibid.*, p. 278.
49. J. Slemrod and J. Bakija, *Taxing Ourselves: A Citizen's Guide to the Debate Over Taxes*, 4th edn., Cambridge, Mass.: MIT Press, 2008 (cited in Bohanon *et al.*, *supra* note 46).
50. Feldstein, *supra* note 11, p. 679.
51. *Ibid.*
52. J. Love and T. Hubbard, The Big Idea: Prizes to Stimulate R&D for New Medicines, *Chi.-Kent L. Rev.* 82, 1519 (2007).
53. *See* Abramowicz, *supra* note 26, and Wei, *supra* note 19.
54. This figure is for 2011. *See* National Science Board Science and Engineering Indicators, National Science Foundation, 2014, p. 4.4, available at http://www.nsf.gov/statistics/seind14/content/etc/nsb1401.pdf.
55. *Ibid.*
56. W. W. Fisher and T. Syed, Global Justice in Health Care: Developing Drugs for the Developing World, *U.C. Davis L. Rev.* 40, 581, 611 (2007) ("Because the money for such expenditures is most often (in developed countries) raised through progressive taxation systems, the net effect of adoption of our proposals would be the allocation of burdens roughly in proportion to household income." This statement mischaracterizes progressive taxation, which of course is designed to increase with household income rather than being

in proportion to household income. Therefore, the allocation of burdens would increase disproportionally with increases in household income.).

57. Arrow, *supra* note 30 (noting that in Arrow's model, the welfare distortion from per-unit royalties on an invention is limited by competition from a less-efficient initial technology).
58. *See* W. D. Nordhaus, *Invention, Growth, and Welfare: A Theoretical Treatment of Technological Change*, Cambridge, MA: MIT Press, 1969; W. D. Nordhaus, The Optimum Life of a Patent: Reply, *Am. Econ. Rev*. 62, 428 (1972); and F. M. Scherer, Nordhaus' Theory of Optimal Patent Life: A Geometric Reinterpretation, *Am. Econ. Rev* 62, 422 (1972).
59. New types of products, referred to as product innovations, may be comparable across technology generations. Quality improvements can include durability, energy efficiency, battery life, screen resolution, microprocessor speed, or digital memory storage capacity. New production technologies, referred to as process innovations, also compete across technology generations. Process innovations lower the costs of production, improve the quality of goods that are produced, or allow the production of new types of products. Process innovations can include new types of assembly lines, use of new materials, new applications of robotics, computer-aided design and manufacturing (CAD/CAM) techniques, and other improvements in manufacturing methods. Transaction innovations also compete across generations and include business method inventions such as e-commerce software and techniques for mobile Internet transactions, *see* D. F. Spulber, Should Business Method Inventions Be Patentable?, *J. Legal Analysis* 3, 265 (2011).
60. Spulber, *supra* note 12.
61. *See* A. Arora, A. Fosfuri, and A. Gambardella, Markets for Technology and their Implications for Corporate Strategy, *Indus. & Corp. Change* 10, 419 (2001); A. Arora and A. Gambardella, Ideas for Rent: an Overview of Markets for Technology, *Indus. & Corp. Change* 19, 775 (2010); M. Benassi and A. Di Minin, Playing in Between: Patent Brokers in Markets for Technology, *R&D Mgmt.* 39, 68 (2009); A. Hagiu and D. B. Yoffie, The New Patent Intermediaries: Platforms, Defensive Aggregators and Super Aggregators, *J. Econ. Perspectives* 27, 45 (2013); and C. Odasso, G. Scellato, and E. Ughettoy, Selling Patents at Auction: an Empirical Analysis of Patent Value, *Indus. & Corp. Change* 24, 417 (2014).
62. Calandrillo, *supra* note 26, p. 337 and Abramowicz, *supra* note 26 recognize the administrative costs of public prize systems.

63. This is an expenditure request for fiscal year 2016, *see* http://www.uspto.gov/about-us/performance-and-planning/budget-and-financial-information.
64. *See* http://www.uspto.gov/web/patents/classification/cpc.html (demonstrating the extensive Cooperative Patent Classification (CPC) developed by the USPTO and the European Patent Office (EPO)).
65. Private groups such as the X Prize Foundation also offer prizes for inventors, *see* http://www.xprize.org/. These prizes generate tournaments in which inventors compete to offer the best invention that satisfies the rules of the competition.
66. http://www.xprize.org/about/what-is-an-xprize.
67. *Ibid.*
68. F. A. Hayek, The Pretense of Knowledge, *Swedish J. Econ.* 77, 433, 520 (1975).
69. Demsetz, *supra* note 12; H. E. Smith, Exclusion versus Governance: Two Strategies for Delineating Property Rights, *J. Legal Stud.* 31, S453 (2002); H. E. Smith, Intellectual Property as Property: Delineating Entitlements in Information, *Yale L.J.* 116, 1742 (2007); H. E. Smith, H. E., Institutions and Indirectness in Intellectual Property, *U. Pa. L. Rev.* 157, 2083 (2009); R. P. Merges, A Transactional View of Property Rights, *Berkeley Tech. L.J.* 20, 1477 (2005); Kieff, *supra* note 12; and Spulber, *supra* note 12.
70. Spulber, *supra* note 12.
71. *See* D. F. Spulber, Market Microstructure and Intermediation, *J. Econ. Perspectives* 10, 135–152 (1996); and D. F. Spulber, *Market Microstructure: Intermediaries and the Theory of the Firm*, Cambridge: Cambridge University Press, 1999.
72. *See* R. Zeckhauser, The Challenge of Contracting for Technological Information, *Proc. Natl. Acad. Sci.* 93, 12743 (1996); and D. F. Spulber, *The Innovative Entrepreneur*, Cambridge: Cambridge University Press, 2014.
73. *See* D. F. Spulber, Tacit Knowledge with Innovative Entrepreneurship, *Int'l J. Indus. Org.* 20, 641 (2012). *See also* A. Arora, Contracting for Tacit Knowledge: The Provision of Technical Services In Technology Licensing Contracts, *J. Dev. Econ.* 50, 233 (1996).
74. D. F. Spulber, Innovation Economics: The Interplay among Technology Standards, Competitive Conduct, and Economic Performance, *J. Competition L. & Econ.* 9, 777 (2013).
75. L. G. Telser, Why Should Manufacturers Want Fair Trade?, *J. L. & Econ.* 3, 86 (1960).

76. *Leegin Creative Leather Prods., Inc. v. PSKS, Inc.*, 551 U.S. 877 (2007). This decision reversed *per se* illegality in *Dr. Miles Med. Co. v. John D. Park & Sons Co.*, 220 U.S. 373 (1911).
77. Kieff, *supra* note 12.
78. *See* A. C. Harberger, The Measurement of Waste, *Am. Econ. Rev.* 84, 58 (1964) and A. C. Harberger, Three Basic Postulates For Applied Welfare Economics: An Interpretive Essay, *J. Econ. Literature* 9, 785 (1971). On the extensive literature on measurement of deadweight welfare loss, including deadweight welfare loss from government taxation, *see* W. E. Diewert, The Measurement of Deadweight Loss Revisited, *Econometrica* 49, 1225 (1981).
79. F. Hayek, The Use of Knowledge in Society, *Am. Econ. Rev.* 35, 519, 526 (1945) (observing that "Fundamentally, in a system where the knowledge of the relevant facts is dispersed among many people, prices can act to coordinate the separate actions of different people in the same way as subjective values help the individual to coordinate the parts of his plan").
80. Technology transfers under the Stevenson–Wydler Technology Innovation Act, Pub. L. No. 96–480, 94 Stat. 2311 (1980) are carried out by the Office of Research and Technology Applications (ORTA). The Stevenson–Wydler Act was amended by the United States Federal Technology Transfer Act, Pub. L. No. 99–502, 100 Stat. 1785 (1986) and the America COMPETES Reauthorization Act Pub. L. No. 111–358, 104 Stat. 3958 (2011).
81. M. Kremer and H. Williams, Incentivizing Innovation: Adding to the Toolkit, *Innovation Pol'y. & Econ.* 1, 11 (2010) ("Mandatory mechanisms for encouraging innovation cannot be costlessly turned on and off because of the dynamic element inherent in any market in which firms make long-term R&D investments").
82. University and Small Business Patent Procedures Act, 35 U.S.C. §§ 200–212 (1980).
83. The Bayh–Dole Act: A Guide to the Law and Implementing Regulations, Council On Governmental Relations, 1–2 (1999), available at http://www.cogr.edu/docs/Bayh_Dole.pdf; cited by J. F. McDonough, The Myth of the Patent Troll: An Alternative View of the Function of Patent Dealers in an Idea Economy, *Emory L.J.* 56, 189, 199 (2006).
84. B. Bayh, J. P. Allen, and H. W. Bremer, Universities, Inventors, and the Bayh–Dole Act, *Life Sci. L. & Indus. Rep.* 3, 1, 3 (2009).
85. *See* T. T. Aldridge and D. Audretsch, The Bayh-Dole Act and Scientist Entrepreneurship, *Res. Pol'y* 40, 1058 (2011), and the references therein.

See also D. S. Siegel, R. Veugelers, and M. Wright, Technology Transfer Offices and Commercialization of University Intellectual Property: Performance and Policy Implications, *Oxford Rev. Econ. Pol'y* 23, 640–660 (2007) and R. Grimaldi, M. Kenney, D. S. Siegel, and M. Wright, Special Issue: 30 Years After Bayh-Dole: Reassessing Academic Entrepreneurship, *Res. Pol'y* 40, 1045 (2011).

86. AUTM, U.S. Licensing Activity Survey, FY2012, Association of University Technology Managers, available at http://www.autm.net/AM/Template.cfm?Section=FY2012_Licensing_Activity_Survey&Template=/CM/ContentDisplay.cfm&ContentID=11435.
87. National Science Foundation, supra note 54.
88. B. D. Wright, K. Drivas, Z. Lei, and S. A. Merrill, Technology Transfer: Industry-funded Academic Inventions Boost Innovation, *Nature*, 507, 297–298 (2014).
89. *Ibid.*
90. According to the US Government Accountability Office, the HEALTH CARE.GOV website was established at an initial cost of $840 million and was subject to significant cost overruns and performance failures. *See* Statement of W. T. Woods, Healthcare.gov Contract Planning and Oversight Practices were Ineffective Given the Challenges and Risks, US Government Accountability Office, July 21, 2014, available at http://docs.house.gov/meetings/IF/IF02/20140731/102587/HHRG-113-IF02-Wstate-WoodsW-20140731.pdf. *See also* Healthcare.Gov: Ineffective Planning and Oversight Practices Underscore the Need for Improved Contract Management, GAO-14-694, July 30, 2014, available at http://www.gao.gov/assets/670/665179.pdf.
91. For example, the Patient Protection and Affordable Care Act involves high transaction costs. *See* O. B. Tracker, U.S. House of Representatives, Committee on Ways and Means, Committee on Education and the Workforce, and Committee on Energy and Commerce (2013), available at http://waysandmeans.house.gov/uploadedfiles/aca_burden_tracker_final_5_6_13.pdf and A. Anderson, The Impact of the Affordable Care Act on the Health Care Workforce, Backgrounder No. 2887, 10, The Heritage Foundation, March 18, 2014, available at http://thf_media.s3.amazonaws.com/2014/pdf/BG2887.pdf ("The ACA has thus far added 109 distinct regulations. The time and effort to comply with these rules and regulations will equal an estimated 190 million hours of paperwork per year imposed on business and the health care industry. Most of

the estimated 13,000 pages of regulations are focused on health care institutions, and compliance with these rules will also reduce the time spent on direct patient care.").

92. *See* D. F. Spulber, *Regulation and Markets*, Cambridge, MA: MIT Press, 1989.
93. Anderson, *supra* note 91, p. 2 ("With the new demand for medical services for the millions who are expected to enroll in Medicaid and the federal and state insurance exchanges, the workforce shortages could become catastrophic.").
94. B. Z. Khan, Premium Inventions: Patents and Prizes as Incentive Mechanisms in Britain and the United States, 1750–1930, in *Understanding Long-Run Economic Growth: Geography, Institutions, and the Knowledge Economy*, Vol. 205, Dora L. Costa and Naomi R. Lamoreaux (eds.), NBER and University of Chicago, 2011; B. Z. Khan, Going for Gold: Industrial Fairs and Innovation in the Nineteenth-Century United States, *Revue Economique* 64, 89 (2013); B. Z. Khan, Selling Ideas: An International Perspective on Patenting and Markets for Technological Innovations, 1790–1930, Bus. Hist. Rev. 87, 39 (2013); and B. Z. Khan, The Social Consequences of Patent Institutions and Prizes in Technology Markets, in *Interdisciplinary Perspectives on Intellectual Property Law*, D. Halbert and W. Gallagher (eds.), forthcoming. *See also* B. Z. Khan and K. L. Sokoloff, History Lessons: The Early Development of Intellectual Property Institutions in the United States, *J. Econ. Perspectives* 15, 233 (2001).
95. B. Z. Khan, Trolls and Other Patent Inventions: Economic History and the Patent Controversy in the Twenty-First Century, Working Paper, Department of Economics, Bowdoin College and NBER, 2014.
96. Khan, *supra* note 94.
97. *See* B. Z. Khan, Going for Gold: Industrial Fairs and Innovation in the Nineteenth-Century United States, *Revue Economique* 64, 89 (2013). *See also* B. Z. Khan, The Social Consequences of Patent Institutions and Prizes in Technology Markets, in D. Halbert and W. Gallagher, *Interdisciplinary Perspectives on Intellectual Property Law* (forthcoming).
98. B. Z. Khan, Of Time and Space: Technological Spillovers among Patents and Unpatented Innovations in Early U.S. Industrialization, Department of Economics, Bowdoin College and NBER, 2014.
99. *Ibid.*
100. http://www.uspto.gov/about/nmti/NMTI_Announcement.jsp.
101. http://www.nsf.gov/od/nms/medal.jsp.

102. http://www.nsf.gov/od/nms/medal.jsp. *See also* the recipient's data base from 1962, available at http://www.nsf.gov/od/nms/results.jsp.
103. http://www.nsf.gov/od/nms/medal.jsp.
104. *See* H. O. Blair, Inventions in the Soviet Union, *Int'l Law* 7, 485 (2014); P. B. Maggs, Restructuring of the Soviet Law in Inventions, *Colum. J. Transnat'l L.*28, 277 (1990).
105. Maggs, *supra* note 104.
106. The medal was awarded from 1983 to 1991; "The Presidium of the Supreme Soviet of the USSR was the main conferring authority of the award based on recommendations from the State Committee for Inventions and Discoveries of the USSR and the Central Council of the All-Union Society of Inventors and Innovators," available at http://en.wikipedia.org/wiki/Honoured_Inventor_of_the_USSR.
107. Kieff, *supra* note 12.
108. Kieff, *supra* note 12. *See also* Abramowicz, *supra* note 26.
109. Love and Hubbard, *supra* note 52, p. 1554.
110. This is quoted in Machlup and Penrose (1950). *See* J. S. Mill, *Principles of Political Economy: With Some of Their Applications to Social Philosophy*, 7th edn., W. J. Ashley (ed.), Longmans, Green and Co., 1909, p. 932 (1st edition 1848), also available at http://oll.libertyfund.org/titles/101.
111. *See* Spulber, *supra* note 12.
112. *Ibid.*
113. Demsetz, *supra* note 12.
114. Epstein, *supra* note 12.
115. For a contemporary overview of price theory, *see* E. G. Weyl, A Short Summary of Price Theory, Department of Economics, University of Chicago, Working Paper, May 2014, under preparation for the *J. Econ. Literature*.
116. F. A. Hayek, The Use of Knowledge in Society, *Am. Econ. Rev.* 35, 519, 523 (1945).
117. *Ibid.*, p. 526.
118. *See* D. F. Spulber, Innovation and International Trade in Technology, *J. Econ. Theory,* 138, 1 (2008) and D. F. Spulber, The Quality of Innovation and the Extent of the Market, *J. Int'l Econ.* 80, 260 (2010).
119. *Ibid.*
120. D. F. Spulber, Competing Inventors and the Incentive to Invent, *Indus. & Corp. Change*, 22, 33 (2013) and D. F. Spulber, How Do Competitive Pressures Affect Incentives to Innovate when there is a Market for Inventions?, *J. Pol. Econ.* 121, 1007 (2013).

121. *Ibid* .
122. For a discussion of technology capital, *see* E. R. McGrattan and C. Prescott, Openness, Technology Capital, and Development, *J. Econ. Theory* 144, 2454 (2009). I employ the term technology capital because it suggests that it can be applied productively by firms. The term "knowledge capital" seems too broad for the purposes of the present discussion. On the production and distribution of knowledge, *see* F. Machlup, *The Production and Distribution of Knowledge in the United States*, Vol. 278, Princeton University Press, 1962 and Z. Griliches, Issues in Assessing the Contribution of Research and Development to Productivity Growth, *Bell J. Econ.* 10, 92 (1979). Technology capital also is distinct from human capital. Gary Becker defines investment in human capital as those "activities that influence future real income through the imbedding of resources in people," *see* G. S. Becker, Investment in Human Capital: A Theoretical Analysis, *J. Pol. Econ.* 70, 9 (1962).
123. C. J. Serrano, The Dynamics of the Transfer and Renewal of Patents, *R and J. Econ.* 41, 686 (2010).
124. R. J. Epstein and P. Malherbe, Reasonable Royalty Patent Infringement Damages after UNILOC, *Aipla Q. J.* 39, 3, 8 (2011).
125. *Ibid.*, p. 8.
126. *Ibid.*
127. *Ibid.*
128. *Ibid.*
129. Contrary to what is commonly believed, Jules Dupuit did not recommend either public subsidies or marginal cost pricing. *See* A. Jules É. J. Dupuit, De la mesure de l'utilité des travaux publics, *Annales des ponts et chaussées* 8, 332 (2nd ser. 1844) *translated in* R.H. Barback, On the Measurement of the Utility of Public Works, *Int'l Econ. Paper,*2, 83 (1952), *reprinted in* K. J. Arrow and T. Scitovsky (eds.), *Readings in Welfare Economics*, 1969, pp. 255–283; R. B. Ekelund, Jules Dupuit and the Early Theory of Marginal Cost Pricing, *J. Pol. Econ.* 76, 462 (1968); and R. Ekelund and R. F. Hébert, *Secret Origins of Modern Microeconomics: Dupuit and the Engineers*, University of Chicago Press, 1999.
130. *See* H. Hotelling, The General Welfare in Relation to the Problems of Taxation and of Railway and Utility Rates, *Econometrica* 6, 242 (1938) (recommending government subsidies to achieve marginal cost pricing for industries with economies of scale such as public utilities).
131. A. C. Pigou, *A Study of Public Finance*, 3rd edn., Macmillan, 1947.
132. *See* R. Coase, The Marginal Cost Controversy, *Economica* 13, 169 (1946) and R. Coase, The Marginal Cost Controversy: Some Further Comments,

Economica 14, 150 (1947). *See also* E. K. Browning, The Marginal Cost of Public Funds, *J. Pol. Econ.* 84, 283 (1976) and D. E. Wildasin, On Public Good Provision with Distortionary Taxation, *Econ. Inquiry* 22, 227 (1984).

133. J. F. Duffy, The Marginal Cost Controversy in Intellectual Property, *U. Chi. L. Rev.* 71, 37 (2004).
134. *See* H. Demsetz, Why Regulate Utilities?, *J. L. & Econ.* 11, 55 (1968); W. J. Baumol, and R. D. Willig, Fixed Costs, Sunk Costs, Entry Barriers, and Sustainability of Monopoly, *Q. J. Econ.* 96, 405 (1981); W. J. Baumol, J. C. Panzar, and R. D. Willig, *Contestable Markets and the Theory of Industry Structure*, Harcourt Brace Jovanovich, 1988; and Spulber, *supra* note 92.
135. This is explained in Chapter 8 of Spulber, *supra* note 92.
136. *See* Spulber, *supra* note 92 at Chapter 8. *See also* Kieff, *supra* note 12, on market pricing of inventions. Roin, *supra* note 24, also points out that two-part tariffs for inventions remove some of the theoretical advantages of "prizes."
137. J. Kornai and Th. Lipták, Two-Level Planning, *Econometrica* 33, 141, 168 (1965) ("The National Planning Bureau wishes to make use of this method too, to obtain sounder foundations for long-term macroeconomic plans.").
138. *See* O. Lange, A Note on Innovations, *Rev. Econ. & Stat.* 25, 19 (1943); O. Lange, On the Economic Theory of Socialism, *Rev. Econ. Stud.* IV(1 and 2) (1936–1937); O. Lange, The Scope and Method of Economics, *Rev. Econ. Stud.* 13, 19 (1945–1946); F. M. Taylor, The Guidance of Production in the Socialist State, *Am. Econ. Rev.* 19, 1 (1929). This is discussed by M. H. I. Dore and M. C. Kaser, The Millions of Equations Debate: Seventy Years After Barone, *Atlantic Econ. J.* 12, 30 (1984).
139. Lange, *supra* note 138.
140. A. P. Lerner, Marginal Cost Pricing in the 1930's, *Am. Econ. Rev.* 67, 235 (1984).
141. On uncertainty, *see* F. Knight, *Risk, Uncertainty and Profit*, University of Chicago Press, 1921.
142. *See* W. J. Baumol and R. D. Willig, Fixed Costs, Sunk Costs, Entry Barriers, and Sustainability of Monopoly, *Q. J. Econ.* 96, 405 (1981). *See also* W. J. Baumol, J. C. Panzar, and R. D. Willig, *Contestable Markets and the Theory of Industry Structure*, Harcourt Brace Jovanovich, 1988 and Spulber, *supra* note 92.
143. D. F. Spulber, Deregulating Telecommunications, *Yale J. Reg.* 12, 25 (1995).

144. *See* E. P. Lazear and S. Rosen, Rank-Order Tournaments as Optimum Labor Contracts, *J. Pol. Econ.* 89, 841 (1981); B. J. Nalebuff and J. E. Stiglitz, Prizes and Incentives: Towards a General Theory of Compensation and Competition, *Bell J. Econ.* 14, 21 (1983); C. R. Taylor, Digging for Golden Carrots: An Analysis of Research Tournaments, *Am. Econ. Rev.* 85, 872 (1995); R. L. Fullerton and R. P. McAfee, Auctioning Entry into Tournaments, *J. Pol. Econ.* 107, 573 (1999); B. Moldovanu and A. Sela, The Optimal Allocation of Prizes in Contests, *Am. Econ. Rev.* 91, 542 (2001); Y.-K. Che and I. Gale, Optimal Design of Research Contests, *Am. Econ. Rev.* 93, 646 (2003); and C. Riis, Efficient Contests, *J. Econ. & Mgmt. Strategy* 19, 643 (2010). Moldovanu and Sela examine the optimal number of prizes that should be awarded for a single tournament.
145. M. R. Baye and H. C. Hoppe, The Strategic Equivalence of Rent-Seeking, Innovation, and Patent-Race Games, *Games & Econ. Behav.* 44, 217 (2003).
146. For models of patent racing, *see* P. Dasgupta and J. Stiglitz, Uncertainty, Industrial Structure, and the Speed of R&D, *Bell J. Econ.* 11, 1 (1980); J. F. Reinganum, Dynamic Games of Innovation, *J. Econ. Theory* 25, 1 (1981); J. F. Reinganum, A Dynamic Game of R and D: Patent Protection and Competitive Behavior, *Econometrica* 50, 671 (1982); and J. F. Reinganum, The Timing of Innovation: Research, Development, and Diffusion, in *Handbook of Industrial Organization*, R. Schmalensee and R. D. Willig (eds.), Elsevier Science Publishers, 1989, pp. 849–908.
147. Baye and Hoppe, *supra* note 145, also show that these models are equivalent to the basic model of rent-seeking.
148. Kitch, *supra* note 15.
149. *See* Spulber, *supra* note 12.
150. Hayek, *supra* note 14, p. 9.
151. *See* the discussion in Spulber, *supra* note 73, and the references therein.
152. Kitch, *supra* note 15.
153. For example, Erkal and Scotchmer consider R&D when decision makers decide whether or not to invest in an idea after observing the idea and the realization of development costs. N. Erkal and S. Scotchmer, *Scarcity of Ideas and R&D Options: Use It, Lose It or Bank It*, National Bureau of Economic Research, Cambridge, MA, Working Paper No. 14940, 2009. Poblete and Spulber show that option contracts are optimal agency contracts for R&D. J. Poblete and D. F. Spulber, Managing innovation: Optimal

incentive contracts for delegated R&D with double moral hazard, Euro. Ec. Rev. 95, 38 (June 2017).

154. *See* A. Pakes, Patents as Options: Some Estimates of the Value of Holding European Patent Stocks, *Econometrica* 54, 755–784 (1986) and M. Schankerman and A. Pakes, Estimates of the Value of Patent Rights in European Countries during the Post-1950 Period, *Econ. J.* 96, 1052 (1986).
155. A. A. Ziedonis, Real Options in Technology Licensing, *Mgmt. Sci.* 53, 1618 (2007).
156. W. Mann, Creditor Rights and Innovation: Evidence from Patent Collateral, Wharton Working Paper, May 1, 2014, available at http://fnce.wharton.upenn.edu/pro_le/1033/.
157. S. J. H. Graham, R. P. Merges, P. Samuelson, and T. Sichelman, High Technology Entrepreneurs and the Patent System: Results of the 2008 Berkeley Patent Survey, *Berkeley Tech. L.J.* 25, 1255 (2009).
158. G. E. Moore, Cramming More Components Onto Integrated Circuits, *Electronics Mag.* 38(8), 114–117 (1965); G. E. Moore, Lithography and the Future of Moore's Law, *Opt./Laser Microlithograp. VIII*: *Proc.* SPE, 2440, 2–17 (1995).
159. *Ibid.*
160. R. A. Schaller, Moore's Law: Past, Present, and Future, *IEEE Spectrum*, June 54 (1997).
161. *Ibid.*
162. G. E. Moore, The Role of Fairchild in Silicon Technology in the Early Days of 'Silicon Valley', *Proc. IEEE* 86(1), 53, 59 (1998).
163. *Ibid.* ("I was not at that meeting, since my responsibility at the time was to oversee the engineering effort to get our transistors into production.").
164. *Ibid.*
165. *Ibid.*
166. Excerpts from A Conversation with Gordon Moore: Moore's Law, Intel Corporation, Video transcript, 2005, available at http://web.eng.fiu.edu/npala/eee6397ex/gordon_moore_1965_article.pdf.
167. Moore, 1995, *supra* note 158, p. 14.
168. A related study of Moore's Law by Ana Aizcorbe and Samuel Kortum provides a detailed empirical analysis that tests a capital vintage model by considering average prices within each generation and examining how prices of each generation decline over time. A. Aizcorbe and S. Kortum, Moore's Law and the Semiconductor Industry: A Vintage Model, *Scandinavian J. Econ.* 107, 603 (2005).

169. I used the bureau of labor statistics calculator, *see* http://data.bls.gov/cgi-bin/cpicalc.pl?cost1=5.25&year1=1980&year2=2013.
170. http://hexus.net/tech/reviews/cpu/37989-intel-core-i7-3770k-22nm-ivy-bridge/
171. http://hexus.net/tech/reviews/cpu/37989-intel-core-i7-3770k-22nm-ivy-bridge/.

Chapter 3

1. *Bilski et al. v. Kappos,* 561 U.S. 593 (2010), hereafter *Bilski.*
2. *See* S. M. Wagner, Business method patents in Europe and their strategic use – evidence from franking device manufacturers. *Economics of Innovation and New Technology* 17 (3) 173–194 (2008) ("a closer look reveals that business methods are eligible for patentability in Europe and are actually being granted by the European Patent Office despite the apparent exclusion in Article 52 EPC.")
3. *Alice Corp. Pty. Ltd. v. CLS Bank Int'l*, 573 U.S. 208, (2014), hereafter *Alice*.
4. *Ibid*, p. 1.
5. *Ibid.*
6. United States Patent and Trademark Office [Docket No. PTO–P–2018–0053] 2019 revised patent subject matter eligibility guidance, Federal Register 50, 84(4) Monday, January 7, 2019,https://www.govinfo.gov/content/pkg/FR-2019-01-07/pdf/2018-28282.pdf
7. *Mayo Collaborative Servs. v. Prometheus Labs., Inc., U.S.* 566, 66 (2012), hereafter *Mayo.*
8. *Mayo*, p. 2.
9. *Mayo*, p. 3.
10. *Mayo*, p. 4.
11. *Association for Molecular Pathology v. Myriad Genetics, Inc.*, U.S. 569, 576 (2013) hereafter *Myriad.*
12. *Myriad*, p. 12.
13. *Myriad*, p. 1.
14. *Ibid.*
15. *Ibid.*
16. USPTO, Automated financial or management data processing methods. USPTO White Paper 2010. Available at: http://www.uspto.gov/web/menu/

busmethp/index.html#origins, p. 2 ("The first financial patent was granted on March 19, 1799, to Jacob Perkins of Massachusetts for an invention for 'Detecting Counterfeit Notes.'")

17. *Ibid.*, citing E. Burke, Commissioner of patents, list of patents for inventions and designs, issued by the United States from 1790 to 1847 (1847).
18. A search conducted by author on July 8, 2010, of the USPTO database for Patent Class 705 yielded 1,143 hits before 1976 and 105,811 hits from 1976 to the present. *See* http://patft.uspto.gov/.
19. *State Street Bank & Trust Co* v. *Signature Financial Group, Inc.*, 149 F. 3d 1368, 1373— (*Fed. Cir.* July 23, 1998.)
20. *See* USPTO, 2010, *supra* note 16, p. 22; and R. M. Hunt, 2010. Business method patents and U.S. financial services. 28 (3) contemporary economic policy 322–352, p. 322. ("The *State Street* decision had an almost immediate effect in terms of business method patenting behavior. About 1,000 issued patents were classified in Class 705 in the first 5 yr after that case; grants are currently running at twice this rate.")
21. At the height of the dot-com bubble, Rivette and Kline wrote "Nowhere is the frenzy over patent rights more intense, however, than in the emerging electronic commerce industries of the Internet, where entrepreneurs are rushing to stake their proprietary claims to this booming new frontier of business." *See* K. G. Rivette, and D. Kline, 2000. Rembrandts in the Attic: Unlocking the hidden value of patents. boston, MA: Harvard Business School Press, p. 6. *See also* M. J. Meurer, Business Method Patents and Patent Floods. *Washington University J. of Law & Poli.* 8, 309–339, (2002) and A. K. Rai, Addressing the patent gold rush: The role of deference to PTO patent denials. *Washington University J. of Law & Poli.* 2, 199–227 (2000).
22. J. Besen and M. J. Meurer, Patent failure: How judges, bureaucrats and lawyers put innovations at risk. Princeton, NJ: Princeton University Press, 2008.
23. J. Besen and M. J. Meurer, *ibid.* p. 187 (2008).
24. *See* D. L. Burk and M. A. Lemley, Patent crisis and how the courts can solve it. Chicago: University of Chicago Press, 2009.
25. D. L. Burk and M. A. Lemley, *ibid.* p. 158, 2009. ("the solution to the problem of bad patents in the software and business method fields is not the creation of absolute rules against patentability, but the application of existing doctrines designed to weed out bad patents, and if necessary the reform of other doctrines that encourage litigation abuse.")

26. S. J. H. Graham, R. P. Merges, P. Samuelson, and T. Sichelman, High technology entrepreneurs and the patent system: Results of the 2008 Berkeley patent survey, 24 (4) *Berkeley Tech. L. J.* 1255–1328 (2009).
27. B. H. Hall, Business and financial method patents, innovation, and policy. *Scot. J. of Pol. Econ.* 56 (s1), 443–473, 445 (2009)) ("There is no precise definition of business method patents": "many scholars make little distinction between business method patents, internet patents, and software patents more broadly, at least when making policy recommendations. This is inevitable in the present day, because many business method patents are in fact patents on the transfer of a known business method to a software and/or web-based implementation, so the distinction is hard to maintain.") *See* S. Wagner, *supra* note 2, 194 2008. ("The concept of business methods is notoriously difficult to define. From an economic perspective, the term 'business method' is very broad and comprises various economic activities such as selling and buying items, marketing or finance methods, schemes and techniques. From a legal perspective, it is hard to find an abstract definition of what exactly constitutes a business method and what makes it different from other 'methods'. Currently, neither European nor US (patent) laws contain a legal definition of the term business method while actually using it frequently.") *See also* Hart, R., P. Holmes, and J. Reid, 2000. The Economic Impact of Patentability of Computer Programs, Report to the European Commission, OECD.
28. The term market microstructure refers to the rules, procedures, and institutions in a market; *see* D. F. Spulber, Market microstructure: Intermediaries and the theory of the firm. Cambridge: Cambridge University Press, 1999.
29. D. F. Spulber, Discovering the role of the firm: The separation criterion and corporate law, *Berkeley Bus. L. J.* 6 (2) 298–347 (2009a); D. F. Spulber, The theory of the firm: Microeconomics with endogenous entrepreneurs, firms, organizations, and markets. Cambridge: Cambridge University Press, 2009b.
30. On the definition of the firm based on a "separation criterion," *see* Spulber 2009a and Spulber, 2009b, *ibid.*
31. The "separation criterion" involves application of the "Fisher Separation Theorem," which is a fundamental concept in Economics and Finance. *See* I. Fisher, 1906. The Nature of Capital and Income. New York: Macmillan; Fisher, Irving. 1907. Rate of Interest: Its Nature, Determination and Relation to Economic Phenomena. New York: Macmillan; Fisher, Irving.

1930. The Theory of Interest: As Determined by Impatience to Spend Income and Opportunity to Invest It. New York: Macmillan.

32. D. F. Spulber, Market microstructure and intermediation, *J. of Econ. Perspectives* 10(3), 135–152 (1996).
33. R. H. Coase, The nature of the firm. *Economica* 4 (16), 386–405 (1937).
34. *See* M. H. Miller, Financial innovation: The last twenty years and the next. 21 *J. of Fina. and Q. Anal.* 21, 459–471 (1986); R. C. Merton,. Financial innovation and economic performance. *J. of Appl.Cor. Fina.* 4, 12–22 (1992).
35. J. Lerner, The new new financial thing: The origins of financial innovations. *J. of Fina. Econ.* 79 (2), 223–255, p. 224 (2006).
36. *See* Lerner, 2006, *ibid. See also* P. Tufano, Financial innovation, in constantinides, G. M. Harris and R. Stulz, eds., *Handbook of the Economics of Finance,* 1A, 307 336 (2003). Amsterdam: North-Holland and B. H. Hall, G. Thoma, and S. Torrisi, Financial patenting in Europe, *Euro. Manag. Rev.* 6 (1), 45–63 (2009).
37. The Oxford English Dictionary (OED). Oxford: Oxford University Press, 1989 2nd ed. Available at: http://www.oed.com, presents a multipart definition of "innovation" that recognizes the Schumpeterian description of innovation: "5. *Comm.* The action of introducing a new product into the market; a product newly brought on to the market." Oxford English Dictionary, s.v. "innovation" http://dictionary.oed.com/. The initial definition is generic: "1. a. The action of innovating; the introduction of novelties; the alteration of what is established by the introduction of new elements or forms," and "2. a. A change made in the nature or fashion of anything; something newly introduced; a novel practice, method, etc." The OED definition of innovation in commerce also cites J. Jewkes, D. Sawers, and R. Stillerman. The sources of invention. New York: St. Martin's Press, 249 (1958). ("It seems impossible to establish scientifically any final conclusion concerning the relation between monopoly and innovation."); E. Rogers, Diffusion of innovations. New York: Free Press, 124 (1962). ("It matters little whether or not an innovation has a great degree of advantage over the idea it is replacing. What does matter is whether the individual perceives the relative advantage of the innovation."); and J. A. Allen, Scientific innovation and industrial prosperity, Amsterdam: Elsevier, 8 (1967). ("Innovation is the bringing of an invention into widespread, practical use … Invention may thus be construed as the first stage of the much more extensive and complex total process of innovation.")

38. J. A. Schumpeter, Business cycles: A theoretical, historical, and statistical analysis of the capitalist process. Philadelphia: Porcupine Press. (Reprinted 1989, abridged version of first edition 1939, 59 (1964).
39. J. A. Schumpeter, The theory of economic development. New Brunswick, NJ: Transaction Publishers (Reprinted 1997) p. 66 (1934).
40. J. A. Schumpeter, *ibid.*, p. 65–66 (1934). J. A. Schumpeter, *supra* note 38 p. 61 (1964), among "changes in the methods of supplying commodities," lists "[t]echnological change in the production of commodities already in use, the opening up of new markets or of new sources of supply, Taylorization of work, improved handling of material, the setting up of new business organizations, such as department stores."
41. J. A. Schumpeter, *supra* note 38 p. 61 (1964).
42. OED, *supra* note 37 (1989), citing J. A. Schumpeter, pp. 1, 3, 84, *supra* note 38 (1964). *See also*, J. A. Schumpeter, *supra* note 39 (1934); J. A. Schumpeter, Capitalism, Socialism, and Democracy. New York: Harper & Row (1942).
43. J. A. Schumpeter, *supra* note 38 p. 84 (1964).
44. J. A. Schumpeter, *supra* note 38, id, p. 60 (1964).
45. A. Smith, *An Inquiry Into the Nature and Causes of the Wealth of Nations.* Washington, D.C.: Regnery Publishing. (Originally published 1776), At 2, 5, 6 (1998).
46. R. H. Coase, The problem of social cost. 3 *J. of L. & Econ.* 3 1–44 (1960); R. H. Coase, The nature of the firm: Origin, meaning, influence, *J. of L. Econ.& Organ.* 4 (1), 3–47 (1988). (Reprinted 1991. In O. E. Williamson and S. G. Winter, eds., *The Nature of the Firm: Origin, Meaning, Influence.* 34–74 (1991). Oxford: Oxford University Press.); R. H. Coase, *Essays on Economics and Economists*. Chicago: University of Chicago Press, 1994.
47. *See* H. Demsetz, The theory of the firm revisited, in O. E. Williamson and S. G. Winter, eds., The nature of the firm, 159–178 (1991). Oxford: Oxford University Press. p. 162. ("It is not so easy to distinguish purchase across a market from in-house production because in-house production involves the use of inputs that are *purchased*. Purchasing inputs (across markets) is substituted for purchasing goods that are more nearly complete (across markets).")
48. Demsetz, *ibid.*, p. 162.
49. Demsetz, *ibid.*
50. Spulber, 2009b, *supra* note 29 p. 63.
51. Emphasis in original, see http://www.uspto.gov/web/patents/classification/uspc705/defs705.htm. The USPTO class 705 also includes the above "in combination with cryptographic apparatus or method."

52. According to the USPTO, http://www.uspto.gov/web/patents/classification/uspc705/defs705.htm, "scope of the class": "1. The arrangements in this class are generally used for problems relating to administration of an organization, commodities or financial transactions. 2. Mere designation of an arrangement as a 'business machine' or a document as a 'business form' or 'business chart' without any particular business function will not cause classification in this class or its subclasses. 3. For classification herein, there must be significant claim recitation of the data processing system or calculating computer and only nominal claim recitation of any external art environment. Significantly claimed apparatus external to this class, claimed in combination with apparatus under the class definition, which perform data processing or calculation operations are classified in the class appropriate to the external device unless specifically excluded therefrom. 4. Nominally claimed apparatus external to this class in combination with apparatus under the class definition is classified in this class unless provided for in the appropriate external class. 5. In view of the nature of the subject matter included herein, consideration of the classification schedule for the diverse art or environment is necessary for proper search."
53. *Ibid.* For other classes that may apply to business methods, *see also* United States Patent and Trademark Office (USPTO). 2009. Data Processing: Financial, Business Practice, Management, or Cost/Price Determination. USPTO Patent Class 705, Section II, 705-1-705-3. For example, other related sections include 186, Merchandising, various subclasses for customer service methods and apparatus in a variety of areas including banking, restaurant, and stores, 235, Registers (e.g., cash registers, voting machines), 283, Printed Matter, various subclasses for business forms and methods of using such forms. 307, Electrical Transmission or Interconnection Systems, 340, Communications: Electrical, 341, Coded Data Generation or Conversion, 345, Computer Graphics Processing and Selective Visual Display Systems, 359, Optics: Systems and Elements, 360, Dynamic Magnetic Information Storage or Retrieval, 365, Static Information Storage and Retrieval, 369, Dynamic Information Storage or Retrieval, 370, Multiplex Communications, 371, Error Detection/Correction and Fault Detection/Recovery, 375, Pulse or Digital Communications, 377, Electrical Pulse Counters, Pulse Dividers, or Shift Registers: Circuits and Systems, 379, Telephonic Communications, 380, Cryptography, 382, Image Analysis, 434, Education and Demonstration, 463, Amusement Devices: Games, (a method or apparatus for moving or

processing information specified as game or contest information), 700, Data Processing: Generic Control Systems, 704, Data Processing: Speech Signal Processing, Linguistics, Language Translation, and Audio Compression/Decompression, 708, Electrical Computers: Arithmetic Processing and Calculating, 709, Electrical Computers and Digital Processing Systems: Multicomputer Data Transferring or Plural Process Synchronization, 713, Electrical Computers and Digital Processing Systems: Support, 714, Error Detection/Correction and Fault Detection/ Recovery, 902, Electronic Funds Transfer.

54. J. R. Allison, and S. D. Hunter, On the feasibility of improving patent quality one technology at a time: The case of business methods, *Berkeley Tech. L. J.* 21 (2), 729–794 (2006).
55. Allison and Hunter, *ibid.*, p. 736 (2006).
56. J. E. Cohen, and M. A. Lemley, Patent scope and innovation in the software industry, *California L. Rev.* 89 (1), 1–57, p. 9 (2001).
57. Cohen and Lemley, *ibid.*, (2001)
58. F. S. Kieff, The case for registering patents and the law and economics of present patent-obtaining rules, *Boston College L. Rev.* 45, 55-123. http://lawdigitalcommons.bc.edu/bclr/vol45/iss1/2, at 112 (2003).
59. 35 U.S.C. 101.
60. 35 U.S.C. 100a, b.
61. 35 U.S.C. 102 and 103.
62. As the court states in *Bilski*, "Section 101 similarly precludes the broad contention that the term "process" categorically excludes business methods."
63. The OED, 1989, *supra* note 37, defines a "process" as "[1]b. *gen.* The fact of going on or being carried on, as an action or series of actions; progress, course" and "8. A continuous and regular action or succession of actions occurring or performed in a definite manner, and having a particular result or outcome; a sustained operation or series of operations. (Now the most common use.)" http://www.oed.com/ .
64. V. R. Fuchs, The service economy. Cambridge, MA: National Bureau of Economic Research, p. 1.
65. Fuchs, id, p. 1–13.
66. The measurement of GDP by industry prepared by the Bureau of Economic Analysis (BEA) is based on the National Income and Product Accounts (NIPAs). According to the BEA: "Current-dollar value added in the annual industry accounts is measured as the sum of industry distributions of

compensation of employees, gross operating surplus, and taxes on production and imports less subsidies." The BEA prepares current-dollar statistics on value added by an industry "by extrapolating industry statistics on compensation of employees, gross operating surplus, and 'taxes on production and imports less subsidies' with published and unpublished industry data from the NIPAs." According to the BEA, "Compensation of employees by industry is extrapolated using the sum of industry wage and salary accruals and supplements to wages and salaries. Gross operating surplus by industry is extrapolated using the sum of industry corporate profits, proprietors' income, capital consumption allowances, net interest, and net business current transfer payments." Additionally, the BEA obtains value added for farms and government from the NIPAs. *See* B. M. Lindberg and J. M. Monaldo, Annual industry accounts advance statistics on GDP by industry for 2007. *Surv. of Curr. Busin.* 88 (5), 38–50 (2008).

67. *See* D. D. Kim, B. M. Lindberg, and J. M. Monaldo, Annual industry accounts: Advance statistics on GDP by industry for 2008. *Surv.of Curr. Busin.* 89 (5), 22–37. An industry's general product by origin (GPO) or value added equals its gross output (sales or receipts and other operating income plus inventory change) minus its intermediate inputs (consumption of goods and services purchased from other industries or imported); *see* R. E. Yuskavage, Gross product by industry, 1991–92. *Surv. of Curr. Busin.*74 (10), 30–34 (1994).
68. Based on U.S. GDP data in Kim, Lindberg, and Monaldo 2009, *ibid.*
69. The Patent Act (35 U.S.C. 103) defines a "biotechnological process" as "(A) a process of genetically altering or otherwise inducing a single- or multi-celled organism to — (i) express an exogenous nucleotide sequence, (ii) inhibit, eliminate, augment, or alter expression of an endogenous nucleotide sequence, or (iii) express a specific physiological characteristic not naturally associated with said organism; (B) cell fusion procedures yielding a cell line that expresses a specific protein, such as a monoclonal antibody; and (C) a method of using a product produced by a process defined by subparagraph (A) or (B), or a combination of subparagraphs (A) and (B)."
70. 35 U.S.C. 103.
71. *Bilski.*
72. *See In re Bilski*, 545 F.3d 943, 88 U.S.P.Q.2d 1385 (*Fed. Cir.* 2008).
73. *Bilski.*
74. *Funk Bros. Seed Co. v. Kalo Inoculant Co.*, 333 U.S. 127 (1948).

75. *Funk Bros.* 333 U.S. 127 (1948).
76. *Funk Bros.* 333 U.S. 127 (1948) at 130.
77. *Gottschalk v. Benson*, 409 U.S. 63 (1972).
78. *Gottschalk v. Benson*, 409 U.S. 63 (1972), p. 71.
79. *Gottschalk v. Benson*, 409 U.S. 63 (1972), p. 73.
80. *Parker v. Flook*, 437 U.S. 584 (1978).
81. *Diamond v. Diehr*, 450 U.S. 175 (1981) p. 185.
82. *Diamond v. Diehr*, 450 U.S. 175 (1981).
83. *Cochrane v. Deener*, 94 U.S. 780, 94 U.S. 787–788 (1877). Cited in *Diamond v. Diehr*, 450 U.S. 175 (1981).
84. *State Street*, 149 F. 3d 1368, 1373 — (*Fed. Cir. Jul.* 23, 1998). "The patented invention relates generally to a system that allows an administrator to monitor and record the financial information flow and make all calculations necessary for maintaining a partner fund financial services configuration."
85. The United States Court of Appeals for the Federal Circuit (CAFC) observes that "for the purposes of a § 101 analysis, it is of little relevance whether claim 1 is directed to a 'machine' or a 'process,' as long as it falls within at least one of the four enumerated categories of patentable subject matter, 'machine' and 'process' being such categories." *State Street*, 149 F. 3d 1368.
86. *State Street*, 149 F. 3d 1368.
87. *State Street*, 149 F. 3d 1368.
88. *State Street*, 149 F. 3d 1368.
89. *State Street*, 149 F. 3d 1368, citing "Office personnel have had difficulty in properly treating claims directed to methods of doing business. Claims should not be categorized as methods of doing business. Instead such claims should be treated like any other process claims." Examination Guidelines, *Fed. Reg.* 61, 7478, 7479 (1996).
90. *AT&T v. Excel Communications, Inc* 172 F. 3d 1352 (*Fed. Cir.* 1999).
91. *See In re Bilski*, 545 F. 3d 943, 88 U.S.P.Q.2d 1385 (*Fed. Cir.* 2008).
92. *See* Patrick, A., Patent Eligibility and Computer-Related processes: A critique of *In re Bilski* and the Machine-or-Transformation Test, *Virginia J. of L. & Tech.* 14 (3), 181–211, 211 (2009).
93. "Nothing in today's opinion should be read as endorsing the Federal Circuit's past interpretations of §101. *See*, e.g., *State Street*, 49 F. 3d, 1373," *Bilski*.
94. *Bilski*.

95. *Bilski.*
96. “The machine-or-transformation test may well provide a sufficient basis for evaluating processes similar to those in the industrial Age — for example, inventions grounded in a physical or other tangible form. But there are reasons to doubt whether the test should be the sole criterion for determining the patentability of inventions in the Information Age.” *Bilski.*
97. A. L. Durham, “Useful Arts” in the Information Age, *Brigham Young L. Rev.* 1999 (4), 1419–1528, 1455 (1999).
98. J. R. Thomas, The patenting of the liberal professions, *Boston College L. Rev.* 40 (5), 1139–1186, 1143 (1999).
99. *Bilski.* Stevens cites Thomas (1999, 1164).
100. *Bilski.* For Stevens, a business method invention often is a mere “series of steps.”
101. *Bilski.*
102. *See* P. Veyne, The Roman Empire. Cambridge, MA: Harvard University Press, 129 (1987).
103. Schumpeter, *supra* note 39, 165 (1934). (“Because there are always entrepreneurs and relatives and heirs of entrepreneurs, public opinion and also the phraseology of the social struggle readily overlook these facts.”)
104. *See* Veyne, *supra* note 102, 129 (1987). (“The key to the mystery lies in the fact that commercial wealth belonged to the newly rich, while the old wealth was based on land. Inherited wealth defended itself against upstart merchants by imputing to them every conceivable vice: merchants are rootless, greedy, the source of all evil; they promote luxury and weakness; they distort nature by travelling to far-off lands, violating the natural barrier of the seas and bringing back what nature will not permit to grow at home.”)
105. This negative characterization is typical of Marxist writings. *See, for example,* J. L. Van Zanden, The rise and decline of holland’s eEconomy: merchant capitalism and the labour market. Manchester: Manchester University Press. 7 (1993). (“merchant capitalism often employed the systems of exploitation that already existed in the pre-capitalist modes of production.”)
106. D. N. McCloskey, *The Bourgeois Virtues: Ethics for an Age of Commerce.* Chicago: University of Chicago Press, 2 (2006). In 1848, a major revolutionary wave swept across Europe, *see* Rapport, Mike. 2009. *1848:* Year of revolution. New York: Basic Books.
107. T. Sowell, *Intellectuals and Society.* New York: Basic Books, 62 (2009).

108. *See* J. T. Dunlop and W. R. Jan, Introduction. In A. B. Stephen, *Revolution at the Checkout Counter: The Explosion of the Bar Code*. 5–9 (1997). Cambridge, MA.: Harvard University Press, 5.
109. US Patent 2,612,994.
110. US Patent 2,612,994.
111. US Patent 2,612,994.
112. Dunlop and Rivkin, *supra* note 108, p. 9 (1997).
113. For an overview of the judicial treatment of software, *see* C. King, Abort, Retry, Fail: Protection for software-related inventions in the wake of State Street Bank & Trust Co. v. Signature Financial Group, Inc. *Cornell L. Rev.* 1118–1180.
114. Laudon, K. C. and C. G. Traver. 2010. *E-Commerce: Business, Technology, Society*, 6th ed. Boston: Prentice Hall.
115. Laudon and Traver. 2010, *ibid,*.p. 210.
116. Laudon and Traver. 2010, *ibid.*, p. 211.
117. Laudon and Traver. 2010, *ibid.*
118. Spulber, 2009b, *supra* note 29.
119. Spulber, 2009b, *supra* note 29.
120. Graham *et al.*, 2009, *supra* note 26.
121. Graham *et al.*, 2009, *supra* note 26, p. 1275.
122. Graham *et al.*, 2009, *supra* note 26, p. 1297.
123. Graham *et al.*, 2009, *supra* note 26, p. 1297.
124. Graham *et al.*, 2009, *supra* note 26.
125. T. S. Simcoe, S. J. S. Graham, and M. P. Feldman, Competing on standards? Entrepreneurship, intellectual property and platform technologies. *J. of Econ. & Manag. Stra.* 18 (3), 775–816, 776 (2009).
126. Simcoe *et al.*, *ibid.*, p. 807.
127. On the choice between patenting and secrecy when there is asymmetric information, *see* I. Horstmann, G. M. MacDonald, and A. Slivinski, Patent as information transfer mechanisms: To patent or (Maybe) not to patent, *J. of Poli. Econ.* 93, 837–858 (1985). *See also* N. T. Gallini, patent policy and costly imitation, *RAND J. of Econ.* 52–63, and F. Cugno and E. Ottoz, Trade secret vs. broad patent: The role of licensing, *Rev. of L. and Econ.* 2 (2), 209–221 (2006).
128. J. S. Gans and S. Stern, Incumbency and R&D incentives: Licensing the gale of creative destruction, *J. of Econ. & Mana. Strat.* 9 (4), 485–511 (2000). Consider the tradeoff between the threat of product market entry

and the threat of expropriation of the technology by the incumbent, and obtain technology licensing in equilibrium. They suggest that entry by a startup is "something of an economic puzzle" in the absence of non-contractible information asymmetries between the incumbent and the entrant. *See also* J. S. Gans and S. Stern, The product market and the market for 'Ideas': Commercialization strategies for technology entrepreneurs, *Rese. Poli.* 32 (2), 333–350 (2003), who find that the issue is the development of a market for ideas: "the main problem is not so much invention but *commercialization*" (333, emphasis in original).

129. D. F. Spulber, How entrepreneurs affect the rate and direction of inventive activity, in J. Lerner and S. Stern eds., The rate and direction of inventive activity revisited, *Nation. Bureau of Econ. Rese.*, Chicago: University of Chicago Press, 277–315 (2012).
130. *See* W. M. Landes and R. A. Posner, The economic structure of intellectual property law. Cambridge, MA: Harvard University Press. For a general discussion of incentives for R&D, *see.* N. T. Gallini and S. Scotchmer, Intellectual property: When is it the best incentive system? *Innovation Poli. and the Econ.* 2, 51–77 (2003) (2002).
131. The effectiveness of the system of IP rights also depends on associated legal and transaction costs. *See*, for example, S. M. Besen and L. J. Raskind, An introduction to the law and economics of intellectual property, *J. of Econ. Perspectives* 5 (1), 3–27, p. 5 (1991). ("The objective of intellectual property protection is to create incentives that maximize the difference between the value of the intellectual property that is created and used and the social cost of its creation, including the cost of administering the system.")
132. A. Devlin and N. Sukhatme, Self-Realizing inventions and the utilitarian foundation of patent law. *William & Mary L. Rev.* 51, 897–955, p. 902 (2009).
133. Burk and Lemley, *supra* note 24, p. 41 (2009).
134. Burk and Lemley, *supra* note 24, p. 39 (2009).
135. Burk and Lemley, *supra* note 24, p. 41 (2009).
136. Burk and Lemley, *supra* note 24, p. 156 (2009).
137. Devlin and Sukhatme, *supra* note 132 (2009).
138. Devlin and Sukhatme, *supra* note 132, p. 910 (2009).
139. Devlin and Sukhatme, *supra* note 132, p. 910 (2009).
140. Devlin and Sukhatme, *supra* note 132, p. 904 (2009).
141. Devlin and Sukhatme, *supra* note 132, p. 904 (2009).
142. Burk and Lemley, *supra* note 24, p. 38–39 (2009).
143. Devlin and Sukhatme, *supra* note 132, p. 904 (2009).

144. Geoff Brumfiel interviewed Andre Geim, who explained why he did not file for a patent: We considered patenting; we prepared a patent and it was nearly filed. Then I had an interaction with a big, multinational electronics company. I approached a guy at a conference and said, "We've got this patent coming up, would you be interested in sponsoring it over the years?" It's quite expensive to keep a patent alive for 20 years. The guy told me, "We are looking at graphene, and it might have a future in the long term. If after ten years we find it's really as good as it promises, we will put a hundred patent lawyers on it to write a hundred patents a day, and you will spend the rest of your life, and the gross domestic product of your little island, suing us." That's a direct quote. In the interview by Geoff Brumfiel, Andre Geim further observes,

> I considered this arrogant comment, and I realized how useful it was. There was no point in patenting graphene at that stage. You need to be specific: you need to have a specific application and an industrial partner. Unfortunately, in many countries, including this one, people think that applying for a patent is an achievement. In my case it would have been a waste of taxpayers' money.

See G. Brumfiel, Andre Geim: In praise of graphene. *Nature*, October 7, (2010). doi:10.1038/news.2010.525, http://www.nature.com/news/2010/101007/full/news.2010.525.html.

145. Royal Swedish Academy of Sciences. 2010. *Scientific Background on the Nobel Prize in Physics 2010: Graphene*, October 5, Stockholm, Sweden. Search Engine History. Available at: http://www.searchenginehistory.com.
146. M. Pollack, The multiple unconstitutionality of business method patents, *Rutgers Comp. & Tech. L. J.* 28 (1), 61–120 (2002). Cited by Judge Dyk, *In re Bilski*, 545 F.3d 943, 88 U.S.P.Q.2d 1385 (*Fed. Cir.* 2008), *en banc* decision of the United States Court of Appeals for the Federal Circuit.
147. *Bilski.*
148. *Bilski.*
149. *Bilski.*
150. M. A. Lemley and D. L. Burk, Policy levers in patent law, *Virginia L. Rev.* 89 (7), 1575–1696, p. 1575–1589 (2003). This is cited by Justice Stevens in *Bilski.*
151. Justice Stevens observes that the marketplace already rewards business methods: "Innovators often capture advantages from new business methods notwithstanding the risk of others copying their innovation." *Bilski.*

152. On the importance of market demand as a driver of inventive activity, *see* J. Schmookler, Invention and economic growth. Cambridge, MA: Harvard University Press; and Landes and Posner, *supra* note 130 (1966).
153. K. L. Sokoloff, Inventive activity in early industrial America: Evidence from patent records, *J. of Econ. Hist.* 48 (4), 813–850, 1790–1846 (1988).
154. *See* N. Rosenberg, Technological change in the machine tool industry, *J. of Econ. Hist.* 23 (4), 414–443 1840–1910 (1963); N. Rosenberg, Factors affecting the diffusion of technology. *Explo. in Econ. Hist.*10 (1), 3–33 (1972a); and N. Rosenberg, *Technology and American Economic Growth*. New York: Harper & Row, 1972b.
155. D. F. Spulber, Competing inventors and the incentive to invent, industrial and corporate change, 22 (1), 33–72 (2013), doi: 10.1093/icc/dts013; D. F. Spulber, How do competitive pressures affect incentives to innovate when there is a market for inventions? *J. of Poli. Econ.*121, 6, 1007–1054 (2013).
156. Policymakers should not neglect the demand side of the market for inventions. Focusing only on the supply side of a market is a familiar problem in economics that echoes the Marxian labor theory of value and even recalls Adam Smith's (1776) famous observation that "The real price of everything, what everything really costs to the man who wants to acquire it, is the toil and trouble of acquiring it." *See* also M. Blaug, *Economic Theory in Retrospect*. Cambridge: Cambridge University Press, 1962.
157. K. J. Arrow, Economic welfare and the allocation of resources for invention. In National Bureau of Economic Research, *The Rate and Direction of Inventive Activity*, 609–626. Princeton, NJ: Princeton University Press, 1962.
158. D. F. Spulber, The quality of innovation and the extent of the market. *J. of Intern. Econ.*80 (2), 260–270 (2010); D. F. Spulber, Innovation and international trade in technology, *J. of Econ. Theo.*138, 1–20 (2008). doi:10.1016/j.jet.2007.06.002.
159. Arrow, 1962, *supra* note 157.
160. *See* J. J. Anton and D. A. Yao, Expropriation and inventions: Appropriable rents in the absence of property rights, *American Econ. Rev.* 84 (1), 190–209 (1994); J. J. Anton, and D. A. Yao, Starts-ups, spin-offs, and internal projects, *J. of L. Econ. & Organi.* 11 (2), 362–378 (1995); J. J. Anton and D. A. Yao, The sale of ideas: Strategic disclosure, property rights, and contracting, *Rev. of Econ. Stu.* 69 (3), 513–531 (2002); J. J. Anton and D. A. Yao, Patents, invalidity, and the strategic transmission of enabling information, *J. of Econ. & Mana. Stra.* 12 (2), 151–178 (2003); J. J. Anton and D. A. Yao,

Little patents and big secrets: Managing intellectual property, *Rand J. of Econ.* 35 (1), 1–22 (2004).

161. Arrow, *supra* note 157, p. 151 (1962).
162. Stevens suggests that businesses can obtain rents from their inventions through trade secrecy and first-mover advantages (branding, technology lock-in, and networking effects). First-mover advantages are far from reliable forms of protections for IP; entrants often fare better than first movers, through improvement, imitation, and strategic capabilities. The notion that technology lock and networking effects provide returns to IP is unsubstantiated and inconsistent with economic analysis; *see* Spulber (2008b, 2008a).
163. K. F. Jorda, Trade secrets and trade-secret licensing. In *Intellectual Property Management in Health and Agricultural Innovation: A Handbook of Best Practices*. A. F. Krattiger, R. T. Mahoney, L. Nelson *et al.* eds., 1043–1057 (2007). Davis, CA: PIPRA. Available at http://www.ipmall.info/ipHandbook-Ch%2011%2005%20Jorda%20Trade%20Secret%20Licensing.pdf.
164. Jorda, *ibid.*, p. 1056.
165. King, *supra* note 113, p. 1158–1159 (2000).
166. G. S. Becker and K. M. Murphy, The division of labor, coordination costs, and knowledge. In R. Febero and P. S. Schwartz, eds., *The Essence of Becker*, 608–632 (1995). Stanford: Hoover Institution Press.
167. I. Ayres and P. Klemperer, Limiting patentees' market power without reducing innovation incentives: The perverse benefits of uncertainty and non-injunctive remedies, *Michigan L. Rev.* 97, 985–1033 (1999).
168. *See* R. P. Merges, Of property rules, Coase, and intellectual property, *Columbia L. Rev.* 94, 2655–2673 (1994): H. E. Smith, The language of property: Form, context, and audience, *Stanford L. Rev.* 55, 1105–1191 (2003); and H. E. Smith, Intellectual property as property: delineating entitlements in information, *Yale L. J.* 116, 1742–1822 (2007).
169. A. Arora and R. P. Merges, Specialized supply firms, property rights and firm boundaries, *Indu. and Corp. Chan.* 13, 451–475 (2004).
170. *See* J. P. Kesan, Carrots and sticks to create a better patent system, *Berkeley J. of L. and Tech.* 17 (2), 763 (2002); J. P. Kesan and M. Banik, Patents as incomplete contracts: Aligning incentives for R&D investment with incentives to disclose prior art, *Washington Univ. J. of L. and Poli.* 2, 23–54 (2000); and V. Denicolò and L. A. Franzoni. The contract theory of patents, *Intern. Rev. of L. and Econ.* 23, 365–380 (2004).
171. P. J. Heald, A transaction costs theory of patent law, *Ohio State L. J.* 66 (3), 473–509 (2005).

172. Spulber, 2009b, *supra* note 29.
173. F. S. Kieff, On coordinating transactions in intellectual property: A response to smith's delineating entitlements in information, *Yale L. J. Pock.Par.* 117, 101–109 (2007); F. S. Kieff, Coordination, property, and intellectual property: An unconventional approach to anticompetitive effects and downstream access, *Emory L. J.* 56 (7), 327–438 (2006).
174. *See* T. Caulfield, R. M. Cook-Deegan, F. S. Kieff, and J. P. Walsh, Evidence and anecdotes: An analysis of human gene patenting controversies, *Nat. Biote.* 24 (9), 1091–1094.
175. *See* Bessen and Meurer, 2008, *supra* note 22 and Burk and Lemley, 2009, *supra* note 24.
176. J. F. McDonough, The Myth of the patent troll: An alternative view of the function of patent dealers in an idea economy, *Emory L. J.* 56, 189–228 (2006).
177. *See* J. F. McDonough, 2006, *ibid.* Market dealers are also referred to as "non-practicing entities" (NPEs).
178. N. R. Lamoreaux and K. L. Sokoloff, Intermediaries in the U.S. market for technology, 1870–1920 (2002). NBER Working Paper No. 9017. Available at: http://www.nber.org/papers/w9017. *See also* N. R. Lamoreaux and K. L. Sokoloff, Market trade in patents and the rise of a class of specialized inventors in the 19th-century United States. *American Econ. Rev.* 91 (2), 39–44 (2001); N. R. Lamoreaux, K. L. Sokoloff, and D. Sutthiphisal, Patent alchemy: The market for technology in US history. *Business Hist. Rev.* 87 (1), 3–38, pp. 37–38 (2013). ("Although only a small number of inventors have ever achieved great riches by selling off or licensing the rights to their intellectual property, their example has encouraged untold thousands to follow in their footsteps, shifting out the economy's technological frontier in the process.")
179. Lamoreaux and Sokoloff, 2002, *ibid.*
180. *Ibid.*
181. *Ibid.*
182. *See,* for example, R. C. Dreyfuss, Are business method patents bad for business? *Santa Clara Computer & High Techn. L. J.* 16 (2), 263–280 (2000) and Hunt, 2010, *supra* note 20.
183. Bessen and Meurer, 2008, p. 219.
184. *See* V. Chiappetta, TRIP-ping over business method patents, *Vanderbilt J. of Trans. L.* 37, 181–202 (2004). *See also* V. Chiappetta, Defining the

proper scope of internet patents: If We Don't Know Where We Want to Go, We're Unlikely to Get There, *Michigan Telecom.s & Tech. Rev.* 7, (2000–2001).

185. Stevens points out that "The Court, in sum, never provides a satisfying account of what constitutes an unpatentable abstract idea." *Bilski.*
186. *Bilski.* Stevens also expresses concerns about the "'potential vagueness' of business method patents, *eBay Inc.*, 547 U. S., p. 397."
187. *See* J. R. Allison and E. H. Tiller, The business method patent Myth, *Berkeley Tech. L. J.* 18 (4), 987–1084 (2003). ("Overall, our data show that Internet business method patents were no worse than patents in general in the late 1990s. Indeed, our empirical evidence suggests that they may have been better than average.")
188. Bessen and Meurer, 2008, *supra* note 22.
189. Significant growth in software patenting is due to relaxed patent standards rather than increased productivity of software patents, *see* J. Bessen and R. M. Hunt, An empirical look at software patents, *J.of Econ. & Manag. Strat.* 16, 157–189, p. 181 (2007), ("Eliminating the subject matter exclusion and reducing the nonobviousness and enablement requirements may have made software patents much easier (less costly) to obtain. Patents with more abstract claims may have had broader scope, increasing the appropriability each patent delivered. Both served to decrease the cost of appropriability.")
190. U.S. Patent No. 5,960,411 (September 12, 1997).
191. U.S. Patent No. 5,797,127 (December 31, 1999). *See* Eugene Quinn (2002).
192. Dreyfuss, 2000, p. 279.
193. E. R. Quinn, The proliferation of electronic commerce patents: Don't Blame the PTO, *Rutgers Comp. & Tech. L. J.* 28 (1), 121–154, p. 124 (2002).
194. *See* J. J. Dratler, Alice in Wonderland meets the U.S. patent system, *Akron L. Rev.* 38, 299–336, pp. 302–303 (2005). ("The alleged 'inventor' there had written a pedestrian computer program to manage a certain type of investment vehicle, a 'hub and spoke' investment partnership. The program made pedestrian arithmetic calculations, mostly as required by rules of the SEC and other accounting and tax authorities. Nothing in the claims at issue addressed any particular algorithm, programming technique or method of programming. For all those claims revealed, the alleged 'inventor' had done nothing more than write a pedestrian computer program for

performing routine arithmetic calculations dictated by legal authority, using programming languages, techniques and computers invented — if at all — by someone else.") *See also* J. J. Dratler, Does Lord Darcy yet live? The case against software and business-method patents, *Santa Clara L. Rev.* 43, 823 (2003).

195. A. B. Jaffe and J. Lerner, Innovation and its discontents, *Capitalism and Soc.*1 (3), 1–36 (2006). Available at: http://www.bepress.com/cas/vol1/iss3/art3.
196. Bessen and Meurer, *supra* note 22, Chapter 11 (2008).
197. *See* R. P. Merges, As many as 6 impossible patents before breakfast: Property rights for business concepts and patent system reform, *Berkeley Tech. L. J.* 14 (2), 577–615 (1999).
198. *See* Merges, 1999, *ibid.* and M. A. Lemley, Rational ignorance at the patent office, *Northwestern Univ. L. Rev.*95, 1495–1532 (2001).
199. Kieff, 2003, *supra* note 58. *See* also F. S. Kieff, The case for preferring patent-validity litigation over second-window review and gold-plated patents: When one size doesn't fit all, How Could Two Do the Trick? *University of Pennsylvania L. Rev.* 157, 1937–1963 (2009).
200. D. A. Hounshell, *From the American System to Mass Production, 1800–1932: The Development of Manufacturing Technology in the United States.* Baltimore, MD: Johns Hopkins University Press, 1985.
201. G. S. Becker, *Human Capital: A Theoretical and Empirical Analysis with Special Reference to Education,* 2nd ed. New York: National Bureau of Economic Research, 1975.
202. Technological change also can affect employment levels and the distribution of income; *see* D. Acemoglu, Changes in unemployment and wage inequality: An alternative theory and some evidence, *American Econ. Rev.* 89 (5), 1259–1278 (1999); D. Acemoglu, Technical change, inequality and the labor market, *J. of Econ. Lite.* 40 (1), 7–72 (2002).
203. E. Hopkins, Working hours and conditions during the industrial revolution: A re-appraisal, *Econ. Hist. Rev.* 35 (1), 52–66 (1982).
204. *See* Hopkins (1982, 66): "It follows that to suggest that during the classic years of the Industrial Revolution the majority of workers in this region (and perhaps elsewhere) were forced to assume new work habits and become the slaves of a new time discipline is really a very doubtful proposition, and its unthinking repetition can serve only to perpetuate a historical myth."

205. *See* S. King and G. Timmins, *Making Sense of the Industrial Revolution: English Economy and Society, 1700–1850.* Manchester: Manchester University Press, p. 68–100 (2001).
206. R. M. Hartwell, Observes that "On any historical accounting, the industrial revolution in England began one of the great discontinuities of history marking 'the great divide' between a world of slow economic growth, in which population and real incomes were increasing slowly or not at all, and a world of much faster economic growth, in which population has increased at an almost frightening rate and in which there have been sustained increases in real income per head." *See* R. M. Hartwell, Editor's Introduction. In *The Causes of the Industrial Revolution in England.* R. M. Hartwell, ed., 1–30. London: Methuen & Co.
207. For the period 1781–1851 of the Industrial Revolution, workers experienced "impressive net gains in the standard of life." *See* P. H. Lindert and J. G. Williamson, English Workers' living standards during the industrial revolution: A new look, *Econ. Hist. Rev.* 36 (1), 1–25 (1983). For a standard pessimistic view, *see, for example,* C. H. Feinstein, Pessimism perpetuated: Real wages and the standard of living in Britain during and after the Industrial Revolution, *J. of Econ. Hist.* 58 (3), 625–658 (1998).
208. D. S. Landes, *The Wealth and Poverty of Nations: Why Some Are So Rich and Some So Poor.* New York: Norton, p. 186 (1998).
209. For an overview, *see* D. S. Landes, *The Unbound Prometheus: Technological Change and Industrial Development in Western Europe from 1750 to the Present.* Cambridge: Cambridge University Press, 1969.
210. Data for the period 1870–1979 exhibit "historically unprecedented growth in productivity, gross domestic product per capita and exports and the remarkable convergence of productivities of industrialized market economies." *See* W. J. Baumol, Productivity growth, convergence, and welfare: What the long-run data show, *American Econ. Rev.* 76 (5), 1072–1085 (1986).
211. Landes, 1998, *supra* note 208.
212. D. H. Autor, F. Levy, and R. J. Murnane, The skill content of recent technological change: An empirical exploration, *Quarterly J. of Econ.* 118 (4), 1279–1333. D. H. Autor, F. Levy, and R. J. Murnane consider data from the period 1960–1998. *See also* D. H. Autor, L. F. Katz, and M. S. Kearney, Trends in U.S. wage inequality: Revising the revisionists, *Rev. of Econ. and Stati.* 90 (2), 300–323 (2008).

213. *See* D. H. Autor, F. Levy, and R. J. Murnane, *ibid*., p. 1279. On complementarity between computers and skilled labor, *see also* Z. Griliches, Capital-Skill complementarity, *Rev. of Econ. and Stati.* 51 (4), 465–468 (1969); C. Goldin and L. F. Katz, The origins of technology-skill complementarity, *Quarterly J. of Econ.* 113 (3), 693–732 (1998); F. Levy and R. J. Murnane, With What Skills Are Computers a Complement? *American Econ. Rev. Pap. and Proce.* 86 (2), 258–262 (1996); E. Brynjolfsson and L. M. Hitt, Beyond computation: Information technology, organizational transformation and business performance, *J. of Econ. Perspectives*, 14 (4), 23–48 (2000).
214. *See* L. Autor and R. J. Murnane, *supra* note 212 p. 1279 ("Translating task shifts into education demand, the model can explain 60 percent of the estimated relative demand shift favoring college labor during 1970–1998.")
215. *See* the survey and discussion in Brynjolfsson and Hitt, *supra* note 213.
216. *See* B. P. Bosworth and J. E. Triplett, The early 21st century U.S. productivity expansion is *Still* in services, *Interna. Produ. Moni.* 14, 3–19 (2007a); B. P. Bosworth and J. E. Triplett, Services productivity in the United States: Griliches' services volume revisited. In E. R. Berndt and C. M. Hulten, eds., *Hard-to-Measure Goods and Services: Essays in Memory of Zvi Griliches.* 413–448 (2007b). Chicago: University of Chicago Press; J. E. Triplett and B. P. Bosworth, *Services Productivity in the United States: New Sources of Economic Growth*. Washington, D.C.: Brookings Institution Press, 2004; J. E. Triplettand B. P. Bosworth, 'Baumol's Disease' Has Been Cured: IT and Multifactor Productivity in U.S. Services Industries. In D. W. Jansen, ed., *The New Economy and Beyond: Past, Present, and Future,* 34–71 (2006). Cheltenham, U.K.: Edgar Elgar. *See also* D. Pilat, The ICT productivity paradox: Insights from micro data, *OECD Econ. Stud.* 2004 (1), 37–64 (2004).
217. *See* Coase, 1937; 1988; 1994, pp. 3–14.
218. J. Deighton, L. Kornfeld, and M. Gerra, Economic value of the advertising-supported internet ecosystem, January, Interactive Advertising Bureau, New York, NY, p. 116 (2017). https://www.iab.com/wp-content/uploads/2017/03/Economic-Value-Study-2017-FINAL2.pdf.
219. Deighton, *et al.*, 2017, *ibid.*
220. *Ibid.*
221. B. K. Atrostic, P. Boegh-Nielsen, K. Motohashi, and S. Nguyen, IT, productivity and growth in enterprises: New results from international micro data. In OECD, *The Economic Impact of ICT—Measurement, Evidence and Implications*. 279–300 (2004). Paris: OECD. *See also* B. K. Atrostic,

J. Gates, and R. Jarmin, Measuring the electronic economy: Current status and next steps. Center for economic studies, U.S. Bureau of the Census, Working Paper No. CES-WP-00-10, 2000. Available at: http://www.census.gov/econ/estats/papers/3.pdf.

222. Atrostic *et al.*, 2004, *ibid.*
223. T. Clayton, C. Criscuolo, P. Goodridge, and K. Waldron, Enterprise E-Commerce: Measurement and impact. In OECD, *The Economic Impact of ICT—Measurement, Evidence and Implications*, Paris: OECD, 241–260 (2004).
224. Clayton *et al.*, *ibid.*
225. *See* Spulber 2009b, 1999, 2009a.
226. Spulber 2009b.
227. Firms provide markets with mechanisms of spontaneous order in addition to prices, including marketing, sales, media, and other types of mass communication. On the role of firms in establishing and operating markets and in the design of market microstructure, see D. F. Spulber, 1998. *The Market Makers: How Leading Companies Create and Win Markets.* New York: McGraw Hill/ Business Week Books; Spulber, 1999.
228. D. F. Spulber 2009b.
229. Based on U.S. GDP data in Lindberg and Monaldo, 2009, *supra* note 68.
230. *See* Lindberg and Monaldo, 2009, *supra* note 68. An industry's general product by origin (GPO) or value added equals its gross output (sales or receipts and other operating income plus inventory change) minus its intermediate inputs (consumption of goods and services purchased from other industries or imported); *see* Yuskavage (1994).
231. United States Department of Commerce. 1994. *U.S. Industrial Outlook 1994.* U.S. Government Printing Office.
232. *Ibid.*, 38–1.
233. *See* U.S. Dept. of Commerce, 1994, *ibid.* pp. 38–2. Measuring the wholesale trade industry can be difficult. As noted (*ibid.*, 38–2), retail sales to industry are no longer included in the Census Bureau's sales totals for wholesale establishments. However, manufacturer's sales branches, and agents, brokers, and commission merchants continue to be included in the GDP. It quotes an industry survey for 1992 in which total wholesale was divided as follows: 45 percent through merchant wholesalers, 7 percent through agents, brokers, and commission merchants, 26 percent through alternative channels, and manufacturer's sales branches distributed 23 percent. Clearly, some of the wholesaler's traditional activities are being

carried out by retailers, and are reflected in value added of the retail trade. Also, some of the strategic alliances between retailers and manufacturers appear to reflect increased wholesaling responsibilities for manufacturers, which show as a contribution to manufacturing value added.

234. In an earlier study (Spulber 1996), I choose to exclude business services that did not represent intermediation. The current focus is on transactions generally so that it includes such activities as accounting and legal services.
235. United States Census Bureau. 2006. *Annual Survey of Manufactures, Statistics for Industry Groups and Industries: 2005.* Washington, D.C.: U.S. Government Printing Office.
236. Census Bureau, *ibid.*
237. *Ibid.*
238. See J. Sikander and V. Sarma, A prescriptive architecture for electronic commerce and digital marketing. Microsoft Corporation white paper (2010). Available at: http://www.microsoft.com/commerceserver/en/us/white-papers.aspx and Microsoft Corporation. 1997. Microsoft Internet Commerce Strategy: A Foundation for Doing Business on the Internet. Available at: http://msdn.microsoft.com/en-us/library/ms953599.aspx.
239. USPTO. 2010.
240. *Ibid.*
241. J. Temple, Google Instant predicts What Users are Searching For. *San Francisco Chronicle,* September 8 (2010).
242. US Patent 6,269,361 (Davis *et al.*, July, 31, 2001). *See also* http://www.searchenginehistory.com/.
243. These included AlltheWeb, Altavista, AskJeeves, Hotbot, IWon, Lycos, Teoma, MSN, and Yahoo! *See* A. Ellam, Overture and Google: Internet Pay-Per-Click (PPC) Advertising Auctions. London Business School Case Study CS-03-022 (2003).
244. US Patent 6,269,361 (Inventors: Davis *et al.*, July, 31, 2001, Assignee: GoTo.com, Pasadena, CA).
245. *Ibid.*
246. *Ibid.*
247. S. Olsen, Google, Yahoo Bury the Legal Hatchet, *CNET News*, August 9 (2004). Available at: http://news.cnet.com/Google,-Yahoo-bury-the-legal-hatchet/2100-1024_3-5302421.html.
248. In 2008, Google search and content had about 75 percent of Internet advertising expenditures, Yahoo! search and content had 20 percent, and

Microsoft had less than 5 percent. *See* Efficient Frontier. 2009. U.S. Search Engine Performance Report: Q4 2008. January, White Paper.

249. www.chemconnect.com.
250. *eBay Inc., et al., Petitioners v. Mercexchange*, L. L. C., 547 U. S. 388 (2006).
251. B. Steil, Changes in the ownership and governance of securities exchanges: Causes and consequences. In R. Herring and R. E. Litan, eds., *Brookings-Wharton Papers on Financial Services: 2002,* 61–91 (2002). Washington, D.C.: Brookings Institution Press.
252. *Ibid.*
253. H. R. Stoll,. Comment and discussion. In R. Herring and R. E. Litan, eds., *Brookings-Wharton Papers on Financial Services: 2002,* 83–90 (2002). Washington, D.C.: Brookings Institution Press.
254. Sikander and Sarma consider business method inventions in relation to Microsoft's e-commerce strategies: "Over time, the e-commerce function has evolved from a component of the retail strategy to a core strategic enabler for businesses. For most retailers, e-commerce represents their fastest growing revenue channel and a key asset from which they can build and maintain relationships with their customers. Retailers today are focused on delivering consistent experiences for customers across channels to enable revenue growth, brand loyalty, and innovation." *See* Sikander and Sarma, *supra* note 238.
255. *See* Sikander and Sarma, *supra* note 238.
256. *Ibid*, p. 14.

Chapter 4

1. *See* W. G. Park, International patent protection: 1960–2005, *Res. Pol'y* 37, 761, 766 (2008); D. Riker, Intellectual property rights and international receipts of royalties and licensing fees 1 (USITC, Working Paper No. 2014-08C, 2014), https://www.usitc.gov/publications/332/ec201408c.pdf.
2. *See* Z. Yang, Damaging royalties: An overview of reasonable royalty damages, *Berkeley Tech. L.J.* 29, 647, 648 (2014); *see also* R. J. Epstein and P. Malherbe, Reasonable royalty patent infringement damages after uniloc, *AIPLA Q.J.* 39, 3, 5 (2011); L. S. Keele, Res'Q'ing patent infringement damages after ResQNET: The dangers of litigation licenses as evidence of reasonable royalty, *Tex. Intell. Prop. L.J.* 20, 181, 183 (2011); E. S. Lee, Historical perspectives on reasonable royalty damages and current

congressional efforts for reform, *UCLA J.L. & Tech.* 13, 1, 1 (2009) ("[T]he issue of patent damages has become a major point of contention and the subject of debate by legal scholars, legislators, and heads of business."); C. B. Seaman, Reconsidering the Georgia-Pacific standard for reasonable royalty patent damages, *BYU L. Rev.* 2010, 1661, 1661 (2010) ("Determining damages for infringement is one of the most important – and controversial – issues in current patent litigation.").

3. P. S. Menell *et al.*, *Fed. Judicial Ctr.*, Patent case management judicial guide 7–17 (3rd ed. 2016), https://www.fjc.gov/sites/default/files/2017/PCMJG3d_2016_final.pdf.
4. Yang, *supra* note 2, p. 648.
5. *Ibid.*, p. 652.
6. *See* D. F. Spulber, Intellectual contract and intellectual law, *J. Tech. L. & Pol'y*, (2018), Fall, 23(1), https://www.journaloftechlaw.org/issues/23-1-spulber/, pp. 1–67.
7. Elsewhere, I introduce the concepts of "Intellectual Contract" and "Intellectual Tort" within the context of new framework that I refer to as "Intellectual Law." *Ibid.*, p. 1.
8. C. Barry *et al.*, PwC, 2017 Patent Litigation Study: Change on the Horizon? 4 (May 2017), https://www.pwc.com/us/en/forensic-services/publications/assets/2017-patent-litigation-study.pdf [hereinafter 2017 Patent Litigation Study].
9. L. B. Pincus, Computation of damages in patent infringement actions, *Harv. J.L. & Tech.* 5, 95, 120 (1991) ("Damages in the form of a reasonable royalty are generally awarded when the calculation of lost profits is considered too speculative, or when no actual damage in the form of lost sales has occurred or has been proven.").
10. 2017 Patent Litigation Study, *supra* note 8, p. 11.
11. *Ibid.*
12. *See* J. S. Masur, The use and misuse of patent licenses, *Nw. U.L. Rev.* 110, 115, 119 (2015) ("But the result has been to leave courts almost entirely at sea and at the mercy of the parties' experts attempting to assess damages."). The courts are rejecting arbitrary heuristics, although some argue in favor of heuristics as a means of lowering legal costs. *See* T. Cotter, Patent damages heuristics, *Tex. Intell. Prop. L.J.* 25, 159, 162–63, 211 (2019).
13. Masur, *supra* note 12, pp. 122–23.

14. *See* C. E. Brixen and C. E. Meis, Codifying the daubert trilogy: The amendment to federal rule of evidence 702, *Jurimetrics* 40, 527, 528 (1999); M. H. Graham, The expert witness predicament: Determining "Reliable" under the gatekeeping test of Daubert, Kumho, and proposed amended rule 702 of the federal rules of evidence, *U. Miami L. Rev*. 54, 317, 356 (2000); M. C. McCarthy, Helpful or reasonably reliable analyzing the expert witness's methodology under federal rules of evidence 702 and 703, *Cornell L. Rev.* 77, 350, 353 (1991); C. L. Montz, Trial judges as scientific gatekeepers after daubert, joiner, kumho tire, and amended rule 702: Is anyone still seriously buying this? *UWLA L. Rev*. 33, 87, 90 (2001).
15. *Daubert v. Merrell Dow Pharmaceuticals, Inc.,* 509 U.S. 579, 592–93 (1993); *see also* Federal Rules of Evidence. 104 ("The court must decide any preliminary question about whether a witness is qualified, a privilege exists, or evidence is admissible."); Federal Rules of Evidence 702 ("A witness who is qualified as an expert by knowledge, skill, experience, training, or education may testify in the form of an opinion or otherwise if: (a) the expert's scientific, technical, or other specialized knowledge will help the trier of fact to understand the evidence or to determine a fact in issue; (b) the testimony is based on sufficient facts or data; (c) the testimony is the product of reliable principles and methods; and (d) the expert has reliably applied the principles and methods to the facts of the case."); *Kumho Tire Co. v. Carmichael*, 526 U.S. 137, 141 (1999); *IP Innovation, L.L.C. v. Red Hat, Inc.*, 705 F. Supp. 2d 687, 691 (E.D. Tex. 2010) ("The parties are reminded that expert testimony on the topic of damages will not be allowed absent a firm basis in accepted economic principles with an eye to the facts of this record."). According to the Federal Rules of Evidence, Rule 702. Testimony by an Expert Witnesses:
"A witness who is qualified as an expert by knowledge, skill, experience, training, or education may testify in the form of an opinion or otherwise if: (a) the expert's scientific, technical, or other specialized knowledge will help the trier of fact to understand the evidence or to determine a fact in issue; (b) the testimony is based on sufficient facts or data; (c) the testimony is the product of reliable principles and methods; and (d) the expert has reliably applied the principles and methods to the facts of the case."
16. R.D. Blair and T. F. Cotter, An economic analysis of damages rules in intellectual property law, *Wm. & Mary L. Rev*. 39, 1585, 1615 (1997); *see also*

M. A. Lemley, Should patent iinfringement require proof of copying? *Mich. L. Rev*. 105, 1525, 1525 (2006) ("Patent infringement is a strict liability offense."); R. P. Merges, Contracting into liability rules: Intellectual property rights and collective rights organizations, *Calif. L. Rev.* 84, 1293, 1294 (1996); R. P. Merges, Intellectual property rights and bargaining breakdown: The case of blocking patents, Tenn. *L. Rev*. 62, 75, 75 (1994).

17. S. E. Sterk, Strict liability and negligence in property theory, *U. Pa. L. Rev.* 160, 2129, 2156 (2012).
18. *See* R. D. Blair and T. F. Cotter, Strict liability and its alternatives in patent law, *Berkeley Tech. L.J.* 799, 800 (2002) ("Patent infringement is often characterized as a strict liability tort, and in some ways it is. But it is not strict liability in the purest sense, or at least not in the sense in which the term is used in general tort law.").
19. T. Sichelman, Purging patent law of private law remedies, *Tex. L. Rev.* 92, 517, 519 (2013); *see also* J. C. Jarosz and M. J. Chapman, The hypothetical negotiation and reasonable royalty damages: The tail wagging the dog, *Stan. Tech. L. Rev.* 16, 769, 786 (2013) ("[R]easonable royalty damages are a form of general damages intended to compensate for the tort of patent infringement.").
20. K. N. Hylton, Enhanced damages for patent infringement: A normative approach, *Rev. Litig.* 36, 417, 421 (2017).
21. B. N. Anand and T. Khanna, The structure of licensing contracts, *J. Indus. Econ.* 48, 103, 103 (2000).
22. P. B. C. Jones, Violation of a patent license restriction: Breach of contract or patent infringement? *IDEA* 33, 225, 226 (1992) ("[A] patent licensing agreement is a contract which is governed by principles of state contract law.")
23. *Licensing Agreement*, Black's Law Dictionary (2d ed. Online), https://thelawdictionary.org/licensing-agreement/ (defining licensing agreement as "[w]ritten contract between the owner/licensor of a patent, copyright, trademark, know-how, service mark, or other intellectual property, and a licensee to use, make, or sell copies of the original .... Commercialization of a technology is a major purpose for licensing agreements. These contracts typically (1) limit the licensee's scope or field, (2) make the license exclusive or nonexclusive, (3) demands royalties or other compensation if further licensing occurs by the licensee.")
24. U.S. Patent and Trademark Office, Manual of Patent Examining Procedure § 301 (9th ed. 2017), https://www.uspto.gov/web/offices/pac/mpep/s301.html#d0e17687.

25. *See* discussion *infra* Section II.C.
26. *See* Spulber, *supra* note 6, at 17.
27. *Ibid.*, p. 12.
28. *Ibid.*, p. 15.
29. 35 U.S.C. § 284 (2012) ("Upon finding for the claimant the court shall award the claimant damages adequate to compensate for the infringement, but in no event less than a reasonable royalty for the use made of the invention by the infringer, together with interest and costs as fixed by the court.").
30. *See* Federal Trade Commission, The evolving IP marketplace: Aligning patent notice and remedies with competition 19–20 (2011), https://www.ftc.gov/sites/default/files/documents/reports/evolving-ip-marketplace-aligning-patent-notice-and-remedies-competition-report-federal-trade/110307patentreport.pdf, ("Patent law appropriately implements this concept by awarding reasonable royalty damages based on what a willing licensor and willing licensee would have agreed to in a hypothetical negotiation."); *see also* Jarosz and Chapman, *supra* note 19, p. 772 ("[T]he hypothetical negotiation construct was originally introduced simply as one of many considerations to estimate such damages. It has since evolved into the primary tool used to determine reasonable royalty damages.").
31. *See, e.g., Fujifilm Corp. v. Benun*, 605 F.3d 1366, 1372 (*Fed. Cir.* 2010) ("To determine a reasonable royalty, a jury must find the royalty that would have been agreed to in a hypothetical negotiation between a willing licensee and willing licensors at the time infringement began."); *Georgia-Pacific Corp. v. U.S. Plywood Corp.*, 318 F. Supp. 1116, 1121 (S.D.N.Y. 1970).
("The ['willing buyer and willing seller'] rule is more a statement of approach than a tool of analysis. It requires consideration not only of the amount that a willing licensee would have paid for the patent license but also of the amount that a willing licensor would have accepted. What a willing licensor and a willing licensee would have agreed upon in a suppositious negotiation for a reasonable royalty would entail consideration of the specific factors previously mentioned, to the extent of their relevance.")
32. *See* Jarosz and Chapman, *supra* note 19, pp. 785–86.
33. *Rite-Hite Corp. v. Kelley Co.*, 56 F.3d 1538, 1554 n.13 (*Fed. Cir.* 1995) (en banc) ("The hypothetical negotiation is often referred to as a 'willing licensor/willing licensee' negotiation. However, this is an inaccurate, and even absurd, characterization when, as here, the patentee does not wish to grant a license.").

34. *See generally* F. S. Kieff and A. Layne-Farrar, Incentive effects from different approaches to holdup mitigation surrounding patent remedies and standard-setting organizations, *J. Competition L. & Econ.* 9, 1091 (2013).
35. For the discussion of the "retrospective or *ex post* model," *see* The Sedona Conference, Commentary on patent reasonable royalty determinations: A project of the Sedona Conference working group on patent damages and remedies, at 22–23 (2016).
"The Retrospective Model states: The royalty shall be determined by considering what (a) fully informed, (b) willing, and (c) reasonable persons (d) in the positions of the patent owner (or owners throughout the period of infringement) and the infringer would agree to at the time of trial as a fair price for the license, (e) taking into account all relevant facts and circumstances occurring before or during that period, while (f) factoring out any switching costs, lock-in costs, patent-holdup costs, or other similar costs that are not attributable to the value of the patented technology.... a. 'Fully informed' means a licensor and licensee who both know all relevant facts available to them, not just the facts actually known to the individuals at the plaintiff and the defendant entities at the relevant times."
Ibid.
36. *Ibid.*, p. 9.
37. *Ibid.*, p. 25.
"Another advantage of the Retrospective Model is that it better aligns with the plain language of the patent damages statute to provide adequate compensation for "the use made of the invention" by the infringer because it allows the trier-of-fact to consider *actual* infringing use, as opposed to only *projected* infringing use. By the same token, the Retrospective Model allows the trier-of-fact to award a reasonable royalty directly related to the actual harm caused by the accused infringer's unauthorized use of the patented invention, instead of the expected harm of the infringement viewed from at a fixed point in time before any infringement has actually occurred."
Ibid.
38. *See In re Innovatio IP Ventures*, No. 11 C 9308, 2013 WL 5593609, at *58–59 (N.D. Ill. October 3, 2012) ("[T]he court will not adjust the RAND rate in light of pre-litigation uncertainty about the essentiality of a given patent."); *see also LaserDynamics, Inc. v. Quanta Computer, Inc.*, 694 F.3d 51, 76 (Fed. Cir. 2012).

39. *See* discussion *infra* Section II.C.
40. *See* O. W. Holmes, Jr., The path of the law, *Harv. L. Rev*. 457, 10, 463 (1897).
41. *See Panduit Corp. v. Stahlin Bros. Fibre Works,* 575 F.2d 1152, 1159 (6th Cir. 1978).
42. *See* Spulber, *supra* note 6, pp. 47–49.
43. *Ibid.,* pp. 17–19.
44. *See* Holmes, *supra* note 40, pp. 463–64.
45. *Ibid.*
46. "In my opinion no one will understand the true theory of contract or be able even to discuss some fundamental questions intelligently until he has understood that all contracts are formal, that the making of a contract depends not on the agreement of two minds in one intention, but on the agreement of two sets of external signs — not on the parties' having meant the same thing but on their having said the same thing."
    Ibid., p. 464.
47. *See generally* P. Dyck, Note, Beyond confusion – Survey evidence of consumer demand and the entire market value rule, *Hastings Sci. & Tech. L.J.* 4, 209 (2011); J. D. Putnam and T. A. Williams, The smallest salable patent-practicing unit (SSPPU): Theory and Evidence (2016), https://ssrn.com/abstract=2835617.
48. *See* Spulber, *supra* note 6, p. 13.
49. *Ibid.,* p. 47.
50. *See ibid.,*p. 28.
51. *Econ. Research Serv. U.S. Dep't of Agric.*, The public policy background and the economic case for intellectual property, USDA, https://www.ers.usda.gov/webdocs/publications/45080/17597_err15b_1_.pdf?v=0 (last visited November 14, 2018).
52. *See generally World Intellectual Prop. Org.,* Licensing of intellectual property assets; Advantages and Disadvantages, WIPO, http://www.wipo.int/export/sites/www/sme/en/documents/pdf/licensing.pdf (last visited Nov. 14, 2018).
53. *Ibid.*
54. For discussions of lost profits, *see* J. J. Anton and D. A. Yao, Finding "Lost" profits: An equilibrium analysis of patent infringement damages, *J.L. Econ. & Org*. 23, 186, 187 (2007); R. J. Epstein, *The* Market share rule with price erosion: Patent infringement lost profits damages after crystal, *AIPLA Q.J.* 31, 1, 4 (2003); J. L. Harrison, The lost profits measure of damages in

price enhancement cases, *Minn. L. Rev*. 64, 751, 753 (1980); M. A. Lemley, Distinguishing lost profits from reasonable royalties, *Wm. & Mary L. Rev*. 51, 655, 656 (2009); R. M. Lloyd, Proving lost profits after daubert: Five questions every court should ask before admitting expert testimony, *U. Rich. L. Rev.* 41, 379, 380 (2007); G. J. Werden *et al.*, *Economic Analysis of Lost Profits from Patent Infringement with and Without Noninfringing Substitutes*, *AIPLA Q. J*. 27, 305, 306 (1999).

55. Epstein, *supra* note 54, pp. 3–4.
56. D. F. Spulber, How patents provide the foundation of the market for inventions, *J. Competition L. & Econ.* 11, 271, 271 (2015).
57. *See generally* R. H. Coase, The problem of social cost, *J.L. & Econ.* 56, 837 (2013).
58. *See generally* K. Binmore, Nash bargaining Theory I-III, in *The* Economics of Bargaining, 27–46, 61–76, 239–56 (K. Binmore and P. Dasgupta eds., 1987); J. C. Harsanyi, A Bargaining model for the cooperative n-person game, in *Contributions to the Theory of Mathematical Studies* 40 (A. W. Tucker and R. D. Luce ed., 1959); A. Roth, *Axiomatic Models of Bargaining* (Springer-Verlag 1979); K. Binmore, A. Rubinstein, and A. Wolinsky, The Nash bargaining solution in economic modelling, *Rand J. Econ.* 176 17, (1986); J. C. Harsanyi, A simplified bargaining model for the n-Person cooperative game, *Int'l. Econ. R.* 4, 80 (1963); J. F. Nash, Jr., The bargaining problem, *Econometrica* 18, 155 (1950); J. Nash, Two person cooperative games, *Econometrica* 21, 128 (1953).
59. R. Zeckhauser, The challenge of contrasting for technological information, *Proc. Nat'l. Acad. Sci. U.S. Am.* 93, 12743, 12743 (1996).
60. The ABCs of licensing intellectual property, *Nutter* (Apr. 1, 2010), https://www.nutter.com/ip-law-bulletin/the-abcs-of-licensing-intellectual-property.
61. This was settled in 2017. *See* D. Palmer, Apple and Nokia Settle Patent Licensing Lawsuit, *ZDNet* (May 23, 2017, 11:35 AM), https://www.zdnet.com/article/apple-and-nokia-settle-patent-licensing-lawsuit/.
62. S. Brachmann, TiVo stock pops 17 percent in trading after ITC judge issues Section 337 final initial determination against comcast, *IPWatchdog* (May 31, 2017), http://www.ipwatchdog.com/2017/05/31/tivo-stock-pops-17-percent-after-itc-judge-issues-section-337-final-initial-determination-against-comcast/id=83868/.
63. *See* Jones, *supra* note 22, p. 229. ("[B]reach of a license restriction may give rise to a suit for breach of contract or an infringement suit."); O.

Ben-Shahar, Damages for unlicensed use, *U. Chi. L. Rev.* 78, 7, 9 (2011) ("This wrongful action by the licensee could be both a breach of the license contract, giving rise to the common law's contract remedies, and an infringement of the licensor's intellectual property, with remedies provided by statute."). On historical jurisdictional issues, *see* D. S. Chisum, The allocation of jurisdiction between state and federal courts in patent litigation, *Wash. L. Rev.* 46, 633, 633 (1971).

64. *Tekelec, Inc. v. Verint Sys., Inc.*, 708 F.3d 658, 663 (5th Cir. 2013).
65. J. C. Paul, D. B. Kacedon, and R. B. Cassady, Licensee's breach of agreement provides licensor with ability to Sue licensee for infringement, *Finnegan LES Insights* (February 10, 2015), https://www.finnegan.com/en/insights/licensee-s-breach-of-agreement-provides-licensor-with-ability-to.html?news=96fbfb22-5002-496d-921d-4d059ce52710.
66. *See, e.g.*, J. Gamet, Ericsson sues Apple after failing to reach patent license agreement, *Mac Observer* (February 27, 2015, 11:20 AM), https://www.macobserver.com/tmo/article/ericsson-sues-apple-after-failing-to-reach-patent-license-agreement.
67. *eBay Inc. v. MerExchange, L.L.C.*, 547 U.S. 388, 390 (2006).
68. *Ibid.*
69. *Unwired Planet v. Huawei*, [2017] EWHC 711 (Pat) [154]–[55], (Eng.).
70. *See* M. Daniels, Comcast, manufacturers infringe 2 Rovi patents: ITC Judge, Law360 (May 31, 2017, 10:23 PM), https://www.law360.com/articles/929807/comcast-manufacturers-infringe-2-rovi-patents-itc-judge. I provided Rovi with an expert report in the form of a rebuttal statement in this matter. Rovi acquired TiVo and changed its name to TiVo. *See* D. Lieberman, Rovi changes Its Name to TiVo as it Closes Acquisition of DVR Pioneer, *Deadline* (September 8, 2016, 7:14 AM), http://deadline.com/2016/09/rovi-buys-tivo-changes-name-1201815210/.
71. *See* Spulber, *supra* note 6, p. 5.
72. *Ibid.*
73. *Ibid.,* p. 19.
74. On relationships and contracts, *see* generally I. R. Macneil, Contracts: Exchange transactions and relations (2d ed. 1978); I. R. Macneil, The relational theory of contract: Selected works of Ian Macneil (David Campbell ed., 2001).
75. D. F. Spulber, Patent licensing and bargaining with innovative complements and substitutes, *Res. Econ. 693*, 70, 693 (2016).

76. *Ibid.,* p. 708.
77. *Ibid.,* p. 694. Licensing contracts offered by patent pools are an exception that proves the rule. The patent pool and licensees usually do not negotiate licensing contract provisions including royalties. Patent owners within the patent pool, however, negotiate among themselves to obtain contract provisions including royalties. *Ibid.,* p. 710, n.23.
78. *Ibid.,* pp. 708–09.
79. J. Stone, How to license a patent & royalties, *Chron*, https://smallbusiness.chron.com/license-patent-royalties-80018.html (last visited October 2, 2018).
80. *Ibid.*
81. *See* Spulber, *supra* note 6, p. 7.
82. This classification is attributed to Marshall Phelps who served as chief of global IP at IBM and Microsoft, *see* N. Östman, How to create the 'Pull' for patent licensing? *LinkedIn* (September 6, 2016), https://www.linkedin.com/pulse/how-create-pull-patent-licensing-niklas-%C3%B6stman?trk=prof-post; *see also* D. L. Cohen, Licensing standard-essential patents on FRAND Terms (2017), http://kidonip.com/wp-content/uploads/2017/07/Cohen_Paper.pdf.
83. Patent licensing and enforcement, *IPOfferings*, https://www.ipofferings.com/patent-licensing-enforcement.html (last visited November 14, 2018).
84. Östman, *supra* note 82.
85. *Ibid.*
86. Cohen, *supra* note 82, p. 2.
87. *Ibid.,* p. 14.
88. *Ibid.,*p. 2.
89. *Ibid.*
90. *Ibid.*
91. *Ibid.*
92. *See* Spulber, *supra* note 56, p. 308.
93. *See* Cohen, *supra* note 82, pp. 8–9.
94. Fed. Trade Comm'n, The Evolving IP Marketplace: Aligning Patent Notice and Remedies With Competition 29 (2011).
95. *Ibid.,* p. 2.
96. *See* Spulber, *supra* note 6, p. 20.
97. *See generally* B. Z. Khan, Trolls and other patent inventions: Economic history and the patent controversy in the twenty-first century, *Geo. Mason L. Rev.* 21, 825, 837 (2014); J. O. Lanjouw and M. Schankerman, Characteristics of patent litigation: A window on competition, *Rand J. Econ.* 32, 129 (2001);

J. O. Lanjouw and M. Schankerman, Protecting intellectual property rights: Are small firms handicapped? J.L. & Econ. 47, 45, 58 (2004); R. D. Katznelson, A century of patent litigation in perspective (November 17, 2014), https://ssrn.com/abstract=2503140 or http://dx.doi.org/10.2139/ssrn.2503140.

98. Katznelson, *supra* note 97, p. 7.
99. The costs of monitoring can affect incentives to infringe, *see* generally C. Crampes & C. Langinier, Litigation and settlement in patent infringement cases, *Rand J. of Econ.* 33, 258, 261 (2002).
100. *See* Cohen, *supra* note 82, p. 2 ("The accumulation of laws, regulations, economic analysis and polite lies licensing executives like to tell each other when negotiating over an SEP license (i.e., the F/RAND framework) helps obscure the fact that if the threats are not credible, SEPs, like other patents, have little inherent value.").
101. *Ibid.*
102. *Ibid.*
103. Östman, *supra* note 82.
104. *See* Spulber, *supra* note 6, p. 12.
105. *See* Cohen, *supra* note 82, p. 2.
106. R. Stitzing *et al.*, Over-declaration of standard essential patents and determinants of essentiality, *Nokia* 12 (September 4, 2018), https://ssrn.com/abstract=2951617.
107. *Ibid.,* p. 25 ("We find that the strongest predictor for essentiality is when the declaration of the SEP refers to a specific technical specification of the standard.").
108. Östman, *supra* note 82.
109. *Ibid.*
110. I. Lunden and J. Russell, Nokia and Xiaomi Ink Patent and equipment Deal, Xiaomi Buys Nokia Patents, *Techcrunch* (July 5, 2017), https://techcrunch.com/2017/07/05/nokia-and-xiaomi-ink-patent-and-equipment-deal-xiaomi-buys-nokia-patents/.

    ("Xiaomi will become a customer of Nokia's for network equipment — specifically 'network infrastructure equipment designed to deliver the high capacity, low power requirements expected by large web providers and datacenter operators' and "optical transport solutions for datacenter interconnect, IP Routing based on Nokia's newly announced FP4 network processor, and a data center fabric solution."")

    Ibid.; *see also* United IPR, NOKIA & XIAOMI: Sign landmark patent licensing agreement, *Mondaq* (August 8, 2017), http://www.mondaq.com/

india/x/617484/Patent/NOKIA+XIAOMI+Sign+Landmark+Patent+Licensing+Agreement.

111. *See NOKIA & XIAOMI*, *supra* note 110.
112. *See* Spulber, *supra* note 75, p. 694.
113. Spulber, *supra* note 56, p. 291.
114. S. S. Harrison and P. H. Sullivan, Einstein in the boardroom: moving beyond intellectual capital to I-stuff 2 (Wiley ed. 2006).
115. *Ibid.*
116. *Ibid.*, p. 62.
117. Spulber, *supra* note 56, p. 281.
118. *See* Spulber, *supra* note 6, p. 16.
119. *Ibid.*, pp. 48–49.
120. *See* Lee, *supra* note 2, pp. 7–8.
121. *See* Spulber, *supra* note 75, p. 710.
122. *See* Spulber, *supra* note 56, p. 274.
123. *Ibid.*, p. 273.
124. S. Kieff, Views of the H. F. S. Kieff, Commissioner, United States International Trade Commission, on the United States Federal Trade Commission's and the United States Department of Justice Antitrust Division's Joint Guidelines for the Licensing of Intellectual Property, *U.S. Int'l Trade Commission* (September 23, 2016), https://www.ftc.gov/system/files/documents/public_comments/2016/09/00006-128911.pdf; *see also* F. S. Kieff and T. A. Paredes, The basics matter: At the periphery of intellectual property, *Geo. Wash. L. Rev.* 73, 174, 185–88 (2004).
125. F. S. Kieff, Property rights and property rules for commercializing inventions, *Minn. L. Rev.* 85, 697, 703 (2000); *see also* J. F. Duffy, Rethinking the prospect theory of patents, *U. Chi. L. Rev.* 71, 439, 439–40 (2004); E. W. Kitch, The nature and function of the patent system, *J.L. & Econ.* 20, 265, 265–90 (1977). *But see* P.J. Heald, A transaction costs theory of patent law, *Ohio St. L.J.* 66, 473, 499–500 (2005).
126. Spulber, *supra* note 56, pp. 290–97.
127. *Ibid.*, p. 295.
128. *See ibid.*
129. *See ibid.*, p. 274.
130. *See ibid.*, p. 307.
131. *See* Jarosz and Chapman, *supra* note 19, p. 803; Zelin, *supra* note 2, p. 651.
132. *See* Jarosz and Chapman, *supra* note 19, pp. 783–84.
133. *Ibid.*, pp. 799–800.

134. *Ibid.*, pp. 785–88.
135. *See ibid.*, pp. 799–807.
136. *See* Spulber, *supra* note 6, p. 32.
137. *Ibid.*, p. 48.
138. *See ibid.*, p. 12.
139. *See ibid.*, p. 17.
140. *See ibid.*, p. 49.
141. *See ibid.*, p. 52.
142. *Cf. ibid.*, p. 18.
143. *Ibid.* p. 47.
144. *See Panduit Corp. v. Stahlin Bros. Fibre Works*, 575 F.2d 1152, 1158–59 (6th Cir. 1978).
145. *See* Lanjouw and Schankerman, *supra* note 97, p. 48.
146. *Ibid.*, p. 56.
147. *See* E. Rasmusen and I. Ayres, Mutual and unilateral mistake in contract law, *J. Legal Stud.* 22, 309, 312 (1993).
148. Spulber, *supra* note 6, p. 21.
149. *See generally* Rasmusen and Ayres, *supra* note 147.
150. *Ga.-Pac. Corp. v. U.S. Plywood Corp.*, 318 F. Supp. 1116, 1120 (S.D.N.Y. 1970).
151. *See ibid.*
152. *Ibid.* ("The amount that a licensor (such as the patentee) and a licensee (such as the infringer) would have agreed upon (at the time the infringement began) if both had been reasonably and voluntarily trying to reach an agreement . . . .")
153. *Panduit Corp. v. Stahlin Bros. Fibre Works*, Inc. 575 F.2d 1152, 1159 (6th Circuit 1978).

     "The amount of a reasonable royalty after infringement turns on the facts of each case, as best they may be determined. Among the relevant facts are: "what plaintiff's property was, to what extent defendant has taken it, its usefulness and commercial value as shown by its advantages over other things and by the extent of its use[.]""

     Ibid. (citations omitted).
154. *Ibid.*, pp. 1158–59.
155. *Ibid.*, p. 1159.
156. In *LaserDynamics*, Judge Reyna states, "[i]n considering the fifteen Georgia-Pacific factors, it is presumed that the parties had full knowledge of the facts and circumstances surrounding the infringement at that time."

LaserDynamics, Inc. v. Quanta Comput., Inc., 694 F.3d 51, 76 (Federal Circuit 2012).

157. *In re Innovatio IP Ventures, LLC*, No. 11-C-9308, 2013 WL 5593609, at *7 (N.D. Ill. October 3, 2013).
158. *Ibid.*
159. *Ibid.*
160. *Ibid.*; *see Lucent Techs., Inc. v. Gateway, Inc.*, 580 F.3d 1301, 1325 (Federal Circuit 2009).
161. *Lucent Techs.*, 580 F.3d at 1325 ("The hypothetical negotiation tries, as best as possible, to recreate the *ex ante* licensing negotiation scenario and to describe the resulting agreement. In other words, if infringement had not occurred, willing parties would have executed a license agreement specifying a certain royalty payment scheme.").
162. Jones, *supra* note 22, p. 240 n.75.
163. *See Halo Electronics, Inc. v. Pulse Electronics, Inc.*, 136 S. Ct. 1923, 1929 (2016).
164. *See ibid.,* p. 18 ("Consistent with nearly two centuries of enhanced damages under patent law, however, such punishment should generally be reserved for egregious cases typified by willful misconduct.").
165. Jones, *supra* note 22, p. 240 n.75 ("In fact, a licensor may be able to obtain the same range of remedies in state court for the breach of a license agreement that the licensor would be able to obtain in federal court for patent infringement under 35 U.S.C. §§ 283–285 (i.e., an injunction, compensatory damages, and attorney fees).").
166. Although Cotter does not examine patent license contracts, he refers to reasonable royalties as "expectation damages," which he defines as "the value of the license that the patentee would have negotiated with the defendant, absent the infringement." T. F. Cotter, Four principles for calculating reasonable royalties in patent infringement litigation, *Santa Clara Comput. & High Tech. L.J* 27, 725, 737–38 (2010); *Ibid.,* p. 727 ("[T]he baseline damages recovery for prevailing patent owners should be the amount that restores them to the position they would have enjoyed but for the infringement.").
167. Spulber, *supra* note 56, p. 274.
168. *Ibid.,* p. 275.
169. *Ibid.,* p. 272.
170. *Ibid.,* p. 303.
171. *Ibid.,* p. 274.

172. *Ibid.*, p. 276.
173. *Ibid.*, p. 280.
174. *Ibid.*, p. 295.
175. H. Demsetz, The exchange and enforcement of property rights, *J.L. & Econ.* 7, 11, 17 (1964) ("The enforcement of the accompanying property rights has an important impact on the ability of prices to measure benefits.").
176. Spulber, *supra* note 56, p. 280.
177. *Ibid.*, p. 288.
178. R. A. Epstein, The clear view of the cathedral: The dominance of property rules, *Yale L.J.* 106, 2091, 2091 (1997).
179. *Ibid.*
180. *Ibid.* ("[A] liability rule denies the holder of the asset the power to exclude others or, indeed, to keep the asset for himself. Rather, under the standard definition he is helpless to resist the efforts by some other individual to take that thing upon payment of its fair value, as objectively determined by some neutral party.").
181. *Ibid.*, p. 2120.
182. G. Calabresi and A. D. Melamed, Property rules, liability rules, and inalienability: One view of the cathedral, *Harv. L. Rev.* 85, 1089, 1092 (1972).
    "An entitlement is protected by a property rule to the extent that someone who wishes to remove the entitlement from its holder must buy it from him in a voluntary transaction in which the value of the entitlement is agreed upon by the seller .... Whenever someone may destroy the initial entitlement if he is willing to pay an objectively determined value for it, an entitlement is protected by a liability rule. This value may be what it is thought the original holder of the entitlement would have sold it for."
    Ibid.
183. *Ibid.*, p. 1119.
184. P. J. Heald, Optimal remedies for patent infringement: A Transactional model, *Hous. L. Rev.* 45, 1165, 1176 (2008) ("The goal of remedies for patent infringement should be to provide incentives for efficient transactions to occur while accounting for the cost of transacting."); *see* J. M. Golden, Principles for patent remedies, *Tex. L. Rev.* 88, 505, 554 (2010).
185. Heald, *supra* note 184, p. 1185.
186. *eBay Inc. v. MercExchange, L. L. C.* 547 U.S. 388, 393–94 (2006).
187. For an overview of these issues, *see* Hylton, *supra* note 20, pp. 417–18.
188. *Aro Mfg. Co. v. Convertible Replacement Tops*, 377 U.S. 476, 505 (1964); Hylton, *supra* note 20, pp. 430–31.

189. 35 U.S.C. § 284 (2018).
190. M. Y. M. Mohamed, Unjust enrichment for patent infringement: A novel idea? *J. Intell. Prop. L.* 4, 123, 125 (1996).
191. *Ibid.*, pp. 125–26.
192. *Ibid.*, p. 155.

    ("What is unacceptable is how courts have managed to read the 1946 amendment of the patent code as eliminating the traditional remedy of an accounting for the infringer's profits. Such a reading is without basis. In fact, Congress appears to have intended to preserve the option of a restitutionary recovery.")

    Ibid., p. 159; *see also* Lord Goff of Chieveley and G. Jones, The law of restitution 12 n.63 (Gareth Jones ed., 4th ed. 1993).
193. See J. Edelman, Gain-Based damages: Contract, tort, equity and intellectual property 1 (2002) ("Restitutionary damages are a reverse which operates to restore wrongful transfers of value from a claimant to a defendant. Disgorgement damages operate to strip a defendant of profit made by wrongful conduct."); *see also* R. Grantham and C. Rickett, A normative account of defenses to restitutionary liability, *Cambridge L.J.* 67, 92, 101 (2008); R. B. Grantham and C. E. F. Rickett, Disgorgement for unjust enrichment? *Cambridge L.J.* 62, 159, 159 (2003) ("Restitution is the giving back of wealth received by a defendant from a claimant, which must be given back or restored because it amounts to an unjust enrichment at the claimant's expense."); R.B. Grantham and C. E. F. Rickett, Property rights as a legally significant event, *Cambridge L.J.* 62, 717, 738 (2003).
194. Her Majesty's Attorney General v. Blake [2000] (HL) (appeal taken from U.K.).

    "Be that as it may, in these types of case equity considered that the appropriate response to the violation of the plaintiff's right was that the defendant should surrender all his gains, and that he should do so irrespective of whether the violation had caused the plaintiff any financially measurable loss. Gains were to be disgorged even though they could not be shown to correspond with any disadvantage suffered by the other party. This lack of correspondence was openly acknowledged. In Lever v. Goodwin (1887) 36 Ch. D. 1, 7, Cotton L.J. stated it was 'well known' that in trade mark and patent cases the plaintiff was entitled, if he succeeded in getting an injunction, to take either of two forms of relief: he might claim from the defendant

either the damage he had sustained from the defendant's wrongful act or the profit made by the defendant from the defendant's wrongful act."
Ibid.

195. *See generally* A. Burrows, The law of restitution 2 (3rd ed. 2011). *See also* P. Birks, An introduction to the law of restitution 2 (rev. ed. 1989); A. Kull, Rationalizing restitution, *Calif. L. Rev.* 83, 1191, 1201 (1995) ("Where the law imposes an obligation to pay for benefits conferred in the absence of contract, the ordinary measure of recovery is therefore defendant's gain, not plaintiff's cost."). Restitution for patent infringement would be subject to a defense of innocence by the infringer. *See* Edelman, *supra* note 193, p. 242.
196. For a guide to license agreements, *see*, e.g., D. M. Cameron and R. Borenstein, Key aspects of IP license agreements, *Ogilvy Renault* (2003), http://www.jurisdiction.com/lic101.pdf; D. Bobrowicz, A checklist for negotiating license agreements, *Concept Foundation* (2007), http://www.iphandbook.org/handbook/ch11/p11/; *see also* U.N. Indus. Dev. Org., Guidelines for evaluation of transfer of technology agreements, 12 development and transfer of technology Series 3 (1979); U.N. Indus. Dev. Org., UNIDO manual on technology transfer negotiation, modules 6, 16 (1996); World Intellectual Prop. Org. [WIPO], *Licensing Guide for Developing Countries*, no. 620 (1977). G. Quinn, Drafting a licensing agreement, A patentee perspective, *IPWatchdog* (April 30, 2016), http://www.ipwatchdog.com/2016/04/30/drafting-licensing-agreement/id=68723; K. Leute, Anatomy of a license agreement, in *AUTM Technology Practice Manual*, 4 (3d.ed.2010),https://www.autm.net/AUTMMain/media/ThirdEditionPDFs/V4/TTP_V4_AnatomyLicense.pdf.
197. *See* Cameron and Borenstein, *supra* note 196, pp. 6–9.
198. *Ibid.*, p. 8.
199. For standard licensing contracts, *see*, for example, Gemalto's license agreement. Standard patent license agreement, *Gemalto,* https://www.gemalto.com/companyinfo-site/about-site/merger-site/download-site/Documents/patent_licence.pdf (last visited November 14, 2018).
200. *See EDGAR | Company Filings*, SEC, https://www.sec.gov/edgar/searchedgar/companysearch.html (last visited November 14, 2018).
201. *See United States International Trade Commission,* USITC, https://www.usitc.gov (last visited November 14, 2018).
202. *See* Cameron and Borenstein, *supra* note 196, p. 6.
203. *Ibid.*, pp. 6–9, 26.

204. *Ibid.*, pp. 1–2, 33.
205. R. C. Nordhaus, Patent license agreements, *Bus. Law*. 643, 21, 643 (1966). "Because of the infinite variety of rights and obligations that may be established between a patent licensor and his licensee, there is no "standard" form of license agreement that may be used in all situations. Each license agreement must be carefully tailored to the specific circumstances of the particular case."
    Ibid.
206. Cameron and Borenstein, *supra* note 196, p. 1, 11.
207. *Ibid.*
208. *Ibid.*, p. 7.
209. M. Sullivan, In its war with Apple, Qualcomm tries to save its business model, *Fast Company* (July 20, 2017), https://www.fastcompany.com/40442789/apple-qualcomm-war-existential-threat.
210. The Ninth Circuit Court determined that "Qualcomm's patent-licensing royalties and 'no license, no chips' policy did not impose an anticompetitive surcharge on rivals' modem chip sales." *Federal Trade Commission v. Qualcomm Incorporated,* United States Court of Appeals for the Ninth Circuit, 19-16122, August 11, 2020.
211. *See* Cameron and Borenstein, *supra* note 196, p. 11, 32.
212. *Ibid.*, p. 32.
213. *See ibid.*
214. *See ibid.*, p. 12, 37.
215. *See, e.g.*, Nordhaus, *supra* note 205, p. 644; G. Parchomovsky and R. P. Wagner, Patent portfolios, *Temple U.*, http://www.temple.edu/lawschool/dpost/ptw/parchomovsky.pdf (last visited Nov. 14, 2018).
216. *See* Cameron and Borenstein, *supra* note 196, p. 1.
217. *Ibid.*, p. 1, 17.
218. 301 Ownership/Assignability of patents and applications, MPEP (9th ed., rev. July 2015).
219. *U.S. Dep't of Just. & Fed.* Trade comm'n, antitrust enforcement and intellectual property rights: Promoting innovation and competition 59 (2007).
220. *Ibid.*, p. 57.
221. Nordhaus, *supra* note 205, pp. 643–44.
222. *Ibid.*, pp. 644–45, 657.
223. *See* Cameron and Borenstein, *supra* note 196, p. 18.

224. *See ibid.*, p. 9, 18.
225. *See* 37 C.F.R. § 3.1 (2018).
"An exclusive license may be granted by the patent owner to a licensee. The exclusive license prevents the patent owner (or any other party to whom the patent owner might wish to sell a license) from competing with the exclusive licensee, as to the geographic region, the length of time, and/or the field of use, set forth in the license agreement. A license is not an assignment of the patent. Even if the license is an exclusive license, it is not an assignment of patent rights in the patent or application."
Ownership/Assignability of patents and applications, 2015 December Comm'r Pat. 301, https://www.uspto.gov/web/offices/pac/mpep/s301.html#d0e17687.
226. Cameron and Borenstein, *supra* note 196, p. 9.
227. *Ibid.*
228. *Ibid.*, p. 12.
229. *Ibid.*, p. 21 ("There is no widely accepted definition for 'improvement' in the context of intellectual property licenses, but it is usually used to mean a development within the field of the licensed technology that enhances the usability, functionality, efficiency, performance or other characteristic of the original technology.").
230. *Ibid.*
231. *Ibid.*, p. 21. "At the end of it all, the royalty fee should account for the bargain struck, and a higher royalty may be justified to the extent the licensee is entitled to the benefit of subsequent licensor improvements. It may also be dealt with through an extension of the term of the Agreement (and a corresponding extension of the length of time during which a licensee must pay royalties), particularly if the improvements are patentable." *Ibid.*
232. *Ibid.*, p. 22.
233. *Ibid.*, p. 21.
"At the end of it all, the royalty fee should account for the bargain struck, and a higher royalty may be justified to the extent the licensee is entitled to the benefit of subsequent licensor improvements. It may also be dealt with through an extension of the term of the Agreement (and a corresponding extension of the length of time during which a licensee must pay royalties), particularly if the improvements are patentable."
Ibid.
234. *Ibid.*

235. *See* Patent cross license agreement between advanced micro devices, Inc. and Intel Corporation, SEC Archives, §§ 2–3 (November 11, 2009), https://www.sec.gov/Archives/edgar/data/2488/000119312509236705/dex102.htm.
236. The articles of the contract are as follows: 1. Definitions, 2. License Grant, 3. Warranties, 4. Additional Covered Standards, 5. Term; Termination, 6. Payment of License Fees, 7. Wireless Local Loop Subscriber Units, 8. Adjustments to Royalties, 9. Payments, 10. Cross Licenses, 11. Advance Payment, 12. Miscellaneous. *See* TDMA Patent License Agreement Between Interdigital Tech. Corp. & Samsung Elec. Co., SEC Archives, https://www.sec.gov/Archives/edgar/data/354913/000119312506230371/dex1085.htm. (last visited November 14, 2018).
237. *See ibid.*
238. *Ibid.,* at art. 2.
239. *Ibid.* at § 11.1.
240. *Ibid.* at § 6.3.
241. *Ibid.* at § 11.1.
242. *Ibid.* at § 6.4.
243. *Ibid.* at § 7.2.
244. *See* L. M. Goldstein and B. N. Kearsey, Technology patent licensing an international reference on 21st century patent licensing, patent pools and patent platforms 70 (2004).
245. *See ibid.*; TDMA patent license agreement between interdigital Tech. Corp. & Samsung Elec. Co., *SEC Archives*, https://www.sec.gov/Archives/edgar/data/354913/000119312506230371/dex1085.htm.
246. *See* Goldstein and Kearsey, *supra* note 244, p. 68.
247. For other patent license agreements, *see* SISVEL, *SISVEL LTE patent pool portfolio license agreement*, http://sisvel.com/images/media/2016/LTE-Portfolio-License-Agreement.pdf; SISVEL, *SISVEL WLAN program license agreement*, http://www.sisvel.com/Wi-Fi/License_Agreement.pdf.
248. *See* Goldstein and Kearsey, *supra* note 244, p. 70.
249. Antitrust guidelines for the licensing of intellectual property, F.T.C § 5.5, p. 31 (U.S. Dep't Just. January12, 2017); *see also* Antitrust Enforcement and Intellectual Property Rights: Promoting Innovation and Competition, F.T.C, Ch. 3 (U.S. Dep't Just. April 2017).
250. MPEG-2 license agreement, *MPEGLA*, http://www.mpegla.com/main/programs/M2/Pages/License.aspx (last visited November 14, 2018).
251. *See* MPEG-2 introduction, *MPEGLA*, http://www.mpegla.com/main/programs/m2/pages/intro.aspx (last visited November 14, 2018).

252. *Ibid.* For a summary of the Agreement, see MPEGLA, *supra* note 250.
253. *See* MPEGLA, *supra* note 250.
254. The licensors of the MPEG-2 patent portfolio license include the following: Alcatel Lucent, ARRIS Technology, Inc. (formerly General Instrument Corporation), British Telecommunications plc, Canon Inc., CIF Licensing, LLC, Cisco Technology, Inc., Fujitsu Limited, GE Technology Development, Inc., Hewlett Packard Enterprise Company, Hitachi, Ltd., JVC KENWOOD Corporation, KDDI Corporation, Koninklijke Philips N.V., LG Electronics Inc., Mitsubishi Electric Corporation, Multimedia Patent Trust, Nippon Telegraph and Telephone Corporation, Orange SA, Panasonic Corporation, Robert Bosch GmbH, Samsung Electronics Co. Ltd., SANYO Electric Co. Ltd., Sharp Corporation, Sony Corporation, The Trustees of Columbia University in the City of New York, Thomson Licensing, and Toshiba Corporation. *See ibid.*; *see also* MPEGLA, *MPEG-2 Licensors*, http://www.mpegla.com/main/programs/M2/Pages/Licensors.aspx (last visited November 14, 2018).
255. MPEGLA, *supra* note 250, at § 7.9.
256. *Ibid.* at § 6.1.
257. *Ibid.* at § 6.2.
258. MPEGLA, *supra* note 251.
259. MPEGLA, *supra* note 250.
260. *See ibid.*
261. *Ibid.* at § 2.
262. *Ibid.*
263. *Ibid.*
264. *Ibid.*
265. *Ibid.*
266. *Ibid.*
267. *Ibid.*
268. *Ibid.*
269. The chapters describe these phases. *See* Menell *et al.*, *supra* note 3, at §§ 2-1–9-3.
270. *See ibid.* pp. 5–8.
271. *See* J. J. Anderson and P. S. Menell, Informal deference: A historical, empirical, and normative analysis of patent claim construction, *Nw. U.L. Rev.* 108, 1, 3–4 (2014).
272. *Microsoft Corp. v. Motorola, Inc.*, No. C10-1823JLR, 2013 WL 2111217, p. *3 (W.D. Wash. April 25, 2013).

273. Infringement generally does not involve complementary knowledge transfers because the patent holder and the infringer are not already involved in a business relationship. However, complementary knowledge transfers may arise when the infringement suit stems from a business dispute between the parties such as a breach of contract.
274. *See* Mennell *et al.*, *supra* note 3, at E-93 (Reproducing Federal Circuit Bar Association Model Patent Jury Instruction).
275. *Ibid.* at § 2–9 ("Patent claims play a central role in patent cases, as they establish and delineate the intellectual property.").
276. *Ibid.* at §§ 2-9–2-26.
277. *Ibid.* at § 2–13.
278. *Ibid.*

     "The Supreme Court's seminal decision in Markman v. Westview Instruments, Inc., 517 U.S. 370, 391 (1996), took claim construction out of the jury's hands and put the responsibility squarely on the district judge to construe patent claim terms. More recently, Teva Pharmaceuticals USA, Inc. v. Sandoz, Inc., 135 S. Ct. 831 (2015), not only confirmed that district courts were authorized to resolve subsidiary factual issues underlying claim construction, but held that such findings of fact should be upheld unless they are clearly erroneous."

     Ibid.
279. *See* Leute, *supra* note 196, p. 5.
280. Menell *et al.*, *supra* note 3, at E-93 (citing the following authorities for model instructions: "*Uniloc USA, Inc. v. Microsoft Corp.*, 632 F.3d 1292 (Federal Circuit 2011) (25% "rule of thumb" inadmissible); *ResQNet.com, Inc. v. Lansa, Inc.*, 594 F.3d 860 (Federal Circuit 2010) (per curiam) (licenses must be related to patent at issue to be relevant to a reasonable royalty); *Lucent Techs., Inc. v. Gateway, Inc.*, 580 F.3d 1301, 1340 (Federal Circuit 2009) *cert. denied*, 130 S. Ct. 3324 (2010) (vacating and rewarding jury award as excessive); *Golight, Inc. v. Wal-Mart Stores, Inc.*, 355 F.3d 1327, 1338 (Federal Circuit 2004); *Maxwell v. J. Baker, Inc.*, 86 F.3d 1098, 1108-10 (Federal Circuit 1996); *Mahurkar v. C.R. Bard, Inc.*, 79 F.3d 1572, 1579–81 (Federal Circuit 1996); *Rite-Hite Corp. v. Kelley Co.*, 56 F.3d 1538, 1554 (Federal Circuit 1995) (en banc); *Georgia-Pacific Corp. v. U.S. Plywood Corp.*, 318 F. Supp. 1116, 1120 (S.D.N.Y. 1970); *Interactive Pictures Corp. v. Infinite Pictures, Inc.*, 274 F.3d 1371 (Federal Circuit 2001); *Trans-World Mfg. Corp. v. Al Nyman & Sons, Inc.*, 750 F.2d 1552 (Federal Circuit 1984)").

281. *Ibid.*
282. G. K. Leonard and S. P. Rusek, Patent purchase price is useful in damages analysis, *Law360* (September 8, 2014), https://www.law360.com/articles/573442/patent-purchase-price-is-useful-in-damages-analysis.
283. Apple Inc. v. Motorola Inc., 757 F.3d 1286, 1315 (Federal Circuit 2014).
284. Leonard and Rusek, *supra* note 282.
285. B. W. Burton and S. Weingust, Misuse of patent purchase price in damages analysis: Part 1, *Law360* (August 11, 2014), https://www.law360.com/articles/562178/misuse-of-patent-purchase-price-in-damages-analysis-part-1 [hereinafter Burton & Weingust, *Part 1*]; *see also* B. W. Burton and S. Weingust, *Misuse of Patent Purchase Price in Damages Analysis: Part 2*, Law360 (August 12, 2014), https://www.law360.com/articles/562184?scroll=1.
286. Burton and Weingust, *Part 1*, *supra* note 285; *see* Spectralytics, Inc. v. Cordis Corp., 649 F.3d 1336, 1345 (Federal Circuit 2011).
287. Spulber, *supra* note 56, at 291, 303, 311.
288. *Ibid.,* p. 274.
289. *Ibid.,* p. 290.
290. *Ibid.,* p. 308.
291. *Ibid.,* p. 291.
292. *See* European Patent Office, Patents and the fourth industrial revolution: The inventions behind digital transformation 14 (2017) ("[T]echnologies are increasingly being integrated into a wide range of business applications, offering new opportunities for innovation and value creation based on data and software.").
293. Burton and Weingust, *Part 1*, *supra* note 285.
294. *Ibid.*
295. For a discussion on the discounting of royalties in contract negotiations to reflect the probability that a patent is found to be valid and infringed, *see* J. Farrell and C. Shapiro, How Strong Are Weak Patents? *Am. Econ. Rev.* 98, 1347, 1348 (2008); *see also* Burton and Weingust *Part 1*, *supra* note 285.
296. M. Vakili, Patent portfolio valuations – Importance of IP and patents, *IPWatchdog* (July 12, 2017), http://www.ipwatchdog.com/2017/07/12/patent-portfolio-valuations/id=85409/ [hereinafter Vakili]. R. K. Kuhnen, Huawei v. ZTE – ECJ Sets framework for injunctive relief regarding SEPs, IAM (April 11, 2016), https://www.iam-media.com/huawei-v-zte-ecj-sets-framework-injunctive-relief-regarding-seps.

297. *See* D. F. Spulber, Standard setting organisations and standard essential patents: Voting and markets, *Econ. J.* 129, April, 1477 (2019)
298. *See ibid.,* pp. 2–3.
299. *Ibid.,* p. 5.
300. Stitzing *et al.*, *supra* note 106, p. 1.
301. S. S. Nair, M. Mathew, and D. Nag, Dynamics between patent latent variables and patent price, *Technovation* 31, 648, 650 (2011).
302. Burton and Weingust, *Part 1*, *supra* note 285 (Expressing concerns about the efficiency of the market for patents).
303. Burton and Weingust, *Part 2*, *supra* note 285.
304. S. Yelderman, Do Patent Challenges Increase Competition? *U. Chi. L. Rev.* 83, 1943, 1953 (2016).
305. *Ibid.,* pp. 1959–60.
306. *See* C. Morah, Patents are assets — Learn how to value them, *Investopedia* (April 23, 2018, 7:03 PM), https://www.investopedia.com/articles/fundamental-analysis/09/valuing-patent.asp.
307. K. King, The value of intellectual property, intangible assets and goodwill, *World Intell. Prop. Org.,* http://www.wipo.int/sme/en/documents/value_ip_intangible_assets_fulltext.html (last visited Nov. 14, 2018).
308. C. J. Serrano, The dynamics of the transfer and renewal of patents, *RAND J. Econ.* 41, 686, 698 (2010).

     "In summary, we find that active patents with a higher number of patent citations received and generality, as well as previously traded patents (especially the recently traded), are more likely to be traded and renewed. The data also reveal that the probability that an active patent will be traded decreases with age, with one exception, which is the year immediately after a renewal date. Finally, we also show that the probability of an active patent being allowed to expire increases with age."

     Ibid. A. Galasso *et al.*, Trading and enforcing patent rights, *RAND J. Econ.* 44, 275, 306 (2013) ("[T]he impact of trade is related to transaction characteristics — specifically, the size of the buyer's patent portfolio and the technological fit of the patent in that portfolio.").
309. Vakili, *supra* note 296.
310. This can be represented by a general function that describes how market value is related to factors that affect patent value, V = F(patent value indicators).
311. *See generally* Ocean Tomo, http://www.oceantomo.com/featured-engagements/ (last visited November 14, 2018).

312. T. Fischer and J. Leidinger, Testing patent value indicators on directly observed patent value — An empirical analysis of Ocean Tomo patent auctions, *Res. Pol'y* 43, 519, 520 (2014).
313. C. Odasso, G. Scellato, and E. Ughetto, Selling patents at auction: An empirical analysis of patent value, *Indus. & Corp. Change* 24, 417, 417 (2014).
314. K. A. Sneed and D. K. N. Johnson, Selling ideas: The determinants of patent value in an auction environment, *R&D Mgmt.* 39, 87, 91 (2009).
315. Nair *et al.*, *supra* note 301, at 650.
316. "The USPTO allows parties to record assignments of patents and patent applications to, as much as possible, maintain a complete history of claimed interests in a patent. The USPTO also permits recording of other documents that affect title (such as certificates of name change and mergers of businesses) or are relevant to patent ownership (such as licensing agreements, security interests, mortgages, and liens). The 2016 update to the Patent Assignment Dataset contains detailed information on 7.2 million patent assignments and other transactions recorded at the USPTO since 1970 and involving roughly 12.2 million patents and patent applications. It is derived from the recording of patent transfers by parties with the USPTO."
Patent Assignment Dataset, U.S. Patent & Trademark Office, https://www.uspto.gov/learning-and-resources/electronic-data-products/patent-assignment-dataset (last visited November 14, 2018).
317. *See generally* S. J. H. Graham, A. C. Marco, and A. F. Myers, Monetizing marks: Insights from the USPTO trademark assignment dataset, *J. Econ. & Mgmt. Strategy*, April 2015.
318. *See* T. R. Varner, Technology royalty rates in SEC filings, 45 les nouvelles 120, 120 (2010).
319. *See* A. D. Marco, G. Scellato, E. Ughetto, and F. Caviggioli, Global markets for technology: evidence from patent transactions, *Res. Pol'y* 46, 1644, 1648 (2017) ("The highest incidence of transactions is recorded for US priority patents (6.37%), and this is followed by EPC priority patents (5.51%). China, Japan and Korea show a lower percentage incidence of traded patents (3.07%, 1.47% and 1.36%, respectively).").
320. K. Richardson, E. Oliver, and M. Costa, 2016 patent market report: Overview, *IPWatchdog* (April 10, 2017), http://www.ipwatchdog.com/2017/04/10/2016-patent-market-report-overview/id=81689/.
321. Announcing AST's IP3 2017 – A fixed price, fixed term collaborative patent buying program, *Allied Security Trust* (May 1, 2017), http://ast.com/

news_article/announcing-asts-ip3-2017-fixed-price-fixed-term-collaborative-patent-buying-program/.

322. "IAM Market aims to simplify the IP transactions market, as well as making it more transparent. It allows IP owners to profile their licensing, sales operations and technology transfer programmes, as well as provide details of specific rights that they are interested in transacting. It allows IP buyers to search IP assets based on industry, technology and transaction type, and it facilitates requests for intellectual property and technology. IAM has no stake in or knowledge of the deals."
About IAM Market, IAM Market, https://www.iam-market.com/node/4 (last visited October 10, 2018).
323. *Valuation*, ICAP Pat. Brokerage, https://icappatentbrokerage.com/valuation (last visited November 14, 2018).
324. C. Arthur, *Nortel Patents Sold for $4.5 bn*, The Guardian (July 1, 2011, 3:08 PM), https://www.theguardian.com/technology/2011/jul/01/nortel-patents-sold-apple-sony-microsoft.
325. *Ibid.*
326. N. Lomas, Kodak agrees to sell digital imaging patent portfolio for $525 M to consortium of 12 licensees, including Apple, Google, Facebook, *TechCrunch* (December 19, 2012), https://techcrunch.com/2012/12/19/kodak-to-sell-digital-imaging-patent-portfolio-for-525m/.
327. *Our Patent Portfolio*, Intell. Ventures, http://www.intellectualventures.com/inventions-patents/patent-portfolio/ (last visited November 14, 2018).
328. *2016 IBM Annual Report*, IBM, p. 119, https://www.ibm.com/annual-report/2016/images/downloads/IBM-Annual-Report-2016.pdf (last visited November 14, 2018).
329. *See ibid.*
330. *Ibid.*, p. 21.
331. *Ibid.*, p. 94.
332. *Ibid.*, p. 35.
333. Hall studies how the ratio of the firm's market value to the book value of its tangible assets is related to the ratio of the firm's stock of R&D assets to the book value of the firm's tangible assets and the ratio of the firm's stock of patents to the stock of R&D assets. *See* B. H. Hall, Exploring the patent explosion, *J. Tech. Transfer* 30, 35, 42 (2005); *see also* B. H. Hall *et al.*, Market value and patent citations, *RAND J. Econ.* 36, 16, 17–23 (2005).
334. *See generally* J. Bessen, Estimates of patent rents from firm market value, *Res. Pol'y* 38, 1604 (2009).

335. *See* U. Akcigit, M. A. Celik, and J. Greenwood, Buy, keep, or Sell: Economic growth and the market for ideas, *Econometrica* 84, 943, 944 (2016).
336. L. Kogan, D. Papanikolaou. and N. Stoffman, Technological innovation, resource allocation, and growth, *Q.J. Econ.* 132, 665, 666 (2017).
337. *Ibid.,* p. 682; *see* P. Giuri *et al.*, Inventors and invention processes in Europe: Results from the PatVal-EU survey, Res. Pol'y 136, 107, 1121 (2007); *see also* D. Harhoff, F. M. Scherer, and K. Vopel, Citations, family size, opposition and the value of patent rights, *Res. Pol'y* 32, 1343, 1349 (2003).
338. J. Bessen, The value of U.S. patents by owner and patent characteristics, *Res. Pol'y* 37, 932, 932 (2008); Y. Deng, Private value of european patents, *Eur. Econ. Rev.* 51, 1785, 1801 (2007); C. Grönqvist, The private value of patents by patent characteristics: Evidence from Finland, *J. Tech. Transfer* 34, 159, 160 (2007); A. Pakes, Patents as options: Some estimates of the value of holding European patent stocks, *Econometrica* 54, 755, 755 (1986); M. Schankerman, How valuable is patent protection? Estimates by technology field, *RAND J. Econ.* 29, 77, 78 (1998); *see also* M. Schankerman and A. Pakes, Estimates of the value of patent rights in European countries during the Post-1950 period, *Econ. J.* 96, 1052, 1059 (1986).
339. D. Harhoff, F. M. Scherer, and K. Vopel, Exploring the tail of patented invention value distributions, *in Econ. L. and Intelle. Prop.* 279, 280 (O. Grandstrand ed., 2003) ("[P]atent renewal studies reveal a highly rightward-skewed distribution of individual patent values . . . .").
340. N. v. Zeebroeck, The puzzle of patent value indicators, *Econ. Innovation & New Tech.* 20, 33, 33 (2011).
341. On surveys of patent holders, *see* A. Gambardella, P. Giuri, and A. Luzzi, The market for patents in Europe, *Res. Pol'y* 36, 1163, 1177 (2007); D. Harhoff, F. Narin, F. M. Scherer, and K. Vopel, Citation frequency and the value of patented inventions, *Rev. Econ. & Stat.* 81, 511, 511 (1999); M. Reitzig, What determines patent value? Insights from the semiconductor industry, *Res. Pol'y* 32, 13, 17 (2003) (discussing surveys evaluated by technical experts); D. Harhoff *et al.*, supra note 339.
342. *See, e.g.*, A. Gambardella, D. Harhoff, and B. Verspagen, The value of European patents, *Eur. Mgmt. Rev.* 5, 69, 69 (2008); J. Suzuki, Structural modeling of the value of patent, *Res. Pol'y* 40, 986, 988 (2011); A. Gambardella *et al.*, The value of european patents evidence from a survey of european inventors 3 (2005), https://www.ipeg.com/wp-content/uploads/2015/02/PatVal-EU-study-2005.pdf.

343. *See generally* Gambardella, Harhoff, and Verspagen, The value of european patents, *supra* note 342.
344. *Ibid.,* p. 80.
345. *Ibid.,* pp. 82–83.
346. *See* J. Lerner and A. Layne-Farrar, Valuing patents for licensing: A practical survey of the literature 7 (March 2006) (unpublished manuscript).
347. *Ibid.,* p. 10.
348. *Ericsson, Inc. v. D-Link Systems, Inc.,* 773 F.3d 1201, 1227 (Federal Circuit 2014).
349. D. F. Spulber and C. S. Yoo, Access to networks: Economic and constitutional connections, *Cornell L. Rev.* 88, 885, 899 (2003).
350. In a competitive market, at the price that equates demand and supply, the value of the good to the marginal buyer equals the cost of the good to the marginal seller. *Ibid.,* p. 895.
351. *Ibid.,* pp. 900–01.
352. J. R. Hicks, Value and capital: An inquiry into some fundamental principles of economic theory 40–41 (1939).
353. S. Ghosh, An economic analysis of the common control exception to gray market exclusion, *U. Pa. J. Int'l Bus. L.* 15, 373, 410–12 (1994).
354. *See* R. A. Mundell, International trade and factor mobility, *Am. Econ. Rev.* 47, 321, 330, 326–30 (1957).
355. *LaserDynamics, Inc. v. Quant Computer, Inc.* 694 F.3d 51, 56 (Federal Circuit 2012); *see also* Lucent Techs., Inc. v. Gateway, Inc., 580 F.3d 1301, 1325–26 (Federal Circuit 2009).
356. *See* H. Demsetz, The exchange and enforcement of property rights, *J.L. & Econ.* 7, 11, 14 (1964); *see also* Lerner and Layne-Farrar, *supra* note 346.
357. Z. Yang, Damaging royalties: An overview of reasonable royalty damages, *Berkeley Tech. L.J.* 29, 647, 651–52 (2014).
358. For a discussion of bargaining in the context of patent licensing and also references to the economics literature on bargaining, *see generally* Spulber, *supra* note 75.
359. *See generally* Coase, *supra* note 57.
360. *See* Spulber, *supra* note 75, p. 695.
361. Masur, *supra* note 12, p. 145 ("The dollar value of a license (roughly) represents the underlying value of the patent discounted by the probability that the patent will be found invalid or not infringed at trial.").
362. As Masur notes, this runs contrary to *LaserDynamics v. Quanta Computer,* 694 F.3d 51 (Federal Circuit 2012). *Ibid.,* p. 127 ("I wish to suggest that the

Federal Circuit had it exactly backwards: the BenQ license, and not the other twenty-eight licenses, was the most accurate indication of the 'true' value of the patent.").

363. *Ibid.*, p. 133 (expressing concerns that a problem would arise because parties would anticipate this adjustment in future litigation, and that this would increase negotiated royalties, leading to an upward spiral as a patent holder increases demands on each consecutive licensee).
364. *Intellectual Prop. Ins. Servs. Corp., AIPLA* 2015 Report of the economic survey (2015), http://www.patentinsuranceonline.com/wp-content/uploads/2016/02/AIPLA-2015-Report-of-the-Economic-Survey.pdf (citing AIPLA, Report of the Economic Survey (2015), https://www.accmeetings.com/AM16/faculty/files/Article_482_7928_LitSpend___AIPLA_2015_Report.pdf).
365. *Ibid.*
366. *Ibid.*
367. *Ibid.*
368. *Ibid.*
369. *See, e.g.*, M. J. Hasbrouck, Protecting the gates of reasonable royalty: A damages framework for patent infringement cases, *J. Marshall Rev. Intell. Prop. L.* 11, 192 (2011); Jarosz and Chapman, *supra* note 19.
370. Masur, *supra* note 12, p. 142 n.108.
371. *Ibid.*, p. 142.
372. *FreecycleSunnyvale v. Freecycle Network*, 626 F.3d 509, 515 (9th Circuit 2010) (quoting *Barcamerica International USA Trust v. Tyfield Importers,* Inc., 289 F.3d 589, 596 (9th Circuit 2002)).
373. *Ibid.*, pp. 515–26 (quoting *Barcamerica*, 289 F.3d 598).
374. B. Zeng, Lucent v. Gateway: Putting the reasonable back into reasonable royalties, *Berkeley Tech. L.J.* 26, 329, 352 (2011) ("The Federal Circuit remanded these cases, in part, because damage experts must present a specific methodology. The court will not accept mere recitations of large royalty rates based on unreliable evidence that may mislead the jury.").
375. Stitzing *et al.*, *supra* note 106, p. 2.
376. Spulber, *supra* note 55, p. 277.
377. Spulber, *supra* note 297, p. 2.
378. *Ibid.*, p. 22.
379. *Ibid.*, p. 2.
380. G. Sidak, The meaning of FRAND, Part II: Injunctions, *J. Competition L. & Econ.* 11, 201, 206 (2015) ("By entering into a FRAND contract, an SEP

holder gives up its right to exclude from the use of the SEPs any implementer willing to pay FRAND compensation.").

381. *Ibid.*
382. *Ibid.*, p. 268.
383. J. P. Kesan and C. M. Hayes, FRAND's forever: Standards, patent transfers, and licensing commitments, *Ind. L.J. 231,* 89, 233 (2014) ("The conceptual framework we propose characterizes FRAND commitments as creating a property interest, instead of merely creating a contract or a condition that affects a competitive relation.").
384. *Ibid.*, p. 313.
385. *Apple Inc. v. Motorola, Inc.*, 757 F.3d 1286, 1332 (Federal Circuit 2014).
386. Case C-170/13, *Huawei Technologies Co. Ltd. v ZTE Corp.*, 2014 E.C.J. 2391, ¶ 103; *see also* R. K. Kuhnen, Huawei v ZTE – ECJ sets framework for injunctive relief regarding SEPs, IAM (April 11, 2016), http://www.iam-media.com/Intelligence/Patents-in-Europe/2016/Europe-f/ocus/Huawei-v-ZTE-ECJ-sets-framework-for-injunctive-relief-regarding-SEPs.
387. *See* Kuhnen, *supra* note 386.
388. R. Jacob and A. Milner, Lessons from Huawei v. ZTE 1 (2016), http://www.4ipcouncil.com/application/files/6314/7928/6022/Lessons_from_Huawei_v_ZTE_-_RJacob_-_24-10-16.pdf.
389. *Ibid.*, p. 2.

    "The judgment of the European Court of Justice (CJEU) in Huawei v. ZTE has provided valuable guidance on the circumstances when a holder of a Standard Essential Patent (SEP) which has given a commitment to license the SEP on FRAND terms is entitled to seek an injunction against an implementer without acting in breach of competition law."

    Ibid., p. 1.
390. *Ibid.*, p. 2.
391. *Apple Inc. v. Motorola, Inc.*, 757 F.3d 1286, 1332 (Federal Circuit 2014).
392. *Unwired Planet v. Huawei* [2017] EWHC (Pat) 711 [155] (Eng.).
393. *Ibid,*. p. 157.
394. *Ibid.*, p. 159.
395. Fed. Trade Comm'n, The Evolving IP Marketplace: Aligning patent notice and remedies with competition 22 (March 2011), https://www.ftc.gov/sites/default/files/documents/reports/evolving-ip-marketplace-aligning-patent-notice-and-remedies-competition-report-federal-trade/110307patentreport.pdf.

396. R. A. Epstein, F. S. Kieff, and D. F. Spulber, The FTC, IP, and SSOs: Government Hold-Up replacing private coordination, *J. Competition L. & Econ.* 8, 1, 27 (2012).
397. Federal Trade Comm'n, *supra* note 395, p. 200.
398. For example, a total royalty of R = $100 is consistent with a fixed fee of $60 and running royalties of 2% on sales of $2,000, or a fixed fee of $25 and running royalties of 1% on sales of $7,500.
399. *See* N. V. Siebrasse and T. F. Cotter, A new framework for determining reasonable royalties in patent litigation, *Fla. L Rev.* 68, 929, 978–80 (2016) (discussing lump-sum versus running royalties).
400. S. Gin, An analysis of cross-licensing with asymmetric patent portfolios, Department of Economics, University of Ottawa, ECO 6999, 16, 18 (2016).
401. *See* 2017 Patent litigation study, *supra* note 8, p. 3.
402. T. R. Varner, An economic perspective on patent licensing structure and provisions, *Bus. Econ.* 46, 229, 235 (2011).
"Combination product royalty reductions can take a number of different forms, but the most common form observed in the data set is one in which the base royalty rate is multiplied by the ratio of the licensed product's stand-alone price ... to the sum of the stand-alone prices of the licensed and unlicensed products .... Other forms of combination product royalty reductions include ratios based on manufacturing or fully allocated costs, the number of active components, and the number of functions performed."
Ibid., pp. 235–36.
403. *See* S. Balganesh, Copyright infringement markets, *Colum. L. Rev.* 113, 2277, 2295 (2013).
404. D. Hegde, Tacit knowledge and the structure of license contracts: Evidence from the biomedical industry, *J. Econ. & Mgmt. Strategy* 23, 568, 568–69 (2014).
405. *Ibid.*
406. Varner, *supra* note 402, p. 234.
407. *Ibid.*, p. 229.
408. Spulber, *supra* note 75.
409. *See generally* K. Arrow, Economic welfare and the allocation of resources for invention, *in* National Bureau of Economic Research, The rate and direction of inventive activity: Economic and social factors 609 (Princeton University Press 1962); N. T. Gallini and R. A. Winter, Licensing in the theory of innovation, *RAND J. Econ.* 16, 237 (1985); M. L. Katz and

C. Shapiro, How to license intangible property, *Q.J. Econ.* 101, 567 (1986). *See also* M.l L. Katz and C. Shapiro, On the licensing of innovations, *RAND J. Econ.* 16, 504, 511 (1985).

410. Arrow, *supra* note 409, pp. 619–22.
411. *See generally* D. F. Spulber, Competing inventors and the incentive to invent, *Indus. & Corp. Change* 22, 3 (2012) [hereinafter Spulber, *Competing Inventors*]; D. F. Spulber, How Do Competitive Pressures Affect Incentives to Innovate When There Is a Market for Inventions? *J. Pol. Econ.* 121, 1007 (2013) [hereinafter Spulber, *How Do Competitive Pressures*].
412. Spulber, How do competitive pressures, *supra* note 411, pp. 1031–32.
413. *See generally* E. Stasik, Royalty rates and licensing strategies for essential patents on LTE (4G) telecommunications standards, *les Nouvelles* 45, 114 (2010).
414. *Ibid.,* pp. 116–17.
415. *Ibid.,* p. 116 (citing B. Kearsey and L. M. Goldstein, Technology patent licensing: An international reference on 21st century patent licensing, patent pools, and patent platforms 53 (2004)).
416. T. R. Varner, Technology royalty rates in SEC filings, *les Nouvelles* 45, 120, 120 (2010).
417. Varner, *supra* note 402, p. 230.
418. *Ibid.,* p. 232.
419. *Ibid.,*p. 230, 233.
420. *Ibid.,* p. 233.
421. M. Sakakibara, An empirical analysis of pricing in patent licensing contracts, *Indus. & Corp. Change* 19, 927, 931 (2010). M. Sakakibara examines 661 patent licensing contracts between 1998 and 2003. *Ibid.*
422. *Ibid.,* p. 928.
423. *Ibid.*
424. *Ibid.,* p. 932.
425. *Ibid.*
426. *Ibid.,* pp. 932–33.
427. *Ibid.,* p. 933.
428. *Ibid.*
429. *Ibid.,* p. 939.
430. *Ibid.,* p. 933.
431. *Ibid.,* p. 940.
432. P. Arqué-Castells and D. F. Spulber, The market for technology: Harnessing creative destruction 1 (Northwestern. University. Pritzker School of Law & Econs. Series No. 18–14, 2018); *see also* N. Bloom, M. Schankerman, and

J. Van Reenen, Identifying technology spillovers and product market rivalry, *Econometrica* 81, 1347, 1347 (2013). *See generally* Sakakibara, *supra* note 421.
433. Arqué-Castells and Spulber, *supra* note 432, p. 40.
434. *Ibid.*
435. Sakakibara, *supra* note 421, p. 941.
436. *Ibid.*, p. 929.
437. Hegde, *supra* note 404, p. 568; *see also* D. F. Spulber, Tacit knowledge with innovative entrepreneurship, *Int'l J. Indus*. Org. 30, 641 (2012).
438. 773 F.3d 1201, 1230 (Federal Circuit 2014).
439. *Ibid.*
440. *Georgia-Pacific Corp. v. U.S. Plywood Corp.*, 318 F. Supp. 1116, 1120 (S.D.N.Y. 1970).
441. J. A. Alfred, Licensing standards essential patents, *les Nouvelles* 52, 223, 224 (2017) (noting that ninety-six cases cite *Georgia Pacific* since 1995, of which thirty-five discuss the *Georgia Pacific* factors).
442. *Georgia-Pacific.*, 318 F. Supp. at 1120.
443. *Ibid.*, p. 1121 (Citing *Horvath v. McCord Radiator & Mfg. Co.*, 100 F.2d 326, 335 (6th Circuit 1938)).
444. *Ibid.*
445. *Ibid.* ("What a willing licensor and a willing licensee would have agreed upon in a supposititious negotiation for a reasonable royalty would entail consideration of the specific factors previously mentioned, to the extent of their relevance.").
446. *Ibid.*, p. 1120.
447. *Ibid.*
448. *See supra* Part III.
449. *Georgia-Pacific*, 318 F. Supp. p. 1120.
450. *See supra* Part IV.
451. *Georgia-Pacific*, 318 F. Supp. p. 1120.
452. Seaman, *supra* note 2, pp. 1665–66.
453. *Georgia-Pacific*, 318 F. Supp. p. 1120.
454. *Ibid.*
455. *Ibid.*
456. *Ibid.*
457. *Ibid.*
458. *Ibid.*
459. G. K. Leonard and M. A. Lopez, Determining RAND royalty rates for standard-essential patents, *Antitrust L.J.* 29, 86, 87 (2014).

460. *Georgia-Pacific*, 318 F. Supp. p. 1120.
461. *Ibid.*
462. *Ibid.*
463. *Ibid.*
464. *Ibid.*
465. *Ibid.*
466. *Ibid.*
467. *Ibid.*
468. *Ibid.*

     "15. The amount that a licensor (such as the patentee) and a licensee (such as the infringer) would have agreed upon (at the time the infringement began) if both had been reasonably and voluntarily trying to reach an agreement; that is, the amount which a prudent licensee — who desired, as a business proposition, to obtain a license to manufacture and sell a particular article embodying the patented invention — would have been willing to pay as a royalty and yet be able to make a reasonable profit and which amount would have been acceptable by a prudent patentee who was willing to grant a license."

     Ibid.
469. *See* Leonard and Lopez, *supra* note 459, pp. 88–91; J. R. Bartlett and J. L. Contreras, Rationalizing FRAND royalties: Can interpleader save the internet of things? *Rev. Litig.* 36, 285, 293 (2017).
470. Bartlett and Contreras, *supra* note 469, p. 292; *see also* Jarosz and Chapman, *supra* note 19, pp. 795–96.
471. Jarosz and Chapman, *supra* note 19, pp. 795–98.
472. *See supra* Section IV.B.
473. *See supra* Section IV.B.
474. *See supra* Section IV.B.
475. The markup of the technology provider's opportunity costs is greater than or equal to one and less than or equal to the ratio of the adopter's benefits to the provider's costs, $1 \leq Y \leq B/C$. The markdown of the adopter's benefits less than or equal to one and greater than or equal to the ratio of the provider's opportunity costs to the adopter's benefits, $C/B \leq X \leq 1$.
476. *See* Leonard and Lopez, *supra* note 459, p. 89.
477. *See, e.g., Rite-Hite Corp. v. Kelley Co.,* 56 F.3d 1538, 1554 n.13 (Federal Circuit 1995) (en banc) ("The hypothetical negotiation is often referred to as a 'willing licensor/willing licensee' negation. However, this is an inaccurate, and even absurd, characterization when, as here, the patentee does not wish to grant a license.").

478. *See* Leonard and Lopez, *supra* note 459, pp. 88–91.
479. *See ibid.,* p. 86; *see also* Seaman, *supra* note 2, pp. 1696.
480. *See* Leonard and Lopez, *supra* note 459, p. 87; *see also* Seaman, *supra* note 2, p. 1696.
481. *See* Bartlett and Contreras, *supra* note 469, pp. 300–01.
482. *See ibid.*
483. *See ibid.,* pp. 297–300.
484. *In re Innovatio IP Ventures, LLC*, No. 11-C-9308, 2013 WL 5593609, at *39 (N.D. Ill. October 3, 2013).
485. Leonard and Lopez, *supra* note 459, pp. 88–89.
486. *Ibid.,* p. 89; *see supra* Section IV.B.
487. *See Microsoft Corp. v. Motorola, Inc.*, No. C10-1823JLR, 2013 WL 2111217 (W.D. Wash. April 25, 2013); *see also* Bartlett and Contreras, *supra* note 469, pp. 293–94.
488. Bartlett and Contreras, *supra* note 469, p. 293.
489. *See, e.g.*, D. J. Durie and M. A. Lemley, A structured approach to calculating reasonable royalties, *Lewis & Clark L. Rev.* 14, 627, 637 (2010).

     "Not surprisingly, a reasonable royalty designed to mimic the results of a hypothetical license negotiation between patentee and infringer should be strongly influenced by the value that the patented technology actually contributes. The more the patented technology is worth, the more a willing buyer would be willing to pay, and the more a willing seller could reasonably demand."

     Ibid.; *see also* A. L. Landers, Patent claim apportionment, patentee injury, and sequential invention, *Geo. Mason L. Rev.* 471, 472 (2012) ("This Article starts with the fundamental premise that a patentee's harm cannot be greater than the patentee's contribution.").
490. Leonard and Lopez, *supra* note 469, p. 88.
491. *Ibid.,* pp. 87–89.
492. *See* Seaman, *supra* note 2, pp. 1718–19.
493. *See ibid.*; *see also* Section IV.B.
494. Such calculations require information about comparable licenses and the costs of design arounds for the licensee, with particular consideration given to "the amount of evidence available for implementing each methodology, the quality of data available to support each methodology, and the economic circumstances of each case." Jarosz and Chapman, *supra* note 19, p. 828; *see also* Seaman, *supra* note 2, p. 1727 (describing a similar approach).

     "Specifically, the cost to the infringer of adopting and implementing an acceptable noninfringing substitute, plus any incremental benefit provided

by the patented technology vis-à-vis the substitute, represents the true economic value of the patent over the prior art. As a result, the cost of the noninfringing substitute represents the maximum amount a rational licensee would have agreed to pay in a hypothetical negotiation."
Seaman, *supra* note 2, p. 1727. This approach should be modified because a buyer's willingness to pay for the new technology would equal its economic value, that is, the incremental benefit of the new technology *plus* the cost of the inferior substitute.

495. *See* Bartlett and Contreras, *supra* note 469, p. 303.
496. *See ibid.*; *see also* Leonard and Lopez, *supra* note 469, p. 86.
497. According to Judge Holderman:
"In essence, the Bottom Up approach suggests determining the cost of implementing reasonable alternatives to the Innovatio patents that could have been adopted into the standard, and dividing that cost by the total number of infringing units to determine the maximum per unit royalty Innovatio' s patents would have merited in the 1997 hypothetical negotiation."
In re Innovatio IP Ventures, LLC, No. 11-C-9308, 2013 WL 5593609, at *37 (N.D. Ill. October 3, 2013).
498. *See generally Panduit Corp. v. Stahlin Bros. Fibre Works*, 575 F.2d 1152 (6th Circuit 1978).
499. *Ibid.*, pp. 1159–62.
500. *Ibid.*
501. *Ibid.*
502. *Ibid.*, p. 1162 n.9.
503. *See* Pincus, *supra* note 9, p. 127.
504. *Ibid.*; *Georgia-Pac. Corp. v. U.S. Plywood-Champion Papers Inc.*, 446 F.2d 295, 299 (2d Circuit 1971).
505. *See Georgia Pacific*, 446 F.2d p. 299.
506. *Ibid.*, pp. 299–300, 300 n.3.
507. *See* Bartlett and Contreras, *supra* note 469, pp. 293–94, 294 n.39; *see also* Pincus, *supra* note 9, p. 127.
508. *See* Spulber, *supra* note 75, p. 693.
509. *See generally ibid.*
510. *See ibid.* at 694.
511. *See ibid.*
512. *Microsoft Corp. v. Motorola, Inc.*, No. C10-1823JLR, 2013 WL 2111217, at *13 (W.D. Wash. April 25, 2013).
513. *Ibid.*

514. *See* Leonard and Lopez, *supra* note 469, pp. 89–91.
515. *TCL Commc'n Tech. v. Telefonaktiebolaget LM Ericsson*, No. 15-cv-2370, 2017 WL 6611635, at *1 (C.D. Cal. December 21, 2017); *In re Innovatio IP Ventures, LLC*, No. 11-C-9308, 2013 WL 5593609, at *37 (N.D. Ill. October 3, 2013); *see* J. Rantanen, *Guest Post by Prof. Jorge Contreras: TCL v. Ericsson: The First Major U.S. Top-Down FRAND Royalty Decision,* Patentlyo Blog (December 27, 2017), https://patentlyo.com/patent/2017/12/contreras-ericsson-decision.html; R. Vary, Supersize this: Unwired Planet American style, Bird & Bird (December 28, 2017), https://www.twobirds.com/en/news/articles/2017/global/supersize-this-unwired-planet-american-style.
516. *TCL Commc'n Tech.*, 2017 WL 6611635, at *8.
517. Leonard and Lopez, *supra,* note 459, p. 89. ("Prior to standardization, the maximum possible royalty burden that would have been considered is that which would have exhausted the total economic profit that manufacturers expected from products compliant with the standard.") Leonard and Lopez also state "Expected economic profits would represent an upper bound on the aggregate royalty burden because some of these profits may be due to the act of standardization itself rather than any of the technologies chosen to be part of the standard; that is, the value of standardization could have been achieved using alternatives to the chosen SEPs."
518. Spulber, *supra* note 6, p. 11.
519. *See supra* Part IV.A.
520. Notice that if we view royalties as a share of the infringer's benefits $R = XB = X(P - A)$, and x is the share of the infringer's profit, $R = xP$, then it follows that the share of profits can be written as $x = X(1 - A/P)$.
521. Epstein and Malherbe, *supra* note 2, p. 29.
522. *Ibid.,* p. 28.
523. *Ibid.,* p. 26.
524. *Ibid.*
525. *Ibid.*
526. *Ibid.,* pp. 11–14.
527. *Uniloc USA, Inc. v. Microsoft Corp.*, 632 F.3d 1292, 1315 (Federal Circuit 2011) (surveying the academic literature on the 20% profits rule).
528. *See ibid.,* p. 1313 (quoting G. K. Leonard and L. J. Stiroh, Economic approaches to intellectual property policy, litigation, and management, 949 PLI/Pat 425, 454–55 (September–Nov. 2008)).
529. *See In re Innovatio IP Ventures, LLC*, No. 11-C-9308, 2013 WL 5593609, at *1, *37–38 (N. D. Ill. October 3, 2013).

530. *Ibid.*, pp. *38–39.
531. *Ibid.*, p. *38.
532. *See ibid.*, pp. *35–38.
533. Leonard and Lopez, *supra* note 459, p. 89.
534. *In re* Innovatio, 2013 WL 5593609, p. *43.
535. *Ibid.* (citing Schankerman, *supra* note 338, at tbl.5 & n.12).
536. *Ibid.*, p. *43.
537. *Ibid.*
538. *See ibid.*
539. *See supra* Part IV.A.
540. Schankerman, *supra* note 338, p. 77.
541. *TCL Commc'n Tech. v. Telefonaktiebolaget LM Ericsson*, No. 15-CV-2370, 2017 WL 6611635, at *1, *18 (C.D. Cal. December 21, 2017).
542. *Ibid.*, pp. *25–26.
543. *Ibid.*, pp. *41–48.
544. *Ibid.*
545. *Ibid.*, p. *11.
546. *Ibid.*, p. *12.
547. *Ibid.*,p. *14.
548. *Ibid.* ("It is also unclear why the drop in the price of phones matters, because Ericsson's public statements were never conditioned on a particular dollar-per-unit return.").
549. *Ibid.*, p. *8.
550. *Ibid.*, p. *9.
551. *Ibid.*, p. *23.
552. *Ibid.*
553. *Ibid.*, p. *10; Vary, *supra* note 515, p. 5 ("The top-down exercise starts from the artificial assumption that all handsets, globally, have an aggregate royalty rate which is a set percentage of the selling price.").
554. J. G. Sidak, Apportionment, FRAND royalties, and comparable licenses after Ericsson v. D-Link, *U. Ill. L. Rev*. 2016, 1809, 1825.
555. Cotter, *supra* note 166, p. 733.
556. *See, e.g.*, *Lucent Techs., Inc. v. Gateway, Inc.*, 580 F.3d 1301, 1339 (Federal Circuit 2009) ("There is nothing inherently wrong with using the market value of the entire product, especially when there is no established market value for the infringing component or feature, so long as the multiplier accounts for the proportion of the base represented by the infringing component or feature.").

557. J. G. Sidak, The proper royalty base for patent damages, *J.L. & Econ.* 10, 989, 990 (2014) ("Royalty compensation for patent infringement must reward the patent holder not only for the individual value of its patented technology, but also for a share of the value arising from complementarity and network effects. Only patent damages that meet this requirement are likely to maintain optimal incentives for investment in innovation.").
558. Varner, *supra* note 416, p. 230.
559. *Ibid.*
560. *Ericsson, Inc. v. D-Link Sys., Inc.*, 773 F.3d 1201, 1226 (Federal Circuit 2014).
561. *Ibid.*, p. 1233.
562. *See supra* Part IV.A.
563. Yang, *supra* note 2, p. 654.
564. *Ibid.*, p. 655.
565. B. J. Love, Patentee overcompensation and the entire market value rule, *Stan. L. Rev.* 60, 263, 293 (2007).
566. E. Hovenkamp and H. Hovenkamp, Patent pools and related technology sharing 1, 2 (April 10, 2017) (unpublished manuscript), http://scholarship.law.upenn.edu/faculty_scholarship/1766.
567. *See* Pincus, *supra* note 9, p. 98 ("If in all reasonable probability, the Patent Owner would have made the sales, which the Infringer had made, what the Patent Owner in reasonable probability would have netted from the sales denied to him is the measure of his loss, and the Infringer is liable for that.") (quoting Lam, Inc. v. Johns-Manville Corp., 718 F.2d 1056, 1065 (Federal Circuit 1983)).
568. *VirnetX, Inc. v. Cisco Sys., Inc.*, 767 F.3d 1308, 1326 (Federal Circuit 2014).
569. Garretson v. Clark, 111 U.S. 120, 121 (1884).
570. *VirnetX*, 767 F.3d p. 1326.
571. *Cornell Univ. v. Hewlett-Packard Co.,* 609 F. Supp. 2d 279, 283 (N.D.N.Y. 2009); *see also LaserDynamics, Inc. v. Quanta Comput., Inc.,* 694 F.3d 51, 67 (Federal Circuit 2012).
572. *Cornell Univ.*, 609 F. Supp. 2d p. 283 ("Hewlett-Packard's primary business did not include a la carte processor sales.").
573. *Ibid.*
574. *Ibid.* ("Hewlett-Packard's primary business did not include a la carte processor sales.").

575. *See* E. C. Surette, *Construction and Application of "Entire Market Value" Rule in Patent Infringement Actions*, 21 A.L.R. Fed. 3d Art. 4 (2017) ("To assess how much value each patented and nonpatented component individually contributes to the overall end product … can be an exceedingly difficult and error-prone task.").
576. Y. K. Ro, J. K., Liker, and S. K. Fixson, Modularity as a strategy for supply chain coordination: The case of U.S. *Auto*, *IEEE Transactions on Engineering Mgmt.* 54, 172, 179 (2007).
577. *Ibid.*
578. Spulber, *supra* note 75, p. 310.
579. *Ibid.,* p. 302.
580. *See generally* D. F. Spulber, Complementary monopolies and bargaining, *J.L. & Econ.* 60, 29 (2017).
581. *Ibid.*
582. *See* Spulber, *supra* note 75, p. 706; *see also* Spulber, *supra* note 580, p. 57.
583. Spulber, *supra* note 580, p. 41.
584. *Ibid.,* p. 30.
585. Spulber, *supra* note 75, p. 693.
586. *Ibid.,* p. 694.
587. *Ibid.,* p. 704.
588. *Microsoft Corp. v. Motorola, Inc.,* No. C10-1823JLR, 2013 WL 2111217, at *1, *86 (W.D. Wash. April 25, 2013).
589. *Ibid.,* p. 74.
590. *Ibid.,* p. 87.
591. *Ibid.*
592. *Ibid.,* p. 89.
593. *Ibid.,* p. 88.
594. *TCL Commc'n Tech. v. Telefonaktiebolaget LM Ericsson*, No. 15-CV-2370, 2017 WL 6611635, at *24 (C.D. Cal. Dec. 21, 2017).
595. *Id.* at 14.
596. Spulber, *supra* note 75, at 704.
597. *Id.* at 711.
598. N. W. Chamberlain and J. W. Kuhn, Collective bargaining 170 (2d ed. 1965); s*ee also* J. Svejnar, Bargaining power, fear of disagreement, and wage settlements: Theory and evidence from US industry, *Econometrica* 54, 1055, 1057 (1986).
599. Svejnar, *supra* note 598, p. 1057.
600. *See supra* Part IV.

601. For discussions on using the Nash Bargaining Solution to calculate reasonable royalties, see D. Kidder and V. O'Brien, *The Nash Bargaining Solution*, 49 les Nouvelles 1, 1 (2014); T. Varner, *Nash Bargaining May Not Be Right for Patent Damages*, Law360 (April 18, 2014, 9:37 PM), https://www.law360.com/articles/529437/nash-bargaining-may-not-be-right-for-patent-damages; *see also* F. R. Denton and P. J. Heald, Random walks, non-cooperative games, and the complex mathematics of patent pricing, *Rutgers L. Rev*. 55, 1175, 1234–40 (2003).
602. W. Choi and R. Weinstein, An analytical solution to reasonable royalty rate calculations, *J.L. & Tech. 49*, 51 (2001).
603. *See* K. Binmore and P. Dasgupta, Nash bargaining theory I, in *The Econ. of Bargaining* 27 (K. Binmore and P. Dasgupta, eds. 1987); A. E. Roth, Axiomatic models of bargaining 8 (1979); K. Binmore, *Nash Bargaining Theory I-III, supra* note 58; K. Binmore *et al.*, The Nash bargaining solution in economic modelling, *Rand J. Econ.* 17, 176, 176–88 (1986); J. C. Harsanyi and R. Selten, A generalized Nash solution for two-person bargaining games with incomplete information, *Mgmt. Sci.* 18, 80, 80–106 (1972); J. F. Nash, Jr., The bargaining problem, *Econometrica* 18, 155, 155 (1950); J. F. Nash Jr., Two-Person cooperative games, *Econometrica* 21, 128, 129 (1953).
604. Choi and Weinstein, *supra* note 602, p. 52.
605. This follows from B – R = R – C = (B – C)/2.
606. *VirnetX, Inc. v. Cisco Sys., Inc.*, 767 F.3d 1308, 1332 (Federal Circuit 2014).
607. *Ibid.*, p. 1331.
608. *Ibid.*, p. 1332.
609. A. Rubinstein, Perfect equilibrium in a bargaining model, *Econometrica* 50, 97, 97 (1982).
610. *Ibid.*, p. 102.
611. *Panduit Corp. v. Stahlin Bros. Fibre Works, Inc.* 575 F.2d 1152, 1159 (6th Circuit 1978).

Chapter 5

1. *See* R. Epstein, Intellectual property and the law of contract: The case against "Efficient Breach," *Eur. Rev. of Cont. L.* 9, 345 (2013); *see also* R. Epstein, Simple rules for a complex world (1995).
2. C. Barry, R. Arad, L. Ansell, M. Cartier, and H. Lee, 2017 Patent litigation study: Change on the horizon? PWC https://www.pwc.com/us/en/forensic-services/publications/assets/2017-patent-litigation-study.pdf (last visited

August 7, 2017). There is also significant trademark litigation. W. Bryner, *U.S. Trademark and Unfair Competition Litigation*, Int'l Trademark Ass'n (September 2017), https://www.inta.org/trademarkadministration/Documents/2017/Bryner%20-%20U.S.% 20Trademark%20and%20Unfair%20Competition%20Litigation%2009142017/Bryner%20-%20U.S.%20Trademark%20and%20Unfair%20Competition%20Litigation%2009142017.pdf.

3. Copyright infringement litigation fell 22% in FY 2016, TracReports (November 21, 2016), http://trac.syr.edu/tracreports/civil/445/.
4. S. Brachman, Lex Machina's 2017 trademark litigation report shows high percentage of overall damages awarded on default judgment, IPWatchdog (December 5, 2017), http://www.ipwatchdog.com/2017/12/05/2017-trademark-litigation-report-damages-awarded-default-judgment/id=90683/.
5. D. Almeling, D. W. Snyder, and M. Sapoznikow, A statistical analysis of trade secret litigation in federal courts, *Gonz. L. Rev.* 45, 291, 293 (2009).
6. *See Patents Through History*, USPTO, https://10millionpatents.uspto.gov/ (last visited November 11, 2018); *Trademark Case Files Dataset*, USPTO, https://www.uspto.gov/learning-and-resources/electronic-data-products/trademark-case-files-dataset-0 (last visited November 11, 2018); *see also* S. J. H. Graham, G. Hancock, A. C. Marco, and A. F. Myers, The USPTO trademark case files dataset: Descriptions, lessons, and insights, *J. of Econ. & Mgmt. Strategy* 22, 669, 669–705 (2013).
7. R. Shapiro and K. Hassett, The economic value of intellectual property, *Sonecon* 2, http://www.sonecon.com/docs/studies/IntellectualPropertyReport-October2005.pdf (last visited November 11, 2018).
8. Y. Ménière *et al.*, European patent office, patents and the fourth industrial revolution: The inventions behind digital transformation, 17 (European Patent Office ed., 2017) ("[T]he combined use of a wide range of new technologies in a large variety of sectors of the economy. These include digitisation and highly effective connectivity, but also technologies such as cloud computing and artificial intelligence that have permitted the development of interconnected smart objects operating autonomously.").
9. K. Schwab, The fourth industrial revolution: What it means and how to respond, *Foreign Affairs* (December 12, 2015), https://www.foreignaffairs.com/articles/2015-12-12/fourth-industrial-revolution ("The First Industrial Revolution used water and steam power to mechanize production. The Second used electric power to create mass production. The Third used electronics and information technology to automate production. Now a Fourth Industrial Revolution is building on the Third, the digital revolution that has been

occurring since the middle of the last century. It is characterized by a fusion of technologies that is blurring the lines between the physical, digital, and biological spheres."); *see also* K. Schwab, The fourth industrial revolution (2017).
10. *See* Méniére, *supra* note 8, pp. 17–18.
11. D. F. Spulber and C. S. Yoo, Networks in telecommunications: Economics and law, 39 (2009).
12. D. F. Spulber and C. S. Yoo, Network regulation: The many faces of access, *J. Comp. L. & Econ.* 1, 635 (2005).
13. *See, e.g.*, C. Dhanasai and A. Parkhe, Orchestrating innovation networks, *Acad. Mgmt. Rev.* 31, 659, 659 (2006); *see generally* E. V. Hippel, Horizontal innovation networks — By and for users, *Indus. & Corp. Change* 16, 293 (2007).
14. K. B. Clark, The interaction of design hierarchies and market concepts in technological evolution, *Res. Pol'y* 14, 235, 235 (1985); R. M. Henderson and K. B. Clark, Architecture innovation: The reconfiguration of existing product technologies and the failure of established firms, *Admin. Sci. Q.* 35, 9, 11 (1990); K. Ulrich, The role of product architecture in the manufacturing firm, *Res. Pol'y* 24, 419, 419 (1995).
15. Henderson and Clark, *supra* note 14, p. 2.
16. D. F. Spulber, Licensing standard essential patents: Bargaining and incentives to invent (February 20, 2019) (Northwestern University Working Paper) (on file with author).
17. *See generally* C. Morris and J. Carvalko, The science and technology guidebook for lawyers; ABA groups: Section of science and technology law, *Am. B.* (2014) Ass'n, https://www.americanbar.org/groups/science_technology/about_us.html (last visited September 19, 2018) ("The mission of the ABA Section of Science & Technology Law is to provide leadership on emerging issues at the intersection of law, science, and technology; to promote sound policy and public understanding on such issues; and to enhance the professional development of its members.").
18. For further discussion of problems related to infringement damages, *see* D. F. Spulber, Finding reasonable royalty damages: A contract approach to patent infringement, *Ill. L. Rev.* 2019, 615 (2019).
19. C. R. Hulten, Stimulating economic growth through knowledge-based investment (*OECD Sci., Tech. & Industry*, Working Paper No. 2, 2013), http://www.observatorioabaco.es/ biblioteca/docs/412_OECD_WP_02_2013.pdf.
20. F. Moris, J. Jankowski, M. Boroush, M. Crawford, and J. Lee, *Nat'l Sci. Found.*, R&D Recognized as Investment in U.S. GDP Statistics: GDP

increase slightly lowers R&D-to-GDP Ratio (2015), https://www.nsf.gov/statistics/2015/nsf15315/.

21. U.S. R&D: Slow growth and opportunities, 2017 Global R&D Funding Forecast, Winter 2017, p. 7.
22. L. I. Nakamura, What Is the U.S. Gross Investment in Intangibles? (At Least) One Trillion Dollars a Year! 5 (Federal Reserve. Bank of Philadelphia, Working paper No. 01–15, 2001).
23. C. M. Elsten and N. Hill, Intangible asset market value study? *J. of the Licensing Exec. Soc'y Int'l* 52, 245, 245–47 (2017); B. Lev, Intangibles: Management, measurement, and reporting (2001); B. Lev, Remarks on the measurement, valuation, and reporting of intangible assets 17 (N.Y.U. Working Paper No. 2451–27468, 2003).
24. *See, e.g.*, T. Sichelman, Purging patent law of "Private Law" remedies, *Tex. L. Rev*. 92, 517, 519 (2013) ("[P]atent remedies mirror traditional tort law remedies by attempting to restore the patentee to the *status quo ante* — namely, the state of the world in which there is no infringement of the patent.").
25. *See* D. A. Crane, Intellectual liability, *Tex. L. Rev*. 88, 253, 254 (2009) ("Innovation incentives, once protected by property rights, are increasingly being protected by liability rights.").
26. *See* Spulber, *supra* note 18.
27. J. C. Paul *et al.*, Courts may enforce covenants not to challenge the validity of licensed patents contained in a license agreement settling litigation when the parties clearly waived future challenges to validity, *Finnegan* (October 23, 2012), https://www.finnegan.com/ en/insights/courts-may-enforce-covenants-not-to-challenge-the-validity-of.html.
28. F. S. Kieff, The case for registering patents and the law and economics of present patent-obtaining rules, *B.C. L. Rev*. 45, 55, 123 (2003) ("The case for an alternative model registration system also is helpful in showing why increased scrutiny of patent applications would worsen, not improve, the present system's performance.").
29. G. Quinn, The cost of obtaining a patent in the U.S., *IPWatchdog* (April 4, 2015), http://www.ipwatchdog.com/2015/04/04/the-cost-of-obtaining-a-patent-in-the-us/id=56485/; *see* R. Tushnet, Registering disagreement: Registration in modern American trademark law, *Harv. L. Rev*. 130, 867 (2017).
30. *See* 17 U.S.C. § 102 (2018).
31. P. S. Menell, The property rights movement's embrace of intellectual property: True love or loomed relationship, *Ecology L. Q*. 34, 713, 747 (2007);

P. S. Menell, Intellectual property and the property rights movement, *Reg.* 30, 36, 39 (2007).

32. *See* 35 U.S.C. § 261 (2018).
33. *eBay Inc. v. MercExchange, L.L.C.*, 547 U.S. 388, 392 (2006).
34. There is non-rivalrous usage of some types of tangible assets if demand is constrained below the capacity of the asset. For example, there is non-rivalrous usage of a bridge or a park if demand is less than capacity and there are no congestion externalities. See C. Mora, *How Is Computer Software Classified as an Asset*? *Investopedia* (May 15, 2018, 11:50 AM), https://www.investopedia.com/ask/answers/09/computer-software-intangible-asset.asp.
35. Epstein, *supra* note 1, p. 6.
36. *Ibid.*, p. 10.
37. *Ibid.*, p. 8.
38. A. Schwartz and J. Watson, The law and economics of costly contracting 2–31 (J. M. Olin Center for *Stud. In L., Econ., & Pub. Pol'y*. Working Paper No. 264, 2001) ("Contract law encourages courts to search thoroughly for the parties' actual intentions in creating the contract and in renegotiating it. We show that this search has yielded mandatory legal rules that make it extremely difficult for parties to restrict renegotiation, and that can increase greatly the cost of creating sophisticated contracts. As a consequence, parties now have legal incentives to use the more simple contract forms …").
39. J. Poblete and D. Spulber, Managing innovation: Optimal incentive contracts for delegated R&D with double moral hazard, *Eur. Econ. Rev.* 95, 38 (June 2017).
40. R. P. Merges, Contracting into liability rules: Intellectual property rights and collective rights organizations, *Cal. L. Rev.* 84, 1293, 1358 (1996).
41. G. Calabresi and A. D. Melamed, Property rules, liability rules and inalienability: One view of the cathedral, *Harv. L. Rev.* 85, 1089, 1092 (1972) ("An entitlement is protected by a property rule to the extent that someone who wishes to remove the entitlement from its holder must buy it from him in a voluntary transaction in which the value of the entitlement is agreed upon by the seller …. Whenever someone may destroy the initial entitlement if he is willing to pay an objectively determined value for it, an entitlement is protected by a liability rule. This value may be what it is thought the original holder of the entitlement would have sold it for.")
42. *Ibid.*
43. *Ibid.*

44. R. A. Epstein, The clear view of the cathedral: The dominance of property rules, *Yale L.J.* 106, 2091, 2091 (1997) ("[A] liability rule denies the holder of the asset the power to exclude others or, indeed, to keep the asset for himself.").
45. M. A. Lemley, Should patent infringement require proof of copying? *Mich. L. Rev*. 105, 1525, 1525 (2006) ("Patent infringement is a strict liability offense."); R. Blair and T. F. Cotter, Strict liability and its alternatives in patent law, *Berkeley Tech. L.J.* 799, 800 (2002) [hereinafter R. Blair and T. F. Cotter, *Strict Liability*] ("Patent infringement is a strict liability tort in the sense that a defendant may be liable without having had any notice, prior to the filing of an infringement action, that her conduct was infringing."); R. Blair and T. F. Cotter, An economic analysis of damages rules in intellectual property law, *Wm. & Mary L. Rev*. 39, 1585 (1998).
46. Blair and Cotter, Strict liability, *supra* note 45, p. 806 (suggesting that liability need not be considered strict because in some cases giving notice is required for liability).
47. *Ibid.*
48. *Ibid.*
49. *eBay Inc. v. MercExchange, L.L.C.*, 547 U.S. 388 (2006).
50. *Ibid.*
51. *Ibid.*
52. *Ibid.*, p. 388, 393 ("The traditional four-factor test applied by courts of equity when considering whether to award permanent injunctive relief to a prevailing plaintiff applies to disputes arising under the Patent Act. That test requires a plaintiff to demonstrate: (1) that it has suffered an irreparable injury; (2) that remedies available at law are inadequate to compensate for that injury; (3) that considering the balance of hardships between the plaintiff and defendant, a remedy in equity is warranted; and (4) that the public interest would not be disserved by a permanent injunction .... [A] permanent injunction will issue once infringement and validity have been adjudged.").
53. A. Beckerman-Rodau, The Supreme Court engages in judicial activism in interpreting the patent law in eBay, Inc. v. MercExchange, L.L.C., *Tul. J. Tech. & Intell. Prop*. 10, 165, 165 (2007).
54. D. McGowan, Irreparable harm, *Lewis & Clark L. Rev*. 577, 579 (2010).
55. *See* R. M. Janutis, The Supreme Court's unremarkable decision in eBay Inc. v. MercExchange, L.L.C., *Lewis & Clark L. Rev.* 14, 597, 601, 604 (2010); B. Peterson, Injunctive relief in the Post-eBay world, *Berkeley Tech. L. J.*

23, 193, 196 (2008); D. Ellis *et al.*, The economic implications (and Uncertainties) of obtaining permanent injunctive relief after eBay v. MercExchange, *Fed. Cir. B. J.* 17, 437, 441 (2008).

56. Janutis, *supra* note 55, p. 605.
57. Epstein, *supra* note 1, p. 5.
58. *Ibid.,* p. 24.
59. *Ibid.,* pp. 6–8.
60. *Ibid.*
61. *Ibid.,* pp. 24–25.
62. J. C. Jarosz and M. J. Chapman, The hypothetical negotiation and reasonable royalty damages: The tail wagging the dog, *Stan. Tech. L. Rev.* 16, 769, 772 (2013) ("[T]he hypothetical negotiation construct was originally introduced simply as one of many considerations to estimate such damages. It has since evolved into the primary tool used to determine reasonable royalty damages.").
63. *Georgia-Pacific Corp. v. U.S. Plywood Corp.*, 318 F. Supp. 1116, 1121 (S.D.N.Y. 1970) ("The [willing buyer and willing seller] rule is more a statement of approach than a tool of analysis. It requires consideration not only of the amount that a willing licensee would have paid for the patent license but also of the amount that a willing licensor would have accepted.").
64. *Ibid.*
65. *Ibid.*
66. G. K. Leonard and M. A. Lopez, Determining RAND royalty rates for standard-essential patents, *Antitrust* 29, 86, 88 (2014). ("The bottom-up approach is consistent with the conceptual definition of RAND and is commonly performed in patent infringement cases.").
67. *Ibid.*
68. *Ibid.,* p. 89.
69. *In re Innovatio IP Ventures, LLC* Patent Litigation, No. 11-C-9308, 2013 WL 5593609 (N.D. Ill. October 3, 2012); *TCL Commc'ns Tech. Holdings, Ltd. v. Telefonaktenbologet LM Ericsson*, No. SACV 14-00341 JVS (ANx), 2016 WL 4150033 (C.D. Cal. July 25, 2016); *see* J. Rantanen, *TCL v. Ericsson: The First Major U.S. Top-Down FRAND Royalty Decision*, PatentlyO (December 27, 2017), https://patentlyo.com/patent/2017/12/contreras-ericsson-decision.html; R. Vary, *Supersize This: Unwired Planet American Style*, Bird & Bird (December 2017), https://www.twobirds.com/en/news/articles/2017/global/supersize-this-unwired-planet-american-style.
70. Leonard and Lopez, *supra* note 66, p. 86–87.

71. *See H. Elecs. Inc. v. Pulse Elecs. Inc.,* 136 S. Ct. 1923, 1925 (2016); *Stryker Corp. v. Zimmer, Inc.,* 782 F.3d 649, 661 (Fed. Cir. 2015); G. W. Jordan III, *Halo v. Pulse:* A New chapter for willfulness and enhanced patent damages, *Landslide* (March–April 2017), https://www.americanbar.org/groups/intellectual_property_law/publications/landslide/2016-17/march-april/halo_v_pulse_new_chapter_willfulness_and_enhanced_patent_damages/.
72. 35 U.S.C. § 283 (2018) ("The several courts having jurisdiction of cases under this title may grant injunctions in accordance with the principles of equity to prevent the violation of any right secured by patent, on such terms as the court deems reasonable.").
73. Spulber, *supra* note 18, p. 21.
74. Spulber, *supra* note 18, p. 7.
75. Spulber, *supra* note 18, p. 3.
76. Spulber, *supra* note 18, p. 7 (describing the "market value method" of calculating reasonably royalty damages).
77. D. F. Spulber, How patents provide the foundation of the market for inventions, *J. Competition L. & Econ.* 11, 271, 274 (2015).
78. Méniére *et al.*, *supra* note 8, p. 20.
79. Int'l Telecomm. Union, Series Y: Global information infrastructure, internet protocol aspects and Next-Generation networks (June 2012), https://www.itu.int/rec/ dologin_pub.asp?lang=e&id=T-REC-Y.2060-201206-I!!PDF-E&type=items.
80. *Ibid.*, p. 2.
81. *Ibid.*, p. 4.
82. Spulber, *supra* note 77.
83. *IAS 38 — Intangible Assets*, Deloitte, https://www.iasplus.com/en/standards/ias/ias38 (last visited February 9, 2019) (Examples of intangible assets include the following: "[P]atented technology, computer software, databases and trade secrets; trademarks, trade dress, newspaper mastheads, internet domains; video and audiovisual material (e.g. motion pictures, television programmes); customer lists; mortgage servicing rights; licensing, royalty and standstill agreements; import quotas; franchise agreements; customer and supplier relationships (including customer lists); marketing rights.").
84. IAS 38 intangible Assets, Int'l Fin. reporting standards found., https://www.ifrs.org/issued-standards/list-of-standards/ias-38-intangible-assets/ (last visited February 9, 2019).
85. R. F. Reilly, Valuation of contract-related intangible assets, The practical lawyer, December 2013, p. 37, 38, http://www.willamette.com/pubs/

presentations3/reilly_ contract_intangibles_tpl2013.pdf ("The contract document (or the oral agreement) itself is not the intangible asset. The legal rights and duties of the contract are the intangible asset.").

86. *See* D. F. Spulber, The innovative entrepreneur 27–29 (2014).
87. D. F. Spulber, Public prizes versus market prices: Should contests replace patents? *J. Pat. & Trademark Off. Soc'y* 97, 690 (2015).
88. R. P. Merges, A transactional view of property rights, *Berkeley Tech. L.J.* 20, 1477 (2005).
89. *Ibid.*, p. 1488.
90. *Ibid.*
91. *Ibid.,* pp. 1514–19.
92. F. S. Kieff, Property rights and property rules for commercializing inventions, *Minn. L. Rev*. 85, 697, 703 (2000); *see also* E. W. Kitch, The nature and function of the patent system, *J.L. & Econ*. 20, 265, 266 (1977); J. F. Duffy, Rethinking the prospect theory of patents, *U. Chi. L. Rev*. 71, 439, 439 (2004); P. J. Heald, A transaction costs theory of patent law, *Ohio St. L.J.* 66, 473, 508 (2005).
93. Email from the Honorable F. S. Kieff, Comm'r, U.S. Int'l Trade Comm'n, to U.S. Fed. Trade Comm'n & Dep't of Justice, (September 23, 2016) [hereinafter Kieff, FTC & DoJ Joint IP-AT Guidelines Email], https://www.ftc.gov/policy/public-comments/2016/09/30/comment-00006 (expressing his views on the United States Federal Trade Commission's and the United States Department of Justice Antitrust Division's Joint Guidelines for the Licensing of Intellectual Property); *see also* F. S. Kieff and T. A. Paredes, The basics matter: At the periphery of intellectual property, *Geo. Wash. L. Rev*. 73, 174, 179 (2004).
94. Kieff, FTC and DoJ Joint IPAT Guidelines Email, *supra* note 93.
95. J. Antonipillai and M. K. Lee, USPTO, intellectual property and The U.S. economy: 2016 Update 3 (last visited March 28, 2018), https://www.uspto.gov/sites/ default/files/documents/IPandtheUSEconomySept2016.pdf.
96. Spulber, *supra* note 77, p. 6.
97. R. T. Nimmer, Breaking barriers: The relation between contract and intellectual property law, *Berkeley Tech. L.J*. 13, 827, 888 (1998). Nimmer also states that "property rights are routinely transferred, waived, released and licensed. Contracts provide the means for the development and commercial exploitation of information assets." *Ibid.,* p. 830.
98. *Ibid*., p. 827.
99. *See* S. K. Sandeen, A contract by any other name is still a contract: Examining the effectiveness of trade secret clauses to protect databases,

IDEA 45, 119, 122 (2005) (discussing the relationship between contracts and IP); D. Friedman, In defense of private orderings: Comments on julie cohen's copyright and the jurisprudence of Self-Help, *Berkeley Tech. L.J.* 13, 1151, 1152 (1998); J. H. Reichman and J. A. Franklin, Privately legislated intellectual property rights: Reconciling freedom of contract with public good uses of information, *U. Pa. L. Rev.* 147, 875, 904 (1999); R. P. Merges, The End of Friction? Property rights and contract in the "Newtonian" world of on-line commerce, *Berkeley Tech. L.J.* 112, 15, 126 (1997).

100. Fed. Trade Comm'n, Antitrust guidelines for the licensing of intellectual property 4 (January 12, 2017), https://www.ftc.gov/system/files/documents/public_statements/ 1049793/ip_guidelines_2017.pdf.
101. *Ibid.*
102. *Ibid.*
103. *See, e.g.*, A. K. Dixit and R. S. Pindyck, Investment under Uncertainty 2 (1994).
104. There are difficulties in forming expectations about future events. *See* discussion *infra* Section IV. Also, calculating the expected present discounted value of a stream of benefits requires adjusting either discount rates or the expected value of benefits to account for the costs of risk. *See* A. A. Robichek and S. C. Myers, Conceptual problems in the use of risk-adjusted discount rates, *J. Fin.* 21, 727, 727–30 (1966).
105. *See* C. J. Goetz and R. E. Scott, Liquidated damages, penalties and the just compensation principle: Some notes on an enforcement model and a theory of efficient breach, *Colum. L. Rev.* 77, 554, 562 32 (1977); I. R. Macneil, Contracts: adjustment of long-term economic relations under classical, neoclassical, and relational contract law, *Nw. U. L. Rev.* 72, 854, 864 31 (1978); A. T. Kronman, Specific performance, *U. Chi. L. Rev.* 45, 351, 352 (1978); A. Schwartz, The case for specific performance, *Yale L.J.* 89, 271, 271 (1979); R. Craswell, Contract remedies, renegotiation, and the theory of efficient breach, *S. Cal. L. Rev.* 61, 629, 630 (1988).
106. See E. A. Farnsworth, Legal remedies for breach of contract, *Colum. L. Rev.* 70, 1145, 1147 (1970); J. H. Barton, The economic basis of damages for breach of contract, *J. Legal Stud.* 1, 277, 278 (1972); R. L. Birmingham, Breach of contract, damage measures, and economic efficiency, *Rutgers L. Rev.* 24, 273, 286 (1970); L. A. Kornhauser, An introduction to the economic analysis of contract remedies, *U. Colo. L. Rev.* 57, 683, 720–21 (1986); W. P. Rogerson, Efficient reliance and damage measures for breach of contract, *RAND J. Econ.* 15, 39, 44 (1984).
107. 35 U.S.C. § 154 (2018).

108. P. B. C. Jones, Violation of a patent license restriction: Breach of contract or patent infringement? *IDEA: J. L. & Tech.* 33, 225, 226 (1993) ("[A] patent licensing agreement is a contract which is governed by principles of state contract law.").
109. *Ibid.*
110. *Ibd.,* p. 240, 75.
111. M. C. Jensen and W. H. Meckling, The theory of the firm: Managerial behavior, agency costs, and ownership structure, *J. Fin. Econ.* 3, 305, 310 (1976) ("[Firms] serve as a nexus for a set of contracting relationships among individuals."); *see* M. A. Eisenberg, The conception that the corporation is a nexus of contracts, and the dual nature of the firm, *J. Corp. L.* 24, 819, 828 (1998).
112. S. N. S. Cheung, The contractual nature of the firm, *J.L. & Econ.* 26, 1, 10 (1983). Cheung states that an input owner has the option of own-use, selling the input to others, or creating a firm through contracts delegating the use of the input: "The firm emerges with the third option: the entrepreneur or the agent who holds a limited set of use rights by contract directs production activities without immediate reference to the price of each activity, and the commodities so produced are then sold in the market." *Ibid,* p. 3. *See also* R. Coase, The nature of the firm, *Economica* 16, 386 (1937).
113. *See* D. F. Spulber, The theory of the firm: Microeconomics with endogenous entrepreneurs, firms, markets, and organizations 415 (2009).
114. *Ibid.*
115. *See generally* Spulber, *supra* note 86.
116. *Ibid.*
117. *See* R. Zeckhauser, The challenge of contracting for technological information, *Proc. Nat'l Acad. Sci. U.S.* 93, 12473, 12473 (1996) ("Contracting to provide technological information (TI) is a significant challenge. TI is an unusual commodity in five ways. (i) TI is difficult to count and value; conventional indicators, such as patents and citations, hardly indicate value. TI is often sold at different prices to different parties. (ii) To value TI, it may be necessary to 'give away the secret.' This danger, despite nondisclosure agreements, inhibits efforts to market TI. (iii) To prove its value, TI is often bundled into complete products, such as a computer chip or pharmaceutical product. Efficient exchange, by contrast, would involve merely the raw information. (iv) Sellers' superior knowledge about TI's value make buyers wary of overpaying. (v) Inefficient contracts are often designed to secure rents from TI.").
118. *See* discussion *infra* Section IV.

119. *See generally* Coase, *supra* 112.
120. *Ibid.*
121. *See* T. J. Sturgeon, Modular production networks: A new American model of industrial organization, *Indus. & Corp. Change* 11, 451, 451 (2002); C. Y. Baldwin, Where Do Transactions Come From? Modularity, transactions, and the boundaries of firms, *Indus. & Corp. Change* 17, 155, 161 (2007); R. J. Gilson *et al.*, Contracting for innovation: Vertical disintegration and interfirm collaboration, *Colum. L. Rev.* 109, 431, 435 (2009) ("Contracting for innovation supports iterative collaboration between firms by interweaving explicit and implicit terms that respond to the uncertainty inherent in the innovation process …"); M. M. Blair *et al.*, Outsourcing, modularity, and the theory of the firm, *BYU L. Rev.* 263, 265–66 (2011).
122. E. Brynjolfsson *et al.*, Intangible assets: Computers and organizational capital, *Brookings Pap. on Econ. Acti.* 1, 137, 138 (2002) ("This paper analytically explores the hypothesis that new, intangible organizational assets complement [information technology] capital just as new production processes and factory redesign complemented the adoption of electric motors over 100 years ago.").
123. K. Firth-Butterfield and Y. Chae, Artificial intelligence collides with patent law, *Ctr. for the Fourth Indus. Revolution* 3, 5 (April 2018) http://www3.weforum.org/docs/WEF_48540_WP_End_of_Innovation_Protecting_Patent_Law.pdf.
124. M. C. Jennejohn, Collaboration, innovation, and contract design, *Stan. J. L., Bus. & Fin.* 14, 83, 84 (2008) ("Rather, deverticalized firms enmesh themselves in webs of collaboration — joint ventures, strategic alliances, just-in-time (JIT) production arrangements, etc. — usually in hope of cost-cutting but also with an eye to securing competitive advantage through innovation.").
125. *Ibid.*
126. D. F. Spulber, Standard setting organizations and standard essential patents: Voting and markets, *Econ. J.* 129, 1477 (April 2019), https://doi.org/10.1111/ecoj.12606.
127. *Ibid.*
128. ISO/IEC Guide 2:2004 at 12 (Int'l Org. for Standardization & Int'l Electrotechnical Comm'n 2004), https://www.iso.org/obp/ui/#iso:std:iso-iec:guide:2:ed-8:v1:en.
129. Int'l Org. for Standardization, Navigating a World in Transition 35 (2016), https://www.iso.org/files/live/sites/isoorg/files/about%20ISO/annual_reports/en/annual_report_2016_en.pdf.

130. *See generally* R. Adner and R. Kapoor, Value creation in innovation ecosystems: How the structure of technological interdependence affects firm performance in new technology generations, *Strategic Mgmt. J.* 31, 306 (2010).
131. U.S. Const. art. I, § 8, cl. 8 ("The Congress shall have Power ... To promote the Progress of Science and useful Arts, by securing for limited Times to Authors and Inventors the exclusive Right to their respective Writings and Discoveries."). *See also* G. Quinn, Patents, copyrights and the constitution, perfect together, IPWatchdog (February 19, 2018), http://www.ipwatchdog.com/2018/02/19/patents-copyrights-constitution/id=93941/.
132. *See* 35 U.S.C. § 271 (2018).
133. *Ibid.*; *see also* Fla. Stat. § 815.04 (2018).
134. *See, e.g.*, R. D. Blair and T. F. Cotter, An economic analysis of damages rules in intellectual property law, *Wm. & Mary L. Rev.* 39, 1585, 1615 (1997) ("A substantial number of the law and economics scholars who have written on this subject appear to agree that it is generally preferable to protect intellectual property rights through the use of property, as opposed to liability, rules.").
135. *Trade Secret Policy*, USPTO, https://www.uspto.gov/patents-getting-started/ international-protection/trade-secret-policy (last visited November 24, 2018). But see World Intellectual Property Organization, What is Intellectual Property? (2003) http://www.wipo.int/edocs/pubdocs/en/int-property/450/wipo_pub_450.pdf; World Intellectual Property Organization, intellectual property handbook 3 (2d ed. 2004), http://www.wipo.int/edocs/pubdocs/en/intproperty/489/wipo_pub_489.pdf ("Generally speaking, intellectual property law aims at safeguarding creators and other producers of intellectual goods and services by granting them certain time-limited rights to control the use made of those productions. Those rights do not apply to the physical object in which the creation may be embodied but instead to the intellectual creation as such. Intellectual property is traditionally divided into two branches, 'industrial property' and 'copyright.'").
136. Convention Establishing the World Intellectual Property Organization art. 2, July 14, 1967, 21 U.S.T. 1749, 828 U.N.T.S. 3.
137. G. Quinn, SCOTUS says patents are a government franchise, not a vested property right, *Ipwatchdog* (April 24, 2018), https://www.ipwatchdog.com/2018/04/24/scotus-says-patents-government-franchise-not-vested-property-right/id=96324/; *see also Oil States Energy Servs., LLC v. Greene's Energy Grp., LLC*, 138 S. Ct. 1365, 1373 (2018).

138. *See* 35 U.S.C. § 2(a) (2018).
139. *See* 35 U.S.C. § 131 (2018); 15 U.S.C. § 1051 (2018).
140. *See* 35 U.S.C. §§ 100–03 (2018).
141. USPTO, Protecting Your Trademark: Enhancing your rights through federal registration 3 (2016), https://www.uspto.gov/sites/default/files/documents/BasicFacts.pdf.
142. *Ibid.*, p. 7.
143. *Overview of the Copyright Office*, U.S. Copyright Office, https://www.copyright.gov/about/ (last visited January 21, 2019).
144. 17 U.S.C. § 102 (2018).
145. R. A. Epstein, The disintegration of intellectual property? A classical liberal response to a premature obituary, *Stan. L. Rev.* 62, 455, 459 (2010) ("As I shall argue, the single adoption of one adjustment, and one adjustment only, goes a very long way to ease the transformation from tangible to intangible property. Just use limited terms of exclusive rights, longer for copyrights than patents, to work the transformation from tangible property to these two vital forms of intellectual property. At that point, the remainder of the rules that deal with tangible property, namely those that concern exclusion, use, and disposition, can be carried over without difficulty.").
146. *Ibid.*
147. USPTO, Patent eligible subject matter: Report on views and recommendations from the public United States Patent and Trademark Office (2017), https://www.uspto.gov/sites/default/files/documents/101-Report_FINAL.pdf.
148. 35 U.S.C. § 101 (2018).
149. *Bilski v. Kappos*, 561 U.S. 593 (2010).
150. *Ibid.*; *see also* D. F. Spulber, Should business method inventions be patentable? *J. Legal Analysis* 3, 265, 267 (2011).
151. *Mayo v. Prometheus*, 132 S. Ct. 1289 (2012).
152. USPTO, *supra* note 147, p. 8.
153. *Alice Corp. v. CLS Bank Int'l,* 134 S. Ct. 2347 (2014).
154. G. Quinn, Protecting ideas: Can ideas be protected or patented? *IP Watchdog* (February 15, 2014), http://www.ipwatchdog.com/2014/02/15/protecting-ideas-can-ideas-be-protected-or-patented/id=48009/.
155. Quinn, *supra* note 29 ("Thanks to the United States Supreme Court, the United States Court of Appeals for the Federal Circuit and ever more regulations from the United States Patent and Trademark Office it has become more difficult over the years to create the type of written description and claim sets required.").

156. J. Green and M. Wirz, Whose Idea Is it Anyway? *10 IP Issues in Deals*, ACC Docket, December 2010, p. 40.
157. *See* B. H. Hall and R. H. Ziedonis, The patent paradox revisited: An empirical study of patenting in the US semiconductor industry, *Rand J. Econ.* 1979–1995 32, 101 (2001); L. Fleming, Breakthroughs and the "Long Tail" of innovation, *MIT Sloan Mgmt. Rev.* 49, 69 (2007); C. Schneider, External knowledge sourcing: Science, market and the value of patented inventions, *Managerial and Decision Econ.* 30, 551 (2009); and G. De Rassenfosse, Do Firms face a Trade-Off between the quantity and the quality of their inventions? *Rese. Poli.* 42, 1072 (2013).
158. G. Quinn, Patentability: The nonobviousness requirement of 35 U.S.C. 103, *IP Watchdog* (June 17, 2017), http://www.ipwatchdog.com/2017/06/17/patentability-nonobviousness-35-usc-103/id=84716/.
159. N. Solomon, The problem of patent valuation, *IP Watchdog* (August 15, 2017), http://www.ipwatchdog.com/2017/08/15/problem-patent-valuation/id=86840/.
160. R. S. Eisenberg, Patent costs and unlicensed use of patented inventions, *U. Chi. L. Rev.* 78, 53, 54–55 (2011).
161. G. Quinn, PTAB judges shockingly inexperienced compared to district court judges, *IP Watchdog* (March 6, 2018), http://www.ipwatchdog.com/2018/03/06/ptab-judges-shockingly-inexperienced/id=94438/ ("The America Invents Act (AIA) invests PTAB judges with extraordinary powers. For example, overwhelmingly institution decisions are not appealable. Yet, there have been numerous lawyers with shockingly little experience appointed to the position of patent judge, and vested with the power to make decisions that cannot be reviewed by any Article III federal court.").
162. *See* J. E. Jankowski, Nat'l Sci. Found., business use of intellectual property protection documented in NSF survey 1 (2012), http://wayback.archive-it.org/5902/20181004073804/https://www.nsf.gov/statistics/infbrief/nsf12307/nsf12307.pdf ("New survey findings from the National Science Foundation (NSF) and the U.S. Census Bureau (Census) indicate that trademarks and trade secrets are identified by the largest number of businesses as important forms of IP protection, followed by copyrights, and then patents."); *see generally* J. Pooley, Trade Secrets (2017).
163. S. E. Olafson, Patents vs. Trade secrets — Giving your business the competitive edge, *Ariz. BioInsider* (April 1, 2007), https://www.lrrc.com/files/Uploads/Documents/ Olafson_AZBioInsider.pdf.

164. I.P.L. Png, Law and innovation: Evidence from state trade secrets laws, *Rev. Econ. & Stat*. 99, 167, 168 (2017).
165. *Ibid*., p. 175.
166. *Ibid*.
167. E. D. Pisegna-Cook, Ownership rights of employee inventions: The role of preinvention assignment agreements and state statutes, *U. Balt. Intell. Prop. L.J*. 2, 163, 163 (1994).
168. Epstein, *supra* note 145, p. 458 ("Any agreement, for example, whereby a trade secret is shared pursuant to a confidentiality agreement involves the simultaneous transmission and retention of information — but only if the contractual arrangements are given strong protection, as they typically are.").
169. Owners of buildings and land can place fences around their properties. Owners of automobiles and other vehicles can equip them with locks and other antitheft devices. Companies have various mechanisms for deterring theft of their goods, equipment, and financial assets.
170. Menell, *supra* note 31, p. 726.
171. P. Arqué-Castells and D. F. Spulber, Measuring the private and social returns to R&D: Unintended spillovers versus technology markets (*Nw. L. & Econ. Research*, Paper No. 18–18, 2019), http://dx.doi.org/10.2139/ssrn.3202870.
172. *See* R. P. Merges and R. R. Nelson, On the complex economics of patent scope, *Colum. L. Rev*. 90, 839 (1990); R. P. Merges and R. R. Nelson, On limiting or encouraging rivalry in technical progress: The effect of patent scope decisions, *J. Econ. Behav. & Org*. 25, 1, 6 (1994).
173. *See* Merges and Nelson, 1990, 1994, supra note 172.
174. M. Boldrin and D. K. Levine, The case against patents, *J. Econ. Persp*. 27, 3, 18 (2013).
175. *See* S. Scotchmer, Standing on the shoulders of giants: Cumulative research and the patent law, *J. Econ. Persp*. 5, 29, 30 (1991).
176. On arguments for broader patent scope, *see* E. W. Kitch, The nature and function of the patent system, *J.L. & Econ*. 20, 265 (1977); D. F. Spulber, How patents provide the foundation of the market for inventions, *J. Comp. L. & Econ*. 11, 271 (2015).
177. Kieff, *supra* note 92, p. 710.
178. Kitch, *supra* note 176, p. 278.
179. A. C. Pigou, The economics of welfare 189 (4th ed. 1932).
180. *Ibid*.

181. R. H. Coase, The problem of social cost, *J.L. & Econ*. 3, 1 (1960).
182. *Ibid.*, p. 6.
183. *Ibid.*, p. 9.
184. *Ibid.*
185. *Ibid.*, p. 3.
186. *Ibid.*, p. 5.
187. *Ibid.*, p. 6.
188. H. Demsetz, Information and efficiency: Another viewpoint, *J.L. Econ*. 12, 1, 13 (1969) ("If the cost of contracting is positive, the kind of property rights system that is established may change the allocation of resources in the production of knowledge.").
189. R. P. Merges, Of property rules, coase, and intellectual property, *Colum. L. Rev*. 94, 2655, 2662 (1994) ("Even though there are many dispersed buyers (and sellers) of IPRs, and even though the transaction costs of IPR exchanges are otherwise high, the strong property rule baseline often works quite well. The frequency of contracting in many markets for IPRs — an underdeveloped theme in most of the entitlements literature — gives rise to a myriad of institutions (broadly defined) designed to streamline the exchange of property rights.").
190. *See* J. R. Green and S. Scotchmer, On the division of profit in sequential innovation, *RAND J. Econ*. 26, 20, 21 (1995); T. O'Donoghue *et al.*, Patent breadth, patent life, and the pace of technological progress, *J. Econ. & Mgmt. Strategy* 7, 1, 2 (1998); J. H. Barton, Patents and antitrust: A rethinking in light of patent breadth and sequential innovation, *Antitrust L.J.* 65, 449, 450 (1997).
191. *See* O'Donoghue *et al.*, *supra* note 190, p. 2; Barton, *supra* note 190, 449.
192. N. T. Gallini, Patent policy and costly imitation, *RAND J. Econ*. 23, 52, 53 (1992).
193. A. L. Landers, Patent claim apportionment, patentee injury and sequential invention, *Geo. Mason L. Rev*. 19, 471, 476 (2012).
194. For some discussion of spillovers and RJVs, *see* C. D'Aspremont and A. Jacquemin, Cooperative and noncooperative R&D in duopoly with spillovers, *Am. Econ. Rev*. 78, 1133 (1988); K. Suzumura, Cooperative and Noncooperative R&D in an oligopoly with spillovers, *Am. Econ. Rev*. 82, 1307 (1992).
195. H. M. Blake, Employee agreements not to compete, *Harv. L. Rev*. 73, 625, 629 (1960).
196. S. Sanga, A theory of corporate joint ventures, *Cal. L. Rev.* 106, 1437, 1438 (2018).

197. *Ibid.*, p. 1454.
198. K. J. Arrow, Economic welfare and the allocation of resources for invention, *Nat'l Bureau of Econ. Res.* 0-87014-304-2 609, 615 (1962), https://www.nber.org/chapters/ c2144.pdf.
199. R. J. Gilson, The legal infrastructure of high technology industrial districts: Silicon valley, route 128, and covenants not to compete, *N.Y.U. L. Rev.* 74, 575, 577 (1999).
200. *Ibid.*
201. 35 U.S.C. § 271 (2018).
202. Menell, *supra* note 31, p. 753.
203. R. P. Wagner, Information wants to be free: Intellectual property and the mythologies of control, *Colum. L. Rev.* 103, 995, 1031 (2003).
204. *Ibid.*, p. 1030.
205. Spulber, *supra* note 77, p. 271.
206. On transaction costs of contract formation, *see* Coase, *supra* note 112, and Coase, *supra* note 181, pp. 15–16.
207. The costs and rules of contract formation affect the incentives of parties involved in contract negotiation, *see* Coase, *supra* note 181; A. Katz, The strategic structure of offer and acceptance: Game theory and the law of contract formation, *Mich. L. Rev.* 89, 215, 230 (1990).
208. Poblete and Spulber, *supra* note 39, p. 39 ("Firms must design and apply incentive contracts for specialized economic agents who conduct R&D because most R&D is a delegated activity. The skills, knowledge and personnel necessary for the invention often differ from those needed for other production and operating activities and generally require independent business units. Companies and government agencies conduct R&D in-house by employing specialized experts such as scientists, engineers, and statisticians.").
209. M. N. Darrough and N. M. Stoughton, Moral hazard and adverse selection: The question of financial structure, *J. Fin.* 41, 501, 501 (1986).
210. *Ibid.*
211. G. Manso, Motivating innovation, *J. Fin.* 66, 1823, 1830 (2011).
212. Poblete and Spulber, *supra* note 39, at n. 6.
213. Darrough and Stoughton, *supra* note 209, p. 501.
214. *See* R. B. Myerson, Perspectives on mechanism design in economic theory, *Am. Econ. Rev.* 98, 586, 587 (2008) ("[I]ncentive constraints express the basic fact that individuals will not share private information or exert hidden efforts without appropriate incentives.").

215. *See* P. Bolton and M. Dewatripont, Contract theory 95–96 (2005); J.-J. Laffont and D. Martimort, The theory of incentives 29 (2002); M. C. Jensen and W. H. Meckling, Theory of the firm: Managerial behavior, agency costs and ownership structure, *J. Fin. Econ.* 3, 305, 308 (1976).
216. Poblete and Spulber, *supra* note 39, p. 54.
217. *Ibid.,* p. 38.
218. F. Andersson, M. Freedman, J. Haltiwanger, J. Lane, and K. Shaw, Reaching for the stars: Who pays for talent in innovative industries? *Econ. J.* 119, F308, F327 (2009) ("We show that software firms that operate in software sectors with highly skewed returns to innovation, or high upside gains to innovation, are more likely to attract and pay for highly talented workers. Such firms do so first by paying more up-front in starting salaries to attract skilled employees and second by rewarding workers handsomely for experience or loyalty.").
219. J. E. Core and W. R. Guay, Stock option plans for non-executive employees, *J. Fin. Econ.* 61, 253, 272 (2001) ("Firms with greater monitoring costs and greater growth options (proxied by firm size, the book-to-market ratio, and R&D expense) provide greater option incentives to non-executive employees.").
220. J. Lerner and J. Wulf, Innovation and incentives: Evidence from corporate R&D, *Rev. Econ. Stat.* 89, 634, 634 (2007) ("Among firms with a centralized R&D organization, a clear relationship emerges: more long-term incentives granted to corporate R&D heads are associated with more heavily cited patents. These incentives also appear to be associated with more frequent awards and patents of greater originality.").
221. A. A. Alchian and H. Demsetz, Production, information costs, and economic organization, *Am. Econ. Rev.* 62, 777, 780 (1972).
222. *See* G. P. Baker, Incentive contracts and performance measurement, *J. Pol. Econ.* 100, 598, 609 (1992).
223. D. M. Anderson, Commercialization, *Half Cost Products*, http://www.halfcostproducts.com/commercialization.htm (last visited Nov. 9, 2018).
224. *Ibid.*
225. T. Dewett, Linking intrinsic motivation, risk taking, and employee creativity in an R&D environment, *R&D Mgmt.* 37, 197, 197 (2007).
226. *Ibid.*; *see also* M. Baer *et al.*, Rewarding creativity: When does it really matter? *Leadership Q.* 14, 569, 571 (2003).
227. Dewett, *supra* note 225, p. 204.

228. K. Murdock, Intrinsic motivation and optimal incentive contracts, *RAND J. Econ.* 33, 650, 653 (2002).
229. *Ibid.*
230. Overview, Mectizan Donation Program, https://mectizan.org/what/overview/ (last visited November 11, 2018).
231. Murdock, *supra* note 228, p. 651.
232. *Ibid.*, p. 667 ("When workers are intrinsically motivated, there are 'gains from trade' that arise when the firm implements a project that has negative financial return but generates large intrinsic returns to the agent.").
233. *Ibid.*
234. R. S. Gruner, Imagination, invention, and patent incentives: The psychology of patent law, *U. Ill. J.L. Tech. & Pol'y* 2017, 375, 435 (2017).
235. *Ibid.*, p. 380.
236. *Ibid.*, p. 382.
237. *See* S. J. H. Graham, A. C. Marco, and R. Miller, The USPTO patent examination research dataset: A window on patent processing, *J. Econ. & Mgmt. Strategy* 27, 554, 557 (2018).
238. *See generally* D. C. Mowery and N. Rosenberg, Technology and the pursuit of economic growth (1989). I do not consider various types of legal uncertainty that may affect ICs. These include uncertainty about approval of a patent application and whether a patent will be found to be valid and infringed in court proceedings.
239. *See* Poblete and Spulber, *supra* note 39, p. 54.
240. *See* R. A. Dye, Costly contract contingencies, *Int'l Econ. Rev.* 26, 233, 233–34 (1985).
241. Schwartz and Watson, *supra* note 38, p. 26; *see* Poblete and Spulber, *supra* note 39 (discussing of renegotiation possibility effects on the form of incentive contracts).
242. *See* L. Wasserman, All of statistics: A concise course in statistical inference 87 (2013), http://static.stevereads.com/papers_to_read/all_of_statistics.pdf.
243. *See* M. Weber and C. Camerer, Recent developments in modelling preferences under risk, *Operations-Research-Spektrum* 9, 129 (1987); *see generally* C. Camerer and M. Weber, Recent developments in modeling preferences: Uncertainty and ambiguity, *J. of Risk & Uncertainty* 5, 325 (1992) (providing examples of useful surveys).
244. *See* Wasserman, *supra* note 242, p. 5.
245. *Ibid.*, p. 90.
246. *Ibid.*

247. *See* D. Dequech, Fundamental uncertainty and ambiguity, *E. Econ. J.* 26, 41, 50–51 (2000) ("Going beyond situations of ambiguity, members of different schools of heterodox economic thought have emphasized situations of uncertainty of a more radical type. These situations are essentially characterized by the possibility of creativity and structural change and therefore by significant indeterminacy of the future. Uncertainty appears here in a dynamic context, in which the passage of time is crucial. The future cannot be anticipated by a fully reliable probabilistic estimate because *the future is yet to be created*.").
248. *Ibid.*; *see generally* J. M. Keynes, Treatise on probability (1921), https://archive.org/stream/treatiseonprobab007528mbp#page/n105/mode/2up/search/uncertainty.
249. Letter from Isaac Newton to Robert Hooke (February 5, 1675) (on file with the Historical Society of Pennsylvania Digital Library), https://digitallibrary.hsp.org/index.php/Detail/objects/ 9792.
250. T. S. Kuhn, The structure of scientific revolutions 2 (2d enlarged ed., 1970).
251. *Ibid.*, p. 24.
252. *Ibid.*, pp. 52–53.
253. I. Scheffler, Vision and revolution: A postscript on kuhn, *Phil. Sci.* 39, 366, 374 (1972).
254. D. Dequech, Expectations and confidence under uncertainty, *J. Post Keynesian Econ.* 21, 415, 416 (1999).
255. European Patent Office & Handelsblatt Research Institute, Patents and the Fourth Industrial Revolution: The Inventions Behind Digital Transformation 20 (2017), https://documents.epo.org/projects/babylon/eponet.nsf/0/17FDB5538E87B4B9C12581EF0045762F/$File/fourth_industrial_revolution_2017__en.pdf.
256. J. Schumpeter, Capitalism, Socialism, and Democracy 83 (Routledge 2006) (1942).
257. 25 U.S.C. §§ 102–03 (2018).
258. 35 U.S.C. § 101 (2018).
259. S. Scotchmer and J. Green, Novelty and disclosure in patent law, *RAND J. Econ.* 21, 131, 146 (1990).
260. G. N. Mandel, Patently non-obvious: Empirical demonstration that the hindsight bias renders patent decisions irrational, *Ohio St. L.J.* 67, 1391, 1393 (2006).
261. F. A. Hayek, The use of knowledge in society, *Am. Econ. Rev.* 35, 519, 520 (1945).

262. *Ibid.*, p. 524.
263. *Ibid.*, p. 526.
264. *Ibid.*, p. 523.
265. *Ibid.*, pp. 523–24.
266. F. A. Hayek, Competition as a discovery procedure, *Q. J. Austrian Econ.* 5, 9, 11 (Marcellus S. Snow trans., 2002) (1968).
267. *Ibid.*, p. 18.
268. Organization for Economic Cooperation and Development & Statistical Office of the European Cmtys., Oslo Manual: Guidelines for collecting and interpreting innovation data 16–17 (3d ed. 2005) ("The Manual defines four types of innovations that encompass a wide range of changes in firms' activities: product innovations, process innovations, organisational innovations and marketing innovations."); *see generally* S. Bryan, L. S. Hwang, and S. Lilien, CEO Stock-Based compensation: An empirical analysis of incentive-intensity, relative mix, and economic determinants, *J. Bus.* 73, 661 (2000) (discussing contracts with executives).
269. Organization for Economic Cooperation and Development, F. Manual 2015: Guidelines for collecting and reporting data on research and experimental development 45 (2015), https://www.oecd-ilibrary.org/docserver/9789264239012-en.pdf?expires=1541275882&id=id& accname =guest&checksum=C5F78E17C5D5D32FCCC469D632ACF256 ("The term R&D covers three types of activity: Basic research, applied research and experimental development.").
270. *Ibid.*, p. 28 ("For an activity to be an R&D activity, it must satisfy five core criteria. The activity must be: novel, creative, uncertain, systematic, transferable and/or reproducible.").
271. *See 2017 Global R&D Funding Forecast*, R&D Mag., Winter 2017, p. 7, https://edisciplinas.usp.br/pluginfile.php/3378934/mod_resource/content/1/RD%202016.pdf ("For 2017, total U.S. R&D spending is expected to increase by 2.9% to $527.5 billion or a 1% increase after accounting for 2017's expected 1.9% inflation rate (EIU/OECD).").
272. *Ibid.*
273. *Ibid.*
274. *See* Z. Griliches, Issues in assessing the contribution of research and development to productivity growth, *Bell J. Econ.* 10, 92, 94–95 (1979).
275. *Ibid.*; *see also* A. B. Jaffe, Technological opportunity and spillovers of R&D: Evidence from firms' patents, profits and market value, *Am. Econ. Rev.* 76, 984, 989 (1986).

276. *See* Myerson, *supra* note 214.
277. B. Shackelford and F. Moris, *Nat'l Sci. Found.: Nat'l Ctr. for Sci. and Eng'g Statistics*, A snapshot of business R&D employment in the United States 1 (2016), https://www.nsf.gov/statistics/2017/nsf17302/nsf17302.pdf.
278. *Ibid.*
279. *Ibid.*
280. D. E. Hecker, High-technology employment: A NAICS-based update, *Monthly Lab. Rev*. 57, 58 (2005).
281. D. C. Mowery, The relationship between intrafirm and contractual forms of industrial research in American manufacturing, *Explorations in Econ. Hist.* 1900–1940 20, 351 (1983).
282. *Ibid.,* p. 369.
283. *Ibid.,* pp. 369–70.
284. Andersson *et al.*, *supra* note 218, at F326.
285. P. O. Ángel and L. S. Sánchez, R&D Managers' adaptation of firms' HRM practices, *R&D Mgmt*. 39, 271, 271 (2009).
286. *Ibid.*
287. *Ibid.,* p. 284.
288. K. D. Martell and S. J. Carroll Jr., The role of HRM in supporting innovation strategies: Recommendations on how R&D managers should be treated from an HRM perspective, *R&D Mgmt*. 25, 91, 92 (1995).
289. C. L. Fisk, Removing the "Fuel of lnterest" from the "Fire of Genius": law and the employee-inventor, *U. Chi. L. Rev*. 1830–1930 65, 1127, 1174 (1998).
290. *Ibid.,* p. 1128.
291. *Ibid.,* pp. 1130–31 ("[M]ost employees who invent are bound by contracts requiring them to assign the patents to their employers.").
292. R. P. Merges, The law and economics of employee inventions, *Harv. J.L. Tech.* 13, 1 (1999).
293. *Ibid.,* p. 37.
294. *Ibid.,* p. 3.
295. *Ibid.,* p. 8.
296. *Ibid.,* p. 5.
297. *Ibid.,* pp. 5–6.
298. *Ibid.,* p. 6.
299. *Ibid.,* pp. 6–7.
300. *Ibid.,* p. 47.
301. *Ibid,*. pp. 26–27.

302. *See* Poblete and Spulber, *supra* note 39.
303. Shackelford and Moris, *supra* note 277, p. 1.
304. *Ibid.*
305. N. Lacetera, I. M. Cockburn, and R. Henderson, Do firms change capabilities by hiring new people? A study of the adoption of science-based drug discovery, *Advances Strategic Mgmt.* 21, 133 (2004); L. G. Zucker. M. R. Darby, and J. S. Armstrong, Commercializing knowledge: University science knowledge capture, and firm performance in biotechnology, *Mgmt. Sci.* 48, 138 (2002).
306. Poblete and Spulber, *supra* note 39, p. 39 ("Companies and government agencies also outsource R&D by contracting with research laboratories, specialized firms, universities, and independent researchers .... Corporations and venture capitalists also engage in delegation of R&D through financing, monitoring, and directing entrepreneurial technology startups, specialized research firms, and independent researchers.").
307. R. Veugelers, Internal R&D expenditures and external technology sourcing, *Res. Pol'y* 26, 303, 308 (1997); P. Teirlinck *et al.*, Corporate decision-making in R&D outsourcing and the impact on internal R&D employment intensity, *Indus. Corp. Change* 19, 1741, 1742 (2010).
308. P. Trott and D. Hartmann, Why 'Open Innovation' is old wine in new bottles, *Int'l J. Innovation Mgmt.* 13, 715, 716 (2009).
309. *Ibid.*, p. 720.
310. H. W. Chesbrough, The era of open innovation, *MIT Sloan Mgmt. Rev.*, Spring 2003, p. 35; H. W. Chesbrough, Why companies should have open business models, *MIT Sloan Mgmt. Rev.*, Winter 2007, p. 22.
311. A. Arora *et al.*, The acquisition and commercialization of invention in American manufacturing: Incidence and impact, Res. Pol'y 45, 1113, 1113 (2016) ("Our results indicate that, between 2007 and 2009, 16% of manufacturing firms had innovated — meaning had introduced a product that was new to the industry. Of these, 49% report that their most important new product had originated from an outside source, notably customers, suppliers and technology specialists (i.e., universities, independent inventors and R&D contractors).").
312. A. Arora and A. Gambardella, The market for technology, in *Handbook of the Economics of Innovation* 1, 641, 651 n.8 (B. H. Hall and N. Rosenberg eds., 2010).
313. W. M. Cohen and D. A. Levinthal, Innovation and learning: The two faces of R&D, *Econ. J.* 99, 569, 589 (1989).

314. *See* World Trade Organization, World Trade Report 2014: Trade and Development: Recent Trends and the Role of the WTO 43 (2014).
315. J. Howells, D. Gagliardi, and K. Malik, The growth and management of R&D outsourcing: Evidence from UK pharmaceuticals, *R&D Mgmt.* 38, 205, 206 (2008).
316. P. Azoulay, Capturing knowledge within and across firm boundaries: Evidence from clinical development, *Am. Econ. Rev.* 94, 1591, 1591 (2004).
317. For a discussion on JVs, *see Am. Bar Ass'n*, model joint venture agreement 359–72 (2006), https://apps.americanbar.org/buslaw/newsletter/0049/materials/book.pdf. For a discussion on R&D consortia, *see* S. E. Majewski, How Do Consortia Organize Collaborative R&D? Evidence from the national cooperative research act (*Harvard Law Sch. John M. Olin Ctr. Law, Econ., Bus.*, Discussion Paper No. 483, 2004), http://dx.doi.org/10.2139/ssrn.615583.
318. *Am. Bar Ass'n*, *supra* note 317.
319. Majewski, *supra* note 317.
320. Deloitte, A study of joint ventures the challenging world of alliances 2 (2010), https://www2.deloitte.com/content/dam/Deloitte/fr/Documents/finance/Publications/ Etude_Joint_Venture_juillet%202010.pdf.
321. K. Gugler and R. Siebert, Market power versus efficiency effects of mergers and research joint ventures: Evidence from the semiconductor industry, *Rev. Econ. Stat.* 89, 645, 651 (2007).
322. *See* J. A. Dobkin, Negotiating an international technology joint venture, *Conn. J. Int'l L.* 1, 81, 83 (1985); J. Poyago-Theotoky, Equilibrium and optimal size of a research joint venture in an oligopoly with spillovers, *J. Indus. Econ.* 43, 209, 209 (1995).
323. According to Y. Caloghirou *et al.*, Company incentives to join an RJV may include one or more of the following:

    1. R&D cost sharing;
    2. Reduction of R&D duplication;
    3. Risk sharing, uncertainty reduction;
    4. Spillover internalisation;
    5. Continuity of R&D effort, access to finance;
    6. Access of complementary resources and skills;
    7. Research synergies;
    8. Effective deployment of extant resources, further development of resource base;

9. Strategic flexibility, market access, and the creation of investment 'options';
10. Promotion of technical standards;
11. Market power, co-opting competition;
12. Legal and political advantages.

See Y. Caloghirou *et al.*, Research joint ventures, *J. Econ. Surv.* 17, 541, 556 (2003).

324. N. S. Vonortas, Research joint ventures in the U.S., *Res. Pol'y* 26, 577, 591 (1997).
325. *See* B. Holmstrom, Moral hazard in teams, *Bell J. Econ.* 13, 324, 325 (1982); K. Morasch, Moral hazard and optimal contract form for R&D cooperation, *J. Econ. Behav. & Org*. 28, 63, 65 (1995).
326. S. Bhattacharya, J. Glazer, and D. E. M. Sappington, Licensing and the sharing of knowledge in research joint ventures, *J. Econ. Theory* 56, 43, 44 (1992).
327. National Cooperative Research and Production Act of 1993, 15 U.S.C. §§ 4301–06 (2018); National Cooperative Research Act of 1984, 15 U.S.C. §§ 4301–05 (1984) (current version at 15 U.S.C. §§ 4301–06 (2018)).
328. Y. L. Doz, P. M. Olk, and P. S. Ring, Formation processes of R&D consortia: Which Path to Take? Where Does It Lead? *Strategic Mgmt. J.* 21, 239, 240 (2000).
329. *See* Majewski, *supra* note 317.
330. J. A. Ordover and R. D. Willig, Antitrust for high technology industries: Assessing research joint ventures and mergers, *J. L. Econ.* 28, 311, 313–14 (1985).
331. Jordan, *supra* note 71, p. 10.
332. K. M. Saunders, The role of intellectual property rights in negotiating and planning a research joint venture, *Marq. Intell. Prop. L. Rev*. 7, 75, 97 (2003).
333. *Ibid.,* p. 95.
334. R. Hernán *et al.*, An empirical evaluation of the determinants of research joint venture formation, *J. Indus. Econ*. 51, 75, 87 (2003).
335. *See* D. M. Cameron and R. Borenstein, Key aspects of IP license agreements 8 (2003), http://www.jurisdiction.com/lic101.pdf.
336. *Ibid.,* p. 7.
337. *Ibid.,* p. 32.
338. *Ibid.,* p. 12.

339. USPTO, Manual of Patent Examining Procedure (MPEP) § 301 (9th ed. 2015), https://www.uspto.gov/web/offices/pac/mpep/s301.html#d0e17687.
340. Cameron and Borenstein, *supra* note 335, p. 21 ("There is no widely accepted definition for 'improvement' in the context of intellectual property licenses, but it is usually used to mean a development within the field of the licensed technology that enhances the usability, functionality, efficiency, performance or other characteristic of the original technology.").
341. *See generally ibid.* (stating the contract also includes representations and warranties, disclaimers and limitations of liability, conflict resolution, contract termination and renewal, and enforceability).
342. R. C. Nordhaus, Patent license agreements, *Bus. Law.* 21, 643, 643 (966) ("Because of the infinite variety of rights and obligations that may be established between a patent licensor and his licensee, there is no 'standard' form of license agreement that may be used in all situations. Each license agreement must be carefully tailored to the specific circumstances of the particular case."); B. N. Anand and T. Khanna, The structure of licensing contracts, *J. Indus. Econ.* 103, 131 (2000) ("Licensing contracts in the Computer and Electronics industries are more likely to be signed with firms with whom the licensor has prior relationships, established either through alliance activity, common board membership, or personnel histories.").
343. *See* D. F. Spulber, Patent licensing and bargaining with innovative complements and substitutes, *Res. Econ.* 70, 693, 695 (2016).
344. *Ibid.,* p. 710.
345. *Ibid.,* p. 693.
346. M. L. Katz and C. Shapiro, How to license intangible property, *Q. J. Econ.* 101, 567, 568 (1986).
347. S. E. Warren Jr., Intellectual property litigation rising: How to protect your company's financial health, IRMI (September 2009), https://www.irmi.com/articles/expert-commentary/intellectual-property-litigation-rising-how-to-protect-your-company-s-financial-health.
348. The demand for licenses is based on "carrots" if the user derives benefits from using the intangible asset. The demand for licenses is based on "sticks" if the user obtains the license to avoid litigation over disputed technology. Finally, the demand for licenses is based on "bundles" if the user obtains the license because it is included in a bundle with complementary goods and services. *See* N. Östman, How to create the 'Pull' for patent licensing? *Linkedin* (September 6, 2016), https://www.linkedin.com/pulse/how-create-pull-patent-licensing-niklas-%C3% B6stman?trk=prof-post.

349. *See* I. Macho-Stadler *et al.*, The role of information in licensing contract design, *Res. Pol'y* 25, 43, 52 (1996) (discussing the role of information in determining the structure of royalties in patent licensing contracts); *see also* N. T. Gallini and B. D. Wright, Technology transfer under asymmetric information, *RAND J. Econ.* 21, 147 (1990).
350. R. Jensen and M. Thursby, Proofs and prototypes for sale: The licensing of university inventions, *Am. Econ. Rev.* 91, 240 (2001).
351. *Ibid.,* p. 248.
352. *Ibid.,* p. 245.
353. D. W. Elfenbein, Contract structure and performance of university-industry technology transfer agreements (July 30, 2009), https://ssrn.com/abstract=1452717.
354. D. F. Spulber, Tacit knowledge with innovative entrepreneurship, *Int'l J. Indus. Org.* 30, 641, 641 (2012).
355. *Ibid.*
356. D. Hegde, Tacit knowledge and the structure of license contracts: Evidence from the biomedical industry, *J. Econ. Mgmt. Strategy* 23, 568, 568 (2014).
357. D. F. Spulber, Market microstructure and intermediation, *J. Econ. Persp.* 10, 135, 141 (1996).
358. *Ibid.,* p. 135.
359. *Ibid.*
360. *Ibid.,* pp. 137–38.
361. *Ibid.,* p. 136.
362. *Ibid.,* pp. 145–46.
363. *Ibid.,* p. 135.
364. *Ibid.,* p. 146.
365. Spulber, *supra* note 77, p. 293.
366. *Ibid.,* at n.168.
367. Spulber, *supra* note 357, p. 145.
368. D. F. Spulber, The economics of markets and platforms, *J. Econ. Mgmt. Strategy* 28, 159, 169–70 (2019).
369. N. R. Lamoreaux and K. L. Sokoloff, Intermediaries in the U.S. market for technology, 1870–1920 28 (Nat'l Bureau of Economic Research, Working Paper No. 9017, 2002), https://www.nber.org/papers/w9017.pdf; J. F. McDonough III, The Myth of the patent troll: An alternative view of the function of patent dealers in an idea economy, *Emory L.J.* 56, 189, 207 (2007).

370. Fed. Trade Comm'n, Patent Assertion Entity Activity: An FTC Study (2016), https://www.ftc.gov/system/files/documents/reports/patent-assertion-entity-activity-ftc-study/p131203_patent_assertion_entity_activity_an_ftc_study_0.pdf.
371. *Ibid.,* p. 100; *see also* J. E. Dubiansky, The licensing function of patent intermediaries, *Duke L. & Tech. Rev*. 15, 269, 273 (2017).
372. Avanci, Avanci: Accelerating IoT Connectivity 2 (2016), http://avanci.com/wp-content/uploads/2017/01/2016-Avanci-WP-Final-_-Jan-24.pdf.
373. *Technology*, Avanci, http://avanci.com/technology/ (last visited January 21, 2019).
374. *Ibid.*
375. R. P. Merges and M. Mattioli, Measuring the costs and benefits of patent pools, *Ohio St. L.J.* 78, 281, 285 (2017) ("The benefit for licensees is easy to appreciate: 'one stop shopping' for many patents at once. This conserves on the cost of licensing numerous patents from dispersed patent holders by, in a sense, compressing that process into a single event.").
376. R. P. Merges, Contracting into liability rules: Intellectual property rights and collective rights organizations, *Calif. L. Rev.* 84, 1293, 1295 (1996) ("Collective Rights Organizations (CROs) will often emerge to break the transactional bottleneck. From patent pools to collective copyright licensing organizations such as ASCAP and BMI, IPR owners in various industries have demonstrated the workability of these private transactional mechanisms. Indeed, these case studies uncover two distinct advantages of CROs: expert tailoring and reduced political economy problems.").
377. *Ibid.,* p. 1302.
378. *Ibid.,* pp. 1340–42.
379. *Ibid.,* p. 1340.
380. L. Horn, Alternative approaches to IP management: One-stop technology platform licensing, *J. Com. Biotechnology* 9, 119, 120 (2003).
381. MPEGLA, https://www.mpegla.com. (last visited February 16, 2019).

Conclusion

1. Quinn, G., The Cost of Obtaining a Patent in the US, April 4, 2015, ipwatchdog.com, https://www.ipwatchdog.com/2015/04/04/the-cost-of-obtaining-a-patent-in-the-us/id=56485/.

2. The USPTO fee schedule for patents and trademarks specifies costs to larger entities of maintaining a patent of $1,600 due at 3.5 years, $3,600 due at 7.5 years, and $7,400 due at 11.5 years, https://www.uspto.gov/sites/default/files/documents/USPTO%20fee%20schedule_current.pdf.
3. https://developer.uspto.gov/ipmarketplace/search/platform.

Index

J

K

M

Q

R

S

T

Lightning Source UK Ltd.
Milton Keynes UK
UKHW021013241122
412758UK00004B/90

9 789811 225635